Shifts toward Image-Centricity in Contemporary Multimodal Practices

This innovative collection builds on current multimodal research to showcase image-centric practices in contemporary media, unpacking the increasing extent to which the visual plays a principal role in modern-day communication. The volume begins by providing a concise overview of the history and development of multimodal research with respect to image-centricity, with successive chapters looking at how image-centricity emerges over time, and how it unfolds in relation to language and other features in global design strategies. Bringing together contributions from both established and emerging researchers in multimodality and social semiotics, the book presents case studies on a variety of image-centric genres and domains, including magazines, advertising discourse, multimedia storytelling, and social media platforms. The aims of the book are to interrogate the new multimodal genres, relations, forms of analysis, and methods of production that emerge from a greater reliance on visual components. Refining and broadening current understandings of image-centricity in today's media sphere, this collection will be of particular interest to scholars and students in multimodality, social semiotics, applied linguistics, language and media, and discourse analysis.

Hartmut Stöckl is full professor of English and Applied Linguistics in the Department of English and American Studies at Salzburg University, Austria. His main research areas are in semiotics, media/text linguistics/stylistics, pragmatics and linguistic multimodality research. He is particularly interested in the linkage of language and image in modern media, typography, and an aesthetic appreciation of advertising.

Helen Caple is an Associate Professor in Communications and Journalism at the University of New South Wales, Australia. Her research interests center on news photography, text-image relations, and discursive news values analysis. Helen has published in the area of photojournalism and social semiotics. Her latest monograph with Routledge is *Photojournalism Disrupted: The View from Australia* (2019).

Jana Pflaeging is a research assistant in English and Applied Linguistics at the University of Salzburg, Austria. Her research interests are in multimodal text/discourse linguistics and genre studies, especially genre change in photojournalism. With a background in linguistics and fine arts, she explores the synergies between both fields when creating visualizations of linguistic and multimodal theories, methods, and data.

Routledge Studies in Multimodality
Edited by Kay L. O'Halloran, University of Liverpool

Multimodality and Aesthetics
Edited by Elise Seip Tønnessen and Frida Forsgren

Multimodal Stylistics of the Novel
More Than Words
Nina Nørgaard

A Multimodal Approach to Video Games and the Player Experience
Weimin Toh

Multimodal Semiotics and Rhetoric in Videogames
Jason Hawreliak

Pictorial Framing in Moral Politics
A Corpus-Based Experimental Study
Ahmed Abdel-Raheem

Design Perspectives on Multimodal Documents
System, Medium, and Genre Relations
Edited by Matthew David Lickiss

A Multimodal Perspective on Applied Storytelling Performances
Narrativity in Context
Soe Marlar Lwin

Shifts towards Image-centricity in Contemporary Multimodal Practices
Edited by Hartmut Stöckl, Helen Caple and Jana Pflaeging

For more information about this series, please visit: https://www.routledge.com/Routledge-Studies-in-Multimodality/book-series/RSMM

Shifts toward Image-Centricity in Contemporary Multimodal Practices

Edited by
Hartmut Stöckl,
Helen Caple, and
Jana Pflaeging

LONDON AND NEW YORK

First published 2020 by Routledge

2 Park Square, Milton Park, Abingdon, Oxon OX14 4RN
605 Third Avenue, New York, NY 10017

Routledge is an imprint of the Taylor & Francis Group, an informa business

First issued in paperback 2021

Copyright © 2020 selection and editorial matter, Hartmut Stöckl, Helen Caple, and Jana Pflaeging; individual chapters, the contributors

The right of Hartmut Stöckl, Helen Caple, and Jana Pflaeging to be identified as the authors of the editorial material, and of the authors for their individual chapters, has been asserted in accordance with sections 77 and 78 of the Copyright, Designs and Patents Act 1988.

All rights reserved. No part of this book may be reprinted or reproduced or utilised in any form or by any electronic, mechanical, or other means, now known or hereafter invented, including photocopying and recording, or in any information storage or retrieval system, without permission in writing from the publishers.

Notice:
Product or corporate names may be trademarks or registered trademarks, and are used only for identification and explanation without intent to infringe.

Publisher's Note

The publisher has gone to great lengths to ensure the quality of this reprint but points out that some imperfections in the original copies may be apparent.

Library of Congress Cataloging-in-Publication Data
A catalog record for this title has been requested

ISBN: 978-1-138-59608-5 (hbk)
ISBN: 978-1-03-217606-2 (pbk)
DOI: 10.4324/9780429487965

Typeset in Sabon
by codeMantra

Contents

List of Contributors ix

1 Shifts toward Image-Centricity in Contemporary
 Multimodal Practices: An Introduction 1
 HARTMUT STÖCKL, HELEN CAPLE AND JANA PFLAEGING

PART 1
Advances in Theory

2 Image-Centricity – When Visuals Take Center Stage:
 Analyses and Interpretations of a Current (News)
 Media Practice 19
 HARTMUT STÖCKL

3 Intertextual Reference in Image-Centric Discourse:
 Analytical Model, Classification, and Case Study 42
 NINA-MARIA KLUG

4 The New Visuality of Writing 64
 THEO VAN LEEUWEN

 Commentary: The Critical Role of Analysis in Moving
 from Conjecture to Theory 86
 JOHN A. BATEMAN

PART 2
Historical Developments in Image-Centric Practices

5 On the Emergence of Image-Centric Popular Science
 Stories in *National Geographic* 97
 JANA PFLAEGING

6 Previewing News Stories: How Contextual Cohesion Contributes to the Creation of News Stories 123
SAMEERA DURRANI

Commentary: Image-Centricity and Change in Journalistic Cultures 146
MARTIN LUGINBÜHL

PART 3
The Relative Status of Image and Language

7 Image-Centric Practices on Instagram: Subtle Shifts in 'Footing' 153
HELEN CAPLE

8 Emoji-Text Relations on Instagram: Empirical Corpus Studies on Multimodal Uses of the Iconographetic Mode 177
CHRISTINA MARGIT SIEVER AND TORSTEN SIEVER

9 "And then he Said … No one has more Respect for Women than I do": Intermodal Relations and Intersubjectivity in Image Macros 204
MICHELE ZAPPAVIGNA

Commentary: Reflections on the Relative Status of Image and Language 226
CAREY JEWITT

PART 4
Image-Centric Practices as Global Design Strategies

10 Multimodal Mobile News: Design and Images in Tablet-Platform Apps 233
JOHN S. KNOX

11 Images as Ideology in Terrorist-Related Communications 253
PETER WIGNELL, SABINE TAN, KAY L. O'HALLORAN, REBECCA LANGE, KEVIN CHAI, AND MICHAEL WIEBRANDS

12 Putting the Data Center Stage: Graphs, Charts, and
   Maps in the News Media   275
   MARTIN ENGEBRETSEN

   Commentary: Image-Centric Practices as Global Design
   Strategies   297
   TEAL TRIGGS

   Index   303

Contributors

John Bateman is full professor of Applied Linguistics in the English and Linguistics Departments of Bremen University, Germany, specializing in functional, computational, and multimodal linguistics. His research ranges over functional linguistic approaches to multilingual and multimodal document design, semiotics, and theories of discourse. His current interests center on the development of robust methodologies for multimodal analysis, the application of functional linguistic and corpus methods to multimodal meaning making, and the construction of ontologically-based computational dialogue systems for situated robot-human communication.

Helen Caple is an Associate Professor in Communications and Journalism at the University of New South Wales, Australia. Her research interests centre on news photography, text-image relations, and discursive news values analysis. She is currently exploring the role of citizen photography in contemporary journalism. Helen has published in the area of photojournalism and social semiotics. Her latest monograph with Routledge is *Photojournalism Disrupted: The View from Australia* (2019).

Kevin Chai is lead data scientist for the Curtin Institute for Computation to provide data, computing, analytics, and machine learning/artificial intelligence expertise to researchers and industry partners. Kevin has experience in developing machine learning and natural language processing models to analyze large datasets and developing predictive models. His research interests and experience include machine learning/AI and its application to solving important problems in domains such as health, medicine, education, science, engineering, the humanities, and many other diverse areas of research.

Sameera Durrani is a lecturer at the University of Technology (UTS), Sydney, Australia. Her main research areas are semiotics, photojournalism, and place branding. She is particularly interested in how visual communication influences the representation of nations within news discourse.

Martin Engebretsen is full professor of language and communication in the Department of Nordic and Media Studies at Agder University, Norway. His research interests include multimodal and visual studies, rhetorics, discourse analysis, and journalism studies. He is particularly interested in the exploration of genre development related to processes of digitization in the public media. A volume on 'Data visualization in society' with Amsterdam University Press (2019), co-edited with Helen Kennedy, is among his recent projects.

Carey Jewitt is Professor of Learning and Technology, UCL Knowledge Lab, University College London. She is Director of IN-TOUCH, a 5-year ERC Consolidator Award (in-touch-digital.com). Previously, Carey led the MODE project on multimodal methods in digital environments (MODE.ioe.ac.uk), and MIDAS, on methodological innovation across digital arts and social science (MIDAS.ioe.ac.uk). Recent books include *Introducing Multimodality* (with Bezemer and O'Halloran, 2016), *The Sage Handbook of Researching Digital Technologies* (with Price and Brown, 2014), and *The Routledge Handbook of Multimodal Analysis* (2014).

Nina-Maria Klug is an Associate Lecturer in Applied Linguistics in the Department of German Studies at Kassel University, Germany. Her research priority is on multimodal text- and discourse analysis. Ongoing, she is preparing a book on multimodal construction of (afro) German identity between the 1980s and today, including language, image, and music as relevant resources to convey meaning. She is co-editor of *the Handbook of Language in Multimodal Contexts* (2016).

John S. Knox is a Senior Lecturer in Linguistics at Macquarie University. He teaches primarily on the postgraduate programs in Applied Linguistics and TESOL. His research interests include multimodality, language in education, social semiotics, and mediated discourse.

Rebecca Lange is a Computational Specialist with the Curtin Institute for Computation. Rebecca completed her PhD in astronomy at the International Centre for Radio Astronomy Research at the University of Western Australia. Throughout her studies and research work, she has gained extensive programming as well as data analytics and visualization experience in various programming languages. She is particularly interested in applying her technical skills to support and train researchers in the digital humanities.

Theo van Leeuwen is Professor of Language and Communication at the University of Southern Denmark and Emeritus Professor at the University of Technology, Sydney. He has published widely in the areas of social semiotics, multimodality, and critical discourse analysis. His most recent book is *Visual and Multimodal Research in Organization* *and Management Studies* (Routledge, 2019), co-authored with Markus Höllerer and others. The 3rd edition of his *Reading Images – The Grammar of Visual Design*, co-authored with Gunther Kress, will appear in 2020.

Martin Luginbühl is full professor for German Linguistics at the University of Basel, Switzerland. His current research focuses on media linguistics, genre studies, conversational analysis, and language and culture. In 2014, he published the book *Medienkultur und Medienlinguistik [Media Culture and Media Linguistics]* (Peter Lang Publishers), a genre-based, multimodal comparison of the American "CBS Evening News" and the Swiss TV news show "Tagesschau" from the 1950s until today.

Kay O'Halloran is Head of Department and Chair in Communication and Media in the School of the Arts at the University of Liverpool. Prior to this, she was Professor and leader of the Multimodal Analysis Group and a member of the Curtin Institute for Computation at Curtin University, Western Australia. Her areas of research include multimodal analysis, social semiotics, mathematics discourse, and the development of interactive digital media technologies and visualization techniques for multimodal and sociocultural analytics. She is currently developing mixed-methods approaches that combine multimodal analysis, data mining, and visualization for big data analytics in areas including online extremism, political rhetoric, and 360° video.

Jana Pflaeging is a researcher in English and Applied Linguistics at the Department of English and American Studies at Salzburg University. She currently pursues a binational PhD at Salzburg University, Austria, and Halle-Wittenberg University, Germany. Her research interests are in multimodal text/discourse linguistics and genre studies, especially genre change in photojournalism. With a background in Linguistics and Fine Arts, she explores the synergies between both fields when creating visualizations of linguistic and multimodal theories, methods, and data.

Christina Siever is a research assistant in the research project *What's up, Switzerland*, at the University of Zurich, and investigates emoji-based communication in the subproject *Language Design in WhatsApp: Icono/Graphy*. Before that, she completed her doctorate on *Multimodal Communication in the Social Web* (2015, Lang). Her main research interests are (multimodal) communication in digital media, especially on the social web, with an emphasis on emoji use.

Up until recently, **Torsten Siever** was a research associate in the German Department at Leibniz University Hannover, Germany. His focus of research is on media linguistics (cf. *mediensprache.net*); in his dissertation, he dealt with texts of the extremely short kind. Among other occupations, he is currently working as the editor of the journal *Muttersprache*.

Hartmut Stöckl is full professor of English and Applied Linguistics in the Department of English and American Studies at Salzburg University, Austria. His main research areas are in semiotics, media/text linguistics/stylistics, pragmatics and linguistic multimodality research. He is particularly interested in the linkage of language and image in modern media, typography, and an aesthetic appreciation of advertising. Together with Nina-Maria Klug, he recently edited the *Handbook of Language in Multimodal Contexts* (2016, de Gruyter).

Sabine Tan is a Senior Research Fellow and member of the Multimodal Analysis Group in the Faculty of Humanities at Curtin University, Western Australia. She has a background in critical multimodal discourse analysis, social semiotics, and visual communication. Sabine's current work involves developing multimodal approaches to big data analytics. She has worked on interdisciplinary projects involving the development of interactive software for the multimodal analysis of images, videos, and 360-degree videos for research and educational purposes.

Teal Triggs is Professor of Graphic Design and Associate Dean, School of Communication, Royal College of Art, London. As a graphic design historian, critic, and educator, she has lectured and broadcast widely, and her writings on design pedagogy, self-publishing, and feminism have appeared in numerous edited books and international design publications. She was previously co-Editor of the academic journal *Visual Communication* (Sage). *The Graphic Design Reader* (Bloomsbury Visual Arts, 2019) is her most recent co-edited book.

Michael Wiebrands is an IT professional with 20 years of experience in the tertiary education sector. He has filled a broad range of IT roles, including software development, system administration, application support, database administration, and project management. His current focus is the use of game engines to facilitate the creation of education tools. He has a particular interest in 3D visualization and virtual reality.

Peter Wignell is a Senior Research Fellow and member of the Multimodal Analysis Group in the Faculty of Humanities at Curtin University, Western Australia. He has an academic background in systemic functional linguistics, discourse analysis, and multimodal analysis. His research has been both theoretical and applied. Peter's current research interests are in systemic functional linguistics, especially in its application to the analysis of multimodal texts, with a recent focus on violent extremist discourse and political discourse.

Michele Zappavigna is a senior lecturer at the University of New South Wales. Her major research interest is the discourse of social media and ambient affiliation. Recent books include: *Searchable Talk: Hashtags and Social Media Metadiscourse* (Bloomsbury, 2018), *Discourse of Twitter and Social Media* (Bloomsbury, 2012), *Researching the Language of Social Media* (Routledge, 2014, with Ruth Page, Johann Unger and David Barton), and *Discourse and Diversionary Justice: An Analysis of Ceremonial Redress in Youth Justice Conferencing* (Palgrave, 2018, with J.R. Martin).

1 Shifts toward Image-Centricity in Contemporary Multimodal Practices
An Introduction

Hartmut Stöckl, Helen Caple and Jana Pflaeging

1 Introduction

This volume explores image-centric practices in the contemporary media sphere, a space that images now dominate. It does this through the application of functional-linguistic, social semiotic, text/genre-linguistic and inter-/transtextual approaches to multimodality, and by drawing on both the established and the emerging research expertise of multimodality scholars from Europe and Australia. These scholars were invited to refine and broaden the general idea of image-centricity and put it to the test in a number of different mass/social media contexts, where language, text structure, and text-image relations are dominated and led by images. These include magazines, advertising, news, and social media platforms. We use the term *image* as a cover term to include a range of visuals: photographs, illustrations, visualizations, and new writing/typography. The resulting volume is a rich investigation of a range of contemporary multimodal practices, examining the relative status of image and language, visual aesthetics, multimodal cohesion/coherence, and the values and ideologies underpinning image selection and presentation.

In this chapter, we chart the path toward image-centricity and review the foundational research that has brought us to our current understanding of the role of images in the contemporary media sphere.

2 Shifts toward Image-Centricity in the Contemporary Media Sphere

What is perceivable as an *image-centric* contemporary media sphere is the result of a *shift* toward image-centricity that has taken place, most notably, since the 19th century. Spurred by the Industrial Revolution, but not solely contingent on technological advancements, visual modes have gradually moved toward the center of the semiosphere.

Conditions for image-centricity were initially set through the tremendous material-technological advances of the 20th century, both in the capture and reproduction of images. This has been further enhanced by the advent of computer technology and desktop publishing software that has inspired innovations in type-setting and page composition. A broad range of typefaces, typographical settings, scalable and movable text boxes, vector-based drawing and coloring tools, and now digitally processed photographs are used to create increasingly image-centric page spaces, often on the basis of standardized templates (Johnson & Prijatel, 1999; see also Pflaeging, 2017a).

Sociocultural changes in the values associated with images have also contributed to the shift toward image-centricity. The affective value of the single still photograph, its ability to move public to action, emerged with the documentary photographers of the late 1800s to 1900s. The photography of PH Emerson and Ansel Adams, for example, became instrumental in advocating for improvements in urban living conditions and in the preservation of nature through the national parks system in the United States. Research by Perlmutter (1998) attributes the iconic status of certain news photographs to a range of editorial factors. These include institutional factors such as the photograph's place on the news agenda, repetition of use, and its transposability to other contexts. Coupled with this are image-internal factors such as the ability of a single photograph to sum up an issue (its metonymic function), its potential for cultural resonance, and its often striking composition. Such factors, along with the ability of an image to project the offer of the ideal, of perfection, have also contributed to the shift in advertising materials toward the visual.

The implications of advancements in technological innovation and in the sociocultural conditions facilitating shifts in the semiotic landscape toward the visual have long been noted by the contributors to this volume. In relation to journalism, Caple and Knox (2015, p. 292) have argued that "we have witnessed a fundamental shift towards visual story-telling", and Bednarek and Caple (2012, p. 111) are convinced that "story structure has shifted and images now tend to dominate the verbal text". Acknowledgment of the aesthetic function of photographs has also led to the rise of image-dominated news story genres in print news (Caple, 2013), while the templated structure of online news portals has facilitated an even wider range of roles for photographs in news story structure (see e.g., Knox, 2009a, 2009b; Caple & Knox, 2017). Similarly, contemporary magazines and advertising materials have taken advantage of both technical and cultural shifts to become more image-centric.

The case of the popular science magazine *National Geographic* vividly illustrates the 'rise of the image' afforded by socio-cultural and material-technological developments. In a small-scale study on the development of *National Geographic* feature articles, Pflaeging (2017a, 2017b) shows that, even though the image-per-page ratio has decreased from 0.91 in 1915 to 0.53 images per page in 2015, the layout space taken up by images increased significantly between 1915 and 2015. In particular, the pattern of covering a double-page solely with an image-caption-cluster has emerged from an insignificant 2.4 percent of the compositional designs in use to a prominent 57.8 percent by 2015.

Similarly, Durrani (2017, p. 163) observes a considerable shift in the size of images in the magazine *Time Asia*. In the 1980s, less than one percent of images took up a full page to two pages. In the 2000s, this figure increased to 7.5 percent, and overall, 26 percent of the images were used at half a page or larger (7 percent in the 1980s). This shift in image size has been accompanied by the aestheticization of image composition (making use of more axially composed images) and by evolving page design strategies in which images, headlines, stand-first text, and negative space interact much more meaningfully with each other, to create an evaluative stance on the story.

Print advertising is another example of a genre whose history reflects a clear shift toward image-centricity (cf. Stöckl, 2014b, pp. 94–98). Long and descriptive-argumentative copy containing simple illustrations of products or their use gave way to graphic spaces that are dominated by artfully designed images and minimal text, which must directly engage with visual image elements to produce a rhetorically complex, multimodal, pictorial argumentation (Kjeldsen, 2012). When in the past it was semantically subordinated to the text, now the image leads in an anchoring or complementary text-image relation, often appropriating and re-contextualizing images that, at first sight, do not seem to be commercially relevant. Molnar (2018, n.p.) calls this modern multimodal format 'minimalistic reminder' to highlight its reduced semiotic form and functionality. Stöckl (2017b, p. 74) emphasizes the visually rich, semantically ambiguous, pragmatically underdetermined, and rhetorically complex nature of modern ads when he calls them 'enigmatic' or 'en-riddled'.

Finally, while increasingly affordable digital cameras have inspired non-professional photographers and text producers since the 1990s, it was the more widespread use of camera phones since the 2010s that has made capturing the everyday in images a common daily routine. The advent of social media platforms, that have, to an increasing extent, afforded the *share-ability* or *curate-ability* (Pflaeging, 2015, in press) of online content, and the emergence of online audiences who take quick scrolls through their Facebook timelines, Instagram and Twitter feeds have made image-centric updates a preferred choice for social online interaction (Adami & Jewitt, 2016).

Possibly the most effective way of summing up the shift toward image-centricity is to demonstrate this through a visualization. Figure 1.1 presents a diachronic snapshot of the shift toward image-centricity

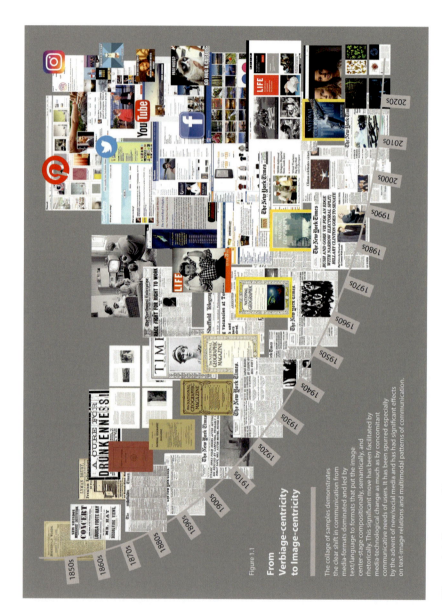

Figure 1.1 From verbiage-centricity to image-centricity.

among the data studied for this volume. Alongside this sits the emergence of new visually-dominated digital media at the turn of the 21st century. Such richly varied and complex modal ensembles in former and contemporary media spheres offer fertile ground for the exploration of image-centric practices, and the contributions to this volume take on this task. In doing so, they build upon the foundational research into multimodality and image-centric practices that precedes this volume.

3 Researching Image-Centric Multimodal Practices

3.1 From Image Nuclearity to Image-Centricity

As Stöckl (2015b, pp. 51–52) notes, the concepts and methods deployed in research on multimodality generally emanate from text linguistics and semiotics and have been mapped onto multimodal phenomena. One such approach stemming from the study of the functional structure of verbiage-centric news reporting (Feez, Iedema, & White, 2008) is Caple's (2008, 2013) works on the functional structure of image-nuclear news stories. The prominent position of image and headline in such texts has been posited to build a propositional nucleus and provide a perceptual and cognitive anchor (in) to the text, which also affects the evaluative stance taken and the (news) values a media story will encode. Accompanying text is dependent on this image-headline nucleus, as it functions to elaborate and extend pictorial content and to disambiguate the visual-verbal play that such stories tend to foreground (Caple, 2013).

While Caple's notion of *image nuclearity* relates to the functional structure of a particular type of news story, it is inextricably linked to a broader communicative trend in popular forms of mass media. In this volume, we broaden the scope of this term and redefine it as *image-centricity* in order to account for its potential as a large-scale multimodal design strategy with far-reaching effects on text structure and perception.

3.2 What Exactly is Image-Centricity?

An explanation of image-centricity works best by exploring the concept in relation to some of the mainstream thinking on text-image relations (cf. Bateman, 2014). *Text-image relations* are understood here as discourse, where "the two modes appear separate yet integrated in both semantics and form" (Martinec & Salway, 2005, p. 338) and "act as a single unit of composition" (Bateman, 2014, p. 28) that constitutes a functional communicative act intentionally designed by a text-maker and consciously attended to by a recipient. Most importantly, arguing that images become dominant and central in a multimodal text implies a shift in the general balance of modes, which is the default assumption in multimodality research. That all modes contribute in their own way and in this sense 'equally' to the overall textual meaning has been expressed in a number of terms, such as 'mutual elaboration' of modes (Jewitt, Bezemer, & O'Halloran, 2016, p. 91), 'dialogicity' of signs (Jewitt et al., 2016, p. 111), 'co-determination' of meaning (Spillner, 1982, qtd. in Bateman, 2014, p. 37), 'complementarity' or 'synergy' (Royce, 1998), and 'meaning multiplication' (Bateman, 2014, pp. 5–7). In contrast, image-centricity clearly implies that images become the superordinate mode in a multimodal text, that the directionality of mode elaboration is from image to text/language, and that the modes have different 'modal intensity' or 'weight' (Norris, 2014, p. 90).

Such mode differences and their varying relative importance have been conceptualized in the term 'status relations' (cf. Martinec & Salway, 2005, pp. 343–349). Clearly, any image-centric text or genre primarily entails 'unequal status', and revisiting Barthes' (1964/1977) original terminology, we can classify image-centricity as a text-image relation of 'anchorage'. Here, mutual mode elaboration is led by a superordinate image, whereas the reverse case, verbiage- or text-centricity corresponds to Barthes' (1964/1977) 'illustration' that implies a direction of mode elaboration from a text to a subordinate image. Martinec and Salway (2005, p. 344) point to the fact that when a text has the leading superordinate status, the image relates to only part of the text, whereas when the image has the leading superordinate status, the text may relate to the whole image or parts of it only. The more strongly image-centric genres, it seems, would be relating a text to an image in its semantic and functional entirety, whereas in weaker forms of image-centricity text may only involve relations to individual image elements.

In addition to an interpretation of image-centricity as *unequal status relations*, with the superordinate image leading mutual mode elaboration, image-centric discourse can also be seen as a special case of *equal status relations*. Martinec and Salway (2005, p. 343) say that "when an image and a text are joined equally and modify one another, their status is considered complementary". This 'equal/complementary' status relation is realized by a whole text and a whole image "combining to form part of a larger syntagm" (Martinec & Salway, 2005, p. 344). Equal and complementary status relation echoes Barthes' (1964/1977, p. 41) classic ideas of *relay* in that "the words, in the same way as the images, are fragments of a more general syntagm and the unity of the message is realized at a higher level, that of the story [...]". It is interesting to see that while Barthes (1964/1977, p. 41) clearly distinguishes relay from *anchorage* (and illustration), he also understood that "the two functions [...] can co-exist". Finally, a wider view of image-centricity as set out and endorsed here must rule out only equal and independent status relations, where "there are no signs of one [mode] modifying the other" (Martinec & Salway, 2005, p. 343).

In our conceptualization of image-centric genres, the most vital element appears to be what Martinec and Salway (2005, p. 345) have called 'text subordination'. In other words, image-centric text-image relations construct a compositional unity of the two modes that is characterized either by an elaboration of the image through text or by a mutual co-elaboration of image and text in a complementary fashion. Consequently, text subordination to us may mean both a semantic centrality of the image that allows it to lead the interpretation of the multimodal text, and a perceptual dominance or salience given to the image that makes it the textual 'entry point' for reading paths and meaning construal. In any case, for an effective elaboration or complementary modification of the superordinate image-meaning to be achieved by the text, linguistic elements are paramount that directly relate to the image and can perhaps only be understood in relation to it. This means that, in image-centric texts, we need to look primarily at deictic elements pointing to the image and at any further expressions that construe intersemiotic cohesion between text and image. How rich and strong are such cohesive chains or networks? What types of ties are there, and which semantic function do they perform? These and other questions need to be raised about image-centricity.

Tracing the theory of text-image relations from its early semiotic beginnings (Barthes, 1964/1977) through systemic functional grammar (Halliday, 1985/1994) to multimodality research (Bateman, 2014; Bateman, Wildfeuer, & Hiippala, 2017) also brings up inherent connections between *status* and the *logico-semantic relations of modes*. It was Martinec and Salway (2005, p. 341) who point out that Barthes' classic unequal status relations of anchorage and illustration can be seen as cases of *elaboration*, where information in one mode is restated or specified/generalized in the other. They differ in the directionality of the elaboration – from text to image (illustration), from image to text (anchorage). The equal status relation of complementary *relay*, on the other hand, exemplifies both *extension*, that is, one mode adding semantically unrelated information to the other, and *enhancement*, that is, one mode qualifying circumstantial info for the other mode. Caple (2013, pp. 130–137), for instance, has shown that in image-centric news stories text accompanying a leading, superordinate image may engage in all three logico-semantic relations. Alongside the specifics of cohesive ties, the logical-semantic functionality of text in image-centric genres should form a major trajectory of research into image-centricity.

Two final points are important to note in relation to a concept of image-centricity. Both raise a critical awareness of the value and reliability of taxonomic approaches to text-image relations, as outlined earlier. The first concerns the ways in which "layout affect[ed] the relationship between image and writing" (Jewitt et al., 2016, p. 80). Bateman (2014, p. 28) touches on the same issue when he points to "the single unit" or "joint composition" of image and text that are "intentionally co-present". Apart from acknowledging the decisive influence of the organization of the multimodal graphic space on semantic construal, he also cautions that "recipients will take from the material on offer what they need in order to get some interpretative task done" (Bateman, 2014, p. 20). This means status and logico-semantics in text-image relation are relative to the text-recipient and are ultimately "task-driven" (Bateman, 2014, p. 20). The second point abstracts from the first and has far-reaching implications. In many ways it would seem justified to distinguish structural text-image relations as deployed in the multimodal text from reconstructed or inferred ones as instantiated by the recipient in a concrete situation (cf. Bateman, 2014, p. 45). If this duality is adequate, the consequence in analysis would be to "not only address [...] text-image relationships as a taxonomic exercise, setting out catalogues of possible connections, but also consider what these relationships are intended to do" (Bateman, 2014, p. 47).

4 Overview of the Book

Our edited volume seeks to explore the notion of *image-centricity* both from a theoretical and an empirical perspective while employing synchronic and diachronic approaches to analysis. We look at all kinds of genres across different media where language, text structure, and text-image relations are dominated and led by images. As noted earlier, we also aim to move beyond the traditional understanding of *image* as 'photograph' to include a range of visuals (photographs, illustrations, visualizations, new writing/typography, among others) that dominate text, although we retain the term *image* as a cover term.

The volume comprises 11 chapters contributed by established and emerging multimodality scholars from Australia, Austria, Denmark, Germany, Norway, Switzerland, and the United Kingdom. The case studies they present draw on the contributors' wide experience in researching magazine genres, advertising discourse, news discourse, social media discourse, multimedia storytelling, and new writing. The chapters are organized around four key objectives: an exploration of advances in theory and methodology (Part 1 of this book), historical developments in image-centric practices (Part 2), the relative status of image and language (Part 3), and image-centric practices as a design strategy (Part 4).

4.1 Part 1: Advances in Theory

Designating current media practices as image-centric presupposes a theory to describe and explain this multimodal trend. First, the concept itself must be fleshed out in detail: What are its defining criteria? How does image-centricity affect semantics and the form of text-image relations?

What are the genre variations in different media? Second, we must ask in which ways the typography, layout, and materiality of the textual artifacts drive and shape image-centricity in the age of new writing (cf. van Leeuwen, 2008; Stöckl, 2014a). Third, image-centric multimodal texts also raise inter- and transtextual questions (cf. Klug, 2016): How do dominant images become frequent points of reference in intertextual relations? How do such images form the fabric of entire discourses? In how far are they instrumental in developing arguments or conveying viewpoints and evaluations? Such questions are explored in Chapters 2, 3, and 4.

Hartmut Stöckl revisits the notion of *image nuclearity* and provides both theoretical argument and empirical evidence for renegotiating the concept's position in relation to a distinctly broader idea of image-centricity. His corpus study of 103 illustrated news stories (sampled from 33 issues of several German- and English-language print newspapers) enables him to identify *Preview, Story Intro, Editorial, Explainer*, and *Gallery* as genres that, just as the image-nuclear news story, employ an image as central element. Noticeable differences in the communicative work accomplished by the image components, however, justify their status as distinct members of an *image-centric genre family*. Drawing on the results of his own and previous related work, Stöckl concludes his chapter by presenting a comprehensive overview of criteria (grouped under the headings of *news type, thematic structure, layout, image type, text-image relations*), which can be applied to map out in further detail the broad terrain of an image-centric genre space.

Nina-Maria Klug raises our awareness of prominent news images that have come to constitute the anchor points of entire discourses. She thereby uncovers a transtextual dimension of the concept of *image-centricity*. From a detailed discussion of discursive moves related to the international reception of Nilüfer Demir's photograph of the dead refugee boy Aylan Kurdi, which has appeared on social media, TV, newspaper front pages, but also on graffiti walls, Klug derives a typology of direct intertextual reference to images that have emerged as discursive focal points. In particular, covering both intra- and intermodal constellations, Klug elaborates on cases of *image quotation, transcription, resemiotization, indexing, meta-textualization, and transformation*. Based on this typology and the analysis that informed it, Klug not only provides a solid framework with which the transtextual dimension of image-centricity can be studied systematically, but also makes a strong case for seeing established notions such as *inter-* and *transtextuality* in a new – *image-centric* – light.

Theo van Leeuwen's contribution is based on the observation that 'new' forms of writing are on the rise whose meaning making relies heavily on contributions from inherently *visual semiotic resources*, such as shape, color, texture of letter forms, or the configuration of textual components on a page. This phenomenon, he argues, could be seen as yet another dimension of image-centricity. After discussing several digital and non-digital examples of *new writing*, he turns to diagrammatic templates, which, due to their conventionalized navigation devices and structural composition, can encourage narrative or conceptual readings. Van Leeuwen interprets his findings against the backdrop of wider socio-cultural contexts. In particular, he assumes functionality/standardization and identity/uniqueness to be two somewhat opposed driving forces of semiotic change. He also considers a striving for aesthetic appeal, a shift from naturalistic representation to modeling, and a declining importance of 'the interpersonal' as further impacting factors. All of these phenomena are regarded as defining characteristics of new writing, which, at the same time, play a crucial role in an ongoing 'marketization' of discourse.

4.2 Part 2: Historical Developments in Image-Centric Practices

The current move toward image-centricity represents a shift in the semiotic landscape of media communication. This implies diachronic change, which is also worth addressing in any theoretical and empirical investigation of multimodal genres. Such research (cf. Pflaeging, 2017a, 2017b; Stöckl, 2017a) needs to show how media and their genres developed from being mainly writing/print and displaying verbiage-nuclear (Caple, 2013, pp. 142–174) multimodality to using image-centric practices. This angle can shed light on changes both in the types and visual composition of images and on shifts in pictorial functionality. Such historical work also promotes our understanding of those factors that have possibly driven the trend toward image-centricity.

Jana Pflaeging investigates the popular science monthly *National Geographic*, a magazine known for its 'image-heavy' journalism, with a focus on the development of the illustrated journalistic short-form genre *Visions* and the communicative circumstances of its emergence in 2004. Configuring nothing but a large, rhetorically central image and a caption on a double-page spread, it lends itself to an exploration of the applicability of *image nuclearity* beyond the realms of hard news reportage. Moving from an analysis of *Visions* in 2015 to a diachronic study of its 2005-predecessor *Visions of Earth*, and from there to an investigation of *Feature Articles* (1985, 1995, 2005, 2015), Pflaeging seeks to shed light on the defining characteristics of *image nuclearity* as construed in other media and genres, and with a view to various developmental stages. Her findings suggest, among other things, the importance of an image's compositional dominance, leading to the conclusion that a theory of image nuclearity can be fruitfully broadened under the heading of image-centricity.

Showing a similar interest in increasingly illustrated print magazine spreads, **Sameera Durrani** reports on key findings from her longitudinal study of *Time Asia*, in particular, 840 photographs featured in its news coverage of Pakistan and Iran. Through a re-application and expansion of frameworks originally put forth for a social-semiotic analysis of image content and composition, Durrani draws out six distinct configurations of central images (single or several) and related verbal units (e.g., headlines, captions, stand-firsts) that have evolved over 30 years of the magazine's publishing history. In all cases, certain representational choices are coupled with compositional ones, for example, when two horizontally aligned images of politicians facing each other convey a sense of confrontation and dispute. Due to their general prevalence in the data set, Durrani assumes that such image-centric configurations function as perceptually salient previews to the content of an adjacent news story and proposes to term them *compositional narrative devices*.

4.3 Part 3: The Relative Status of Image and Language

This book shares Caple's (2013, pp. 130–137) view that determining both *experiential orientation and contextual extension* in the captions and specifying their nature is a fruitful way of looking at text functions in relation to the image. This can be refined and adapted to suit the needs of different genres by adding various text linguistic or rhetorical angles of analysis. How exactly the two text functions of describing the central image(s) and extending its/their context are realized linguistically is a prime objective here. The three contributions in this section also afford some insight into how types of media and genres shape and constrain text-image relations.

In her chapter, **Helen Caple** investigates communicative practices on *Instagram*, a social media platform that is inherently image-centric, with a view to the realization of speaker roles and point of view as construed in the visual and verbal components of the posts. Her analysis of 92 posts made in relation to the 2016 Australian federal elections sheds light on the *logico-semantic relations* between the image and verbiage, the overall functions they serve, and the similarities they bear to captioning practices in news discourse, comic book writing, and photo-album sharing. Given the particularity of her data, that is, posts by dog owners and/or their dogs collected under *#dogsatpollingstations*, Caple is able to draw out subtle shifts in the conflation and separation of speaker roles between pets and their owners that put different demands on the work of image and verbiage in meaning making.

Like Caple's contribution to this section, **Christina Siever** and **Torsten Siever**'s chapter enriches our understanding of image-centric practices on the social media platform *Instagram*. Their particular focus, however, is on *emoji-text relations* in the captions of *Instagram* posts. Scrutinizing a corpus of 6,142 posts, they discover that emojis frequently replace parts of an otherwise verbally expressed proposition. When standing in for nouns, verbs, adjectives, or prepositional phrases, and, in some cases, even complex propositions, emojis take over functions usually performed by writing. The authors posit, however, that emojis cannot be equated with writing either, but rather preserve a potential for iconic and symbolic meaning making and thereby blur the usual distinction between writing and image, a phenomenon the authors capture with the term *iconographetic communication*.

Michele Zappavigna turns to *image macros* as image-centric Internet memes designed to traverse various communicative contexts and to proliferate across social media platforms and beyond. Her particular interest lies in the visual-verbal co-construction of intersubjectivity and the quoted voice. Using the example of *and then he said*-image macros, Zappavigna raises awareness of the complexity of multimodal projection induced through practices of user-based content curation. Expanding previous work in systemic functional linguistics and social semiotics, she presents methodological tools to tease apart the diverse *intermodal ties* between the obligatory and central image, its superimposed caption, the posts into which the meme may be embedded, and further tags and responses. In this context, she probes particular cases of reference resolution which show that a strict alignment of coherence and cohesion measures can be easily dispensed with in social media communication – on platforms that prioritize intersubjectivity to encourage participation and even contribution to what Zappavigna calls an *unfolding social stream*.

4.4 Part 4: Image-Centric Practices as Global Design Strategies

Finally, if we posit and describe a trend toward *multimodal image nuclearization* in current media practices, that is, an ever more effective combination of headlines/captions and large, central, and dominant images, we must ask what general design strategies and multimodal techniques are at work in image-centricity and also what forces drive such processes of genre development. Likely candidates to be considered here are a desire for an increased perceptual salience and faster traversal of genres, a greater selectivity of reading, an atomization of text items in a medium, as well as the de-linearization of pages and the creation of visual tableaus (cf. Knox, 2007 and Pflaeging, 2017b for some of these issues). Such choices may also be motivated by the values and ideological positioning the media products share with their audiences.

The contribution of **John S. Knox** investigates *news apps* on tablet devices, which have, in recent years, gained currency as outlets for news institutions to reach audiences. In particular, he draws attention to the unique design possibilities offered by their comparatively larger screens and further technological affordances. Rooted in the tradition of previous social-semiotic work on news design, Knox examines 12 English-language news apps from Australia, the UK, and the USA, with a view to the overall *visual design of the page,* and the use of images as functional components of a news story. On the basis of these distinctions and his findings, Knox proposes to reserve the term *image-nuclear* for cases in which an image is an obligatory element of a (news story) genre, and to establish *image-centric* as a superordinate term for cases in which images are essential design elements of texts – regardless of their status as s genre component.

Peter Wignell, Sabine Tan, Kay L. O'Halloran, Rebecca Lange, Kevin Chai, and **Michael Wiebrands** explore image-centric design strategies pursued by the violent-extremist organization of ISIS in the production of their online propaganda magazines *Dabiq* and *Rumiyah.* Their analysis, firmly couched in the tradition of systemic functional multimodal discourse analysis, reveals that images central to propaganda purposes are not only textually prominent layout elements but are charged with interpersonal meanings. Through processes of iconization, pictorial elements such as heroes, relics, scripture, or enacted creeds evolve into *bonding icons* that convey values inextricably linked to an extremist world view. Due to their reduced ideational meaning, such images are open to multiple interpretations and lend themselves to a *re-contextualization* across mainstream and social media platforms. Here, they distribute swiftly and widely as image-centric anchor points of entire discourses – findings that, in some respects, also echo Klug's research. The authors conclude by suggesting innovative ways of utilizing automated image analysis to, ultimately, also support actions against a continuing legitimization of extremist mind-sets and an incitement of further violence.

Martin Engebretsen's chapter acknowledges the central role that image-centric, *stand-alone data visualizations* have come to play in contemporary data-driven news media discourse. In his analysis of two sample graphics taken from a Norwegian tabloid news site, he combines concepts from several strands of research (social semiotics, but also cross-disciplinary work on data visualization). In particular, he teases apart the complex – and in some respect idiosyncratic – workings of multimodal meaning making on an ideational, interpersonal, and compositional level. Evolving from this discussion, he raises awareness of the new forms of media literacy that the comprehension of such image-centric visualizations require. Tying his argument to even broader questions of the development of journalistic practice, Engebretsen discusses *datafication, visualization,* and *digitization* as possible driving forces behind the rise of stand-alone data visualizations, and the repercussions their growing prevalence may have on other journalistic genres.

The volume also features short commentaries by **John A. Bateman, Martin Luginbühl, Carey Jewitt,** and **Teal Triggs.**

5 Concluding Remarks

In sum, the principle aim of this volume is to explore image-centric practices in the contemporary media sphere. It argues that a greater reliance of text producers on visuals has repercussions on the *genre space* (Bateman, 2014, p. 70) of a medium and leads to new multimodal genres (and *genre repertoires*, cf. Stöckl, 2017a) with novel and specific *text-image relations* (Stöckl, 2015a, pp. 239–241). We also take into consideration the social context in which contemporary media genres are produced, acknowledging a number of driving forces that shape this trend toward image-centricity, for example, a concern with visual aesthetics, an increase in perceptual and cognitive salience, the values and ideologies underpinning image selection, a de-linearization and atomization of media content, and the creation of visual tableaus. We hope that it inspires future scholars to continue to research the vital role that images play in the shaping of our cultural conscience.

References

Adami, E., & Jewitt, C. (2016). Special issue: Social media and the visual. *Visual Communication, 15*(3), 263–270.

Barthes, R. (1964/1977). The rhetoric of the image. In R. Barthes (Ed.), *Image – Music – Text* (pp. 32–51). London: Fontana.

Bateman, J. (2014). *Text and image: A critical introduction to the visual-verbal divide*. New York, NY: Routledge.

Bateman, J., Wildfeuer, J., & Hiippala, T. (2017). *Multimodality: Foundations, research and analysis – A problem-oriented introduction*. Berlin: de Gruyter.

Bednarek, M., & Caple, H. (2012). *News discourse*. London: Bloomsbury.

Caple, H. (2013). *Photojournalism: A social semiotic approach*. Basingstoke: Palgrave Macmillan.

Caple, H. (2008). Intermodal relations in image-nuclear news stories. In L. Unsworth (Ed.), *Multimodal semiotics: Functional analysis in contexts of education* (pp. 125–138). London: Continuum.

Caple, H., & Knox, J. (2017). Genre(less) and purpose(less): Online news galleries. *Discourse, Context & Media, 20*, 204–217.

Caple, H., & Knox, J. S. (2015). A framework for the multimodal analysis of online news galleries: What makes a "good" picture gallery? *Social Semiotics, 25*(3), 292–321.

Durrani, S. (2017). *Representing nations through visual narratives: Pakistan and Iran in Time Magazine (1981–2010)* (Unpublished doctoral dissertation). University of New South Wales, Sydney, NSW.

Feez, S., Iedema, R., & White, P. R. R. (2008). *Media literacy*. Surry Hills, NSW: NSW Adult Migrant Education Service.

Halliday, M. A. K. (1985/1994). *An introduction to functional grammar*. London: Arnold.

Jewitt, C., Bezemer, J., & O'Halloran, K. (2016). *Introducing multimodality*. London: Routledge.

Johnson, S., & Prijatel, P. (1999). *The magazine from cover to cover: Inside a dynamic industry*. Lincolnwood: NTC Publishing Group.

Kjeldsen, J. E. (2012). Pictorial argumentation in advertising: Visual tropes and figures as a way of creating visual argumentation. In F. H. van Eemeren & B. Garssen (Eds.), *Topical themes in argumentation theory: Twenty exploratory studies* (pp. 239–255). Dordrecht etc.: Springer.

Klug, N.-M. (2016). Multimodale Text- und Diskurssemantik. In N.-M. Klug & H. Stöckl (Eds.), *Handbuch Sprache im multimodalen Kontext* (pp. 165–189). Berlin: de Gruyter.

Knox, J. S. (2009a). Visual minimalism in hard news: Thumbnail faces on the smh online home page. *Social Semiotics, 19*(2), 165–189.

Knox, J. S. (2009b). Punctuating the home page: Image as language in an online newspaper. *Discourse & Communication, 3*(2), 145–172.

Knox, J. S. (2007). Visual-verbal communication on online newspaper homepages. *Visual Communication, 6*(1), 19–53.

Martinec, R., & Salway, A. (2005). A system for image-text relations in new (and old) media. *Visual Communication, 4*(3), 337–371.

Molnar, S. (2018). *Advolution. A systemic functional perspective on the diachronic development of advertising since the 17th century* (Unpublished doctoral dissertation). University of Salzburg, Salzburg.

Norris, S. (2014). Modal density and modal configurations. In C. Jewitt (Ed.), *The Routledge handbook of multimodal analysis* (pp. 86–99). London: Routledge.

Perlmutter, D. D. (1998). *Photojournalism and foreign policy: Icons of outrage in international crises*. Westport: Praeger.

Pflaeging, J. (in press). From image to text, from list to story: Diachronic perspectives on social interaction through viral online genres. In C. Thurlow, C. Dürscheid, & F. Diémoz (Eds.), *Visualizing digital discourse. Interactional, institutional and ideological perspectives* (t.b.a.). Berlin: de Gruyter.

Pflaeging, J. (2017a). Communicative potentials and their use: The case of popular science journalism. In A. Brock & P. Schildhauer (Eds.), *Communication forms and communicative practices: New perspectives on communication forms, affordances and what users make of them* (pp. 181–208). Frankfurt am Main: Peter Lang.

Pflaeging, J. (2017b). Tracing the narrativity of National Geographic feature articles in the light of evolving media landscapes. *Discourse, Context and Media: Special Issue 'Media Evolution and Genre Expectations', 20*(4), 248–261.

Pflaeging, J. (2015). "Things that matter, pass them on": ListSite as viral online genre. *10plus1: Living Linguistics, 1*, 156–181.

Royce, T. (1998). Synergy on the page: Exploring intersemiotic complementarity in page-based multimodal text. *JASFL Occasional Papers, 1*(1), 25–48.

Stöckl, H. (2017a). Multimodality in a diachronic light: Tracking changes in text-image-relations within the genre space of a printed medium. *Discourse, Context and Media: Special Issue 'Media Evolution and Genre Expectations', 20*(4), 262–275.

Stöckl, H. (2017b). The multimodal enigmatic advertisement: 'En-riddling' as a rhetorical strategy in commercial persuasion. In P. Handler, K. Kaindl, & H. Wochele (Eds.), *Ceci n'est pas une festschrift* (pp. 69–81). Berlin: Logos.

Stöckl, H. (2015a). Bewegung auf der Titelseite: Ausdifferenzierung und Hybridisierung durch Sprache-Bild-Texte. In S. Hauser & M. Luginbühl (Eds.), *Hybridisierung und Ausdifferenzierung: Kontrastive Perspektiven der Medienanalyse* (pp. 235–259). Bern: Lang.

Stöckl, H. (2015b). From text linguistics to multimodality: Mapping concepts and methods across domains. In J. Wildfeuer (Ed.), *Building bridges for multimodal research: International perspectives on theories and practices of multimodal analysis* (pp. 51–75). Frankfurt am Main: Peter Lang.

Stöckl, H. (2014a). Typography. In S. Norris & C. D. Maier (Eds.), *Interactions, images and texts: A reader in multimodality* (pp. 283–295). Berlin: de Gruyter.

Stöckl, H. (2014b). "He begs to inform every person interested": A diachronic study of address and interaction in print advertising. *Anglistik/International Journal of English Studies, 25*(2), 81–196.

van Leeuwen, T. J. (2008). New forms of writing, new visual competencies. *Visual Studies, 23*(2), 130–135.

Part 1
Advances in Theory

2 Image-Centricity – When Visuals Take Center Stage
Analyses and Interpretations of a Current (News) Media Practice

Hartmut Stöckl

1 Introduction: Image-Centricity

The specific shifts highlighted in the title of the present book mirror a more general idea in multimodality research: Fix (2001, p. 115) points out that in the semiosphere or the semiotic landscape (Kress, 1998, pp. 57–66), some semiotic modes may become more dominantly used, whereas others lose importance. Such shifts from periphery to center over time have been described for typography and aptly labeled *new writing* (cf. van Leeuwen, this volume) to emphasize their serious repercussions on communicative processes (van Leeuwen, 2008). A similar, technology-driven shift concerns the increased significance of sound in modern audio-visual media (van Leeuwen, 1999). Here, I will be concerned with an obvious and well-attested move of various media to more strongly rely on visuals as a representational resource (Kress & van Leeuwen, 1996; Pflaeging, 2017; Stöckl, 2017). This shift seriously affects the status and functionality of language, text-image relations, and the development of multimodal genres.

Looking to current journalistic practices, perhaps four image-centric trends seem noteworthy. First, in magazines and newspapers – print and online alike – images have come to be used frequently, in effect, to optimally survey for the reader the stories or media content available. Such multimodal genres in previewing function (on homepages and contents pages of magazines) have been called newsbites or newsbits (Knox, 2007). They cue the reader into a story's main topic and its newsworthy elements but also often convey an evaluative stance (Economou, 2006, pp. 214–215). Second, maps, charts, and data visualizations have been accepted as largely self-sufficient media content (cf. Engebretsen, this volume) rather than serving as illustrations for parts of stories, that is, textual themes (Stöckl, 2012). In such infographic genres, visuals serve as a graphic organizing principle for content and text structure. Third, in social media, for example, Facebook or Instagram, major content posted is increasingly photographs or videos, which users comment on. In this case, images are communicative points of departure; they lead multimodal texts and initiate verbal commentary and explanation (Caple, 2019). Finally, images can constitute a story largely in and of themselves, when photographs are accompanied by a headline and extended caption only – something that has been researched intensively by Caple (2008, 2013) and called *image-nuclear news story*. Here, the cohesive ties between image and text elements as well as the functions of text to either describe the image or extend its context have been at the center of attention. This is a very fruitful methodological perspective applicable to the multimodal genres or the image-centric genre family mentioned here.

Based on these general observations, the chapter posits a shift toward image-centricity, which manifests itself in the diversification of image-centric genres. I seek to explore this trend in multimodal (journalistic) practices on a small English-German national newspaper-corpus sampled in 2016. My two main aims will be to draw up a typology of image-centric newspaper genres and to sketch out the levels and criteria needed in multimodal genre description and differentiation. Rather than limit image-centricity to news media, I regard it as a general principle of media story writing adopted for a variety of reasons rooted in changing habits of media-production and reception. Essentially, image-centricity is conceptualized here as including two complementary elements: First, images are more frequently used and come to dominate layout and story format due to size and impact – this aspect could be called *image dominance*. Second, images become more semantically and rhetorically potent; both in their own right but also in their intersemiotic relations to text – this aspect could be termed *image centrality*. Image dominance and centrality together make visuals important entry points for readers and steer their perception and evaluation of media content.

The chapter first critically reviews current research on multimodal genre change and image versus verbiage nuclearity (Section 2). Section 3 presents the material, hypotheses, and results of the corpus study. Section 4 then introduces the levels and criteria in the type of multimodal genre analysis needed to distinguish individual image-centric genres. Section 5 finally summarizes main points and offers potential explanations of and driving forces behind image-centricity.

2 Multimodal Genre Practices in Motion

2.1 The Rise of the Visual

Caple and Knox (2015, p. 292) say about the recent developments at issue here: "we have witnessed a fundamental shift toward visual story telling. Images dominate the verbal story space". They also emphasize the fact that the newly emerging multimodal genres pose "challenges for practitioners and analysts alike" (Caple & Knox, 2015, p. 292). From the perspective of linguistic and multimodal research, these challenges have been met mainly by a fusion of systemic-functional genre analysis (cf. Martin & Rose, 2008) and the study of text-image relations from the perspectives of intersemiotic cohesion and appraisal theory (cf. Bateman, 2014, Chapters 8, 10, and 11). The former accommodated images as stages in a multimodal discourse structure (van Leeuwen, 2005b, pp. 76–81); the latter identified functions of images in relation to text and vice versa, especially highlighting the evaluative aspect of images on the one hand, and the descriptive and explanatory orientation of text accompanying images on the other.

Let us very briefly review three types of studies here to indicate the spectrum and direction of relevant approaches. First, following on from early research (Kress & van Leeuwen, 1998), Stöckl (2015) sketches the emergence of a new image-centric front-page genre in the *Frankfurter Allgemeine Zeitung*. He argues that lead images, which are initially part of a front-page story and form *single image-caption complexes* (Caple & Knox, 2015, p. 295) in a *verbiage-nuclear news story* (Caple, 2013, Chapter 6), over time attract more text and become independent story nuclei in *image-nuclear stories* (Caple, 2013, Chapter 5). This new hybrid genre, a multimodal newspaper editorial, serves multiple functions: to point to various stories inside the paper, to voice the editorial opinion about a topical news item, to establish news values, and to entertain through intersemiotic play (Stöckl, 2015, 238–239). Such studies focus on genre emergence and change; they demonstrate how generic functions and structure give rise to specific text-image relations.

Second, studies of online news media (Caple & Knox, 2012, 2015, 2017) have drawn attention to interesting multimodal genre effects of the intensified availability and use of images in journalism. News or picture galleries, which thrive online and have had a wash-back effect on print media, are a case in point. Rather than using them for the study of intersemiotic relations, Caple and Knox found that news galleries offer a window onto intrasemiotic relations, that is, the ways in which multiple images establish a narrative or encyclopedic structure and the ways multiple captions work together to build a coherent text. Again, such studies show new image-centric multimodal genres in the making and focus on their typical and variable discourse structures.

Third, another type of study opts to consider entire media as collections of multimodal genres and traces their change over larger periods (Pflaeging, 2017; Stöckl, 2017). The focus of such diachronic multimodal studies can either be on the development of one genre (e.g., feature article in *National Geographic*, Pflaeging, 2017) and its *image-caption clusters* or on *multimodal rhetorical clusters* across various genres (Stöckl, 2017, for the *MIT Technology Review*). These studies show shifts in multimodal practices over larger stretches of time (e.g., increasing narrativity, Pflaeging, 2017) driven by a whole host of contextual factors as well as a close interrelation between image use or text-image relations and genre change.

2.2 The Image-Nuclear News Story

It was Helen Caple's work (2008, 2013) on what she called *image-nuclear news stories* (INNSs) that gave the type of research outlined earlier in the chapter a very decisive orientation in that it helped us understand exactly what a rise of the visual might entail. Following on from Iedema, Feez, and White's work (1994) on story nuclei and satellites, Caple argues some news genres use an image to relay the nucleus of a story, that is, its most important kernel of information usually included in headline and lead. What results is a rhetorical structure in which a central image plus headline form the nucleus, which is elaborated in an extended caption providing one or more story satellites. Verbiage-nuclear stories, by contrast, relate the story nucleus through text and use images to serve as story satellites. In terms of genre change from verbiage-nuclear to image-nuclear, we witness here a shift in the discourse-structural status of the image. It becomes central so that accompanying text directly refers to the content and style of the image.

INNSs – which show some resemblance to newsbites (Knox, 2007, p. 23; Caple, 2008, p. 125) and standouts (Economou, 2012, p. 246) – have been defined by recourse to a number of typical genre features:

(1) a large, aesthetically pleasing image (Caple, 2010, p. 119);
(2) a heading and a prosodic tail, that is, beginning of caption, both directly relating to the image (Caple, 2008, p. 126; Caple, 2013, pp. 127–130);
(3) verbal-visual play between image, headline, and caption (Caple, 2010; Caple & Bednarek, 2010; Stöckl, 2015, pp. 243–245);
(4) an extended caption containing both linguistic elements describing pictorial content (experiential orientation) and elements providing its wider story context (contextual extension) (Caple, 2013, pp. 130–131);
(5) an evaluative stance (often in line with editorial opinion, ideological angles, and news values determined by the medium) expressed through the combination of headline/image (Economou, 2006, 2012; Caple, 2008, p. 126).

It is two approaches to INNSs in particular that have consolidated methods for researching text-image relations in general: First, scrutinizing accompanying text for its function in relation to the image has resulted in a clearer awareness of what kind of semiotic work the cohesive ties between lexis and pictorial elements actually perform. The types of semantic relations known from clause-connections and rhetorical structure (cf. Bateman, 2014, pp. 161–174, pp. 205–221) have proved very helpful in drawing up a repertoire of common and typical text-image relations. This is an analytical toolkit that adapts well to any other multimodal genre. Second, the notion that "prominent images can function as

Macrotheme [...] for a whole text" (Economou, 2006, p. 214) and may – explicitly or implicitly – evoke an evaluative or attitudinal response in the reader, which accompanying text can reinforce, modify, or counteract, is crucial for multimodal analysis. This train of thought has rightly drawn attention to the news or ideological values that are inscribed or provoked by images and has made available analytical distinctions developed in linguistic/social-semiotic appraisal theory (Bednarek & Caple, 2012, Chapters 3 and 6) that apply to images and text alike.

2.3 The Image-Centric Genre Space

The theory and practical study of INNSs has, however, also raised some questions. Observations in my corpus show quite clearly that the INNS as initially described by Caple (2013) is a very specific and narrowly defined genre, while some of its defining features seem general enough to apply to a whole range of similar and related genres. Among others, we might raise the following questions: Are both headline and prosodic tail needed to form a multimodal story nucleus? How extensive are extended captions or can whole stories also function as image-central accompanying text? Are both experiential orientation and contextual extension obligatory elements in the text? And finally, how constitutive is verbal-visual play for the genre? The hypothesis I am advancing here is that modern media display quite some variety of image-centric genres, which form what could be called an image-centric *genre space* or *genre family*, that is, a network of related genres all of which share important multimodal features, above all, of course, image-centricity. The INNS à la Caple is a constitutive element of this genre space or genre family; its defining features may be scrutinized for what they are worth in describing other image-centric genres. So what exactly may we best understand by image-centricity?

In Barthes' (1964/1977) early account of *text-image relations*, image-centricity is captured in the notion of *anchorage*, which is one type of *unequal status relations* (Martinec & Salway, 2005, p. 349), the reverse being *illustration*, where the text is in the lead. So for a multimodal text to be image-centric, the text needs to comment on or semantically 'anchor' the image. However, Barthes says: "Obviously, the two functions of the linguistic message (i.e., anchorage and relay, H.S.) can co-exist in the one iconic whole, but the dominance of the one or the other is of consequence for the general economy at work" (Barthes, 1964/1977, p. 41). He understood the crucial nature of status relations, yet conceded that unequal and equal status can co-occur. This clearly raises doubt about a simplistic dichotomy of image-centric and verbiage-centric multimodality. Unequal status also in some way runs counter to the very principle of multimodality that postulates mutual mode integration and reciprocal meaning multiplication, regardless of which mode may be in the lead.

However, if we wish to maintain the practically useful distinction, we must stipulate two major defining criteria for image-centricity already suggested by Caple: (1) the image is large and dominant in the layout – its content and design have the power of arresting viewer attention, and (2) the largest part of the accompanying text directly relates to the image so that strong intersemiotic cohesive ties emerge. I have labeled these two aspects image dominance and centrality (cf. Section 1) and contend they are the hallmarks of image-centric genres; the other criteria set up by Caple to define the more specific and narrow INNS need not hold for the entire genre space.

It may be elucidating to relate image-centricity to the three general perspectives on multimodality: production, product, and reception. Producers need to select images that can function as cognitive points of departure for texts; products must display rich and direct intersemiotic cohesion, and recipients need to really be attracted to the images and be led by them in(to) the engagement with the entire multimodal story. Having thus defined image-centricity, we are still free to interpret the image-centric shift in current multimodal communication as either a deterministic process of change driven by technological development, as a genre- or media-specific trend or as an intensifying pattern of image use, which may also reverse. Whatever stance we take on this, based on a small explorative corpus, the present study advances a two-part hypothesis: (1) image-centric newsstory writing forms a superordinate genre family comprising a whole range of individual genre members, and (2) this image-centric genre space is potentially large and diverse – it is shaped by the journalistic cultures of the media in question and by a principle of an aesthetic reversal (Cook, 2001, pp. 224–230) in multimodal practices.

3 Studying Image-Centric Journalistic Cultures and Practices

3.1 Corpus, Questions, and Aims

The corpus underlying my general observations was sampled between March and May 2016 and includes altogether 33 complete issues of different German/Austrian and British/American print newspapers of national distribution. From this material, a smaller, more balanced corpus was collated (24 issues – four time sets from April/May 2016 with six papers each, three German, three British/American; cf. Table 2.1),

Table 2.1 Small exploratory German-English newspaper corpus

NEWSPAPERS	FAZ	SZ	W	GW	INYT	UT
Set 1 | Dates	08-04-16	13-04-16	13-04-16	08-04-16	08-04-16	12-04-16
Set 2 | Dates	20-04-16	20-04-16	16-04-16	15-04-16	12-04-16	19-04-16
Set 3 | Dates	27-04-16	27-04-16	27-04-16	22-04-16	19-04-16	26-04-16
Set 4 | Dates	08-05-16	08-05-16	07-05-16	06-05-16	26-04-16	06-05-16

FAZ = Frankfurter Allgemeine Zeitung | **SZ** = Süddeutsche Zeitung | **W** = Die Welt | **GW** = The Guardian Weekly | **INYT** = International New York Times | **UT** = USA Today.

Image-Centricity – When Visuals Take Center Stage 25

which I used to draw up the typology of image-centric news stories (ICNSs) and conduct a few inter-newspaper comparisons and quantifications. This corpus yielded a total of 103 ICNSs.

The corpus proper exclusively represents national quality newspapers with a large distribution; this decision was made to record established journalistic practices likely to lead markets and design trends. The inclusion of two language cultures, German and English, was to allow for a broader culture-contrastive analysis, even though ultimately, the focus was primarily on individual journalistic cultures and their comparison. The large majority of the issues are weekday ones; the German corpus, however, contains three (out of 12) weekend issues, which usually contain some more pictorial material so that given the British/American papers are international editions with no weekend issues, the quantification may be slightly skewed in this respect.

Based on this material, I was interested in the following aspects:

1. What ICNSs feature in the corpus? How can the respective genres be distinguished and labeled on the basis of typical generic features? The resulting typology draws on selected aspects of multimodal genre description presented in Figures 2.5 and 2.6.
2. How do the various types distribute in the corpus generally, and in the various newspapers in particular? What can such frequencies tell us about newspaper cultures and about how prominent ICNS genres are in different journalistic cultures as compared with verbiage-centric genres?

Generally, the qualitative analysis of the corpus aims at outlining the current uses of image-centric news media practices in big national newspapers and seeks to establish a sub-genre repertoire of the image-centric genre space (or genre family). Here the focus is on the dimensions of multimodal genre description in which image-centricity can differ, a concern that will be taken up again in Section 4. The quantitative elements of the analysis are to indicate that genre profiles (cf. Luginbühl, 2011, pp. 311–315) may be a suitable way to compare newspaper cultures with regard to image-centric news media practices and relating these to verbiage-centric ones. It goes without saying that the value of the present quantification is rather limited. Given a larger corpus, however, spanning a long(er) period of time and looking at many different newspapers and journalistic cultures, such a quantitative angle could be quite productive and revealing.

3.2 Qualitative Analysis: Image-Centric News Story Genres

The 103 exemplars of ICNSs were determined by applying the two general criteria for image-centricity set up earlier (cf. Section 2.3): large and dominant image in the layout (dominance) and accompanying text relating directly to the image (centrality). The corpus represents different medial practices and different genres; altogether six distinct genres were differentiated, which I decided to label as follows: (1) Preview, (2) Story Intro, (3) INNS, (4) Editorial, (5) Explainer, and (6) Gallery. What I seek to describe below is genre prototypes, that is, typical exemplars of the respective category – it is useful to accommodate the notion of intra-genre variability. Rather than attempt a very fine-grained genre description at this stage, my aim is a valid distinction of the six genres on the basis of some effective generic descriptors as contained in Figures 2.5 and 2.6. So I scrutinized the ICNS genres for their function (the predominant semiotic work they do), their location in the medium, their internal structure and layout, the size/nature of the accompanying text, the type of image used, and, where obvious, details of the text-image relation. In Section 4, I will refine the multimodal genre analysis by suggesting other levels and criteria of description.

Previews are situated either at the top of the front page or of individual sections. As the genre label suggests, they preview and highlight major stories by indicating their story nuclei (e.g., *The skinny on eating less. Why food companies are pushing smaller portions.* ut_26-04-16_top-bar, cf. Figure 2.1 – ❶). In contrast to online newsbits/newsbites, I decided to label them preview. These paratextual previews often, but not always, contain explicit references or pointers to the location of the actual story (e.g., *in money*, ut_26-04-16_top-bar). In terms of structure, a headline and subhead combine with a usually smaller format, specially cropped image, while an extended caption is missing. As previews are usually accommodated in a graphic bar, left-right compositions seem most plausible, with either image or text placed first in the linear sequence. Whereas the very brief text must be capable of relating the story nucleus, the image typically shows a news actor, object, or situation that is central to the story. Consequently, repetition, synonymy, meronymy, hypo-/hyperonymy, and collocation seem useful and expectable intersemiotic sense relations (cf. Royce, 1998, p. 31). It is interesting to see that online newspaper homepages are essentially accumulations of such ICNS previews; Knox (2007) calls them newsbits or newsbites, which need not necessarily feature images, but increasingly do so. In print newspapers, they occur much more rarely and serve to signpost to the reader stories that are given special news value in the issue.

Story Intros, like previews, announce and highlight a story. However, they are located at the top of the very story they introduce and take up a lot of page space. Economou (2012) calls them standouts, apparently for their graphic/image salience but has also characterized them as *macrothematic* (2006, p. 232) and as *story introductions* (2008, p. 254). In story intros, a rather large and appealing image combines with typographically marked text that, while still following the headline-subhead logic, can be extended to include author, type of story, and major subtopics covered, and grammatically resembles a text comprised of three to four clauses rather than a clause or clause-complex (e.g., *Der beste Freund. Kuscheltiere*

Image-Centricity – When Visuals Take Center Stage   27

Figure 2.1 ❶ Preview – *USA Today* ut_26-04-16_1, ❷ Story intro – *Süddeutsche Zeitung* (weekend edition) szw_08-05-2016_50, ❸ INNS – *International New York Times* inyt_12-04-16_7.

werden von ihren kleinen Besitzern überall hin mitgenommen Aber wehe, wenn sie plötzlich mal verschwinden. szw_08-05-16_50_kuscheltiere, cf. Figure 2.1 – ❷). Consequently, besides relating to the image, accompanying text also extends the context in that it sets the scene for the story to be told. Most importantly, the story intro can also incorporate a caption in addition to headline and subhead. In terms of layout, the image serves as a graphic background for the text, which needs to be set off against it – this explains the extra effort with its typographic design. The multimodal composition allows for maximum flexibility and variety. Much strategic thought goes into the selection and design of the images, which often are conceptual as well as montaged rather than narrative press photographs; they can supply the visual elements crucial for cueing readers into the knowledge frame of the story.

INNSs (cf. Figure 2.1 – ❸) – in my corpus often explicitly labeled Photos of the Day/Week – use a high-impact photograph to tell a brief story by relating all accompanying text to the event/action represented in the image. Any paratextual or sign-posting function as in preview and story intro is absent from such ICNSs. The multimodal text structure of headline + image + extended caption represents a self-sufficient story, where some text elements realize ekphrasis, while others extend the context of the image by elements we do not see in the image but that are contiguously or episodically related to it. In many ways, this ICNS-genre presupposes a narrative image or at least a configuration of objects and/or people that suggests potential action in a scenario. Also, given the wealth of photographs available to editors and authors at a given point in time, images in INNSs need to be spectacular either for form/design (cf. Caple's criteria for aesthetics in the balance network, Caple, 2013, Chapter 4) or capture content that is highly topical or rarely captured in pictures at all. Again this does not hold at all for the kind of generic/repetitive (but not unimaginative) conceptual images in previews and story intros. As accompanying text engages in either experiential orientation or contextual extension, the ensuing intermodal cohesive ties will be close in the first, and more loose/indirect in the latter function. Finally, my corpus suggests that INNSs can occur in both the soft news and the hard news sections. They vary greatly with regard to structure (i.e., presence of headline and prosodic tail), scope, and playfulness between language and image.

Editorials (cf. Figure 2.2 – ❶) resemble INNSs regarding their layout and structure; they also combine a large striking image with a headline and extended caption, which is also often introduced by a playful prosodic tail. However, their functionality is different: rather than tell an image-centered story, the text may pursue altogether four functions. It explicitly points to one or more stories inside the paper, links and contextualizes various news items, evaluates and comments on one or more news themes, and evokes semantic incongruities and tensions in the interest of building a humorous attitude or ironic distance to the news item(s) (cf. Stöckl, 2015, pp. 238–239). (The editorial in Figure 2.2 – ❶ associates social democratic policy-making and electorate with the atmosphere in corner-pubs.) This complex semiotic work, which mirrors some of the tasks of magazine editorials (Thompson & de Klerk, 2002), can only be performed effectively if the editorials are placed on the front page or in a prominent position on the comments pages. The latter placement is typical of editorial cartoons (cf. van den Hoven & Schilperoord, 2017), which are treated as a subtype of the editorial in my account of ICNS

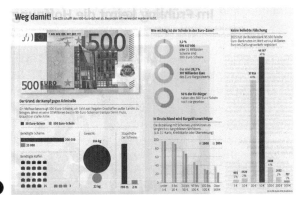

Figure 2.2 ❶ Editorial – *Frankfurter Allgemeine Zeitung* – faz_20-04-16_1, ❷ Explainer – *Süddeutsche Zeitung* (weekend edition) szw_08-05-16_7, ❸ Gallery – *Guardian Weekly* gw_22-04-16_24.

genres. In contrast to image-centric front-page editorials (evidently typical of German news culture currently), such editorial cartoons feature little text; usually just a short one-clause caption (and speech/thought balloons, of course), whose main function is a humorous commentary expressing the voice of the paper. Contrary to generic press photography, the images in newspaper editorials often do not show news-relevant visual elements (the example in Figure 2.2 – ❶ shows a typical Berlin corner-pub), make reference to fictional or historical worlds, and represent conceptual images in the form of drawings, paintings, or depictions of cultural artifacts. The editorial in Figure 2.2 – ❶ is a textually explicated allusion to E. Hopper's *Nighthawks*. A focus on form (i.e., frames, perspectives, colors, lighting, etc.) over and above their content is apparent (cf. Stöckl, 2015, p. 249). Besides rather inconspicuous uses of accompanying text as experiential orientation, the text-image relations are typically based on multimodal metaphor, metonymy, analogy, or comparison (cf. Stöckl, 2015, pp. 250–252).

Explainers (cf. Figure 2.2 – ❷) reflect the increased importance of the infographic and data-visualizing format for news writing (cf. Engebretsen, this volume). They fuse diagrammatic and pictorial material with short text in one graphic space, which is typically neatly segmented into info-blocks. The internal structure of explainers is flexible because headlines, captions, or language labels (legends) may be placed in various relations to images and graphics. As the term suggests, explainers fulfill the function of providing explanatory background to topical news themes by locating, quantifying, and comparing data items and by showing the internal structure and processes of objects and systems (cf. Stöckl, 2012, pp. 181–184). The types of graphics and data visualizations are diverse owing to the increase in available software and displayable data. Image-centricity shows in the largely self-sufficient readability of the graphic/pictorial information, which is elaborated by verbal labels denoting colors and graphic shapes but also by short or extended captions providing context. Explainers can either be largely independent texts treating individual news topics, or they may complement a longer story. In any case, they are framed as separate texts – either with or without a reliance on intertextual relations. The more self-sufficient the explainers are, the more complex and manifold the data and its display and the more strongly they foreground their aesthetic qualities. Such qualities show in more images, more diverse visualization types, and the adaptation of different medial patterns (cf. Stöckl, 2012, pp. 191–194).

Galleries have extensively been treated by Caple and Knox (2012, 2015, 2017) as an online ICNS-genre promoted by the wide availability of excessive amounts of images and medial affordances of the screen, as, for instance, scrollable or hyperlinked content. Be they digital or printed, the semiotic hallmark of galleries is multiple images that give rise to intrasemiotic relations, that is, cohesive ties establishing coherence between individual images and between individual captions. Even though Caple and Knox (2017, p. 1) seem to doubt this when in current practice they observe "an incohesive series of image-caption complexes collected under a headline", potentially, images can easily be sequenced to either report an event as temporally connected series of actions and situations (event-based) or as parts of a scenario, object, or frame of knowledge (theme-based). Consequently, captions in such coherent galleries usually use systematic cohesive ties to construe an overall coherent caption text across individual images. My corpus contains both largely incoherent collections of single image-caption complexes under a heading like *eyewitnessed* (gw_22-04-16_24, cf. Figure 2.2 – ❸) and coherent theme-based galleries with richly cohesive captions (w_07-05-16_2_bilder-d-tages_5). The first type features a very economical use of the captions in the service of mainly experiential orientation and minimal contextual extension (e.g., *A Greenpeace activist abseils down Nelson's column in Trafalgar Square, London after fitting a face mask to the 52-metre high monument to highlight pollution fears*, gw_22-04-16_24); the latter makes an effort to produce more extensive captions that feature mainly contextual extension and develop a story or explanatory commentary to coherently link mainly theme-based images. The function of galleries, which exclusively feature photographs, is either to survey and highlight major recent news events or to showcase spectacular, aesthetically rewarding photos and contextualize them in an explanatory or evaluative fashion.

3.3 Quantitative Analysis: Genre Profiles and News Cultures

After briefly surveying and comparing the nature of the six ICNS-genres, I will now look at how these distribute in the corpus. The relative-frequency breakdown of the genres across the six newspapers informs us about the popularity of individual genres and their respective communicative functions in the medium. Story intros (37.9 percent) are the most frequent ICNS-genre – we may conclude from this that image-centricity primarily serves to attract readers to key stories. Very generally, the image-centric principle lends a particular news value to those stories and makes them stand out on the page. Essentially, the same functionality is realized by the previews, which are the second most ICNS-genre in the corpus (17.5 percent). Here image-centricity promotes intertextual relations between a paratext and the actual story, which are located in different parts of the newspaper. INNSs make up 17.5 percent of the total number of ICNS-genres. They demonstrate the narrative potential of images and their function of relating a brief news story in conjunction with just an extended caption and headline. Explainers (10.7 percent) are the next most frequent ICNS-genre overall and highlight the function of infographic and data-visualizations for explaining issues either as self-sufficient news or as news background. Editorials follow in frequency, with 9.7 percent highlighting the evaluative and commenting function of ICNSs. In this genre, leading news combines with images and cartoons to give voice to the editorial opinion of the medium. Finally, galleries represent the least frequent ICNS-genre in the present corpus. On the one hand, this may indicate the suboptimal suitability of galleries for the printed medium as compared with online newspapers. On the other hand, the very presence of galleries testifies to the importance of surveying news events and showcasing particularly striking photographs regarding content and aesthetics. The most important conclusion from the overall frequency breakdown seems that an intertextual previewing function that leads into stories and highlights them is paramount in the medial logic of newspapers as it underlies story intros, previews, and editorials, totting up to a total of 65.1 percent of all ICNS-genres.

Newspapers as a *super-* or *macro-genre* (Bhatia, 2004, p. 57) are characterized by specific collections or configurations of individual genres. Looking at their types, frequencies, and the relations between them establishes what Luginbühl (2011, pp. 311–315) has called a *genre profile*. This idea favorably adapts to our concerns with image-centricity, and a profile of the ICNS-genres in each newspaper of the corpus (cf. Figure 2.3) can be drawn up. If we compare the individual image-centric genre profiles, represented in Figure 2.3 as bars constituted of segments in different colors, we are able to form an idea of differences and similarities between journalistic cultures regarding image-centricity in multimodal news writing.

A first observation tells us that each newspaper in the corpus features its own very special genre profile, that is, a certain mix of ICNS-genres, which reflects the editorial conventions and the journalistic news

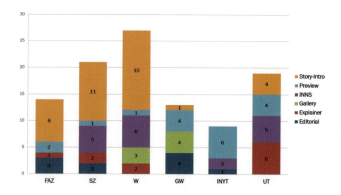

Figure 2.3 Image-centric genre profiles for the six newspapers in the corpus.

culture at a given point in time. So, for instance, the W features galleries, whereas the UT does not, and both fail to use editorials. Disregarding details, a second observation suggests a marked contrast between the German (three bars to the left) and the English/American newspapers (three bars to the right): Whereas story intros appear in roughly equal measure to be typical of the German papers, they do not frequently occur in the English/American corpus. Conversely, previews seem typical of English/American news culture and rarely feature in the German papers. This may mean that German news culture has a penchant for highlighting and more strongly illustrating the very news stories themselves, while English/American news culture prefers to paratextually signpost major stories visually. A third observation aims at the number of different ICNS-genres in the various papers and produces a plausible distinction between high and low genre-diversity, as exemplified by W and SZ (high), and INYT (low), respectively. Such results may give rise to identifying trends toward stronger visualization or tabloidization in the case of papers that display a rich ICNS-genre diversity.

It is probably easy to gauge the general methodological potential of genre profiles, which – given a large corpus and an additional focus on the positioning or sequencing of the genres in the medium – has much to offer for an in-depth enquiry into news cultures and their use of image-centric genres. Finally, a comparison of the frequency of ICNS-genres with that of verbiage-centric ones for two selected newspaper issues (i.e., W 3 June 16 vs. UT 16 June 16, cf. Figure 2.4) produces a strong overall dominance of verbiage-centric stories, making up 81 percent and 85 percent of all stories, respectively (W: N = 83; UT: N = 165). This allows for the general conclusion that image-centric genres still represent a marked case of news reporting. Note, however, that this does not mean that verbiage-centric stories are un-illustrated; however, in them, images, while perhaps even

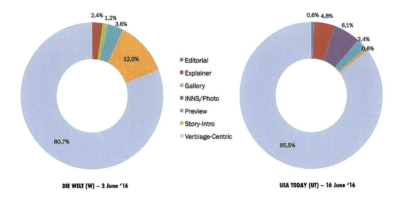

Figure 2.4 Frequencies of image- and verbiage-centric news genres in two newspapers.

being dominant, are not central/nuclear as they do not realize the story nucleus but a satellite. An evident shift toward visual newswriting, then, does not seem to be driven by an increase in image-centric genres alone but rather by an increased number of images across all kinds of genres.

4 Multimodal Genre Analysis

While the present corpus study has provided a plausible repertoire of the image-centric media genre family drawn up on the basis of just few central typological criteria, it cannot claim an exhaustive description of this image-centric genre space nor has it been able to tease out intra-genre variability. For multimodal genre analysis to achieve these goals, that is, a comprehensive and detailed genre differentiation of the image-centric applicable to all kinds of media, it needs to be equipped with clear analytical criteria on a number of levels of text description. The present section sketches out such an analytical framework and suggests *news (media content) type*, *compositional* and *thematic* generic *structure*, *image type*, and *text-image relations* as five global levels of enquiry, each offering its own set of criteria and choices. The analytical suggestions made here draw on and redevelop well-established work in multimodality (cf. Bateman, 2014, pp. 161–174, pp. 186–221) and previous work on specific multimodal news genres (cf. Caple, 2013, pp. 91–141; Knox, 2014; Caple & Knox, 2015). Visualized in Figures 2.5 and 2.6 as an analytical heuristic for analysis, the proposed framework may easily be enhanced or supplemented by increasing the number of criteria or choices.

4.1 News (Media Content) Type

Image-centric news media practices may, first of all, be shaped by the kinds of contents they convey. *News categories* like hard/soft news, culture, travel, or sports are a first suitable differentiating criterion to ascertain whether different media sections develop their own image-centric (sub-)genre conventions. Another aspect to investigate is the type or degree of intertextuality, which allows for a distinction between largely self-sufficient (i.e., isolated, e.g., INNS) and multiply-related media image-centric genres (e.g., editorial). Finally, it may also be profitable to scrutinize the prominence of the story/content, as image-centric genres might be sensitive to differences between leading, breaking, and headline-making front-page items and trivial, minor consecutive stories.

4.2 Compositional Structure

A second analytical level is concerned with the form of the generic structure as indicated by layout, typography, and length/size of text. The present study suggests that this kind of *compositional or formal structure* is quite versatile and can effectively signal different image-centric genres. First, we may profitably ask which stages (i.e., headline, subhead,

Image-Centricity – When Visuals Take Center Stage   35

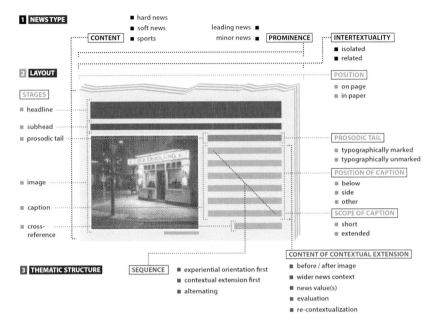

Figure 2.5 Framework for multimodal genre analysis: ❶ *News type* | ❷ *Layout* | ❸ *Thematic structure* (Visualization: J. Pflaeging).

prosodic tail, caption, cross-reference, etc.) the genre exemplars contain and which ones are obligatory or optional. Second, regarding the salience of the caption's initial part, it is useful to look at practices of typographically marking the prosodic tail, like font choices, color, or size. Third, the overall gestalt of the image-centric genre will heavily depend on where captions are placed in relation to the central image. Such choices predispose recipients to reading paths like top-bottom or left-right and give varying prominence to caption and image. Fourth, the scope of the captions may be calculated in number of words. These sizes indicate differing potentials for accommodating experiential orientation/contextual extension and for elaborating varying densities of cohesive ties between visual image elements and verbal expressions in the captions. Finally, even though not strictly part of the genre exemplar, every image-centric genre must be placed in the space of the medium, that is, in a thematic section and somewhere on a page/screen. Again, this formal criterion of positioning characterizes genres and turned out to be indicative of different types of genre in the present study.

4.3 *Thematic Structure*

Generic structure can also be studied with an eye to how subtopics and propositions are sequenced in the (extended) captions. This is a

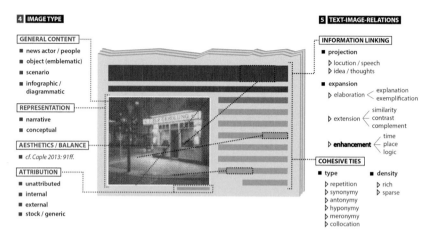

Figure 2.6 Framework for multimodal genre analysis ❹ *Image type* | ❺ *Text-image relations* (Visualization: J. Pflaeging).

perspective focused on thematic development and on how images are contextualized through caption text. First, more generally, one may ask about the sequencing of information in the service of experiential orientation or contextual extension, which might also produce alternating patterns and give varying prominence to the two caption functions. A predominance of experiential orientation characterizes more descriptive or narrative genre variants, while a predominance of contextual extension may point to more evaluative or argumentative genre variants. Second, more specifically, propositions and subtopics may be scrutinized for exactly how they add context to the image. Caple (2013, pp. 130–137) has already looked into this in quite some detail, but further content types and functions may be possible if the genre space embraces more than news (e.g., author, type of story, source of data etc.).

4.4 Image Type

Image-centric genres naturally are also greatly shaped by the types of images predominantly used, as each of them affords different meaning potentials. A first analytical criterion on the level of *image type* looks at what kind of generalized content the image relays, that is, news actors (typically) and emblematic objects, to name just two very different content categories. Second, with a view to descriptions of images in theories of visual grammar (cf. Kress & van Leeuwen, 1996), quite some detail is available to categorize how images represent their content. Most fundamentally, we must ask about any image whether it provides a narrative or a conceptual process, that is, does the image show action or static objects in relation and their symbolic attributes. This has immediate repercussions for the kinds of captions, as accompanying text will either help specify the scenario and unfold the pictorial action or it will describe and elaborate on the objects depicted. Third, the compositional structure of professional media images may be designed to achieve aesthetic effects. Caple (2013, pp. 91–120) has described some of the major semiotic choices and structures available to image makers in her *balance network*, arguing that aesthetic pleasure and balance derive from "organizing the visual information in the image frame into regular and symmetrical patterns" (Caple, 2013, p. 95). Applying this notion to the image-centric genre space, it is important to take into account that each genre (and medium) may develop its own prototypical *balance*, that is, compositional choices, whose aesthetic effects are bound to wane through repeated use. This is why truly aesthetic effects in the sense of making the form of an image stand out and leading the recipient to reflect on its impact on visual meaning are only to be had through continuous change and innovation (cf. *principle of reversal* – Cook, 2001, p. 224). Fourth, given that prominent images are capable of conveying an attitudinal stance or an evaluative angle (Caple & Knox, 2012, pp. 220–224), it is useful to scrutinize images for any more or less clear affect orientations, positive/negative and neutral being the most general, while other more specific ones like shock, awe, sympathy, and adoration are also possible. Finally, the images used may differ greatly with regard to their source or attribution (cf. Caple & Knox, 2017, p. 7), which can essentially range from professional (agency – media external/ staff – media internal) to amateur or unattributed images sampled from unknown or undisclosed sources. The type of source or explicit attribution in image use greatly impacts on the credibility and authority, as well as on the singular or generic quality of the represented reality or pictorial message. Image-centric genres clearly differ as to their practices of sourcing and attributing images – while some (INNSs) require singularity, others (story intros) may trade in generic stock images.

4.5 Text-Image Relations

It would seem plausible to argue that differences in image-centric genres show most clearly on the descriptive level of text-image relations. Based on the substantial theoretical work already done on intersemiotic relations of text and image (cf. Bateman, 2014, pp. 161–174), at least two major analytical criteria seem essential: the logical-semantics of information linking (cf. van Leeuwen, 2005a, pp. 220–226; Bateman, 2014, pp. 188–190, pp. 195–197) and intersemiotic cohesion or texture (cf. Royce, 1998; Bateman, 2014, pp. 165–172). Regarding the first criterion, text accompanying a centric image may project what depicted people say or think, and elaborate, extend, or enhance pictorial information and messages. Looking into more detail, we may inspect conjunctive relations distinguishing a temporal, spatial, or logical basis (i.e., cause, effect, purpose, etc.). Emerging linking patterns for different image-centric genres will be shaped among others by the type of story content and by the general functionality of the genre (e.g., evaluative/argumentative vs. narrative). With regard to intersemiotic cohesion, we can first look at the types of intersemiotic sense relations that form cohesive ties between visual message elements and verbal expressions. Simple repetition or synonymy will create a different texture than hyper-/hyponyms, for example. Second, disregarding the specific types of ties, we can simply count all their instances and form an idea of how richly or sparsely intersemiotic cohesion is realized in the texture of the multimodal genre.

It is vital to realize that distinct image-centric genres and sub-genres always emerge on the basis of differences on all the levels and criteria set out earlier. So, ultimately, each image-centric genre must come as a specific bundle or configuration of properties. However, it may well be – and my corpus explorations indicate this – that selected criteria are more salient and strongly genre-distinguishing than others. These would then have to count as prototypical features of the image-centric genre space at large. Such strongly genre-distinctive features are: intertextuality of media content, presence/configuration of stages, scope of caption, type of contextual extension, general image content and narrative/conceptual type, and intersemiotic cohesion. Corpus studies would perhaps be well advised to make these features analytical priorities.

5 Summary and Conclusion: Driving Forces of Image-Centric Media Practices

Based on a conceptual clarification of image-centricity, this chapter has advanced and illustrated the idea that image-centricity materializes in different genres that cumulatively create a diversified image-centric genre space or genre family. A small-scale exploratory corpus study was used to draw up an inventory of image-centric (news) media genres in current German and British/American journalistic print culture, highlighting the observation that each newspaper creates its own image-centric genre profile, which contrasts with those of other papers. Adopting central descriptive criteria of a multilevel framework for genre analysis, each image-centric genre was characterized. Naturally, the study merely represents a selective snapshot of the current state of image-centric genre development. Such research may favorably be expanded by looking into the historical making of image-centricity (cf. Stöckl, 2015, pp. 239–241; Pflaeging, 2017) and by studying newly emerging or *nascent genres* (Martinec, 2013). Caple and Knox (2017, p. 11) argue that, generally, new genres are likely to emerge "when social activity and social purpose are aligned in new contexts". The present chapter suggests that in order to track down image-centric genres within linguistic multimodality studies, we need an analytical framework with clear levels and criteria. Such a guiding rationale and toolbox for empirical analysis has been fleshed out here (cf. Figures 2.5 and 2.6). It may be useful in adding to the repertoire of image-centric genres or sub-genres across various media and in enriching the description of the individual genres.

Finally, studies such as this raise the question of whether there really is a trend towards image-centricity in current media practices, and, if so, what drives this trend and what it entails. First, form a media-producer's perspective, image-centricity increases the perceptual salience of stories on pages and screens, as images effectively attract attention and lure recipients into reading. Second, from a reader's perspective, image-centricity promotes the easy selectivity and faster traversal of entire media (offers) (cf. Knox, 2007, p. 48). While *atomization* (Knox, 2007, p. 19), that is, decreasing size/scope of news items as in newsbites, seems primarily an online media screen phenomenon, it may, in the long run, turn out to affect printed media too and create de-linearized pages and visual tableaus rather than continuous reading matter. On a critical discourse analytical note, increasing image-centricity may also imply less real discursive storytelling and explanation in exchange for more inscribed or evoked attitudinal and evaluative meanings in the multimodal story nuclei.

References

Barthes, R. (1964/1977). The rhetoric of the image. In R. Baths (Ed.), *Image, music, text* (pp. 32–51). London: Fontana.

Bateman, J. A. (2014). *Text and image: A critical introduction to the visual/verbal divide*. London: Routledge.

Bhatia, V. K. (2004). *Worlds of written discourse: A genre-based view*. London: Continuum.

Bednarek, M., & Caple, H. (2012). *News discourse*. London: Bloomsbury.

Caple, H. (2019). "Lucy says today she is a Labordoodle": How the dogs-of-Instagram reveal voter preferences. *Social Semiotics, 29*(4), 427–447.

Caple, H. (2013). *Photojournalism: A social semiotic approach*. New York, NY: Palgrave Macmillan.

Caple, H. (2010). Doubling up: Allusions and bonding in multi-semiotic news stories. In M. Bednarek & J. R. Martin (Eds.), *New discourse on language: Functional perspectives on multimodality, identity, and affiliation* (pp. 111–133). London: Continuum.

Caple, H. (2008). Intermodal relations in image nuclear news stories. In L. Unsworth (Ed.), *Multimodal semiotics: Functional analysis in contexts of education* (pp. 125–138). London: Continuum.

Caple, H., & Bednarek, M. (2010). Double-take: Unpacking the play in the image-nuclear news story. *Visual Communication, 9*(2), 211–229.

Caple, H., & Knox, J. (2017). How to author a picture gallery? *Journalism, 9*, 1–20.

Caple, H., & Knox, J. (2015). A framework for the multimodal analysis of online news galleries: What makes a 'good' picture gallery? *Social Semiotics, 25*(3), 292–321.

Caple, H., & Knox, J. (2012). Online news galleries, photojournalism and the photo essay. *Visual Communication, 11*(2), 207–236.

Cook, G. (2001). *The discourse of advertising*. London: Routledge.

Economou, D. (2012). Standing out on critical issues: Evaluation in large verbal-visual displays in Australian broadsheets. In W. L. Bowcher (Ed.), *Multimodal texts form around the world: Cultural and linguistic insights* (pp. 246–269). London: Palgrave Macmillan.

Economou, D. (2008). Pulling readers in: News photos in Greek and Australian broadsheets. In E. A. Thomson & P. R. R. White (Eds.), *Communicating conflict: Multilingual case studies of the news media* (pp. 253–280). London: Continuum.

Economou, D. (2006). The big picture: The role of the lead image in print feature stories. In I. Lassen, J. Strunck, & T. Vestergaar (Eds.), *Mediating ideology in text and image: Ten critical studies* (pp. 211–233). Amsterdam: Benjamins.

Fix, U. (2001). Zugänge zu Stil als semiotisch komplexer Einheit. In A. Rothkegel & E.-M. Jakobs (Eds.), *Perspektiven auf Stil* (pp. 113–126). Tübingen: Niemeyer.

Iedema, R., Feez, S., & White, P. R. R. (1994). Stage two: Media literacy. A report for the write it right literacy in industry research project by the Disadvantaged Schools Program, NSW. Sydney: Department of School Education.

Knox, J. (2014). Online newspapers. In C. Jewitt (Ed.), *The Routledge handbook of multimodal analysis* (pp. 440–449). London/New York: Routledge.

Knox, J. (2007). Visual-verbal communication on online newspaper homepages. *Visual Communication, 6*(1), 19–53.

Kress, G. (1998). Visual and verbal modes of representation in electronically mediated communication: The potentials of new forms of text. In I. Snyder (Ed.), *Page to screen: Taking literacy into the electronic era* (pp. 53–79). London: Routledge.

Kress, G., & van Leeuwen, T. (1998). Front pages: (The critical) analysis of newspaper layout. In A. Bell & P. Garrett (Eds.), *Approaches to media discourse* (pp. 186–219). Malden, MA: Blackwell.

Kress, G., & van Leeuwen, T. (1996). *Reading images: The grammar of visual design*. London: Routledge.

Luginbühl, M. (2011). Genre profiles and genre change: The case of TV news. In J. Androutsopoulos (Ed.), *Mediatization and sociolinguistic change* (pp. 305–330). Berlin: de Gruyter.

Martin, J. R., & Rose, D. (2008). *Genre relations: Mapping culture*. London: Equinox.

Martinec, R. (2013). Nascent and mature uses of a semiotic system: The case of image-text relations. *Visual Communication, 12*(2), 147–172.

Martinec, R., & Salway, A. (2005). A system for image-text relations in new (and old) media. *Visual Communication, 4*(3), 337–371.

Pflaeging, J. (2017). Tracing the narrativity of *National Geographic* feature articles in the light of evolving media landscapes. *Discourse, Context and Media: Special Issue 'Media Evolution and Genre Expectations', 20*(4), 248–261.

Royce, T. D. (1998). Synergy on the page: Exploring intersemiotic complementarity in page-based multimodal text. *JASFL Occasional Papers, 1*(1), 25–48.

Stöckl, H. (2017). Multimodality in a diachronic light: Tracking changes in text-image relations within the genre profile of the *MIT Technology Review*. *Discourse, Context & Media: Special Issue 'Media Evolution and Genre Expectations', 20*(4), 262–275.

Stöckl, H. (2015). Bewegung auf der Titelseite: Ausdifferenzierung und Hybridisierung durch Sprache-Bild-Texte. In S. Hauser & M. Luginbühl (Eds.), *Hybridisierung und Ausdifferenzierung: Kontrastive Perspektiven der Medienanalyse* (pp. 235–259). Bern: Lang.

Stöckl, H. (2012). Finanzen verbalisieren: Die Text-Bild-Sorte Infographik. *OBST Osnabrücker Beiträge zur Sprachtheorie, 81*, 177–199.

Thompson, S., & de Klerk, V. (2002). Dear reader: A textual analysis of magazine editorials. *Southern African Linguistics and Applied Language Studies, 20*, 105–118.

van den Hoven, P., & Schilperoord, J. (2017). Perspective by incongruity: Visual argumentative meaning in editorial cartoons. In A. Tseronis & C. Forceville (Eds.), *Multimodal argumentation and rhetoric in media genres* (pp. 137–163). Amsterdam: Benjamins.

van Leeuwen, T. (2008). New forms of writing, new visual competencies. *Visual Studies, 23*(2), 130–135.

van Leeuwen, T. (2005a). *Introducing social semiotics*. New York, NY: Routledge.

van Leeuwen, T. (2005b). Multimodality, genre, and design. In S. Norris & R. H. Jones (Eds.), *Discourse in action: Introducing mediated discourse analysis* (pp. 73–94). New York, NY: Routledge.

van Leeuwen, T. (1999). *Speech, music, sound*. London: Macmillan.

3 Intertextual Reference in Image-Centric Discourse
Analytical Model, Classification, and Case Study

Nina-Maria Klug

1 Defining Discourse

First, the use of the term *discourse* in this chapter must be specified, as the term is interpreted differently across the social sciences. Some use *discourse* to describe small communicative units of spoken or written language on the local level of the single text or individual interaction (cf. Bateman, 2016, p. 45). This kind of discourse is the object of, for example, *conversation analysis* as an approach in the study of social action, for example, turn-taking organization in everyday conversation (e.g., Cameron, 2001; Sacks, 1995; Ten Have, 1999). Bateman, Wildfeuer, and Hiippala (2017, p. 133) label this *small d* discourse, which involves "fine-grained analyses of particular instances of communication and the mechanics by which utterances, turns, sentences, etc. can be flexibly joined together to make 'larger' texts".

Big D Discourse (Bateman et al., 2017, p. 133) aligns with the theory of Foucault (1969/2002) and characterizes a phenomenon of a much broader dimension (e.g., Angermuller, 2014; Gardt, 2007). I will refer to this second concept of discourse that reaches far beyond the individual text: in my paper, *discourse* is understood as a *transtextual* semantic unit. The term is used in a way that is more or less synonymous with the communicative construction of a social *discussion* of a topic in which several social actors/groups with different point of views participate and argue (Reisigl & Wodak, 2016, p. 27). A single discourse is reflected in all texts dealing with the same topic (Busse & Teubert, 1994, p. 14; cf. Gardt, 2007, p. 30). As the sum of these texts, the transtextual semantic unit *discourse* is characterized by "a dialectical relationship" that is "socially shaped, but is also socially shaping – or socially *constitutive*" (Fairclough, 1995, p. 55; Reisigl & Wodak, 2016, p. 27). It represents and constitutes the knowledge of social groups, that is, people who share a particular topographical, temporal, and/or cultural space, and views about certain topics, such as global warming, Donald Trump, women, squirrels, love, the pursuit of happiness, or how to behave on a first date. The way people think and feel about their world, others, and themselves is manifested discursively (cf. van Dijk,

2016, p. 68). Discursive practices regulate their "ways of doing things" (Fairclough, 2016, p. 87; van Leeuwen, 2008, p. 6).

Discourses may also have "major ideological effects – that is, they can help produce and reproduce unequal power relations between (for instance) social classes, women and men, and ethnic/cultural majorities and minorities through the ways in which they represent things and position people" (Fairclough & Wodak, 1997, p. 258). Texts constituting a discourse are using "strategies that appear normal or neutral on the surface, but which may in fact be ideological and seek to shape the representation of events and persons for particular ends" (Machin & Mayr, 2012, p. 9). In a nutshell, discourses determine and represent our *social reality* (cf. Berger & Luckman, 1966). In order to analyze and understand social reality, a type of discourse analysis that can contribute to social and cultural analysis (cf. Fairclough, 1995, p. 53; Gardt, 1999; Machin & Mayr, 2012) thus functions as the 'silver bullet'.

However, since discourses are virtual semantic units, and because it is never possible to analytically grasp all the texts that constitute them, discourse analyses must always be based on a subset of discourse, on a selection of individual texts in the understanding of concrete realizations of human knowledge (cf. Lemke, 1995). In defining a corpus, practical aspects such as the availability of the sources as well as relevance criteria with regard to content, actors, genre, or media are critical. However, the particular interest of the researchers who compile the text corpus and their subject-matter orientations (Busse & Teubert, 1994, p. 14) must always be regarded as the decisive factor in the text choices and compilation. Regardless of the specific research question and the descriptive or critical attitude on which the transtextual approach is based, linguistic discourse analyses often have one thing in common: with the exception of *Multimodal Critical Discourse Analysis* (MCDA) (cf. Machin & Mayr, 2012), most of them only include texts or parts of texts consisting of language. In this chapter, I point out some reasons why linguists should not limit themselves to language when compiling a corpus for discourse analysis, no matter whether they follow a descriptive approach, which aims at patterns of the construction of social reality, or whether they adhere to Critical Discourse Analysis, concentrating on the relations of discourse and power.

2 The Multimodal Construction and Representation of Social Reality in Discourse

Without a doubt, language plays an important role in the discursive construction and representation of social reality. But even a cursory glance at conventions of human interaction tells us that communication is never limited to language. People always use several semiotic resources (*modes*) when it comes to meaning making (cf. Stöckl, 2016). They embed spoken and written language in contexts of other semiotic modes, like gestures, facial or body expressions, music, sounds, or images. In this sense, *multimodality* is understood as the functional use of more than one mode of expression, more than one semiotic system for the purpose of communication (cf. Stöckl, 2016, p. 4). A *multimodal text* is "one in which two or more different meaning-making systems combine to produce a text that is one complete semantic unit, not of form, but of meaning" (Caple, 2008, p. 131).

Print media such as newspapers or books can be carriers of texts, composed of visual signs such as written language and static images. Audio media like radio or CD can be used to transport multimodal texts consisting of language spoken or sung, music, and sound. Media such as TV or smartphones allow texts in which both visual and auditory signs of a static or moving kind are used. If, therefore, multimodality is a typical characteristic of the individual text (Kress & van Leeuwen, 1998, p. 186), this must all the more apply to discourse: multimodality determines its very essence. Social reality is *discursively constructed* through language use, but, crucially, also by incorporating other modes, such as the semiotic system of images (cf. Bednarek & Caple, 2012, p. 2; Machin & Mayr, 2012, p. 9), which are the subject of this article.

3 Intertextuality as a Means of Accessing Discourse

If discourses are conceived as transtextual units of texts, which are united in that all these texts are linked to each other by semantic relationships, intertextuality must be understood as the most obvious characteristic of the discursive construction of social reality (cf. Spitzmüller & Warnke, 2011, p. 189). The term *intertextuality*, which dates back to the 1960s (Bakhtin, 1968/1984), refers to all implicit and explicit relations between texts (Broich & Pfister, 1985, p. 11; Broich, 2000, p. 175), that is, all more or less visible traces of other texts in a given text (Berndt & Tonger-Erk, 2013, p. 7). These relationships between texts are usually differentiated into two global types of intertextuality (cf. Klug, 2018, pp. 109–110).

Firstly, there are forms of intertextuality described as *typological* (cf. e.g., Holthuis, 1993). They pertain to the reference of a specific text (*token*) to one or more underlying categories (*type*). *Typological intertextuality* is important when it comes to a description of the relationship between a single text and its genre (e.g., Fairclough, 1995, pp. 77–79), in the sense of a "socially conventionalized type and pattern of communication that fulfills a specific social purpose in a specific social context" (Reisigl & Wodak, 2016, p. 27; see also Bateman, 2008). Forms of typological intertextuality are also taken into consideration in discourse analyses that seek to describe other socially conventionalized patterns. Through these patterns, the individual texts of a discourse are *indirectly* connected with each other. Mental categories like *conceptual metaphors* (cf. Lakoff & Johnson, 1980), *frames* as conceptual units of knowledge representation (cf. Ziem, 2014), or *topoi* as categories of argumentation (Wengeler, 2003) should be mentioned here (examples of such analyses can be found in Klug, 2012, 2016). They all share their important role in the communicative handling of discourse topics. Secondly, there are *direct* forms of intertextuality described as *referential* (cf. Holthuis, 1993). *Referential intertextuality* refers to the relationships between specific texts, for example, in the form of quotations, allusions, adaptations, translations, paraphrases, montages, or plagiarisms (see Genette, 1993).

In the contemporary media sphere, images, too, play an important role as intertextual anchors. It does not come as a surprise why images must be understood as constitutive parts of discourse: not only are they only indirectly linked with other non-linguistic and linguistic texts by sharing certain conceptual patterns, but they also stand in manifold direct intertextual relations to them, that is, they are syntagmatically linked to each other. A discourse can thus be seen as a coherent *and* cohesive transtextual unit of a multimodal character. In the case of the typological connection between texts in a discourse, linguists can freely decide which texts to select for analysis. In the case of referential intertextuality, the text in question determines which other texts it relates to intertextually; they form a necessary background to adequately understand it. The need for including these texts – regardless of the modalities which helped to constitute them – becomes particularly apparent when several texts refer to the same text in the discourse: they highlight it as particularly relevant within the discourse.

Just like verbal texts, images can form the center of a dense network of direct intertextual references to other texts of a verbal or pictorial nature (Klug, 2018, pp. 115–116). What is more, not only can an image take on a key position in individual texts (cf. Caple, 2013, pp. 128–141; Manghani, 2013, p. xxi), it can even be the *key text* (cf. Spieß, 2013) itself. In other words, images can function as discourse nuclei in that they convey a newsworthy event or raise a socially central issue. Their key position in discourse is expressed in the fact that they are "followed by a series of satellites" (Caple, 2008, p. 126). All kinds of text can function as satellites to the centric image as they develop the discourse initiated by it or surrounding it.

4 Modal Affordances of Images

If an image appears as the nucleus of a discourse through intertextual references of various kinds and modes, it must have certain characteristics that justify its special relevance for the meaning making in other texts. Factors conditioning image-centricity may mainly be found in the specific *affordances* of images (see Bednarek & Caple, 2012, pp. 112–118 for press photography).

> Modal affordance is used to refer to what it is possible to express and represent easily with a mode. Affordance is a concept connected to both the material and the cultural, and social historical use of a mode. In other words, the affordance of a mode is shaped by what it offers materially, how it has been repeatedly used to mean, in part by its provenance, and the social conventions that inform its use in context. Kress (2013, 61) suggests that, each mode, as it is realized in a particular social context, possesses a specific 'logic' which points to key features of modes, such as the way some modes are inevitably temporally instantiated, and which in turn provide different communicational and representational potentials. [...] As a result of these different material and cultural affordances, some things can be signified more easily in an image, others in speech. (Jewitt & Hendrikson, 2016, p. 148)

With regard to the semiotic affordances of images, for instance, five features may be distinguished (others are discussed in Stöckl, 2016, pp. 9–18), the first three of which illustrate why images can be perceived particularly well (cf. Sachs-Hombach, 2003, pp. 73–78; Klug, 2018, pp. 116–118). Firstly, images have advantages over language when it comes to attracting the attention and interest of recipients. For example, the components of images are perceived simultaneously. Language is perceived in a linear way, that is, one word is perceived (heard or read) after the other, and this takes time (cf. Nöth, 2000, p. 481). Secondly, images can also be memorized more effectively than words. This retention advantage has been described as the *picture superiority effect* (see e.g., Kroeber-Riel, 1993, pp. 155–156; Weidenmann, 1988, pp. 135–138). Thirdly, the interpretation of pictorial signs is 'easier' and 'faster', because they are not firmly linked to knowledge of a *symbolic* character, which is based on conventionality like the fully arbitrary signs of language (cf. Peirce, 1931–1958, Collected Papers 4, § 447). With a view to Peirce's commonly used semiotic categories, images can usually be interpreted (at least) *iconically*, through inferences based on similarity (cf. Peirce, 1931–1958, Collected Papers 4, § 418; see also Jappy, 2013; Schmitz, 2016, pp. 343–344). Sometimes (especially in the case of the photographic image) they can be interpreted *indexically*, because they are related causally to their referents (cf. Peirce, 1931–1958, Collected Papers 2, § 281–283). In other words: it takes an existing object to be photographed. The fourth point is closely related to the indexical interpretation: photographs seem superior to verbal texts when it comes to suggesting credibility. Photographic images that only seem to reproduce what the camera captures in real objects are far more credible than language-based texts (Holly, 2016, p. 405). We believe to see the world through the photo as it really is (cf. Burke, 2003; Klug, 2015, pp. 508–509), although we know exactly how easy it is to retouch/doctor photographs (cf. Holly, 2016, p. 405). And finally, the processing of images in the right brain hemisphere and their iconic richness of representation also generate a high emotional activation potential (Stöckl, 2016, p. 16). Images have a special emotionalizing or appealing influence that far exceeds the affordances of language with regard to the potential for evoking compassion.

5 Intertextual Reference to a Nuclear Image in Discourse: Case Study and Typology

The specific affordances of images are reflected not least in events of collective grief evoked by iconic images that have affected our collective memory and spread throughout the world and over generations, such as the so-called *Napalm Girl*. This photograph, taken by Nick Út, captures a moment of the U.S. war in Vietnam in 1972, when a young naked Vietnamese girl runs screaming in agony toward the camera after a U.S. napalm attack near her village. The iconicity and strong impact of this photo is demonstrated in the following two comments: on the 40th anniversary of Út's photograph on June 3, 2012, the *National Public Radio, Inc.* (US) wrote on its website: "Whatever your age, you've probably seen this photo. It's a hard image to forget" ("Napalm Girl"). *New Zealand Geographic* noted how such images assisted in "turning the tide of resentment against the war and accelerating its end" (Colton, n.d.).

A similar discourse-shaping relevance applies to recent photos such as the one of the dead Syrian refugee boy Aylan Kurdi (2015, by Nilüfer Demir, see Figure 3.2). In the following, I seek to shed some light on ways in which a transtextual discourse can develop from such an image. Major options for enabling direct intertextual reference that can be classified as either intra- or intermodal are listed in the following overview (Figure 3.1, see also Klug, 2018, pp. 118–128). All of them create cohesion and coherence between the satellite texts and the image-nucleus in a discourse.

To illustrate the different types of intertextuality as shown in Figure 3.1, I will focus on the discursive processing of the aforementioned photograph, which was taken by the Bodrum-based photojournalist Nilüfer Demir for the Turkish news agency DHA on the morning of September 2, 2015. It depicts a toddler with short, dark brown hair, dressed in a red T-shirt, blue trousers, and sandals, lying dead, face down, in the surf (Figure 3.2).

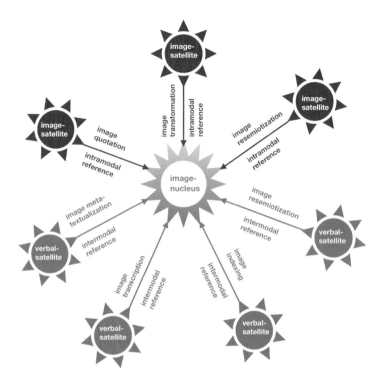

Figure 3.1 Classification of direct intertextual reference to images in discourse.

Figure 3.2 taz, Das Foto von Aylan Kurdi ging Anfang September 2015 um die Welt [The photo of Aylan Kurdi went around the world at the beginning of September 2015], http://www.taz.de/!5284043/, Photo: dpa.

5.1 Image Quotation

Images such as the photo of the little refugee boy first gained prominence in the discourse by *quotation*, which can be characterized as *intramodal reference* (cf. Klug, 2018, p. 119; see also Bednarek & Caple, 2012, pp. 121–123). On the very day in September 2015, when the picture was taken, it spread all over the world through the (social) web, television, and the front pages of newspapers. It was quoted in other texts and thus integrated into subsequent texts of various genres, such as in (online) newspaper articles, which will form the basis of the following discussion. In this process, Demir's photograph was either reproduced without any changes or modified in reproduction by means of pixelation, blurring, and similar techniques. Modifications of this kind are *partial quotations* from the previous image.

The fact that the photo was quoted in different ways seems at first to be a rather banal statement. However, the frequency of a complete or partial re-inclusion of a particular image in other texts is the most obvious way of indicating the central role the image plays in specific discourses. The citation identifies the cited photograph as a nucleus around which a whole series of satellite-texts orbit.

Moreover, the way in which the quotations are taken up again allows some conclusions to be drawn about the actors who use them. In the case of the image discussed here, the way in which it is cited, for example, sheds light on how the actors deal with social taboos. Nilüfer Demir's photograph shows an apparently dead child. In many contemporary societies, there has been a social taboo in the press for many years: one must not show dead human bodies in such a way that the individual becomes identifiable. Against the background of this social convention, it makes an important difference whether, for example, actors in discourse choose to quote a photograph, which depicts the child with his face turned toward the viewer, or if they show a picture of the dead boy being photographed from behind, so that at least his face cannot be identified. It also makes a difference whether an editorial team decides for the complete reproduction of the image rather than a form of the quote, which pixelates or blurs parts of the image (Figure 3.2). Finally, the choice of those image details that are rendered unrecognizable also illustrates the actors' different ways of dealing with corresponding image templates in discourse.

Newspapers from different countries quoted the image in a number of ways: the editors of *Channel 4* (UK) (Aylan Kurdi, 2015) decided in favor of a complete blurring of the picture, to a degree which makes the entire scene vaguely visible. The German *Westfalen-Blatt*, in its online edition of September 4 (Kemper, 2015), chose a complete black and white pixelation of the child, which makes the reference to Demir's photograph (rear view) visible only through the direct partial quotation of the environment. The online edition of the German *taz* (Figure 3.2) and the British newspaper *Mirror*, September 2 (2015), just softened the facial features of the boy, while the reference text (front view) was quoted in full. Other newspapers, such as *The New York Times* (Barnard & Shoumali, 2015), opted for the direct quotation of the complete front view – at least in the online edition. In the print version of the newspaper, the editorial team decided against using a direct citation of the photograph, that is, against depicting the dead boy's body.

For each of the countries mentioned here, further examples could be given that demonstrate a different handling of the picture quotation. Regardless of the type of citation, they point to the central role of photographs in news discourse.

5.2 Image Indexing

Intertextual references that highlight a pictorial nucleus are also found in texts that do not contain any image quotation. One such strategy of *intermodal* reference to an image (further strategies are discussed in Bednarek & Caple, 2012, pp. 121–123; Caple, 2013, pp. 142–160) is called *indexing* of the image and uses a linguistic expression that replaces the quotation (cf. Klug, 2018, pp. 120–121). This reference may be of a general nature. This is the case, for example, when an article in the German newspaper *Süddeutsche Zeitung* (Plöchinger, 2015 Example (1)) points out:

1 *Die Bilder von Bodrum sind allerorten im Internet zu finden*
[The pictures of Bodrum can be found everywhere on the Internet].

The intertextual reference can also be more specific, for instance, if the linguistic text includes an external link and thus hypertextually links to the pictorial nucleus. This strategy can be found in an article in the online edition of the German newspaper *Der Tagesspiegel* ("Presserat", 2015), which says:

2 *Wer das Bild des toten Flüchtlingsjungen Aylan Kurdi am Strand von Bodrum gesehen hat, wird es wohl nie wieder vergessen*
[Anyone who has seen the <u>picture of the dead refugee boy Aylan Kurdi</u> on the beach in Bodrum will probably never forget it].

A link (underlined in Example (2)) allows recipients direct access to the pictorial nucleus.

5.3 Image Meta-Textualization

Regardless of whether the image is quoted intramodally or is 'only' intermodally indexed, it is typically reflected in a verbal commentary.

Certainly, the frequency of *meta-textual references* increases with the nature of the nucleus, which can be regarded as highly emotionalizing, even taboo-breaking in the case of the example discussed in this chapter.

When contextualized by meta-textual reference, images are, for instance, *evaluated* linguistically. The emotional effect of the pictures is reflected upon and confirmed by the intertextual reference which characterizes them as "heart-breaking images of a Syrian toddler lying dead on a Turkish beach" ("Aylan Kurdi", 2015), or as "disturbing" (Moyer, 2015). They are evaluated as "die traurigsten Fotos auf der Welt" [the saddest photos in the world], which are "unerträglich" [unbearable] ("Toter Flüchtlingsjunge in Bodrum", 2015) and "conmociona[n] al mundo" [shock the world] ("La foto del chico sirio muerto", 2015).

In addition, verbal texts refer meta-textually to highly emotionalizing, taboo-breaking images when it comes to a *justification* of why such an image is either completely or partially quoted or why it is not presented at all. With regard to the image of a dead child discussed here, the justification seems almost self-evident. Demir's photograph reveals three patterns of argumentation in international discourse by which the handling of the picture is meta-textually substantiated (cf. Klug, 2018, pp. 121–122). Less direct forms of intertextual reference are typically substantiated by the social obligation to protect victims and their human dignity (cf. Example (3)) or to protect recipients (Example (4)).

3 *Warum wir hier kein totes Kind zeigen. [...] Aus Respekt vor der Menschenwürde haben wir den Jungen gepixelt*
   [Why we are not showing a dead child here. [...] Out of respect for human dignity we pixelated the boy] (Kemper, 2015).
4 *Das Bild zeigen oder nicht? [...] Ist es tatsächlich so, dass Menschen dem Tod erst ins Auge sehen müssen, um das tödliche Potenzial politischer Entscheidungen zu verstehen? Reichen nicht Worte wie zu Beginn dieses Artikels, um begreifbar zu machen, was vor jenem Strand passiert ist, was an vielen Orten gerade vielen Menschen passiert? Vulgär formuliert: Muss man Ihnen als Leserin oder Leser das Bild eines toten Kindes zum Frühstück zumuten, damit unmenschliche Aspekte der Asylpolitik in Ihren persönlichen Diskurs rücken?*
   [Show the picture or not? [...] Is it true that people first have to face death to understand the lethal potential of political decisions? Aren't words like the ones used at the beginning of this article enough to make us understand what happened at that beach, what is happening to many people in many places? To put it in a vulgar fashion: does it need confronting you, the readers, with the image of a dead child for breakfast so that inhumane aspects of asylum policy become part of your personal discourse?] (Plöchinger, 2015, cf. Endnote 9).

However, the complete image quotation is generally justified by the semiotic power of the image (cf. Examples (5) and (6)) and the obligation to document the event (Example (7)).

5 *If these extraordinarily powerful images of a dead Syrian child washed up on a beach don't change Europe's attitude to refugees, what will? [...] The Independent has taken the decision to publish these images because, among the often glib words about the 'ongoing migrant crisis', it is all too easy to forget the reality of the desperate situation facing many refugees* (Withnall, 2015).

6 *Le Monde.fr avait choisi de diffuser la vidéo montrant ces images dès mercredi après-midi. La photographie du petit garçon figure également sur notre 'une' jeudi 3 septembre, accompagnée d'un éditorial rédigé par notre directeur appelant à 'ouvrir les yeux'*
[Le Monde.fr has chosen to broadcast the video showing these images from Wednesday afternoon. The photograph of the little boy also appears on our front page on Thursday, 3 September, accompanied by an editorial written by our director calling for 'opening our eyes'] ("La photo d'un enfant mort", 2015).

7 *Auch wir haben uns entschieden, das Foto zu zeigen. Jeden Tag sterben Menschen an den europäischen Grenzen. Daran wollen und dürfen wir uns nicht gewöhnen. Wir wissen, das Bild ist schwer zu ertragen, aber es dokumentiert das Versagen Europas in der Flüchtlingskrise. Deshalb müssen wir unsere Leser damit konfrontieren*
[We have also decided to show the photo. Every day people die at European borders. We do not and must not get used to this. We know the picture is difficult to bear, but it documents Europe's failure in the refugee crisis. That is why we have to confront our readers with it] ("Toter Flüchtlingsjunge in Bodrum", 2015).

5.4 Image Transcription

Another strategy of intermodal reference to previously published images that identifies them as discourse nucleus is the practice of *transcription* (cf. Klug, 2018, pp. 122–123). The term *transcription* refers to the translation or transmission of image content into language (cf. on the concept of *transcriptivity*, Jäger, 2002; cf. the concepts of *transmutation* or *intersemiotic translation* as suggested by Jakobson, 1981, p. 190). Linguistic paraphrases, interpretations, explanations, or commentaries of a pictorial text are also included in the concept of transcription (see also the concept of the *translational intertextuality* in Krause, 2000, p. 66, and the intermodal relations of *identification*; cf. Caple, 2013, p. 145; Royce, 2002, pp. 193–194). In this sense, attempts are repeatedly made to translate the pictured into language (cf. Examples (8) and (9)).

8 *The picture, taken on Wednesday morning, depicted the dark-haired toddler, wearing a bright-red T-shirt and shorts, washed up on a beach, lying face down in the surf not far from Turkey's fashionable resort town of Bodrum* (Smith, 2015).
9 *The pictures show a small boy lying face down in the sand on a Turkish beach as an official stands over him* (Withnall, 2015).

Other forms of transcription explicate elements in pictorial reference not easily depicted due to the limitations of the pictorial mode and the fact, "that an image captures only one fleeting moment in an entire event" (Caple, 2013, p. 148). In this case of intermodal reference to the image, which Caple terms "intersemiotic expansion" (Caple, 2013, p. 154), words "add more or alternative information" (Caple, 2013, p. 154). For example, we learn something about the specific location of the event (cf. intermodal relation of *circumstances*, Royce, 2002, pp. 193–194; cf. Caple, 2013, p. 145), about the name, geographic origin, and age of the depicted child, and about his family (intermodal relations of *identification* and *attributes*, Royce, 2002, pp. 193–194; cf. Caple, 2013, p. 145). Only through intertextual reference do we find out that this toddler is a refugee and get to know about the circumstances of his flight and death (see Examples (10)–(13)).

10 *Flüchtlingsjunge Aylan Kurdi [...] Tot am Strand angespült* [Refugee boy Aylan Kurdi [...] washed ashore dead] (taz, 2016, see Figure 3.2).
11 *The boy was part of a group of 11 Syrians who drowned off the coastal town of Bodrum in Turkey after an apparent failed attempt to flee the war-ravaged country* (Withnall, 2015).
12 *The pictured boy is reported to be three-year-old Aylan, who drowned along with his five-year-old brother Galip and their mother, Rihan. Their father, Abdullah Kurdi, survived* (Migrant crisis, 2015).
13 *The family may have been trying to reach Canada. In June [...] Aylan's family 'desperately' tried to get permission to emigrate to Canada – where Abdullah's sister, Teema Kurdi, lives in Vancouver – but their refugee application was rejected by Canadian authorities* (Moyer, 2015).

Language specifies and concretizes the image in the intertextual reference by giving further information about the depicted participants or, for example, the circumstances that "may be locative (setting – including 'time' [...])" (Caple, 2013, p. 145). At the same time, it broadens the meaning of the image where it appears necessary: the photographically documented, individual death of the three-year-old Syrian refugee boy Aylan Kurdi is extended to the misery and death of "refugees" in general and to Europe's political failure in overcoming the refugee crisis (Examples (14)–(18)). The linguistic text suggests a certain symbolic interpretation of the image.

14 *First this photo became viral on the internet, shared everywhere, eliciting worldwide demands for aid to these families who are risking death and all their life's savings to get out of Syria, Iraq or Afghanistan, to reach Europe and safety* (Huffington Post, 2015).
15 *La foto de un chico sin vida tirado en una playa de Turquía tras el naufragio de dos botes con sirios que huían de la guerra conmocionó hoy profundamente al mundo, reflejando como quizás ninguna otra imagen hasta ahora el drama y la tragedia que persiguen a los refugiados y la fatal inacción europea*
 [The photo of a lifeless boy lying on a beach in Turkey after the shipwreck of two boats with Syrians fleeing the war today deeply shocked the world, reflecting, as perhaps no other image so far, the drama and tragedy that haunt the refugees and the fatal European inaction] ("La foto del chico sirio muerto", 2015).
16 *Manche Bilder vergisst man nicht. Sie prägen das Bild des Krieges. Das Foto des dreijährigen Ailan wird lange verbunden sein mit dem Tod der Flüchtlinge*
 [Some pictures are unforgettable. They shape the face of war. The photo of three-year-old Aylan will be associated with the death of the refugees for a long time] ("Presserat", 2015).
17 *[D]as Foto von Aylan Kurdi wurde zum Symbol der Flüchtlingskrise*
 [The photo of Aylan Kurdi became the symbol of the refugee crisis] (taz, 2016, see Figure 3.2).

By embedding the image in multimodal contexts of language, it is provided with a symbolic meaning that goes far beyond what is actually depicted. Today, Demir's photographs are regarded worldwide as a strong *symbol* of the current refugee crisis:

18 *It is an image that captures the human tragedy of Europe's migrant crisis* ("Image of drowned boy", 2015).

5.5 Image Transformation

As examples taken from the contemporary media landscape show, Demir's photographs have not only been linguistically indexed, metatextualized, or transcribed, they have been repeatedly transformed into other images that go hand in hand with a change of genre and media. One of many examples of such a *transformation*, which refers intertextually to the photograph, is the following (cf. Klug, 2018, pp. 124–126): at

Intertextual Reference in Image-Centric Discourse 55

Figure 3.3 Graffiti referring to Demir's photograph of the dead boy at beach, Frankfurt am Main (*Wikimedia Commons (creative commons)*, Photo: Frank C. Müller, Frankfurt am Main, 2016).

the beginning of March 2016, two German graffiti artists, Justus Becker and Oğuz Şen, transformed the photo of the dead toddler into a 120 sqm graffiti piece at East Harbor in Frankfurt am Main (see Figure 3.3).

The graffiti piece, which functions as a *pictorial satellite* that orbits the photographical nucleus intramodally, provides evidence for the intertextual handling of discourse-forming photos. There are a number of consequences of this transformation, which affect the impact of the text. As such, the transformation of the photo into the typically *transgressive* genre *graffiti*, for instance, has a somewhat provocative potential (cf. Heinemann, 1997). In other words, the more difficult it is for the public to ignore a transgressive text, the higher is its efficiency in achieving its communicative goals (Auer, 2009, pp. 296–297). The graffiti piece confronts the viewers in public space without asking for their consent. In their spatial environment, they come face to face with a pictorial representation so large and colorful that it is difficult to avert the eyes. It can be seen from passing trains, walkways, and important buildings of the city, for example, from the windows of the *European Central Bank* (ECB), which is located near the East Harbour. The graffiti piece urges its recipients to deal with the issues it encodes. This, among others, involves a processing of *indexical, iconic,* and *symbolic* signs and sign complexes, which requires knowledge of the intertextual embedding of the depiction. If we recognize in the piece the original photograph, we can understand it *indexically* as a "*Spurbild*" [trace picture] (Doelker, 2002, p. 70), which stands in an existential causal relationship to its referential object, that is, to what happened off the coast in Bodrum, Turkey, in late summer 2015.

Against the background of discursive knowledge, we can interpret the graffiti piece *iconically* and *indexically* as a sign of the individual fate of Aylan Kurdi. This is possible because we have come to know many details about his life, family, and circumstances of death through the continuous multimodal embedding of the nuclear photograph since September 2015 (see e.g., Examples (8)–(13)). Against the background of its dense discursive network, we can also interpret the image as a conventional *symbolic* sign that shows us Europe's failure in dealing with the refugee crisis (see Examples (14)–(18)). We can understand it as an appeal that admonishes us to perceive the suffering and death of those who have fled. It implicitly implores us to do something about it (see Examples (5) and (6)).

If we consider the meta-textual ideas of the two Frankfurt-based artists, which were published in the German press, further information is added, which specifies the symbolic interpretability of the image. The artists state the title of their work: "Europa, Geld und Tod" [Europe, money, and death]. The positioning of the image close to the ECB intensifies the symbolic interpretation.

> Ich dachte, es wäre wichtig, das auch mal hierher zu bringen. Weil's die Leute ja erst interessiert, wenn es vor der Haustür passiert
> [I thought it was important to bring this to this place as well. Because people are only interested when it happens on their doorsteps].
> ("Graffiti zeigt ertrunkenen Flüchtlingsjungen", Frankfurter Allgemeine Zeitung, March 11, 2016).

The opposition between European wealth and extra-European poverty becomes visually tangible to its viewers in their everyday environment.

5.6 Image Resemiotization

Almost four weeks later, on the night of June 22, 2016, the graffiti piece undergoes an intertextual *resemiotization*, that is, a more or less complex form of consecutive meaning making, in which, through the modification of already existing signs of various kinds, a meaning different from the original one is created (Pappert, 2017). It was *overlaid* with the words "Grenzen retten Leben! Fuck Antifa!" [Borders save lives! Fuck Antifa!] (see Figure 3.4).

This form of intertextual reference reacts discursively to its pictorial nucleus. It assigns a meaning to it which is clearly different from the

Intertextual Reference in Image-Centric Discourse 57

meaning it was given before. The polyphony of discourses is expressed in answers such as the one given with the *overlay* of the piece (cf. Klug, 2018, p. 127). Through texts of the verbal and pictorial kind, individual actors/groups engage with the artifact in a direct dialogue. This direct dialogic relationship between the image-nucleus and its following satellites can be characterized by action and reaction, by call and response. This existence of a mutual relationship through the interplay of verbal and non-verbal texts is further substantiated by a new pictorial response. It comes a few weeks later, from the artists themselves. They rewrite the graffiti again, in quite a different intramodal way: now, it depicts a dark-haired toddler, laughing, in a red T-shirt, surrounded by teddy bears (see Figure 3.5).

Figure 3.4 Graffiti crossing: Grenzen retten Leben! Fuck Antifa! [Borders save lives! Fuck Antifa!] (Photo: Nina-Maria Klug, Frankfurt am Main, 2016).

Figure 3.5 Repainted graffiti piece of the laughing refugee boy (Photo: Nina-Maria Klug, Frankfurt am Main, August 13, 2016).

6 Conclusion

The aim of this chapter was to argue that the concept of image-centricity on which this volume is based does not only apply to intratextual analyses. Images employed in discourses, too, can shape the social construction of reality to a great extent. They can dominate entire discourses, which are considered to be transtextual semantic units of texts.

Images enrich discourses with their particular semiotic potential. They provide an individual contribution to the communicative handling of specific topics and can even take a central position in discourses, which can then be characterized as *image-centric*. In this sense, the photograph of a dead refugee toddler on the beach of Bodrum, taken by the Turkish journalist Nilüfer Demir as discussed here, has shaped the discourse on the contemporary refugee crisis in an image-centric fashion – not least because of its outstanding powers of emotionalization and authorization, which results from the specific affordances of the pictorial mode. Within the image-centric discourse, images such as the ones discussed in this case study form the textual nucleus around which many verbal and non-verbal satellites orbit. Together they form a coherent and cohesive semantic unit, a *multimodal discourse*. As a consequence, the satellites cannot be properly understood without their nucleus, nor can the nucleus be understood without its satellites. It gains its discursive meaning only from the intertextual embedding in the multimodal contexts of language on the one hand, and the intramodal embedding in the context of other images on the other hand. This embedding process expands and specifies the discursive meaning potential through direct and indirect references. This applies in particular to the graffiti piece that confronts us on the wall at Frankfurt's East Harbor today (Figure 3.5). Like the previous ones, this image makes us reconsider our actions in view of the current refugee crisis by depicting what consequences a change in behavior could have had: Aylan Kurdi – and with him many other refugees who died during their flight – could still be alive like the little laughing boy depicted in the mural. We can only understand this appeal if we interpret the image against the background of the texts with which it is intertextually connected. In this chapter I have introduced six major types of direct intertextual reference, some of an intramodal nature, others of an intermodal nature: (1) *image quotation*, (2) *image indexing*, (3) *image transformation*, (4) *image resemiotization*, (5) *image metatextualization*, and (6) *image transcription* (Figure 3.1). A transtextual analysis of such direct forms of intertextual reference reveals the close symbiosis of verbal texts and images in discourse. It proves the claim that we do well to regard images as a central part of a genuinely multimodal discourse in which social reality is construed and represented. Images should at all costs be taken into account when compiling and researching a corpus in linguistic discourse analysis.

References

Angermuller, J. (2014). *Poststructuralist discourse analysis: Subjectivity in enunciative pragmatics*. Basingstoke: Palgrave Macmillan.

Auer, P. (2009). Sprachliche Landschaften. In A. Deppermann & A. Linke (Eds.), *Sprache intermedial: Stimme und Schrift, Bild und Ton* (pp. 271–298). Berlin: de Gruyter.

Bakhtin, M. M. (1968/1984). *The problems of Dostoevsky's poetics*. (Carly Emerson, Ed. and Trans.) Minneapolis: University of Minnesota Press.

Bateman, J. A. (2016). Methodological and theoretical issues in multimodality. In N.-M. Klug & H. Stöckl (Eds.), *Handbuch Sprache im multimodalen Kontext* (pp. 36–74). Berlin: de Gruyter.

Bateman, J. A. (2008). *Multimodality and genre. A foundation for the systematic analysis of multimodal documents*. Basingstoke: Palgrave Macmillan.

Bateman, J., Wildfeuer, J., & Hiippala, T. (2017). *Multimodality: Foundations, research and analysis – A problem-oriented introduction*. Berlin: de Gruyter.

Bednarek, M., & Caple, H. (2012). *News discourse*. London: continuum.

Berger, P. L., & Luckman, T. (1966). *The social construction of reality: A treatise in the sociology of knowledge*. Garden City, NY: Anchor Books.

Berndt, F., & Tonger-Erk, L. (2013). *Intertextualität: Eine Einführung*. Berlin: Erich Schmidt.

Broich, U. (2000): Intertextualität. In G. Braungart, H. Fricke, K. Grubmüller, J.-D. Müller, F. Vollhardt, & K. Weimar (Eds.), *Reallexikon der deutschen Literaturwissenschaft* (Vol. 2, pp. 175–179). Berlin: de Gruyter.

Broich, U., & Pfister, M. (Eds.). (1985). *Intertextualität: Formen, Funktionen, anglistische Fallstudien*. Tübingen: Niemeyer.

Burke, P. (2003). *Augenzeugenschaft: Bilder als historische Quellen*. Berlin: Wagenbach.

Busse, D., & Teubert, W. (1994). Ist Diskurs ein sprachwissenschaftliches Objekt? Zur Methodenfrage der historischen Semantik. In D. Busse, F. Hermanns & W. Teubert (Eds.), *Begriffsgeschichte und Diskursgeschichte* (pp. 10–28). Opladen: Westdeutscher Verlag.

Cameron, D. (2001). *Working with spoken discourse*. London: SAGE Publications.

Caple, H. (2013). *Photojournalism: A social semiotic approach*. New York: Palgrave Macmillan.

Caple, H. (2008). Intermodal relations in image nuclear news stories. In L. Unsworth (Ed.), *Multimodal semiotics: Functional analysis in contexts of education* (pp. 125–138). London: continuum.

Doelker, C. (2002). *Ein Bild ist mehr als ein Bild: Visuelle Kompetenz in der Multimedia-Gesellschaft* (3rd ed.). Stuttgart: Klett-Cotta.

Fairclough, N. (2016). A dialectical-relational approach to critical discourse analysis in social research. In R. Wodak & M. Meyer (Eds.), *Methods of critical discourse studies* (pp. 86–108). London: Sage.

Fairclough, N. (1995). *Media discourse*. London: Hodder Education.

Fairclough, N., & Wodak, R. (1997). Critical discourse analysis. In T. van Dijk (Ed.), *Discourse as social interaction* (pp. 258–284). London: Sage.

Foucault, M. (1969/2002). *The archaeology of knowledge* (2nd ed.). (A. M. Sheridan, Trans.). London: Routledge.

Gardt, A. (2007). Diskursanalyse: Aktueller theoretischer Ort und methodische Möglichkeiten. In I. Warnke (Ed.), *Diskurslinguistik nach Foucault: Theorie und Gegenstände* (pp. 27–52). Berlin: de Gruyter.

Genette, G. (1993). *Palimpseste: Die Literatur auf zweiter Stufe.* (W. Bayer & D. Hornig, Trans.). Frankfurt am Main: Suhrkamp.

Heinemann, M. (1997). Graffiti und Losungen: Eine intertextuelle Korrelation? Ein Beitrag zur Intertextualität von Textsorten. In J. Klein & U. Fix (Eds.), *Textbeziehungen: Linguistische und literaturwissenschaftliche Beiträge zur Intertextualität* (pp. 373–382). Tübingen: Stauffenburg.

Holly, W. (2016). Audiovisueller Text: Nachrichtenfilm. In N.-M. Klug & H. Stöckl (Eds.), *Handbuch Sprache im multimodalen Kontext* (pp. 392–409). Berlin: de Gruyter.

Holthuis, S. (1993). *Intertextualität: Aspekte einer rezipientenorientierten Konzeption.* Tübingen: Stauffenburg.

Jäger, L. (2002). Transkriptivität: Zur medialen Logik der kulturellen Semantik. In L. Jäger & G. Stanitzek (Eds.), *Transkribieren: Medien/Lektüre* (pp. 19–41). München: Fink.

Jakobson, R. (1981). Linguistische Aspekte der Übersetzung. In W. Wills (Ed.), *Übersetzungswissenschaft* (pp. 189–198). Darmstadt: Wissenschaftliche Buchgesellschaft.

Jappy, T. (2013). *Introduction to Peircean Visual Semiotics.* London: Bloomsbury.

Jewitt, C., & Hendrikson, B. (2016). Social semiotic multimodality. In N.-M. Klug & H. Stöckl (Eds.), *Handbuch Sprache im multimodalen Kontext* (pp. 145–164). Berlin: de Gruyter.

Klug, N.-M. (2018). Wenn Schlüsseltexte Bilder sind: Aspekte von Intertextualität in Presse und öffentlichem Raum. In S. Pappert & S. Michel (Eds.), *Multimodale Kommunikation in öffentlichen Räumen: Texte und Textsorten zwischen Tradition und Innovation* (pp. 109–132). Stuttgart: ibidem.

Klug, N.-M. (2016). Multimodale Text- und Diskurssemantik. In N.-M. Klug & H. Stöckl (Eds.), *Handbuch Sprache im multimodalen Kontext* (pp. 165–189). Berlin: de Gruyter.

Klug, N.-M. (2015). 'Ich habe es doch mit eigenen Augen gesehen!': Zur Eigentlichkeit bildlicher Zeichen. In C. Brinker-von der Heyde, N. Kalwa, N.-M. Klug, & P. Reszke (Eds.), *Eigentlichkeit. Zum Verhältnis von Sprache, Sprechern und Welt* (pp. 501–522). Berlin: de Gruyter.

Klug, N.-M. (2012). *Das konfessionelle Flugblatt 1563–1580: Eine Studie zur historischen Semiotik und Textanalyse.* Berlin: de Gruyter.

Krause, W.-D. (2000). Kommunikationslinguistische Aspekte der Textsortenbestimmung. In W.-D. Krause (Ed.), *Textsorten: Kommunikationslinguistische und konfrontative Aspekte* (pp. 34–67). Frankfurt am Main: Lang.

Kress, G. (2013). What is Mode? In C. Jewitt (Ed.), *The Routledge handbook of multimodal analysis* (pp. 60–76). London: Routledge.

Kress, G., & van Leeuwen, T. (1998). Front pages: The (critical) analysis of newspaper layout. In A. Bell & P. Garrett (Eds.), *Approaches to media discourse* (pp. 186–219). Oxford: Blackwell.

Kroeber-Riel, W. (1993). *Bildkommunikation.* München: Vahlen.

Lakoff, G., & Johnson, M. (1980). *Metaphors we live by.* Chicago: University of Chicago Press.

Lemke, J. L. (1995). *Textual politics.* London: Taylor & Francis.

Machin, D., & Mayr, A. (2012). *How to do critical discourse analysis: A multimodal introduction*. London: Sage.
Manghani, M. (2013). *Image studies: Theory and practice*. London: Routledge.
Nöth, W. (2000). *Handbuch der Semiotik*. Stuttgart: Metzler.
Pappert, S. (2017). Plakatbusting: Zur Umwandlung von Wahlplakaten in transgressive Sehflächen. In M. Wengeler & H. Kämper (Eds.), *Protest – Parteienschelte – Politikverdrossenheit: Politikkritik in der Demokratie* (pp. 55–75). Bremen: Hempen.
Peirce, C. S. (1931–1958). *Collected papers* (vols. 1–6) (C. Harshone & P. Weiss, eds.) (vols. 7–8) (A. W. Burks, ed.). Cambridge, MA: Harvard University Press.
Reisigl, M., & Wodak, R. (2016). The discourse-historical approach (DHA). In R. Wodak & M. Meyer (Eds.), *Methods of critical discourse studies* (pp. 23–61). London: Sage.
Royce, T. (2002). Multimodality in the TESOL classroom: Exploring visual-verbal synergy. *TESOL Quarterly*, 36(2), 191–205.
Sachs-Hombach, K. (2003). *Das Bild als kommunikatives Medium: Elemente einer allgemeinen Bildwissenschaft*. Köln: Halem.
Sacks, H. (1995). *Lectures on conversation*. Oxford: Blackwell Publishing.
Schmitz, U. (2016). Multimodale Texttypologie. In N.-M. Klug & H. Stöckl (Eds.), *Handbuch Sprache im multimodalen Kontext* (pp. 327–347). Berlin: de Gruyter.
Spieß, C. (2013). Texte, Diskurse, Dispositive: Zur theoretisch-methodischen Modellierung eines Analyserahmens am Beispiel der Kategorie Schlüsseltext. In K. Roth & C. Spiegel (Eds.), *Angewandte Diskurslinguistik: Felder, Probleme, Perspektiven* (pp. 17–42). Berlin: Akademie.
Spitzmüller, J., & Warnke, I. H. (2011). *Diskurslinguistik: Eine Einführung in Theorien und Methoden der transtextuellen Sprachanalyse*. Berlin: de Gruyter.
Stöckl, H. (2016). Multimodalität: Semiotische und textlinguistische Grundlagen. In N.-M. Klug & H. Stöckl (Eds.), *Handbuch Sprache im multimodalen Kontext* (pp. 3–35). Berlin: de Gruyter.
Ten Have, P. (1999). *Doing conversation analysis: A practical guide*. Thousand Oaks: Sage.
van Dijk, T. (2016). Critical discourse studies: A sociocognitive approach. In R. Wodak & M. Meyer (Eds.), *Methods of critical discourse studies* (pp. 62–85). London: Sage.
van Leeuwen, T. (2008). *Discourse and practice: New tools for critical discourse analysis*. Oxford: University Press.
Weidenmann, B. (1988). *Psychische Prozesse beim Verstehen von Bildern*. Bern: Hogrefe.
Wengeler, M. (2003). *Topos und Diskurs: Begründung einer argumentationsanalytischen Methode und ihre Anwendung auf den Migrationsdiskurs (1960–1985)*. Tübingen: Niemeyer.
Ziem, A. (2014). *Frames of understanding in text and discourse: Theoretical foundations and descriptive applications*. Amsterdam: Benjamins.

(Online-)Newspaper articles cited in this chapter

Aylan Kurdi: Images that changed UK views on refugees? (2015, September 3). *Channel 4*. Retrieved from https://www.channel4.com/news/aylan-kurdi-refugee-crisis-dead-beach-uk-crisis-syrian

Barnard, A., & Shoumali, K. (2015, September 4). Image of drowned Syrian, Aylan Kurdi, 3, brings migrant crisis into focus. *The New York Times*. Retrieved from https://www.nytimes.com/2015/09/04/world/europe/syria-boy-drowning.html

Colton, J. (n.d.). The Napalm Girl: What happened after the shutter clicked. *New Zealand Geographic*. Retrieved from https://www.nzgeo.com/photography/the-napalm-girl/

Frankfurter Allgemeine Zeitung. (2016, March 11). Graffiti für Flüchtlingsjungen: Großflächige Botschaft. Retrieved from http://www.faz.net/aktuell/rhein-main/frankfurt-graffiti-fuer-ertrunkenen-aylan-kurdi-14117844.html

Gage, J. (2015, September 4). About the photo of the dead boy on the beach. *Huffington Post*. Retrieved from https://www.huffingtonpost.com/joan-gage/about-the-photo-of-the-dead-boy-on-the-beach_b_8085270.html?guccounter=1

Graffiti zeigt ertrunkenen Flüchtlingsjungen. (2016, March 11). *Stuttgarter Zeitung*. Retrieved from https://www.stuttgarter-zeitung.de/inhalt.kuenstlerin-frankfurt-graffiti-zeigt-ertrunkenen-fluechtlingsjungen.5b3be5b7-c0c9-4a4a-85e9-17930d74850d.html

Image of drowned boy washed up on Turkey beach highlights plight of migrants. (2015, September 3). *The Sydney Morning Herald*. Retrieved from https://www.smh.com.au/world/image-of-drowned-boy-washed-up-on-turkey-beach-highlights-plight-of-migrants-20150903-gjdwvu.html

Kemper, D. (2015, September 4): Das Drama um Aylan Kurdi aus Syrien bewegt die Welt: Warum wir hier kein totes Kind zeigen. *Westfalen-Blatt*. Retrieved from http://www.westfalen-blatt.de/Ueberregional/Artikel/2102154-Das-Drama-um-Aylan-Kurdi-aus-Syrien-bewegt-die-Welt-Warum-wir-hier-kein-totes-Kind-zeigen

La foto del chico sirio muerto conmociona al mundo. (2015, September 2). *Clarin*. Retrieved from https://www.clarin.com/mundo/chico-sirio-muerto-conmociona-mundo_0_H1le4iQtvQe.html

La photo d'un enfant mort sur une plage turque à la « une » de la presse européenne. (2015, September 3). *Le Monde*. Retrieved from http://bigbrowser.blog.lemonde.fr/2015/09/03/la-photo-dun-enfant-mort-sur-une-plage-turque-a-la-une-de-la-presse-europeenne/

Migrant crisis: Photo of drowned boy sparks outcry. (2015, September 3). *BBC News*. Retrieved from http://www.bbc.com/news/world-europe-34133210

Moyer, J. Wm. (2015, September 3). Aylan's story: How desperation left a 3-year-old boy washed up on a Turkish beach. *The Washington Post*. Retrieved from https://www.washingtonpost.com/news/morning-mix/wp/2015/09/03/a-desperate-refugee-family-a-capsized-boat-and-3-year-old-dead-on-a-beach-in-turkey/?noredirect=on&utm_term=.b907bbb168c8

Napalm Girl: An iconic image of war turns 40. (2012, June 3). *National Public Radio, Inc.* (US). Retrieved from https://www.npr.org/2012/06/03/154234617/napalm-girl-an-iconic-image-of-war-turns-40

Plöchinger, S. (2015, September 3). Was uns der tote Junge von Bodrum lehrt. *Süddeutsche Zeitung*. Retrieved from http://www.sueddeutsche.de/medien/foto-eines-fluechtlingskinds-was-uns-der-tote-junge-von-bodrum-lehrt-1.2632557

Presserat: Foto von Aylan Kurdi ist "Dokument der Zeitgeschichte". (2015, December 12). *Der Tagesspiegel*. Retrieved from http://www.tagesspiegel.de/medien/presserat-ueber-bilder-von-toten-fluechtlingen-foto-von-aylan-kurdi-ist-dokument-der-zeitgeschichte/12675860.html

Robson, S. (2015, September 2). The innocent victims of Europe's migrant crisis: Syrian children wash up on beach after drowning trying to reach Greek island. *Mirror*. Retrieved from https://www.mirror.co.uk/news/world-news/innocent-victims-europes-migrant-crisis-6368163

Smith, H. (2015, September 2). Shocking images of drowned Syrian boy show tragic plight of refugees. *The Guardian*. Retrieved from https://www.theguardian.com/world/2015/sep/02/shocking-image-of-drowned-syrian-boy-shows-tragic-plight-of-refugees

Toter Flüchtlingsjunge in Bodrum: Das traurigste Foto der Welt. (2015, September 3). *Express*. Retrieved from https://www.express.de/news/toter-fluechtlingsjunge-in-bodrum-das-traurigste-foto-der-welt-22533380

Withnall, A. (2015, September 2). If these extraordinarily powerful images of a dead Syrian child washed up on a beach don't change Europe's attitude to refugees, what will? *The Independent*. Retrieved from https://www.independent.co.uk/news/world/europe/if-these-extraordinarily-powerful-images-of-a-dead-syrian-child-washed-up-on-a-beach-don-t-change-10482757.html

4 The New Visuality of Writing
Theo van Leeuwen

1 Introduction

The growing centrality of images can be observed, not only in new roles of the image and new, *image-centric genres*, but also in new forms of writing, where meaning derives as much from the shape, color, and texture of words as from their lexical meanings, and where words connect to form meaningful units, not through grammatical structures and linguistic cohesion, but through the visual structures of layout and diagrammatic *templates*.

New technologies have merged the page and the screen, the printed word and the image. The pages of PowerPoint presentations and websites now have the landscape format of movie and television screens, while images can be produced and viewed on the page-shaped screens of smartphones, and mobile devices allow us to switch between page- and screen-aspect ratios at the flick of the wrist. But this is not just an effect of such new technologies. Rather, new technologies have made available to all what formerly was available to only professional artists and designers, bringing into the mainstream what artists and designers had already been doing with old technologies – making words invade the domain of the image, and images the domain of the word, often merging the two into unified wholes in which neither the images nor the words any longer make sense on their own. Artists began to experiment with this from the early 20th century onward. Marinetti advocated forms of writing in which words would be "liberated" from syntax and punctuation (not unlike today's word clouds) and "redouble their expressive force" with color and a multitude of different typefaces (Apollonio, 2009, p. 105), while Futurists such as Carra and Depero, Dadaists such as Schwitters, and Constructivists such as Lissitzky and Rodchenko used words as visual elements in paintings and poster designs, aiming for a 'painterly typography'. As Marinetti wrote in 1913:

> When necessary we shall use three or four columns to a page and twenty different typefaces. We shall represent hasty perceptions in italic and express a scream in bold types ... a new, painterly,

typographic representation will be born out of the printed page. (Marinetti 1913, qtd. in Spencer, 1982, p. 17)

Soon popular genres, too, began to integrate words and images – posters and magazine pages; the comic strip which had, until the 1930s, neatly separated words and images, but now began to develop its arsenal of dialogue balloons, thought bubbles, and onomatopoeic words; animated film titles such as those of *King Kong* (1933) which had massive letters emerging from behind large jungle leaves; and, today, the animated texts in television commercials as well as in art films such as Peter Greenaway's *Prospero's Books* (1991), in which the protagonist writes the play that he himself lives and acts out, courtesy of the artistry of Brody Neuenschwander, who used his calligraphic skills to "blend [words] into complex multimedia images" (Neuenschwander, 1993, p. 95).

The tools for producing words and images also merged. On writing tools such as PowerPoint and Word, the same colors, textures, animations, and other options can be applied by means of the same operations to words as well as to pictures, and image-oriented software such as Instagram, too, facilitates and encourages the blending of words and images in multiple ways. There are even multimodal keyboards that combine letters and emoji icons. As Danesi (2017, p. 183) has commented: "The emoji code has resurrected visuality in phonetic writing, allowing our eyes to recapture the visual modality that was there in early writing systems".

This chapter will describe and exemplify the key characteristics of this *new writing*. It will argue that this requires a new multimodal analytical approach which applies equally to all modes of spatial meaning making, just as in earlier work I proposed an analytical framework that encompassed all modes of temporal meaning making – speech, music, and other sounds (van Leeuwen, 1999). And, in the spirit of social semiotics, it will relate semiotic change to social change, the characteristics of the new writing to the characteristics of the social developments that gave rise to them.

2 Visual Textuality

Most web pages contain many words. But their cohesion as texts is achieved *visually*, by means of layout, color, and typography, so much so that without them, the texts would be near incomprehensible. One web page (the layout is reproduced in Figure 4.1) would read something like this:

> HOUSE Your Account Fonts Merchandise LetterSetter Free Catalog News Licensing Tech Support Contact Custom Work Free Fonts Search Find It Jump to font kit Try fonts before you buy with

66 Theo van Leeuwen

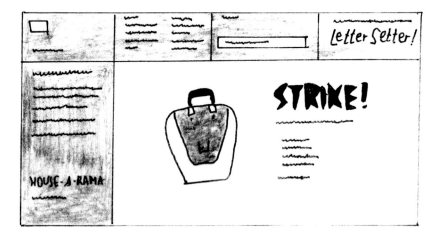

Figure 4.1 Web page (after HOUSEIND.COM website, 2004).

LetterSetter! Strike! House-a-Rama Font Kit $100 Three fonts 54 Dingbats 14 Illustrations Four Patterns BUY IT NOW! House-a-Rama $100 View Fonts View Font Specimens View Illustrations View Patterns & Dingbats Try Fonts with LetterSetter House-a-Rama Buy it Now!

Writing still plays an important role here. With the exception of the font kit bag in the center, the products advertised are all verbally referred to. The connection between the written words, however, is visual. The textual coherence that allows them to make sense is created by layout, color, and typography. Visuality re-enters phonetic writing here, resulting in a text that can no longer be meaningfully read aloud.

This applies not only to the overall cohesion of texts, it also applies to the level of what, in the verbal mode, is expressed by clause structure. Menus and bullet-pointed, for instance, are *visual* structures of the kind Kress and van Leeuwen (2006) call *analytical*, analogous to a possessive relational clause such as (in the case of the House Industries site): *The House-a-Rama Font Kit contains three fonts 54 dingbats, 14 illustrations and four patterns.* Linguistically, there is therefore no process, and hence no clause structure. The *process* function is taken over by the symmetrical list arrangement and the bullet points, "governed by the logic of space, which is typically associated with images and consequently blurs the boundaries between language and image" (Djonov & van Leeuwen, 2014, p. 235).

Figure 4.2 reproduces an advertisement for cat food, which shows a fluffy gray kitten lying on a soft, shiny sheet, with a row of tins of cat

The New Visuality of Writing 67

Figure 4.2 Cat food advertisement (after advertisement in *Vogue*, November 2001).

food at the bottom. A linguistic analysis of the text of this ad will not yield much. There are only four participles "spoilt, spoilt, spoilt, spoilt". But together with the picture, these words create a structure that is analogous to an attributive clause, with the kitten as Carrier, a verbal process, and a set of visual circumstances of means (the tins of cat food at the bottom). Multimodally, it says something like: 'this kitten is spoilt four times over, by each of the four varieties of the brand'. Subtle forms of visual rhyme – correspondences between the fluent folds of the sheet and the flowing letterforms, and between the yellow of the tins of cat food and the kitten's eyes – weld these elements together, and at the same time enhance the text's aesthetic appeal.

In short, in the new writing, words continue to have a lexical function, but syntax and cohesion are visual. The textual metafunction is visually realized, creating a division of metafunctional labor between the modes in the multimodal mix. In what follows, I will describe the textual role of color, typography, and layout in more detail, to then show how they work together to realize the generic structures of new writing texts.

2.1 Color and Textuality

Color contributes to the *textuality* of the new writing in three ways. First, it plays a role in segmenting the text into functional units by giving them distinct colors, so *framing* them (van Leeuwen, 2005). In Figure 4.1, for instance, local navigation (left column) is black, branding and global navigation (top) are a slightly greenish gray, and specific content (center) is white. As well as providing framing, color can of course at the same time provide identity and aesthetic appeal – an increasingly important aspect of the new writing which will be discussed in more detail later in the chapter.

Color can also provide salience, helping to draw attention to elements that are meant to be understood as particularly important. On the House Industries web page, for instance, the color red stands out, drawing attention to the *font kit* in the center.

Finally, and most importantly, color can provide overall cohesion. In website design, cascading style sheets are used to give websites an integrated, "uniform appearance" (Smith, 2005, p. 158), allowing a single external file to dictate the color (and typography) of every page of the site, and when, in a PowerPoint presentation, a background color is chosen, this color remains constant across all slides, thus creating a sense of unity, while, again, at the same time, expressing *identity*, whether the identity of the speaker, the organization for which he or she works, or the identity of the genre of presentation. A chief accountant at one of the universities I have worked at presented the university's annual budget figures against a pale blue background in which the outlines of a calm blue ocean and sky could only just be discerned. He also inserted some quotations from business gurus between the slides presenting the budget figures. Thus, he presented his identity as that of a man with strategic vision rather than a bean counter.

Machin (2004) has pointed out that the photos available from editorial image banks often use just one or two color accents, with the rest of the image in neutral tints – white, light grays, and light blues, and so forth. This allows editors to 'pick up' these colors in the overall layout of pages, and repeat them, for instance, in the colors of headlines and text boxes. For the same reason, many editorial images ensure that there is space for words to be superimposed on the image without conflicting with the visual background. Such images, like the background images of PowerPoint slides, are designed to be integrated with text rather than used as freestanding images: "the photograph is now used as part of the page layout alongside fonts, colors and borders (in) ads, features and fashion alike" (Machin, 2004, p. 334).

Figure 4.3 Women's magazine advice feature (after *Cosmopolitan Magazine* original).

2.2 Typography and Graphic Shape

The magazine text reproduced in Figure 4.3 exemplifies the use of *typography* in realizing textual structure (the text has been paraphrased for copyright reasons). The different functional elements of the text – the headlines (*The Guy* and *Does he want to be your new dude?*), the photo caption (*a forced stare means he's keen*), the sub-headline (*Here are the hints that your best guy friend would prefer some romance*), the headings of each bullet point, and the text of each bullet point – use distinctive fonts, font sizes, and font colors. Only the link between the headline and the four bullet points (*here are the hints*) uses linguistic means to realize the relation between the elements.

The textual role of typography is here again partially a matter of framing, of creating typographic contrasts and typographic similarities between functional elements, and partially a matter of salience, of creating a hierarchy of importance amongst them by means of size and boldness, and so on.

The features which create these contrasts, similarities, and degrees of salience characterize not only letterforms but also more abstract graphic forms, such as the boxes that may enclose text elements or the frame lines that may separate them. Like letterforms, these can all be large or small, bold or light, angular or rounded, regular or irregular, simple or endowed with flourishes of different kinds – as well as have different colors, textures, and so on (cf. van Leeuwen, 2006, 2011).

2.3 Layout

Layout includes three dimensions. Two of these have already been mentioned briefly earlier – framing and salience. The third is composition – the placement of functional elements in the visual field.

As mentioned, *framing* separates, and gives distinct identity to, the functional elements of texts, whether through frame lines or through contrasts in color or typography, and it can also create a sense of connection between functional elements, through similarities in color, typography, or graphic shape generally, thus expressing that these elements are meant to be understood as similar in some sense. It has always existed in print, for instance, through indentation and spacing between paragraphs. It has also always existed in images, where depicted objects can create framing. Arnheim (1982) has described how this happens in Noli Me Tangere [Do not touch me], a painting by Titian which depicts Christ after his resurrection, and Magdalen, on her knees, reaching out to him to see if he is real or a vision. Christ's staff divides the painting in two zones, the zone of Magdalen, who is in the realm of earthly existence, and the zone of Christ who is already beyond this, though still endowed with the presence of a living man. The horizon, says Arnheim, forms another frame line "separating the lower half of the painting from the upper realm of free spirituality in which the tree and the buildings on the hill reach heavenward" (Arnheim, 1982, pp. 112–113). But it is in blended writing that framing acquires its function of combining heterogeneous elements in a multimodal composition.

Salience creates a hierarchy of importance between the functional elements of a page or screen, for instance through differences in size, sharpness of focus, tonal contrast, color contrasts, placement in the visual field, and perspective. *Perceived* salience is, of course, also based on the personal or cultural importance of the depicted elements to reader or viewer. Differences in salience between functional elements can then create a reading path that begins with the most salient element, wherever it is found, and from there moves to the next most salient element, and so on. Such reading paths may not necessarily follow the left-right, top-bottom reading order of traditional printed pages. They may, for instance, start bottom-left and move in a circle, as in Figure 4.4, which

The New Visuality of Writing 71

Figure 4.4 Buy a car, plant a tree (after feature in *Geared Magazine*).

reproduces a page from a magazine produced by the Government of the State of New South Wales to induce good road behavior in young drivers. Here, the eye is first attracted by the bold red headline and the car, bottom left, sharply outlined against the white background, then moves to the tree, top left, then to the text, top right, again in red, and the image of the cockroach, and finally to the article. But even if the article is not read, the message will come across: driving must be related to nature, and then to ways in which car drivers can help limit environmental damage.

Actual readers may follow different reading paths, based on their different interests, especially in text types that are designed to facilitate this, such as newspapers. Eye-tracking studies have shown, for instance, how *editorial readers* avoid advertisements, even when they are objectively the most salient item on a page; *entry point overview readers* scan the headlines, pictures, and ads without any detailed reading; and *focused readers* read one article in detail and ignore the rest (Holsanova et al., 2006, p. 87).

Spatial composition, the placement of functional elements on a screen or page, is the third key aspect of new writing layout. While the words of traditional printed pages also form a spatial arrangement, this arrangement is subjugated to a temporal order in which meaning unfolds as the text is read linearly, from left to right, and top to bottom. Images, on the other hand, are perceived instantaneously, as a whole. Since the Renaissance, they have used perspectival *grids* of lines converging to a vanishing point to guide the placement of elements, thus creating foreground and background, and central and peripheral zones, as well as enhancing naturalism. 20th century designers such as Jan Tschichold have turned the modular paintings of Van Doesburg and Mondrian into layout techniques for commercial printers and designers. Grids now became *proportional regulators* for bringing heterogeneous content together into meaningful, effective, and aesthetically attractive wholes, rather than for naturalistic representation. Building on the ideas of Tschichold and others, post-World War II Swiss designers created the grids that could produce the contemporary multimodal page, with its capacity for almost endless variation. As described by Lupton:

> Whereas a traditional book would have placed captions, commentary and folios within a protective margin, the rationalist grid cut the page into multiple columns, each bearing equal weight within the whole [...] Pictures were cropped to fit the modules of the grid, yielding shapes of unusual proportions. (Lupton, 2004, p. 125)

Grids also became fundamental in web design, where the HTML code had included tables to allow the display of tabular data, in the rigidly modular way that can be seen, for instance, in the catalogs of online shops (see Figure 4.8). But graphic designers soon began to use these tables for the layout of images and captions. However, in contrast to the layout of, for instance, magazine pages, the layout of web pages became increasingly standardized, with clearly framed and predictably placed functional elements (logo top-left, global navigation bar on top, local navigation bar on the left, main content in the center, sub-content and links on the right). In a similar way, the 2007 version of PowerPoint moved from providing 27 *layout templates* that could accommodate any type of content, to just nine *functional templates* with specific semantic functions: *comparison, content with caption, picture with caption*, and so on (Djonov & van Leeuwen, 2013). This trend had already begun before it became embedded in the design of semiotic software. In the late 1960s, designers such as Massimo Vignelli had argued that "design should reject the individual impulse for expression in favor of developing overall systems" (Samara, 2002, p. 20) and had begun to use the grid, not as a proportional regulator, but as a template, with specific zones allocated to specific functional elements. Design began to move from a flexible approach, guided by content, to an emphasis on generic formats that could accommodate a range of different contents and so allow organizations and publications to unify their brand identity across different contents and contexts. Figure 4.3 is an example. At the time Machin and I studied the magazine, *Cosmopolitan* used this 'hot tips' format (Machin & van Leeuwen, 2007) in exactly the same way, even with the same colors, for other items of advice, whether related to health, beauty, relationships, or sexuality: a captioned image followed by a 'bridge' (*Here are the hints that your platonic guy would prefer some passion*), and a bulleted list of items, each starting with a 'tip' in bold white font and followed by a plain font statement elaborating on the tip. The placement of these elements, their framing, and their distinct uses of color and typography *visually* realize a generic structure in a way that makes the item immediately recognizable as a 'hot tips' genre before it is even read. Today, software like Microsoft Word include catalogs of such generic templates for a wide range of document types. In short, as the visual continues its ascendancy, it becomes more conventionalized, more subject to regulation (Kress, 2010, p. 151).

2.4 Diagram Templates

Diagrams, too, provide a kind of syntax for *visually* linking words-in-boxes together into meaningful wholes. In the age of visualization, they play an increasingly important role in the representation, or rather, the *modeling* of the world. A resource like Microsoft *SmartArt* (many similar resources are now available on the Internet) provides no less than 233 different diagram templates. They are clearly oriented to the written word. Only two are said to "also work well with no text". But they all arrange words and text fragments *visually* in meaningful ways, with Microsoft glossing their textual meaning potential, for instance, as being able to "show hierarchical relationships progressing across groups", "show two opposing ideas, or ideas that diverge from a central point", and so on.

However, Microsoft's 233 templates are, in fact, variations and combinations of a limited number of diagram types. Some of these are dynamic, modeling actions and events, while others are static, modeling structures in which depicted elements are understood as parts in a part-whole structure or categories in a classification. In other words, diagrams, like other visuals, are, in Kress and van Leeuwen's terms (2006), either *narrative* or *conceptual*. In narrative visuals, a vector will emanate from one of the elements (the Actor, the element that initiates the action) and lead to another element (the Goal, the element that is

74 *Theo van Leeuwen*

affected by the action), a vector being a line with a sense of directionality, for instance, an arrow.

The most common narrative diagrams are *linear processes, cycles,* and *flowcharts*. Shannon and Weaver's communication model, of which Figure 4.5 shows one version (googling 'communication model' will produce a myriad of others), is an example of a linear process. Here, an Information Source does something to a Transmitter, which, in turn, does something to a Channel, which, in turn, does something to a Receiver, which, in turn, does something to a Destination.

Figure 4.6 is an example of a cycle, taken from the website of a Norwegian engineering company, Kongsberg Maritime, which has a *Cybernetics R&D Group* to "contribute to the cutting edge of research-based and market-oriented innovation" (Kongsberg Maritime, 2007). A Controller acts to input something into a System, instructing it to act in a certain way. The System then provides feedback about its actual behavior to the Controller, who adjusts the input accordingly, for example, by making the message more persuasive or insistent, or by reassessing strategy. But there is also an arrow that comes from nowhere, the (green) arrow on the left. Kress and van Leeuwen (2006, p. 64) call this an Event – there is a process, represented by a vector, and there is a Goal, an affected party, the Controller. But there is no Actor who

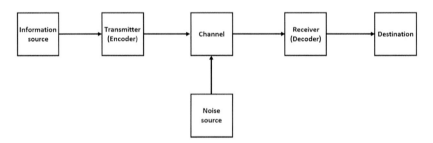

Figure 4.5 Shannon and Weaver's communication model (after Shannon & Weaver, 1949).

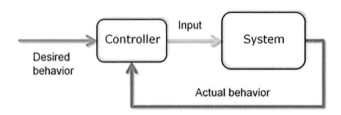

Figure 4.6 Cybernetic model (Kongsberg Maritime, 2007).

decides what is to be desired. This is not included in the model, and therefore not necessarily taken into account in research or management processes based on this model.

In flowcharts, the link between elements is sequential. Here the arrows realize temporal ('and then'), alternative ('or'), or conditional ('if then') connections rather than processes. Like other types of narrative diagram, flowcharts can represent technological processes (e.g., automated production processes) as well as social practices (e.g., medical consultations), and they can represent as well as regulate them. Ventola (1987), for instance, used flowcharts to describe the way service encounters unfold. The chart in Figure 4.7 was designed by an Australian public health professional for nurses in African clinics, where a shortage of ophthalmologists necessitated 'task shifting' – training nurses to conduct medical consultations. A close reading reveals a range of issues. Why are there no arrows between 'ask', 'assess', and 'action'? Why are there no downward 'no' arrows between 'severe pain', 'mild pain', and 'no pain'? More generally, does this diagram foresee all the possible situations the African nurses could be confronted with? Such questions become even more important when flowcharts become the algorithms of the digital programs that today regulate so many of the things we do, whether in our work or as private citizens, requiring us to conform with pre-envisaged options in ways that are often entirely non-negotiable.

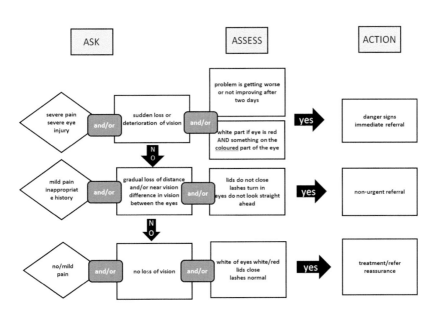

Figure 4.7 Flowchart for medical consultation.

76 *Theo van Leeuwen*

The most common types of conceptual diagram are *analytical diagrams*, *classification diagrams*, *tables*, *networks*, and *mind maps*.

Analytical diagrams show the parts of a whole and the way they fit together to form that whole. Maps are a clear example, as are diagrams that represent abstract 'things' as part-whole structures. A pie chart in a magazine for employees of Rank Xerox, for instance, depicted the outcome of a staff survey, showing the company as consisting of three groups of employees – 'can do' employees who welcome innovation and say things like "we need to work together with management", 'maybe ... if' employees who worry about change and say things like "so and so tried and look what happened to him", and competitive 'yes but' employees who say things like "why should I help when I am not going to win?" Analytical diagrams are often embedded in other diagrams. If, for instance, the elements in narrative diagrams are depicted in enough detail to distinguish their various parts, they can themselves be interpreted as analytical diagrams. Diagrams of tectonic activity may, for instance, use arrows to show erupting volcanoes and rising magma, while also depicting how the Earth's crust consists of different layers.

Figure 4.8 shows how a symmetric arrangement of participants can realize classification. The words or phrases in a list, with or without bullet points, are also symmetrically arranged in this way, and also position elements as belonging to the same category. Tree diagrams are yet another way of visually realizing classification, with overarching categories

Figure 4.8 Online catalog (after page from the website of *Zalando*).

branching out into subcategories that are of the same kind and belong to the same order or rank, as, for instance, in zoology, where orders such as mammals branch out into families such as bears, which branch out again into genera such as black bear and brown bear, and into species such as Asiatic black bears. But branching can also be used to signify hierarchy, as in org charts, or lineage, as in family trees. Like arrows, branches can mean different things in different contexts, and for this reason they may be less precise and definitive than they are often made out to be.

Tables combine the analytical and the classificational, analyzing along one axis, and classifying along the other. However verbal the content of tables may be, their structure is again visual – even the words can, in principle, be replaced by visuals, provided suitable icons are available.

Networks originated in studies of social relations focused on metrics rather than meaning, replacing specific forms of association such as kinship, class, and workplace relations with mere association (cf. Freeman, 2004). This principle was later also applied to information, making the frequency of the links between items of information more important than their semantic relations. But networks are also used to reshape social practices, including the work of academics, through sites like ResearchGate, which replaces the peer review of quality with popularity (ranking in terms of number of followers), and publishing with posting and networking, and which includes everyone with a university email address on an equal basis ("11+ million researchers"), ignoring the hierarchical management systems in which academics work. Arrangements of this kind are then legitimized by buzzwords such as *community, collaboration, self-organization, flexibility, diversity, multiplicity,* and *democratization*.

Mind maps, finally (originally called *idea maps*), were developed in advertising in the late 1940s as a brainstorming technique. They can be seen as a new analytical model with a central concept in the middle and a set of associations with this concept as the parts of a concept-cluster. Here, again, semantic relations are replaced by spatial relations, which can then place different concepts at different distances from the central concept to symbolize their relative centrality or marginality.

3 The Marketization of Discourse: Semiotic Change and Social Change

In this final section of the chapter, I will try to place the new writing in its broader social and cultural context under four headings: the relation between functionality and identity in the new writing, the importance of aesthetics in the new writing, the move from representation to modeling, and the relation between the ideational and interpersonal resources of language and the new writing.

3.1 Functionality and Identity

A key characteristic of the new writing is its dual focus on functionality and identity. As we have seen, functionality and identity are realized by the same stylistic signifiers – color, texture, and the shape of letterforms and other graphic elements at once demarcate the functional elements of spatially realized genres and signify identities through their expressive affordances and cultural connotations.

Functionality, in the sense in which I use the term here, has, over the past 50 years or so, become a key focus, not only in linguistic text research but also in human-computer interaction design. Linguistic descriptions of genre and the algorithms that structure human-computer interaction have moved in the same direction and both provided models for restructuring practices, the former, for instance, in education, the latter in a much wider range of practices. Already in the 1980s, a paper presented at a human-computer interaction conference used a genre analysis of receptionist appointment making phone calls as a model for computer interfaces which would "limit the kinds of response that are possible" and act as a "master-slave relationship in which the slave has the expertise" (Falzon et al., 1986, pp. 97–98).

New writing has developed in the same direction, replacing an approach based on content with an approach based on interaction, on functional templates that accommodate a wide variety of contents. Over time, these functional templates have become increasingly standardized and homogenized, as we have seen, for instance, in web pages, PowerPoint slides, and other digitally mediated text formats.

The expression of identity in these same texts, however, has become more and more varied and heterogeneous, driven by the need for brand differentiation and the need for individuals to express their personal identity, to 'brand the self' (Machin & van Leeuwen, 2008). PowerPoint, for instance, provides a wide range of decorative designs for a very limited set of text patterns such as *title plus list of bullet points* – backgrounds range from abstract patterns to tranquil seascapes and soft focus rust-colored autumn leaves, and the frame lines that divide titles from *content spaces* range from abstract Bauhaus-inspired motifs in red and black to late 19th-century flower flourishes. As a result, we can all do the same things in our own way, even if that way is ultimately not uniquely individual (in the way our handwriting is, for example) but a choice from a wide range of deliberately designed and globally marketed semiotic resources (a large set of pre-selected fonts, for example): "Something is provided for all, so that none may escape", as Adorno once said (Horkheimer & Adorno, 1972/1985, p. 123).

New writing's focus on functionality and identity is therefore based on the same principles as contemporary product design, and an integral part of what Fairclough (1993) called the *marketization of discourse*.

Different kinds of spectacles, for instance, have, in the past, had different functionalities – the monocle, the pince-nez, the quizzer, the lorgnette, scissor glasses, opera glasses, and so on. More recently the functional design of spectacles has become increasingly homogeneous. However, this homogeneous model comes in a bewildering variety of styles – Luxicotta, a $100 billion Italian company which has a near monopoly on the design and manufacture of frames, currently produces 27,000 different models (Knight, 2018). Choosing one of these has become crucial for our identity, for our 'image' as a particular kind of person with particular affiliations and values (Chaney, 1996, p. 12).

3.2 Aesthetics

The new importance of style has reintroduced *aesthetics* into everyday communication. Even highly functional documents such as invitations, invoices, company brochures, annual reports, and course materials must now 'look good'. "If you think a document that looks this good has to be difficult to format, think again!" says a Word template for company brochures, and "We have created styles that let you match the formatting in this brochure to your company fonts and colors with just a click". As pointed out by Caple (2013), aesthetics has even invaded formerly content-driven, functional, rather than artistic, image genres such as photojournalism. Aesthetics, which ever since Kant has been seen as non-functional and a matter of taste, has now acquired important strategic functionality in marketized discourse genres.

Perhaps the emphasis on pleasure in post-structuralism was an early sign of the return of aesthetics. In *Le Plaisir du texte*, and elsewhere, Roland Barthes contrasted the world of meaning, by definition social and cultural, with an experience of pleasure that somehow escaped the social and the cultural. The paradox is, of course, that this very move helped reintroduce pleasure into the social and cultural world. Today, pleasure is not, or no longer, private, detached from society and culture, but deeply interwoven with it. We are called upon to invest pleasure in everything we do and write and to make everything we write pleasurable for the reader or user. This, too, is part and parcel of the marketization of discourse. Already in the 1920s, advertising started to combine functional communication with an appeal to pleasure and desire, and today its communicative strategies have spread well beyond advertising of goods and services.

The emphasis on pleasure is based on the view, pervasive in the world of marketing and branding, and increasingly also in academic discourses, that human action is driven by emotion, a view which also underlies, for instance, the new visual language of emoji. In introducing, in 2016, five redesigned likes (*love, haha, wow, sad,* and *angry*), Facebook offered its users a resource for reacting emotionally rather than rationally – no icons were provided for saying 'agree' or 'disagree', or 'true' or 'false'. Emotional reactions are, of course, also the kind of information Facebook and other platforms collect for commercial purposes. They play a key role in the marketization of discourse and the industries that support it. Companies such as General Sentiment mine data from 60 million sources each day to work out what people like and do not like, and psychologists at Pittsburgh University analyze 50 million tweets a day with an algorithm based on 500 words that are rated on a happiness scale from 1 to 9 (Davies, 2015, pp. 223, 226).

Even diagram templates can now include an aesthetic dimension, for instance, through embellishments such as relief or color. It is not for nothing that Microsoft uses the term *art* in the branding of text production resources such as SmartArt and ClipArt (Kvåle, 2016).

3.3 Representation and Modeling

Kvåle (2016) has described how Microsoft originally supplied only organizational charts and in their manuals explicitly referred to them as such. As their diagrams began to be used beyond their original purpose, for instance, in education, they became *relationship diagrams*, and finally SmartArt in its current form. But the org chart, the structure of corporate governance, remained the dominant model. She concluded that, today,

> [t]he most effective style of organizational charts is infused into all social practices, including education – not explicitly, by verbal instruction, but by being buried in the templatized formats for multimodal representation. (Kvåle, 2016, p. 269)

The history of PowerPoint shows a similar development. It started in the Bell Laboratories, as a device combining different earlier technologies to effectively pitch ideas to management for funding, but it soon found application in many other domains, including, again, education. However, PowerPoint did not adapt itself to these new users – they had to adapt to it, and learn to remodel their modes of communication to the genre of pitching ideas.

The shift from the 'old' writing and the 'old' image to the new writing has also been a shift from representation to modeling. The image, which for centuries had developed ever more sophisticated techniques for the naturalistic representation of the variety of appearances, now moved away from observing the physical world to designing models for representing it – through image lexicons such as Getty Images and through computer-generated images, which must necessarily be built on the basis of modeling what is to be represented. Diagrammatic writing, too, is based on models which originally often applied only to limited technical or other domains, but subsequently influenced the way many other phenomena were represented. Cybernetic cycle diagrams, for instance, originated in the 1920s as a blueprint for electronic control systems, but have subsequently become a template for thought and representation in many other fields including psychology, sociology, neurology, philosophy, and organization studies, so showing, as cybernetics' main proponent, Norbert Wiener, put it (1947/1973, p. 38), that "the thought of every age is reflected in its technique". Networks, as we have seen, were first developed by American sociologists, also in the 1920s, to study who interacts with whom, how often, and how (e.g., friendly or antagonistically), in especially schools and workplaces. But they were soon applied to many other scientific and practical domains – the natural sciences, including neurology, city planning, the classification of information, and of course the Internet. In all these applications, they became an authoritative way of understanding the world and a blueprint for the radical reshaping of social life and its institutions which we are witnessing today.

3.4 *The Ideational and the Interpersonal in the New Writing*

The table in Figure 4.9, represented only in part for reasons of legibility, was taken from a document prepared by the Pro Vice Chancellor Research of an Australian University to explain the criteria for setting Faculty Research Grant income KPIs (Key Performance Indicators) and, at the same time, for imposing these KPIs on Faculty Deans, with the aim of improving the university's research income from government grants and other sources.

R3 fx SAMPLE "BUSINESS AS USUAL" FACULTY TARGETS - BUSINESS FACULTY (NOTE FINAL TARG

SUMMARY REPORT PERFORMANCE DOMAIN: RESEARCH

UTS HISTORICAL PERFORMANCE							UTS FUTURE PERFORMANCE	
KPI REF NO.	KPI TITLE	KPI METRIC	SPONSOR	PREVIOUS RESULT (usually 2003)	BASELINE RESULT (usually 2004)	TARGET TYPE T=Threshold I=Improvement	2005 TARGET	2006 TARGET (TENTATIVE)
R1	Grant application success	% of national competitive grants received by agency and scheme	PVC (Research)	ARC DISCOVERY: 1.44% (2004) ARC LINKAGE: 3.89% (2004)	ARC DISCOVERY: 2.01% (2005) ARC LINKAGE: 4.00% (2005)	T	ARC DISCOVERY: 2.00% (ACTUAL) ARC LINKAGE: 4.00% (ACTUAL)	ARC DISCOVERY: 2.00% ARC LINKAGE: 4.00%
		% of Category 1 Income from non-ARC funds		34%	35% (TARGET)	I	37% (21% NHMRC, 16% OTHER)	39% (22% NHMRC, 17% OTHER)
R2	Research commercialisation outcomes	No. of IP disclosures made & provisional patents filed	PVC (Research)	IP DISCLOSURES: 7 PROVISIONAL PATENTS: 1	IP DISCLOSURES: 28 PROVISIONAL PATENTS: 7	I (beyond 2005)	IP DISCLOSURES: 10 PROVISIONAL PATENTS: 10 STRETCH	IP DISCLOSURES: 11 PROVISIONAL PATENTS: 5
		$ commercial income (trade sales, start up dividends, royalties, licence fees, IP assignments, licensing and sales) - 3 yr moving average		n/a	$75,879	I	$91,055	$109,266

Figure 4.9 Research KPIs in an Australian University.

The words in this table are, again, held together by a visual syntax, which means that there are no verbs, and hence no mood or modality. This causes the writing to lose most of its interpersonal dimension. It is the *mood* element which necessitates a choice between declarative, interrogative, and imperative, and thereby makes every clause into a speech act, and it is the *modality* element, expressed by modal auxiliaries such as 'may', 'will', and 'should', which necessitates every declarative to express a degree of probability, or, more generally, truth value, and every imperative a degree of permission or obligation. In conjunction with the direct address created by first- and second-person pronouns, mood and modality make language, in Halliday's (1985, p. 70) words: "Something that can be argued about – something that can be affirmed or denied, and also doubted, contradicted, insisted on, accepted with reservation, qualified, tempered, regretted, and so on". Without mood, modality, and direct address, information becomes a *fait accompli* that cannot be argued about. Yet a document such as Figure 4.9 still has interpersonal power – it is authoritative and definitive, an order, signed off by an authority.

The same table also lacks the logical connectives which, in traditional writing, play a fundamental role in explaining things. A partial translation of Figure 4.9 in linear prose might read something like this:

> The Key Performance Indicator *Grant Application Success* is the responsibility of the PVC (Research). Success is measured as the percentage of national competitive grants received by a particular agency or scheme. *To* set a target historical performance should be taken into account, and the previous year's results taken as a baseline. *If*, say, the percentage if ARC Discovery Grants was 1.44 and the percentage of ARC Linkage grants 3.89 in 2004, and *if* the percentages were 2.01 and 4.00 in 2005, *then* the 2006 thresholds could be 2.00 and 4.00.

As shown by the italics, conjunctions such as "(in order) to" and "if ... then" create logical connections between the items of information displayed in the table. But tables have no resources for expressing this kind of connection. They objectify the information, fitting it into a rigid classification system.

As a result of this de-personalization and objectification, the same diagram can be interpreted, talked about and around, in different ways, as Kress and van Leeuwen (2006, p. 61) have shown in relation to Shannon and Weaver's communication model (Figure 4.5). However precise diagrams may seem, their meaning is context-dependent, in need of complementation by spoken discourse to re-personalize it and de-objectify it – in the case of Figure 4.9, a meeting between the university's senior management and faculty deans. This kind of context-dependency is characteristic of the new writing. It also characterizes PowerPoint slides, for instance, where the bullet-pointed lists tend to lack mood, modality, and direct address, so that it is up to the presenter to supply the explanations and the interpersonal element and attune the slides to the specific needs of the audience they are presented to.

4 Coda

Some 20 years ago, I had, for the first time, a PhD student who wanted to write a thesis on the language of websites. She began by printing off some 30-odd corporate homepages, planning to analyze them with the methods of linguistic analysis she had learned. But it did not work. The methods were based on clause analysis, and there were hardly any clauses on these pages. There were plenty of words, but they were nouns and nominal groups, not clauses. And the few clauses she did find stood alone, as isolated morsels of information, rather than as part of a running text held together by linguistic forms of cohesion.

My student had also expected to be able to analyze images. And yes, there were some images on these pages. But the methods of image analysis she had learned – semiotics and iconology – did not take her very far, because they assume that images have symbolic meanings and realize some kind of complete message, and most of these images did not. They were either small, bland pictograms or vague monochrome backgrounds for words on which the faint outlines of clouds or rippling water could only just be discerned. Yet the pages were very visual. Plenty of color. Plenty of line. Plenty of visual texture.

It was this experience that made me realize that it was, at least in relation to new writing texts of this kind, no longer possible to speak separately about language and image, and to analyze them separately and in turn, to then and only then look at the kind of image-text connections Barthes (1964/1977) first discussed in the 1960s. It was then that I realized that *cross-modal* principles had to be found which would apply equally and simultaneously to text and image and reveal their profound imbrication.

In this chapter, I have discussed two key cross-modal resources, the generic structures that realize functionality and the stylistic means of expression – color, texture, (typo-)graphic shape – and composition that simultaneously demarcate the functional elements of texts and the identities they express. These multimodal means of expression apply to all spatial semiotic practices, including three-dimensional ones such as architecture and interior decoration (Ravelli & McMurtrie, 2016), and it is one of their key characteristics that they cannot stand alone, that they must be part of multimodal configurations – that color must always be the color *of* something, texture the texture *of* something, and graphic shape the shape *of* something, whether letterforms or the lines that separate title and bullet-pointed lists on PowerPoint.

None of this is to say that the new writing has completed replaced the old writing, or the new image the old image. The old continues to exist alongside the new. Nothing ever changes all at once. But the characteristics of the new writing do need our urgent attention, as they realize the priorities and values of the new order that is so rapidly and radically changing the world we live in.

References

Apollonio, U., (Ed.). (2009). *Futurist manifestos*. London: Tate Publishing.
Arnheim, R. (1982). *The power of the center*. Berkeley: University of California Press.
Barthes, R. (1964/1977). *Image, music, text*. London: Fontana.
Barthes, R. (1973). *Le Plaisir du texte*. Paris: Editions du Seuil.
Caple, H. (2013). *Photojournalism: A social semiotic approach*. Basingstoke: Palgrave Macmillan.
Chaney, D. (1996). *Lifestyles*. London: Routledge.
Danesi, M. (2017). *The Semiotics of emoji*. London: Bloomsbury.
Davies, W. (2015). *The Happiness industry: How the government and big business sold US well-being*. London: Verso.
Djonov, E., & van Leeuwen, T. (2014). Bullet points, new writing and the marketization of public discourse: A critical multimodal perspective. In E. Djonov & S. Zhao (Eds.), *Critical multimodal studies of popular discourse* (pp. 232–250). London: Routledge.
Djonov, E., & van Leeuwen, T. (2013). Between the grid and composition: Layout in PowerPoint's design and use. *Semiotica*, 197, 1–34.
Fairclough, N. (1993). Critical discourse analysis and the marketization of public discourse: The universities. *Discourse and Society*, 4(2), 133–169.
Falzon, P., Amalberti, R., & Carbonell, N. (1986). Dialogue control strategies in oral communication. In K. Hopper & I. A. Newman, (Eds.), *Foundations for human computer communication*. Amsterdam: Elsevier Science Publishers B.V.
Freeman, L. C. (2004). *The development of social network analysis: A study in the sociology of science*. Vancouver, BC: Empirical Press.
Halliday, M. A. K. (1985). *An introduction to functional grammar*. London: Arnold.
Holsanova, J., Rahm, H., & Holmqvist, K. (2006). Entry points and reading paths on newspaper spreads: comparing a semiotic analysis with eye-tracking measurements. *Visual Communication*, 5(1), 65–93.
Horkheimer, M., & Adorno, T. (1972/1985). *Dialectic of enlightenment*. New York, NY: Continuum.
Knight, S. (2018, May 10). The spectacular power of big lens: How one giant company will dominate the way the whole world sees. *The Guardian*. Retrieved from https://www.theguardian.com/news/2018/may/10/the-invisible-power-of-big-glasses-eyewear-industry-essilor-luxottica
Kongsberg Maritime. (2007). *Kongsberg Maritime established cybernetic R&D group*. Retrieved from https://www.simrad.com/www/01/nokbg0238.nsf/NewsPrintKM?ReadForm&cat=DEDAB2A5E1391F4AC12579D0002CB585

Kress, G. (2010). *Multimodality: A social semiotic approach to contemporary communication*. London: Routledge.
Kress, G., & van Leeuwen, T. (2006). *Reading images: The grammar of visual design* (2nd ed.). London: Routledge.
Kvåle, G. (2016). Software as ideology: A multimodal critical discourse analysis of Microsoft Word and SmartArt. *Journal of Language and Politics, 15*(3), 259–273.
Lupton, D. (2004). *Thinking with type: A critical guide for designers, writers, editors & students*. New York: Princeton Architectural Press.
Machin, D. (2004). Building the world's visual language: The increasing global importance of image banks in corporate media. *Visual Communication, 3*(3), 316–336.
Machin, D., & van Leeuwen, T. (2008). Branding the self. In C. R. Caldas-Coulthard & R. Iedema (Eds.), *Identity trouble: Critical discourse and contested identities* (pp. 43–57). Basingstoke; Palgrave Macmillan.
Machin, D., & van Leeuwen, T. (2007). *Global media discourse: A critical introduction*. London: Routledge.
Neuenschwander, B. (1993). *Letterwork: Creative letterforms in graphic design*. London: Phaidon.
Ravelli. L. J., & McMurtrie, R. J. (2016). *Multimodality in the built environment: Spatial discourse analysis*. London: Routledge.
Samara, T. (2002). *Making and breaking the grid: A graphic design layout workshop*. Beverly, MA: Rockport Publishers.
Shannon, C., & Weaver, W. (1949). *The mathematical theory of communication*. Urbana: University of Illinois Press.
Smith, C. (2005). *Photoshop and dreamweaver interaction: Creating high-impact web pages*. New York, NY: McGraw-Hill/Osborne.
Spencer, H. (1982). *Pioneers of modern typography*. Cambridge, MA: MIT Press.
van Leeuwen, T. (2011). The semiotics of decoration. In K. L. O'Halloran & B. A. Smith (Eds.), *Multimodal studies: Exploring issues and domains* (pp. 115–130). London: Routledge.
van Leeuwen, T. (2006). Towards a semiotics of typography. *Information Design Journal, 14*(2), 139–155.
van Leeuwen, T. (2005). *Introducing social semiotics*. London: Routledge.
Ventola, E. (1987). *The structure of social interaction: A systemic approach to the semiotics of service encounters*. London: Frances Pinter.
Wiener, N. (1947/1973). *Cybernetics: Or control and communication in the animal and the machine*. Cambridge, MA: MIT Press.

Commentary
The Critical Role of Analysis in Moving from Conjecture to Theory

John A. Bateman

It is now a truism that communication, and culture more broadly, has become more *visual*. An assumption that some kind of *shift* has occurred toward image-centricity is, as a consequence, quite common. This is well reflected both in this volume as a whole, and in the three chapters of the present section, which attempt in particular to deepen the discussion by setting out some theoretical commitments, motivations, and consequences for the study of image-centricity as such. Each of the chapters addresses a rather different area of concern, although all three, to different extents, set out examples of analysis drawing on the aspects of theory they consider. The first chapter, that of Hartmut Stöckl, attempts to extend our understanding of the diversity of genres that, arguably, assign *images* a central position. The second chapter, that of Nina-Maria Klug, offers a detailed tracing of discursive moves made with respect to culturally prominent news images, suggesting that the core notion of intertextuality must also be extended to include image-like materials. And the third chapter, that of Theo van Leeuwen, focuses on what he has for some time argued to be the *new visuality of writing*, where written language is considered to crucially involve image-like contributions from several domains, including typography, layout, and more. All three chapters show, in their own ways, the need to extend our understanding of multimodality theoretically, methodologically, and practically, if our accounts of image-centricity are to rise to the challenges that many contemporary communicative artifacts present.

The area is complex, however, and all three chapters are exploratory to a greater or lesser extent. Nevertheless, the descriptions they present are all good illustrations of how concrete analysis can, and arguably should, be seen as a way of working on, and extending, theory. Engaging with the demands of concrete analysis is a crucial task facing multimodal analysis at this time, and the more an account is able to support this, the more likely it is for progress to be achieved. Remaining hypothetical, or conjectural, for too long brings a variety of negative consequences, some of which I will return to later in the chapter.

The principal point argued in this commentary will be that good ideas require testing; otherwise they remain at the level of (potentially) good ideas. To turn conjectures, regardless how compelling or insightful, into reliably applicable theory is not straightforward and demands not only considerable investment of effort but also appropriate methodologies. Concretely, then, I will pick up the proposals made in each chapter and consider them from this perspective of joining theory and analysis, asking to what extent they already do this and whether there are particular decisions made that might limit progress toward their own stated goals or additions that could help advance those goals. I will also draw, in part, on my own approach to multimodal analysis, both with respect to the theoretical distinctions drawn and to the methods of empirical analysis which led to them (cf. Bateman, 2016).

The opening chapter from Stöckl is then a natural place to start since his focus on a corpus-based approach to genre and multimodality echoes not only his own detailed investigations carried out from the early 1990s onward on genre and its multimodal expression (cf. Stöckl, 1992, 1997, and further references in the chapter) but also the similarly corpus-based approach begun by Judy Delin and myself in the late 1990s and early 2000s in the scope of the Genre and Multimodality (GeM) project (cf. Allen, Bateman, & Delin, 1999; Bateman, Delin, & Henschel, 2004; Bateman, 2008). Stöckl brings these areas of experience to bear on more recent work on news journalism and the emergence of the very specific image-centric news genre identified by Caple (2008) called the *image-nuclear news story*. Stöckl raises the question as to whether other genres beyond that described by Caple can be found where image materials also play a central, but perhaps different, role.

Stöckl's approach is firmly anchored in corpus-based text linguistics, operating with respect to a selection of news articles from several different English-language and German-language newspapers. In several respects, the approach echoes Martin and colleagues' (cf. Martin, 1992) multiple refinement of Labov and Waletsky's well-known account of the *story genre* into an entire family of closely related genres, such as recounts and reports, on the basis of the varying linguistic features exhibited by the stages of the genres identified. Stöckl's conclusion is that, indeed, an ongoing diversification of image-centric genres can be observed as well as different patterns of genre use across newspapers and language cultures. Moreover, since there also appear to be differences in the kinds of communicative work performed by the image-components of the revealed genres, the results are clearly important for discussions of text-image relations (which are still far too often considered independently of genre) as well as for the general question of what Kress (2010, pp. 83–84) describes as the *reach* of a semiotic mode, that is, the uses that a society typically makes of a given mode. Image-centric genres may consequently be argued to function as one carrier of changes for the reach of images in (at least) Western news culture.

In order to take the work further, Stöckl presents a detailed *coding scheme* for characterizing the use of images in static news media intended to help map out the *image-centric genre space* in more detail. His classification framework covers five levels of enquiry: the type of news, the layout (or compositional structure), the thematic structure, the image type, and the text-image relation (his Figures 2.5 and 2.6). Most of the distinctions included in the framework draw on previous work and the literature, refined as suggested by the analyses required for the corpus work Stöckl describes. Although the categories are by and large plausible, it remains to be seen if they can all be used reliably, and also if they are sufficient to successfully characterize genre differences as desired. The best way to show this would be, as suggested earlier, to apply the framework to a sufficient body of data so that, first, reliability results could be reported for the coding categories (cf. Bateman, Wildfeuer, & Hiippala, 2017, pp. 198–204), and, second, patterns of co-occurrence could be sought that would, indeed, suggest characterizations of particular genres within the space of possibilities as a whole. Examples and methods for finding patterns in this way are given with respect to the very different medium of comics in Bateman, Veloso, and Lau (2019). Carrying out such studies must be seen as a clear priority not only for work on image-centric genres, but for multimodal studies as a whole, as the feedback obtained concerning the usability and relevance of the categories proposed is critical for deciding how to proceed further.

Addressing reliability and relevance would also be valuable for establishing relations *between* descriptive accounts: for example, most of Stöckl's 'layout' characterization overlaps with the more general scheme for layout given in the GeM framework mentioned earlier (Bateman, 2008), albeit at a far reduced level of detail. One criticism commonly made of the GeM scheme has been that it is just *too* detailed for practical work; whether or not this is the case, Stöckl's distinctions could also be seen as configurational 'pre-sets' which, although expressible within the GeM model, might, for particular research questions, be more desirable, as the data might not always require unraveling according to all of the dimensions of organization in principle possible. Variable focus annotation of this kind could be pursued beneficially for many areas of multimodality and may even be posited as a methodological guideline.

The chapter by Klug opens up the discussion of multimodality and the potential centricity of images to go far beyond the confines of individual texts. Drawing on some prominent recent examples of news reporting and responses to that reporting, Klug shows convincingly that the web of intertextual relations established must also be extended so that non-textual, or combined image-text ensembles, are seen as equal partners. Indeed, in reference to the famous case of the press photograph of a young refugee boy lying dead in the waves on a beach and the ensuing discussion not only of the event but of the acceptability of use or non-use of the visual material itself, Klug demonstrates beyond question that images can function equally well, and sometimes more effectively, as the central components of intertextuality in action. To support her discussion, Klug takes a broadly Foucauldian notion of *discourse*, which she contrasts with some more fine-grained and intratextual notions of discourse semantics already used in multimodality (cf. Bateman & Wildfeuer, 2014). For Klug, following a wide range of authors, discourse is crucially a "trans-textual semantic unit" that is "more or less synonymous with a *discussion* of a topic". As emphasized in Bateman, Wildfeuer, and Hiippala (2017, p. 133), however, there can be no conflict between these distinct uses of discourse as both the intratextual dynamic development of meaning, which we distinguish following Martin (1992) as *discourse semantics*, and the societal intertextual unfolding of discourses are essential, and different, facets of communication. Klug's extension of the latter to properly include visual materials is clearly necessary, as entire discourses of discussion can be pursued via visual means not only with contemporary technological support but also, as Klug illustrates, via appropriation of public spaces for visual comment and response (e.g., graffiti, murals, and similar).

Klug also goes further and uses the analysis of her selected case study to argue for a typological classification of the kinds of relationships that might hold to bind such intertextual discourses together, thus moving from description to theory (her Figure 3.1). Although there are no doubt mechanisms that operate at the large-scale discourse level rather than on the intratextual level, it was not yet clear to me whether the categories proposed were really distinct from the kinds of relations also necessary within intratextual analysis. Here, also as argued at length in Bateman, Wildfeuer, and Hiippala (2017, pp. 204–211), it depends crucially on the potentially complex materiality of any multimodal communicative situation being analyzed.

In a class-room situation using a whiteboard, for example, the teacher might well take some image, *transcribe* it in written (or spoken) language, or adjust it by removing or emphasizing part of it (Klug's *transformation*), *index* it by talking about it while walking around the class-room or by referring to it by a reference on another part of the whiteboard, and so on. Evaluation, justifications (Klug's *meta-textualization*) as well as critical revisions (Klug's *resemioticization*) would be equally possible. This suggests a stronger analogy between large-scale Foucauldian discourse and face-to-face conversation, which is itself interesting, and, indeed, between socially constitutive large-scale discourse and fine-grained discourse in general. Perhaps in this respect, arguments could be made that (at least these) issues of intertextuality and intratextuality are matters of fractally differentiated spatiotemporal scales and so should follow naturally from any sufficiently powerful account of (multimodal) communication. Clearly there is much to research.

In the final chapter of the section, van Leeuwen sets out further consequences of the basic tenet that written language engages a broad diversity of visual forms of expression. Certainly, to a large part due to van Leeuwen's own earlier work in this area, this tenet can now be seen as relatively uncontentious, although the important question of just how the study of the phenomenon is to be taken further remains. Van Leeuwen argues that it is beneficial to focus on a set of closely related semiotic *practices* that may 'enlist' a range of semiotic modes and which crucially involve the spatiality of the communicative artifacts or events analyzed. This is further suggested to apply to any practices that mobilize spatiality, such as "packaging, product design and architecture". Van Leeuwen's main focus of interest is then how semiotic change and social change relate; changes in practices involving an extended view of *writing* are consequently interpreted in social critical terms. This is clearly an important undertaking, relating to the broader aims of critical discourse analysis and social critique. However, just as has been the case with linguistically oriented critical discourse analysis, being able to offer analyses that are accurate, revealing, and convincing rests crucially on the application of well-grounded and empirically tested descriptive frameworks.

This is an important issue because, as the complexity of the media artifacts engaged with increases, so too does the need for analytic rigor. Without such rigor, descriptions remain looser than necessary and conjecture cannot advance to build theory. In fact, given insufficient constraint, it even becomes unclear just what 'the phenomenon' at issue for study might be. I will show this very briefly here with respect to some of the analyses that van Leeuwen offers, although the methodological concerns and distinctions employed are of general relevance when attempting multimodal analysis. Two aspects addressed by the first two chapters of the section are particularly relevant here: the first is attention to corpus results rather than handpicked examples; the second is the critical notion of fine-grained discourse semantics *in addition to* larger-scale discourse. Discourse semantic mechanisms are commonly effaced in van Leeuwen's account, with the consequence that discourse-based decisions are constantly being made, but remain implicit in the very terms employed in the analysis rather than emerging as the results of that analysis.

Consider the analyses offered of diagrams in van Leeuwen's chapter. First, the extension to talk of diagrams is itself anything but straightforward. Are diagrams simply further examples of the 'new style' of writing? What kinds of artifacts are demarcated in this way? Diagrams and other *page-based* media certainly share aspects of their materiality as visual (still often static – although dynamic diagrams are on the increase), but they also differ substantially from pictorial images, comics and graphic novels, press photography, news articles, and much else besides. Recognizing this helps when deciding what kinds of analytic levels to employ and is one of the valuable results of genre-based work such as that of Stöckl. Moreover, in our earlier work applying the GeM model, several levels of analysis were proposed for organizing empirical description. As noted earlier, one of these was the layout layer, a visually-oriented and highly restrictive description of the units and relative placements of those units within a framed page-like (static) canvas. The role of such descriptions is often misunderstood in more informal approaches: the point of a restrictive analysis is not to claim that all artifacts work in the same way, but rather to make it compellingly clear that some artifacts, in fact, operate *differently*. If an account is sufficiently loose that is applies to 'everything', theory cannot advance precisely because exceptions and descriptive gaps are not rendered visible.

One of the most important results of the GeM studies in this regard, therefore, was that there are a host of types of media products where the descriptive results did *not* apply, and so other units and relationships would be necessary. Diagrams are one such case. Their layout structure (i.e., use of the visually demarcated possibilities of the 'page', 'spread', 'canvas') is distinctive, which leads to different questions being asked and different hypotheses concerning design variations being entertained.

Furthermore, within the account of semiotic modes articulated in Bateman (2016) and elsewhere, units and relationships within a layout-oriented level of description must in addition receive discourse interpretations (which will often be influenced by genre) in order to be understood and used. It is not possible to directly read off the 'meanings' of visual forms, social or otherwise; one must first establish (empirically) which units are provided by the layout level of the mode and then consider their discourse purposes in order to (abductively) assign interpretations.

Van Leeuwen's interpretation of the Shannon and Weaver diagram for information transmission (his Figure 4.5) proceeds very differently: his description, still based on Kress and van Leeuwen's (1996) *narrative* visual category because of the presence of vectors (in this case, explicit arrows), assigns functional participant roles of *actor* and *acted-upon* to the items connected by the vectors in the diagram. As a consequence, since it is the boxes in the diagram that are connected by arrows, van Leeuwen proposes transcriptions of the form "an Information Source 'does something' to a Transmitter, which in turn 'does something' to a Channel". This, arguably, misreads the diagram; in fact, it misreads the *type* of the diagram. In this case, the arrows are in all likelihood not 'acting-on' vectors at all but rather characterize iconically and indexically the material that is being passed between the various boxes. It is not the boxes that act on the other boxes, but rather that the boxes act (and act differently) on what is being passed through them or which originates or ends with them.

Note that this is, of course, an empirical issue: it may be possible to find support for van Leeuwen's interpretation, but the work of finding that support needs to be done, rather than assuming that the meanings can be read off a 'grammar' of the visual design. There are meanings to be read off the diagram, but these will typically be far less abstract and more schematized. The particular interpretation is not, however, what is at issue here; what is central is the mechanisms by which the diagram is capable of supporting any such readings. And this is the role of discourse as the abductive search for the 'best explanation' of the cues as deployed in the interpreted artifact (cf. Bateman & Wildfeuer, 2014). These 'best explanations' may become fossilized in particular diagram types, which is the case here, as this is an information flow diagram. Related diagrammatic genres within this medium are electric circuits, water courses, and polarized light displays. Indeed, it may be the case that the entire search for *narrative* readings is of quite limited applicability in this genre; further studies similar to that of Stöckl (this volume) will be valuable here as well. Students and educators in particular need to be trained to follow such paths of interpretation rather than being locked into potentially inappropriate analyses and 'meta-languages'.

A misreading also appears to occur in van Leeuwen's listing of questions concerning a flowchart diagram for medical consultation (his Figure 4.7). Here, the lack of an empirically-derived account of the layout structure of the semiotic mode leaves open more variation than is warranted by the actual artifact. It is often not the case that a decomposition directly into vectors will be appropriate, as van Leeuwen himself notes later in his chapter when talking of the necessity for considering substructure in 'images'. It is, however, characteristic of approaches that have not engaged substantially with empirical investigation that this problem is noted but not dealt with – for reliable analyses, however, this issue simply cannot be sidestepped. Appropriate structures are essential in order to avoid raising hypotheses or suggestions that are not motivated by the semiotic modes in question. In the present case, the flowchart as used has a structure that needs to be captured in order both to talk about its design and to suggest critiques. Van Leeuwen instead asks why there are "no downwards 'no' arrows between 'severe pain', 'mild pain', and 'no pain'?". However, given an appropriate layout structure for this diagram, this question makes little sense precisely because the arrows are already present. The 'missing' arrows are simply located with respect to the layout units formed by the complex sets of 'and/or'-conditions running horizontally across the chart rather than solely to the starting condition on the left-hand side (which would, in fact, have brought its own problems for constraining discourse interpretation).

The diagram certainly has a range of potential design problems, but that these arrows are missing is not one of them. Again, it is crucial to be far more explicit about the (visuospatial) structure of any artifact being analyzed, and that demands empirical work first to ascertain that structure; only then can the space of hypotheses for reasonable discourse interpretations be appropriately constrained and the layout structure engaged with as perhaps requiring correction or improvement. Hiippala and Orekhova (2018) introduce ongoing multimodal work on an empirically motivated account of diagram organization of precisely this kind.

The kinds of questions and issues that van Leeuwen raises are without doubt central for our understanding of the social contexts of contemporary communication, but to do the most justice to those questions, it will be necessary to move from more conjectural accounts to positions and frameworks that have been subjected to more direct empirical investigation. This does not mean that those positions are correct; but it does mean that they are more likely to stand a little longer before their limitations are found and more complete accounts proposed. And, indeed, showing just where those accounts have their limitations is the necessary crucial first step toward making progress beyond them.

To conclude, therefore, the three chapters discussed here show well that there are strong reasons for giving far closer attention to the role of images in combined text-image communication. They also show, however, that just what is to count as *images* exhibits considerable variation, itself supportive of a range of distinct functionalities. While these all depend on the affordances of visuospatial materialities, just what is done with those affordances demands not only close empirical investigation but also theoretical frameworks that are responsive to what those investigations reveal.

References

Allen, P., Bateman, J. A., & Delin, J. L. (1999). Genre and layout in multimodal documents: Towards an empirical account. In R. Power & D. Scott (Eds.), *Proceedings of the AAAI Fall Symposium on Using Layout for the Generation, Understanding, or Retrieval of Documents* (pp. 27–34). Cape Cod, MA: AAAI Technical Report FS-99-04.

Bateman, J. A. (2016). Methodological and theoretical issues for the empirical investigation of multimodality. In N.-M. Klug & H. Stöckl (Eds.), *Handbuch Sprache im multimodalen Kontext* (pp. 36–74). Berlin: de Gruyter.

Bateman, J. A. (2008). *Multimodality and genre: A foundation for the systematic analysis of multimodal documents*. Basingstoke: Palgrave Macmillan.

Bateman, J. A., Delin, J. L., & Henschel, R. (2004). Multimodality and empiricism: Preparing for a corpus-based approach to the study of multimodal meaning-making. In E. Ventola, C. Charles, & M. Kaltenbacher (Eds.), *Perspectives on multimodality* (pp. 65–87). Amsterdam: John Benjamins.

Bateman, J. A., Veloso, F. O., & Lau, Y. L. (2019). On the track of visual style: A diachronic study of page composition in comics and its functional motivation. *Visual Communication*. Advance online publication.

Bateman, J. A., & Wildfeuer, J. (2014). A multimodal discourse theory of visual narrative. *Journal of Pragmatics*, 74, 180–218.

Bateman, J. A., Wildfeuer, J., & Hiippala, T. (2017). *Multimodality: Foundations, research and analysis. A problem-oriented introduction*. Berlin: de Gruyter.

Caple, H. (2008). Intermodal relations in image nuclear news stories. In L. Unsworth (Ed.), *Multimodal semiotics: Functional analysis in contexts of education* (pp. 127–138). London: Continuum.

Hiippala, T., & Orekhova, S. (2018, May). Enhancing the AI2 diagrams dataset using rhetorical structure theory. In N. Calzolari, K. Choukri, C. Cieri, T. Declerck, S. Goggi, K. Hasida, H. Isahara, B. Maegaard, J. Mariani, H. Mazo, A. Moreno, J. Odijk, S. Piperidis, & T, Tokunaga (Eds.), *LREC 2018. Proceedings of the Eleventh International Conference on Language Resources and Evaluation* (pp. 1925–1931). Miyazaki: European Language Resources Association (ELRA).

Kress, G. (2010). *Multimodality: A social semiotic approach to contemporary communication.* London: Routledge.

Kress, G., & van Leeuwen, T. (1996). *Reading images: The grammar of visual design.* London: Routledge.

Martin, J. R. (1992). *English text: Systems and structure.* Amsterdam: Benjamins.

Stöckl, H. (1997). *Textstil und Semiotik englischsprachiger Anzeigenwerbung.* Frankfurt: Peter Lang.

Stöckl, H. (1992). Der 'picture relation type': Ein praktischer Analysemodus zur Beschreibung der vielfältigen Einbettungs- und Verknüpfungsbeziehungen von Bild und Text. *Papiere zur Linguistik, 46*(11), 49–61.

Part 2

Historical Developments in Image-Centric Practices

5 On the Emergence of Image-Centric Popular Science Stories in *National Geographic*

Jana Pflaeging

1 Introduction, First Observations, and Research Questions

A plethora of terms has recently been suggested in different publications in multimodality to refer to similar communicative phenomena: contemporary journalism is pervaded by "multisemiotic news stor[ies]," in which images are said to be "prominent" (Caple & Bednarek, 2010, p. 212), "dominant" (Caple, 2013, p. 129), or "focused" (Caple & Bednarek, 2010, p. 212). Genre labels such as *picture stories* or *picture side-bars* have been used among journalists (cf. Caple & Bednarek, 2010, p. 212); *standouts* (Economou, 2012, p. 246; see also 2008), *stand-alones* (Bednarek & Caple, 2012, p. 136; Economou, 2012, p. 248), *news bites* (Knox, 2007, p. 23), *image-nuclear news bites* (Caple, 2008, p. 125), and *image-nuclear news stories* (Caple, 2006, 2008, 2013; see also Caple & Bednarek, 2010) are further category labels that have been proposed in the research literature.

The *image-nuclear news story* (INNS hereafter), in particular, has been identified by Caple as a self-contained and relatively stable newspaper genre. Through extensive empirical work, she found its typical generic stages to be "heading^image^(prosodic tail)^caption" (Caple, 2013, p. 129), with heading, image, and (an optional) prosodic tail constituting the genre's rhetorical core, or nucleus. Caple's study was focused on the image-nuclear practices of one particular medium, the *Sydney Morning Herald*, at a particular period of time, between 2004 and 2006. Since a 'rise of the image' has been generally attested (see Stöckl et al., this volume), it seems a plausible next step to scrutinize other media and genres at different points in time for any tendency to empower the image "with the ability to tell the story itself" (Caple, 2006, p. 1). This will be one of the main concerns of this chapter.

On the American (and international) magazine market, the popular science magazine *National Geographic* (NG hereafter) has built a reputation for an 'image-heavy' popular science journalism that acknowledges a photograph's "power to [do] infinitely more than document" (Draper, 2013, p. 32). In a modern-day world in which photographic equipment has become hyper-accessible and the photographic practice itself pervasive, the growing number of images that surround us may not only prompt an appreciation of the artistic mastery of the medium, but may also trigger a sense of banality, randomness, and even elusiveness. NG clearly distances itself from everyday photographic practices by "wresting a precious particle of the world from time and space and holding it absolutely still [to create] a great photograph [that] can explode the totality of our world, such that we never see it quite the same again" (Draper, 2013, p. 32).

The magazine's emphasis on photography has a long-standing tradition, dating back to its turn to the popular around 1900: NG was first published in 1888 as an *academic* journal of the *National Geographic Society*. Its editors quickly realized, however, that the *Society*'s declared goal "to increase and diffuse geographic knowledge" (NG, Oct 1888, p. i) could only be reached if large mainstream audiences were targeted. Photographic reproduction proved one of the most effective popularization strategies. In 1905, for the first time, a larger number of photographs were used to fill the pages of an issue, and what was meant only as a makeshift solution proved extraordinarily popular with a contemporary audience (Johns, 2013, n.p.). When readership numbers multiplied (Hawkins, 2010, p. 48), the course for the development of NG as a magazine and, soon, as a global brand, was set: a *popular* science journalism covering "themes of exploration and education" that allows their audiences "to travel from their armchair" (Davis, 2005, p. 52).

Figure 5.1 offers both a synchronic and a diachronic view on NG's publishing practices between 1888 and 2015. From a synchronic perspective, each horizontal bar indicates how an individual issue unfolds from front to back cover. Each color stands for a *genre* whose distinctiveness is indicated, among others, by the use of ethno-categorical genre labels (see Pflaeging, 2019): *From the Editor, Members' Forum, Geographica,* or *On Assignment* are examples of short-form *Departments*-genres;[1] *Feature Article* is a prominent long-form genre. Thus, each multicolored bar visualizes a so-called *genre profile*, which provides insight into a medium's *genre repertoire* at a given time, and the *frequency* of their instantiation (Luginbühl, 2014a, pp. 311–313; cf. Orlikowski & Yates, 1994, p. 547). From a diachronic perspective, genre profiles are given at ten-year intervals (if possible). They show that, since the 1980s, an increasingly broad range of short-form genres populates the *Departments*-section of NG; *Feature Article* is the most traditional genre in NG.

Based on the graphic, two observations can be made that seem particularly relevant in light of *shifts toward image-centricity in contemporary multimodal practices*:

Firstly, the most recent genre profile (NG July 2015) includes a short-form genre labeled *Visions* (Figure 5.1, marked by ▽). It features large, aesthetically appealing images that are accompanied by short captions. In book-form publications by NG, these multimodal texts are advertised as "rais[ing] a curtain on the wonders of the world and thrill[ing]

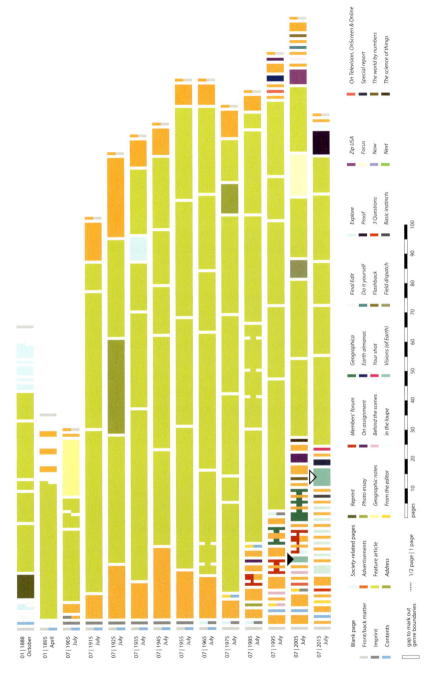

Figure 5.1 Genres profiles of *National Geographic*, 1888–2015.

us with nature's opulence and humanity's splendor. Each image alone exposes a nugget of our planet's magnificence" (Hitchcock, 2013, n.p.). The integrating of large, striking images attests to a parallel between INNS and *Visions*, which makes *Visions* a plausible object for further investigations. Through a synchronic corpus analysis, I seek to ascertain whether both genres differ with respect to their features, and if so, how. Minor alterations could indicate that the INNS is (or at least was at the time) a more widespread phenomenon that has also been instantiated in media other than the *Sydney Morning Herald*. If noticeable differences are found, the assumption that the INNS is a subtype of what ought to be grasped more generally as *image-centric* news media practices (cf. Stöckl et al., this volume) could be put on a more solid empirical footing.

Secondly, the graphic shows that the genre *Visions* is already published in July 2005, at the times labeled *Visions of Earth* (Figure 5.1, marked by ▼). Genres are generally seen as "essentially historically and socially situated" (Bateman, Evangelisti, & Bhatia, 2014, p. 10) phenomena, which do not appear *ex nihilo* but evolve from established generic patterns (Lemke, 1999, n.pag.). Thus, an understanding of the structural, semantic, and functional constellations that facilitate *image nuclearity* (or potentially *image-centricity*) can be deepened through an investigation of earlier developmental stages of a genre. Consequently, a diachronic approach will be adopted in the form of two case studies, focusing first on *Visions/Visions of Earth*, and second on *Feature Article* as a potential genre ancestor, since it has always included a multitude of large, aesthetic photographs.

In the following, I will briefly introduce some theoretical concepts relevant to the subsequent analysis, including *image nuclearity, news* and *popular science journalism, genre, genre profile, genre emergence*. Afterward, I present my synchronic and diachronic case studies before I finally turn to implications of my findings for a theoretical modeling of *image-centricity*.

2 Theoretical Inroads

2.1 Point of Departure: Image-Nuclear News Stories

The INNS has been modeled through extensive empirical analyses. Based on her investigation of 1000 genre exemplars sampled from issues of the newspaper *Sydney Morning Herald* published in 2004–2006 (Caple, 2013, p. 16), Caple identifies heading^image^(prosodic tail)^caption (Caple, 2013, p. 129) as typical generic stages. A striking image in a dominant position on the page (Caple, 2013, pp. 129, 127) usually forms the rhetorical nucleus of the genre, together with a heading and an optional prosodic tail. The heading, typically placed right above the image, serves to evoke a playful stance through word-image play, for example, by using "puns or allusions to other discourses" (Caple, 2013, p. 129; Caple 2008,

p. 131). It thus engages with the audience interpersonally (Caple, 2013, p. 11). The play extends to the prosodic tail, which, if realized, is placed before the caption (Caple, 2013, p. 129).

INNS commonly draw on the remainder of the caption to instantiate two different satellites that *expand* (Caple, 2013, p. 130) the story: on the one hand, this expansion is accomplished through *experiential orientation* (Caple, 2013, p. 131). It serves to set the scene by "anchor[ing]" the image (Barthes, 1964/1977, p. 39), that is, by narrowing down the image's semantic potential through a direct reference to "participants, their actions, circumstances and attributes" (Caple, 2013, p. 130). This is done by means of verbal cues, such as class/group assignment (general) or naming (specific) for participant identification, adverbial/prepositional groups (explicit) to identify location in time, or locative phrases/regional classifiers (more specific and more general) to identify location in space (Caple, 2013, pp. 132–134).

A second part of the caption "provide[s] the wider context" (Caple, 2008, p. 137; see Caple, 2006, p. 11) of a news event and is thus called *contextual extension*. It expands the meaning beyond what is depicted in the image by "focus[ing] our attention on the news angle" and "pointing to its newsworthiness" (Caple, 2013, pp. 134, 130). This is also where news values, that is, "the factors that take an event into the news," are construed verbally and visually (see Bednarek & Caple, 2017). Common news values are, among others, timeliness (an event's relevance in terms of time), proximity (an event's geographical or cultural nearness), personalization (an event's personal or human interest aspect), unexpectedness (an event's unusuality, rarity, or surprising deviance from a default), superlativeness (an event's aspects of intensification), and aesthetic appeal (an event's beauty or pleasure-inducing aspects). Aesthetic appeal, timeliness, and proximity are the three most common news values in Caple's (2013, p. 32) corpus of INNS.

Before applying this concept of *image nuclearity* to my data, I shall comment on its transferability to popular science discourse, and I will also introduce my take on genre and related terms, with a particular focus on magazine journalism.

2.2 From News Journalism to Popular Science Journalism

Per definition, news stories in news journalism (of which the INNS is a subtype) focus on "actions of important people", on "ordinary people who have done extraordinary things", "aberrant behavior, or disruptions to the moral order", and "the impact that events and issues have on our everyday lives" (Caple, 2018, pp. 1–2). Popular science journalists, in contrast, engage in communicative exchanges between the social sphere of science (here understood to include geology, geography, and the social sciences) and the wider public with the aim to make scientific information accessible (Bucchi & Trench, 2014, p. 3; cf. Stöckl &

Pflaeging, 2018, ch.2). The science events and occurrences they report on are not (hard) *news* in a strict sense. Thus, my adopting of *news values* as part of the *image-nuclearity* framework for an analysis of popular science stories needs commenting.

Since *news values* research gained momentum in the 1960s (with Galtung & Ruge, 1965), the concept has received much scholarly attention in various journalism-close research areas (see Caple, 2018 for an overview). Among the neat definitions put forth in these contexts is Bednarek and Caple's (2017) framework from a discourse analysis perspective (as we have just seen, they were among the first to include press photography, too, cf. Caple, 2013). *News values*, in their view, concern the "the newsworthiness of events – their potential newsworthiness in a given community, their newsworthiness as evaluated and determined by newsworkers in news practice, or their newsworthiness as constructed through discourse" (Bednarek & Caple, 2017, p. 42).

With due care and the awareness that such proposals need further investigation (which may, ultimately, prompt the coining of a new (set of) term(s)), I suggest that there is great potential in transferring such considerations to popular science discourse. Within a given community of reader-viewers, such as NG's audience(s), popular science events/occurrences – in the sense of *soft news* events – may be regarded worthy of being published. NG staff evaluate and determine this *news-worthiness*, not least against the backdrop of NG's publishing tradition and its audiences' expectations. Cues of a *news-worthiness* are traceable in the multimodal texts. I assume, for the moment, that what was outlined as *news values* in a narrow sense earlier constitutes a useful starting point for an exploration of *news values* in popular science journalism (cf. Craig, 1994, qtd. in Caple, 2018, who investigated *news values* in *feature photography*).[2] Furthermore, such an approach seems in line with Brighton and Foy's (2007, p. 1) general framing of *news values*: "In its sense everything that happens in the world is a new event, and somebody, somewhere, will have some level of interest in that occurrence". Since the dimension of *news values* in an analysis of INNSs seems to be specific to *news stories* but not necessarily to *image nuclearity*, it seems legitimate to stick with the term *image nuclearity* and its analytical dimensions in the subsequent analysis.

2.3 Genre, Genre Profiles, and Genre Development in Print Magazines

Genre. The satisfaction of social and communicative needs is deeply intertwined with communicative exchanges among individuals and groups (see, e.g., Miller, 1984; Swales, 1990; Bhatia, 1993). *Genres* are "bundles of strategies for achieving particular communicative aims in particular ways" (Bateman, Wildfeuer, & Hippala, 2017, p. 131). In particular, following Swales (1990, p. 58), they are conceptualized as "class[es] of communicative events that share a recognizable communicative purpose, that exhibit a schematic structure supporting the achievement of that purpose, and which show similarities in form, style, content, structure and intended audience". Concrete texts or text exemplars instantiate or participate in genres (cf. Bateman et al., 2017, p. 129).

Many multimodal extensions of the *genre*-concept emphasize a "genre-typical multimodal configurations of text parts" (Stöckl, 2015, p. 62) as necessary descriptive dimension. In other words, while "genre remains a linear, staged activity," *genres* present "relatively stable semiotic configurations for interpretation, and reading paths, [...] to dynamically *select* those stages that a reader is piecing together" (Bateman, 2008, p. 199). The layout of a text has "clearly also [has] consequences for interpretation" (Bateman, 2014c, p. 163); accordingly, the perceptual dominance of a large image on the page can be seen as indicative of its nuclearity (Bateman, 2014c, p. 166; cf. the concept of *image dominance*, in Stöckl, this volume).

In anticipation of studying publication practices of mass market periodicals, it seems furthermore useful to frame genres as "socio-cognitive devices for sensemaking" (Lomborg, 2014, p. 45). Those patterns that prove particularly effective in fulfilling communicative purposes tend to recur (Bateman, 2014a, p. 241; also Lemke, 1999) and, over time, leave imprints in a participant's mind. It is the similarities (and distinctive differences) between concrete textual patterns that give rise to genres as prototypically organized mental abstractions, which guide text production and reception (Lomborg, 2014, p. 3; cf. Iedema, Feez, & White, 1994, p. 76). With issues appearing only once a month, editors face the challenge of "delayed feedback" (Bell, 1991, p. 70), that is, text producers will only learn about any commercial success of their output after the process of text production has already been concluded. Thus, an audience's genre expectations are anticipated, and it is a promising strategy to adhere to patterns that they have already approved of in the past (Pflaeging, 2017, p. 259; see also Lomborg, 2014, p. 3).

Genre profiles. *Genres* are cultural practices that are discursively constructed, recognized, and reinforced among participants with multiple social needs interacting in various different constellations and situations. Therefore, it is not surprising that a discourse community "rarely depend[s] on a single genre for their communication" (Orlikowski & Yates, 1994, p. 542). As socio-historical contexts change and communicative purposes diversify, an increasingly broad variety of communicative patterns may become routinely enacted in a community and cognitively stored in a participant's mind. This may result in comprehensive "sets" or "system[s] of genres," (Bazerman, 1994), which have also been called a community's "genre repertoire" (Orlikowski & Yates, 1994, p. 546). The notion of *genre repertoire* has been complemented by *genre frequency* and *genre networks*, that is, the "intertextual relations between genre" detectable "on the formal, functional and/or content level" (Luginbühl, 2014a, p. 314), which together characterize *genre profiles*. Figure 5.1, for instance, showed the *genre profiles* of NG over time.

Genre emergence. Such notions of genres allow for tracing developmental trajectories of genres at different analytical levels. Individual genre features, or patterns, may emerge, stabilize, experience *pattern strengthening* or *weakening* over time (Pflaeging, 2017, p. 259). If a formerly prototypical conceptual core becomes increasingly atypical due to "the production of more texts of one kind than of another" (Lemke, 1999, n.pag.), the genre category's center is said to have *changed* (cf. Luginbühl, 2014b, p. 336).[3] If certain features/patterns within a genre's constellation of patterns are strengthened, they might get "re-purposed, re-designed and re-deployed" (Bateman et al., 2014, p. 10; also Lemke, 1999, n.pag.) to emerge ultimately as self-contained genres. These are often indicated through a genre name. In cases where the assumed source genre(s) persist(s), one speaks of an instance of *genre emergence* through *genre split* (Lemke, 1999, n.pag.; Schildhauer, 2016, p. 41; see "Verzweigung," Luginbühl, 2014b, p. 335, or "Teilung von Genres," Brock, 2015, p. 207). Such processes ultimately result in a diversification of a community's genre repertoire (Bhatia, 2014, pp. 65–66; Luginbühl, 2014a, pp. 312, 327) – or their magazine media.

For a journalistic community, for example, the editorial staff of NG, the perpetuation and strengthening of their own selling points, that is, popular science journalistic practices that draw heavily on photographic materials, provides an opportunity to "reproduce important aspects of [their] community's [professional, J.P.] identity" (Orlikowski & Yates, 1994, p. 546). Thus, NG's most traditional and prominent genre feature article, whose exemplars have been increasingly photographic since the early 20th century (see Pflaeging, 2017, pp. 252–254), has likely been a fertile ground for (potentially) *image-centric* patterns to gain salience and emerge as self-contained genres.

Given these considerations, it seems worthwhile to juxtapose a synchronic analysis with diachronic perspectives to gain further insight on the 'felicity conditions' of *image nuclearity* or *image-centricity*, respectively.

3 A Synchronic View – Case Study I: NG's *Visions* in 2015

In this section, I adopt a synchronic view on NG's short-form genre *Visions* as published in 2015, to investigate in how far the *Visions*-genre shows typical characteristics of *image nuclearity*.

3.1 Data and Methods

In 2015, text exemplars of the *Visions*-genre extended over three consecutive double-page spreads. Upon closer examination, it becomes apparent that what is published on an individual spread, on a very general note, shows spatial juxtaposition and logico-semantic ties between a large

Emergence of Image-Centric Popular Science Stories 105

image and a short caption. However, it does generally not show any ties to the two others spreads published under the same label, *Visions*. This made me conclude that what appears on one double-page constitutes a self-contained exemplar of the genre *Visions*.[4] Accordingly, each NG-issue includes three *Visions*-exemplars. The only exception was the November 2015-issue, a special issue, that does not feature any *Visions*-exemplars.

Aiming for a comprehensive sample, I collected all available genre exemplars that appeared in NG's monthly issues throughout 2015, a total of 33. All data were screen-captured from the *National Geographic Online Archive* at archive.nationalgeographic.com. The language-parts of the screen-captures were then processed with optical character recognition (OCR) software in order to facilitate further analyses, including an assessment of the caption's scope. Also, the data were manually annotated for features typical of *image nuclearity*, as defined and slightly adapted for an investigation of popular science stories. Results of qualitative annotations were quantified using Excel spreadsheets.

3.2 Results

Visions-exemplars published in 2015 show a very regular pattern of configuring an image and a caption within the layout space of a double-page: in all instances, images extend into all margins of the spread, which makes them perceptually salient and thus prominent layout components. Captions are always super-imposed onto the image and placed in one of the corners of the double-page (except for top-left, since this is where the genre label *Visions* appears on the first spread). Captions are composed from up to four elements (cf. Figure 5.2 ❶, ❷, ❸): (1) All captions include a short sequence of word-forms ($\bar{x}$ = 1.24 word-forms; σ = 0.44) that is typographically marked through bolding and placed right above the first line of the caption; based on their placement and similarity in typographical emphasis, I call this type of component *caption heading*. Furthermore, all captions feature (2) longer stretches of verbal text, which do not show typographical emphasis ($\bar{x}$ = 39.42 word-forms; σ = 4.87); I shall refer to them as *caption bodies*. Also, in all instances of captions, the photographer(s)/photography agency are indicated as author(s)/copyright holders of the image; I call this type of element *authorship note*. Finally, captions may include an *index to online resources*, as illustrated in Figure 5.2 (❸).

In 2015, caption headings always construct a more general reference to the place shown in the image, for example, *Costa Rica, Estonia, Bulgaria*, or, as Figure 5.2 (❶,❷,❸) illustrates, *United States, Japan*, or *Antarctica*. More specific references to place are made in 85.3 percent of the caption bodies, for example, through prepositional phrases such as *In Baltimore's Druid Hill Park* (❶), *at the Sunshine Aquarium [...] on the top-floor of a Tokyo high-rise* (❷), and *On Cuverville Island* (❸). In addition to a disambiguation of location, most caption bodies (70.4 percent) identify central pictorial participants generically, using nouns with some

106 *Jana Pflaeging*

❶ NG April 2015 | 1st image

United States In Baltimore's Druid Hill Park, a dog named Phoebe faces off with a dandelion. To make this shot, the photographer held the flowering weed at arm's length, several feet from Phoebe's face, and used his camera flash to make the seed head glow.

PHOTO: MICHAEL NORTHRUP

❷ NG Dec 2015 | 2nd image

Japan As part of an annual Christmas event, a diver dressed as Santa Claus swims with a zebra shark at the Sunshine Aquarium. The facility is located on the top floor of a Tokyo high-rise. It has no reindeer but about 15,000 animals of some 450 species.

PHOTO: SHIZUO KAMBAYASHI, AP IMAGES

❸ NG Jun 2015 | 3rd image

Antarctica On Cuverville Island bright feet fill the frame as a long-tailed Gentoo penguin leaps from near-freezing water to rocky shore. The largest colony of this species in the Antarctic Peninsula region—more than 9,000 breeding pairs—lives in this rugged spot.

PHOTO: PAUL SOUDERS, BIOSPHOTO

↖ **Order prints** of select *National Geographic* photos online at **NationalGeographicArt.com**.

Figure 5.2 Text exemplars of the genre *Visions* as published in 2015-issues of NG.

pre-modifying adjectives and numerals, and also post-modifying prepositional phrases (e.g., *playful Japanese pensioners, 81 dancers from the New York City Ballet, Children, local women, a former Soviet gymnast*). Specific references to image participants are less frequent (14.8 percent), but they do occur (e.g., *Sophie Gilotti displays her Kim Kardashian cell phone, Fatme Inus*). References to time are mostly not explicit (88.9 percent) and are only deducible from verbal time deixis, for example, *a dog named Phoebe faces off with a dandelion*, cf. Figure 5.2 (❶). On a more general note, these aspects of experiential orientation are very regularly realized in the first part of the caption body (84.8 percent).

Emergence of Image-Centric Popular Science Stories 107

The remainder of the caption is frequently used to accomplish contextual extension. As Figure 5.2 ❶ exemplifies, more elaborate information is, for instance, provided on the unconventional paths the photographer has chosen to succeed in *make[ing] this shot*, which is likely to construe the news value of Unexpectedness as well as a certain degree of Personalization. Unexpectedness is also conveyed through a remark on the location of a *Sunshine Aquarium* being *on the top floor of a Tokyo high-rise*, in Figure 5.2 ❷. Proximity is construed for a primarily U.S. American audience through generic references to the *United States* as depicted location in 20.6 percent of the cases. Superlativeness seems to be a prominent news value in Figure 5.2 ❸, where the caption reveals that *the largest colony* of *Gentoo penguin[s] [...] lives in this rugged spot* shown in the image. Even though Figure 5.2 does not provide any examples, Superlativeness is often construed in the images themselves, for example, through repetitive pictorial elements in wide-angle shots of people, fish swarms, architectural structures, a forest of gnarled trees, or in close-ups of colorful reptile skins. Not surprisingly, all of these images construct Aesthetic Appeal.

4 Diachronic Views – Case Study II: NG's *Vision of Earth* in 2005

As Figure 5.1 suggests, the genre *Visions* was already part of NG's genre profile in 2005,[5] at the time called *Visions of Earth*. Their historical relatedness can, on the one hand, be deduced from their strikingly similar genre names. On the other hand, *Visions of Earth* – a stable member of NG's genre repertoire between August 2004 and February 2006 – made way for *Visions* in March 2006, which from then on appeared in the same place in the genre profile as its predecessor. Consequently, studying text exemplars of the genre *Visions of Earth* means studying *Visions* at an earlier stage of its generic development. By adopting such a diachronic approach, I seek to gain further insight into the emergence of *image nuclearity*, or *image-centricity*, if we subscribe to adopting the broadened notion.

4.1 Data and Methods

In 2005, genre exemplars of *Visions of Earth* do not yet extend over a page space of three double-pages, but is confined to only one spread. As with the 2015-data set, I collected all available genre exemplars published in 2005-issues of NG, which were 12 in total. The data were collected, processed, and analyzed as outlined for the first case study.

4.2 Results

In all 2005-exemplars of *Visions of Earth*, the image covers almost the entire page space of a spread; only the top margin features a white header

108   *Jana Pflaeging*

area. It integrates the phrase *Through A Photographer's Eye*, given in a small font size and small caps, as one part of the genre's label. As in 2015, captions are superimposed onto the image and consist of several component parts, which are marked out through distinct typographical settings: they feature a (1) caption heading ($\bar{x}$ = 3.5 word-forms; σ = 1.24), a label that seems justifiable still on the basis of its use of typographical emphasis and its placement right above an actual caption body (2). In contrast to 2015, caption bodies feature a short sequence of bolded word-forms right at the beginning, which I call (3) a caption teaser. Similar to 2015, all captions end in (4) an authorship note and (5) a cross-medial reference, that is, prompt to engage with NG's online content. Figure 5.3 ❶ to ❸ exemplifies these findings.

❶   NG Dec 2005

CANADIAN ARCTIC
Hundreds of beluga whales pack an inlet at the north end of Somerset Island, where the fresh water of the Cunningham River mingles with the cold, salty Arctic Ocean. On July and August days the river becomes a breathtaking natural spectacle of whales nursing their young and molting—rubbing off their tired last-season skin. Their collective mass gave me the feeling I could walk over the river atop their backs, as if I were crossing a pontoon bridge to the other side. — *Norbert Rosing*

▶ Decorate your desktop with this image of beluga whales in an Arctic inlet, in Fun Stuff at **ngm.com/0512**.

❷   NG Aug 2005

ISLAND OF MAURITIUS
Green leaf platters on a quiet pond, these giant Amazonian water lilies at first seemed perfectly suited to the old botanical garden at Pamplemousses, laid out in the 1700s as a manicured French estate. But when the sun suddenly backlit the leaves, the lilies' wilder side shone through. Hidden jungle patterns and vibrant color exploded. I've often found that I have to sit back and wait for a scene's secrets to reveal themselves. —*David Lyons*

▶ Decorate your desktop with these illuminated lily pads, in Fun Stuff at **nationalgeographic.com/magazine/0508**.

❸   NG Jan 2005

OFF CHICHAGOF ISLAND, ALASKA
It takes just a split second to swap a kayak paddle for a camera, and that's all you have when a whale's jaw suddenly shatters the sea surface. For over 20 years now I've kayaked the waters off Southeast Alaska, photographing humpbacks. Seeing these creatures close-up is as exhilarating to me today as it ever was. This barnacle-laden beauty surprised me when it came up right next to my kayak. Catching it on film was a bit of a miracle. —*Duncan A. Murrell*

▶ Bring this behemoth of the deep to your desktop and download free wallpaper at **nationalgeographic.com/magazine/0502**.

Figure 5.3 Text exemplars of the genre *Visions of Earth* as published in 2005-issues of NG.

Emergence of Image-Centric Popular Science Stories 109

Just as in 2015, caption headings are exclusively used to refer to the place at which an image was captured. In 58.3 percent of the cases, the identification of spatial location is construed through a combination of both a specific and a general reference to place, as in LUANGWA VALLEY LODGE, ZAMBIA or WEST OF GREAT EXUMA IS-LAND, BAHAMAS. Only two in 12 caption headings locate an occurrence in the United States (as in OFF CHICAGOF ISLAND, ALASKA, Figure 5.3 ❸), which suggests that Proximity, in 2005, is not among those news values that are most frequently construed.

Caption teasers are an important juncture between caption body and image. In all sample texts except one, they are grammatically tied to the remainder of the first clause in the caption. On the one hand, they are constituents of a more complex clause that is about to unfold, for example, a complex noun phrase as in **Hundreds of beluga whales** pack an inlet at the north end of Somerset Island (Figure 5.3 ❶) or a part of a more complex noun phrase as in **Green leaf platters** on a quiet pond (Figure 5.3 ❷). However, its typographical marking (through larger font size and bolding) already implies a specific function with respect to the image. Caption teasers afford a first step to disambiguate pictorial participants that might not be clearly identifiable at initial glance. Accordingly, a somewhat mesmerizing accumulation of white dots on blue-brownish background (Figure 5.3 ❶) is identified as beluga whales. What may appear as the cracked skin surface of a prehistoric reptile or extravagant serving trays (Figure 5.3 ❷) is revealed as aquatic plants. The amazement at such perceived incongruities may draw a reader-viewer into reading the caption body, as it seems to keep in store more unexpected information. Figure 5.3 ❷ offers another dimension of semantic play between caption teaser and image. Whereas the term *platter* is, in fact, a technical term for specific kinds of water lilies, it is unlikely to be a more generally known synonym. Therefore, the noun *platters* in the caption teaser *Green leaf platters* is more likely to trigger its metaphorical meaning of 'tableware' at first – which may, as suggested, match a recipient's first interpretation of the image. Figure 5.3 ❸ does not follow this pattern; what may seem as a rugged rock structure in the surf is not revealed as *barnacle-laden whale* until reader-viewers reach the fifth line of the caption body.

The caption body comprises a mean of $\bar{x} = 77.17$ word-forms ($\sigma = 7.85$), and is thus almost twice as extensive as in 2015. All caption bodies are composed from elements that accomplish further experiential orientation and contextual extension. However, sample texts differ noticeably with regard to the degree to which these functions are fulfilled and the order in which this is done. The first two examples in Figure 5.3 follow a comparably straightforward pattern of performing experiential orientation in the first half of the caption body. This is accomplished, for instance, by identifying the location depicted in Figure 5.3 ❶ as an inlet at the north end of Somerset Island, or by disambiguating the Green leaf platters referred to in the caption teaser of Figure 5.3 ❷ as giant

Amazonian water lilies, which can be found on a quiet pond in the old botanical garden at Pamplemousses. The second half of the caption in Figure 5.3 ❶ elaborates more on the context of taking this picture: first, on the conditions that have led to the natural spectacle it shows and, second, on the circumstances that have led to such a spectacular shot. While at least half of the Visions of Earth-exemplars follow this pattern, Figure 5.3 ❷ suggests that there is more variation to the distribution of experiential orientation and contextual extension across a caption. After first identifying main pictorial participants (as explained earlier), some contextual information on the botanical garden follows, which was laid out in the 1700s as a manicured French estate. The next two sentences refer directly to what can be seen in the image, the sun that suddenly backlit the leaves, which caused that the lilies' wilder side shone through. Hidden jungle patterns and vibrant color exploded. The caption closes by providing some further contextual extension, even though, one might argue, contextual information that is of a different kind: the photographer shares his experiences with taking such shots and thereby shifts the focus from the event captured on camera to activity of picture-taking itself[6]: I've often found that I have to sit back and wait for a scene's secrets to reveal themselves. Figure 5.3 ❸ contains similar information (**It takes just a split second** to swap a kayak paddle for a camera, and that's all you have when a whale's jaw suddenly shatters the sea surface.), but gives it at the beginning of the caption. This attests once more to a higher degree of variation both with regards to distributing experiential orientation and contextual extension across the caption, and the kind of contextual information that is provided.

As the discussion of examples has also indicated, superlativeness, unexpectedness, aesthetic appeal, and personalization are among the news values most frequently construed in 2005-texts. Superlativeness, as construed through intensification (*Java's highest mountain, these giant Amazonian water lilies*), comparison (*as exhilarating to me as it ever was*), or references to emotion (*the people at this lodge were astonished*), features prominently in almost all corpus texts. Unexpectedness is likely construed in the process of finding and resolving an incongruity between image and caption; an unexpected use of angle, lighting, color, contrast, composition/texture (cf. Caple, 2013, p. 50) in images also plays its part in construing both unexpectedness and aesthetic appeal. Personalization seems a default feature of a genre whose extended label is *A Photographer's Journal* – featuring subjective views and an individual's voice.

5 Diachronic Views – Case Study III: NG's *Feature Article* 1985–1995–2005–2015

I now expand the diachronic view by scrutinizing exemplars of the genre feature article for any traces of pattern strengthening and weakening that can be related to the phenomenon of *image-centricity* as described for *Visions (of Earth)*.

5.1 Data and Methods

Keeping the 10-year gap between the *Visions (of Earth)*-data sets, I established a diachronic corpus of exemplars of the genre feature article with data sets for 1985, 1995, 2005, and 2015. The first two sets allow for investigating a potential strengthening of image-centricity-related genre features that might have led to the introduction of *Visions of Earth* through genre split. The latter two sets allow for exploring the development of the feature article-genre after the introduction of *Visions (of Earth)*. An analysis of all available feature article-exemplars would have gone beyond the scope of this chapter, which is why I aimed for a balanced set per year of sampling. For every second month, I collected one exemplar (through randomized selection), a total of six articles per year of sampling. In particular, my data sets comprised 71 double-pages for 1985 (with 119 image-caption ensembles), 76 double-pages for 1995 (with 94 image-caption ensembles), 67 double-pages for 2005 (with 101 image-caption ensembles), and 74 double-pages for 2015 (with 75 image-caption ensembles).

5.2 Results

As previous analyses suggest, *Visions (of Earth)* have shown great stability in their spacio-textual coupling of one large, salient image and a caption. It is now interesting to see that the layout pattern of combining nothing but a large image and caption in the page space of a double-page in feature articles had experienced pattern strengthening between 1985 and 2015.

As Figure 5.4 shows, while only every fifth double-page employed the compositional pattern *1 image + caption only* in 1985, almost two-thirds of the spreads did so in 2015. More importantly, however, when *Visions of Earth* was introduced in 2004, its layout pattern had already been the most prominent compositional choice in feature articles for almost 10 years. Its prominence in frequency is complemented by three further characteristics that make the pattern *1 image + caption only* stand out, namely, contrastive choices with respect to image participants, typography, and caption scope.

Contrastive use of main image participants. Compared to all other layout patterns, the pattern *1 image + caption only* showed a preference for landscape motives in 1985 (73.3 percent) and still in 1995 (35.1 percent), often shot in wide-angle (cf. Figure 5.5). By 2005, when *Vision of Earth* emerged and included many landscape depictions (50.0 percent), the *Feature-pattern 1 image + caption only* incorporated landscape

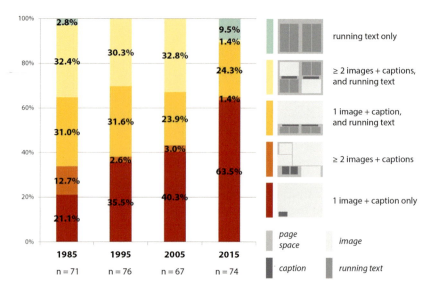

Figure 5.4 Feature article: relative frequencies of layout patterns as instantiated on double-page spreads of NG 1985, 1995, 2005, 2015.

❶ NG July 1995

Presiding over a bend in the Bow River since 1888, the baronial Banff Springs Hotel to transformed a whistle-stop on a wilderness railroad into a fashionable resort visited by royalty and movie stars.

❷ NG July 1995

Plying the mirror-smooth surface of Lake Louise, paddlers soak up the surreal beauty of Banff's most celebrated mountain tarn. Glacial meltwater laden with silt lends the lake its incandescent color, which changes with the seasons. "People ask us what we put in the water to make it that color," says a park employee. "They can't believe it's real."

Figure 5.5 Feature article-spreads of the type *1 image + caption only* and *1 image + caption, and running text* in 1995.

photographs only in 11.5 percent of the cases; people had evolved into the most prominent main image participants (61.5 percent). This observation substantiates the assumption that the 'needs' for prominent landscape formerly fulfilled in the *1 image + caption only* pattern could now be met by the genre *Visions of Earth*, while feature article-images have shown a strong preference for photographs of people.

Contrastive use of typography. In 1985, the feature article "Home to Kansas" (NG 1985 September) capitalizes a short sequence of word-forms in those captions integrated into a *1 image + caption only*-spread, while it draws on bolding in all other captions. The feature article "Excavating a 400-year-old Basque Galleon" (NG 1985 Jul) shows the same typographical distinctions. In the 1995-data set, the feature article "Rocky Times for Banff" (NG 1995 Jul) draws on a contrastive of bolding for all captions part of *1 image + caption only*-layout patterns (cf. Figure 5.5 ❶), while all other captions in this article are set in regular typeface (cf. Figure 5.5 ❷). Similarly, in "Essence of Provence" (NG 1995 Sept), the first letter of captions embedded into all *1 image + caption only-spreads* is initialized, while all other captions do not draw on initialization. In 2005, the "African Oil: Whose Bonanza?" (NG 2005 Sept) and "The Secrets of Long Life" (NG 2005 Nov) capitalize the first few words of a caption included in a *1 image + caption only*-pattern, while all other captions of these articles remain non-capitalized (except for one in "The Secrets of Long Life"). While only less than half of the corpus texts in the first three data sets actually make these distinctions, they show remarkable consistency if they are made.

Contrastive use of caption scope. A comparison of caption scope reveals furthermore a noticeable difference between various types of captions. As Figure 5.6 shows, in 1985, 1995, and 2005, feature article-captions embedded into a *1 image + caption only*-page layout (red) show a tendency to be longer than captions that are part of other layout patterns (yellow).

These observations suggest that the distinctiveness of the *image-centric* pattern had increased by 2005, and one may cautiously conclude that this development is likely to have spurred the introduction of *Visions of Earth* in NG's August 2004-issue. Its status as an autonomous communicative pattern with ethno-categorical genre status is suggested by three observations: first, the fact that, from then on, the double-page spreads employing a *1 image + caption only*-page layout appeared in a different place in the magazine's genre profile. Second, the fact that it received its own label – *Visions of Earth*. Third, the fact that the newly established genre employs, among others, a much more extended caption ($\bar{x}$ = 80.66 word-forms, cf. Figure 5.6, 2005).

Finally, between 2005 and 2015, captions integrated into *Visions*-texts and *all* types of layout patterns in feature articles have become much more alike. They have generally leveled out at about 38 word-forms (see Figure 5.6) and do not generally show any typographical emphasis.[7]

114 *Jana Pflaeging*

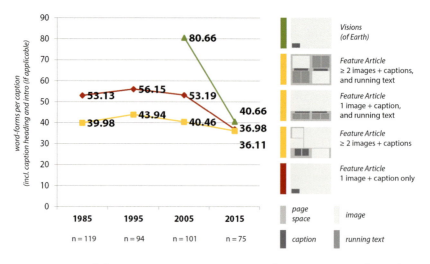

Figure 5.6 Word-forms per caption (mean) as used in *Feature Articles* and in *Visions (of Earth)*, 1985–2015.

❶ **NG May 2015**

Relative to body size, the brains of bottlenose dolphins, like these at the Roatán Institute for Marine Sciences in Honduras, are among the largest in the animal kingdom. Scientists are attempting to decode dolphins complex vocalizations.

❷ **NG May 2015**

Dolphins are extraordinary problem solvers. These two bottlenose dolphins off the Florida Keys quickly learned that the only way to pull the cap off a PVC pipe filled with fish was to cooperate.

Figure 5.7 Feature article-spreads of the type *1 image + caption only* and *1 image + caption, and running text* in 2015.

Also, even though this observations needs to be validated further, they seem to show similarities in their rhetorical structure (cf. Figures 5.2 and 5.7), while image-caption ensembles on layout patterns other than *1 image + caption only* compete with extensive sections of running text for a reader-viewer's attention.

6 Theoretical Implications

Caple's conceptualization of the INNS has already shown how previous modelings of the rhetorical structure of (hard) news stories can be productively adapted: Iedema et al.'s (1994) and White and Thomson's (2008) accounts of journalistic news genres shed light on verbiage-centric (or even verbiage-only) nuclei. Caple's model of the INNS, then, did justice to the tendency to elevate the image to a story Nucleus in contemporary newspaper journalism. With the help of synchronic and diachronic exploration of popular science journalism in a print magazine, I sought to show that a theory of *image nuclearity* can be fruitfully broadened and renegotiated under the heading of *image-centricity*, with regard to the following three aspects (many of which are already traceable in earlier works by Caple, as I will show):

Much variation around INNS's prototypical core. While Caple was able to identify image, headline, and caption as stable, obligatory elements of the INNS genre, the prosodic tail was classified as optional. Furthermore, with respect to those INNSs that employed a prosodic tail, Caple suggested that they could "make an alternative heading" (Caple, 2008, p. 129). Unlike INNS, *Visions (of Earth)*-texts neither have headings nor prosodic tails. Instead, they integrate a large image and a caption which comprises a caption heading and body (which, in 2005, included a caption teaser), a note on authorship, and sometimes a prompt to engage with online content. An INNS's potential for interpersonal engagement and bonding attested for INNS in the *Sydney Morning Herald* is not paralleled in NG. Also, the regularity with which INNSs perform experiential orientation and contextual extension could not be found in early *Visions of Earth*-exemplars. While aesthetic appeal features as prominently in *Visions (of Earth)* as in INNS, the highly frequent construal of superlativeness and unexpectedness seems to be an idiosyncrasy of NG. Despite all these differences, both INNSs and *Visions (of Earth)* generally employ a perceptually dominant and rhetorically central image as nucleus, and a caption with Satellite components.

Importance of compositional dominance. Caple's description of INNS plausibly focuses on logico-semantic relations between image and caption. However, she also remarks that INNSs feature "large" and "striking" images (Caple, 2013, p. 127) and that captions are of the short kind, "usually one to two sentences long" (Caple, 2013, p. 131). If one adopts a view of genre that integrates characteristics of layout/form, one may argue that the layout pattern of juxtaposing a large image and a short caption could be conducive to *image nuclearity*. This seems to be supported by the observation that the layout pattern *1 image + caption only* had gained considerable prominence in feature articles in the years before the introduction of *Vision of Earth*. The importance of compositional dominance could be given more emphasis as part of a theory of *image-centricity* (as also suggested by Stöckl, this volume).

Page space affording focused attention. An emphasis on the layout-side of *image nuclearity* is closely tied to the question of perceptual salience as influenced by what is co-present on a page. Caple and Bednarek (2010, p. 213) explain that an "introduction of more white spaces within and between news stories" paved the way for the emergence of INNS in the *Sydney Morning Herald*. Caple furthermore states that "the fact that there are rarely any other images used on the same page" enables the recipient to "engage with the image in its own right" (Caple, 2008, p. 127). This effect, I suggest, is likely intensified when image and caption are not only "intentionally co-present within a joint composition" (Bateman, 2014b, p. 28), but where a page space as self-contained "[site] of integration" (Bateman, 2008, p. 106) juxtaposes nothing *but* a large image and a caption. On these grounds, instances of *image-centricity* can also be attested in more complex journalistic pieces, such as feature articles. In contrast to INNSs whose verbal text "never extends beyond the caption" (Caple, 2013, p. 134), feature articles contain long stretches of running text and extend over several double-pages. Their images, which would normally be confined to satellite status (cf. Iedema et al., 1994), can be classified as *centric* if they occur as part of the layout pattern *1 image + caption only* on a double-page.[8]

All these findings seem to suggest that *image-centricity* could be established as a more general, flexible, and dynamic notion that could complement the neatly defined concept of *image nuclearity*.

7 Final Remarks

In contemporary multimodal media practices, images tend to dominate the verbal text they accompany in terms of sheer frequency, as well as in spatio-textual scope and status as rhetorical cores. While Caple reconstructed the genre INNS on the basis of a large data set collected from the newspaper *Sydney Morning Herald* published in 2004–2006, my study focused on the image-heavy journalism of the popular science magazine NG at several points in time. This was done to gain insights into a potentially more general prevalence of *image nuclearity* as described for INNS, or to explore the potentials of establishing *image-centricity* as a broader concept, while paying attention to factors contributing to its emergence.

My study of NG's *Visions*-genre (2015) revealed several similarities to INNS in the combination of a large, rhetorically central image, and the distribution of experiential orientation and contextual extension across the caption. However, I also found differences with respect to its generic stages, the degree of playfulness, and the construal of news values. My second case study on NG's *Visions of Earth* (2005) revealed even greater divergences from INNS, while still featuring a compositionally prominent image, which is typically elevated to be the popular science story's rhetorical core. A growing emphasis on image-dominant layout patterns could be attested for the feature articles of previous decades, which has suggested image dominance (cf. Stöckl, this volume) to play a crucial role in the emergence of *image-centricity*. As mentioned earlier, all these findings seem to suggest that *image-centricity* could be established as a more general, flexible, and dynamic notion that could complement the neatly defined concept of *image nuclearity*.

I close this chapter with some final remarks on the driving forces of such developments. An editorial team's anticipation of their audiences' genre expectations drives dynamic pattern evolution on the levels of genre and the genre profile in magazine journalism. Editorial staff may adhere to their magazine's own selling points by strengthening certain generic patterns. This may, ultimately, result in genre emergence through genre split, as we have seen with the *1 image + caption only*-layout pattern in NG. Changes attestable across genres and media may then point to more general shifts in contemporary communicative practices, for example, toward a clusterization (Püschel, 1992; Bucher, 1996) or "atomization" (Knox, 2007, p. 29) of textual artifacts in print media, be they newspapers or magazines. Such developments have been classified as "wash-back" effects (Jewitt, 2017, p. 454, in ref. to Knox, 2017), that is, the impact that an increased engagement with online media has on the design of print products: contemporary audiences spend less time reading newspapers and magazines and more time engaging in *hyper-extensive* reading.[9] This is assumed to have influenced reading paths (Caple & Knox, 2012) and has led to "shallower and less in-depth reading" (Liu, 2005, p. 707).

As suggested earlier, editors of market-prominent magazines such as NG, who target a comparably broad and potentially heterogeneous audience, try to meet their expectations. Connie Phelps, former NG-editor, explains that NG seeks to "[capture] the attention of both the browser and the committed reader" (Phelps in Ryan & Conover, 2004, p. 505). While extensive feature articles cater for more committed reading, both their *image-centric* double-pages and the *image-centric* genre *Visions (of Earth)* meet the demands of quick browsing. On a more general note, the fact that feature articles have been drawing much more frequently on *image-centric* spreads (even to build narratives across sequences of image-centric spreads, see Pflaeging, 2017), and that *Visions (of Earth)* "is consistently our top-rated department" (Hitchcock, 2013, p. 19) attests furthermore to the observation that *shifts toward image-centricity in contemporary multimodal practices* are the *zeitgeist* of our times.

Acknowledgments

I wish to thank Helen Caple, Michaela Hausmann, and Hartmut Stöckl (in alphabetical order) for making valuable comments on an earlier version of this manuscript.

Notes

1 According to journalism scholars Johnson and Prijatel (1999, pp. 117–119), magazines typically realize a repertoire of informing, entertaining, and participatory short-form genres, which are called *Departments*. In fact, NG used the label *Departments* on the *Contents*-page(s) of their issues between June 1995 and September 2012 to refer to such short-form genres.
2 In that sense, I am also responding to a call made in Bednarek and Caple (2017, p. 78) to see whether DNVA applies beyond the prototypical news story:

> Consequently, the inventory applies to prototypical news stories rather than say, business or sports news or letters to the editor, obituaries, current affairs programs, and so on. […] Since there are clear linguistic differences between different types of news and between different semiotic modes, further research will need to be undertaken into such areas.

3 Such shifts typically happen gradually and involve various *metamorphic* changes, for example, with regard to all descriptive dimensions of a genre (Stöckl, 2010, p. 162).
4 This is furthermore suggested by the fact that, in 2005, the semiotic configurations on one double-page only served as self-sufficient genre exemplars.
5 In fact, it was introduced to NG's repertoire of short-form genres in August 2004.
6 I would like to thank Helen Caple for pointing this out to me.
7 This process of standardization can most plausibly be explained by the fact that NG employs legend writers, as managing editor David Brindley reports, whose main responsibility is the captioning of all sorts of NG images. The fact that they are asked to describe what is in the picture but also to "provide a lot more information than what you can just see" on "that story *behind* the photo" (Poynter, 2015, n.p.) could have resulted in further standardization with respect to experiential orientation and contextual extension.
8 The rigidity of the *nuclearity*-concept seems to originate in early applications of Rhetorical Structure Theory (RST) to news journalism. Assumedly, it can be mitigated by tracing the concept back to its roots (see Lenk, 2017 for a similar suggestion). In RST, rhetorical relations are binary at one hierarchical level but split up into smaller binary structures. Accordingly, nuclei exist on different levels of analytical abstraction (Mann & Thompson, 1988, pp. 265–267); even though an image-caption ensemble serves as a satellite in the overall story structure, it can become, I suggest, a salient component on a – *spatially orbital* (Economou, 2012, p. 249) – double-page that earns nucleus-status at a lower level.
9 The time an average U.S. consumer spends daily on reading magazines decreased from 24 minutes in 2010 to an estimated 15 minutes by 2018 (Zenith, 2018a). Similarly, the daily time an average U.S. consumer spends on reading newspapers decreased from 25 minutes in 2010 to an estimated 12 minutes by 2018 (Zenith, 2018b). In contrast, an average U.S. consumer used to spend 85 minutes per day with the Internet, which has increased to 235 minutes by 2018 (Zenith, 2018c).

References

Data

Issue of National Geographic

1888 Oct | 1895 Apr | 1905 Jul | 1915 Jul | 1915 Jul | 1925 Jul | 1935 Jul | 1945 Jul | 1955 Jul | 1965 Jul | 1975 Jul | 1985 Jul | 1995 Jul | 2005 Jul | 2015 Jul

Visions (of Earth)

2015 Jan | Feb | Mar | Apr | May | Jun | Jul | Aug | Sept | Oct | Dec
2005 Jan | Feb | Mar | Apr | May | Jun | Jul | Aug | Sept | Oct | Nov | Dec

Feature Articles

1985 Jan: "Yosemite-Forever?" | Mar: "Susquehanna: America's Small-town River" | May: "Vietnam Veterans Memorial: America Remembers" | Jul: "Excavating a 400-year-old Basque Galleon" | Sept: "Home to Kanvas" | Nov: "Kluane: Canada's Icy Wilderness Park"

1995 Jan: "Close Encounters With the Gray Reef Shark" | Mar: "Dead Or Alive: The Endangered Species Act" | May: "The Cherokee: Two Nations, One People" | Jul: "Rocky Times for Banff" | Sept: "Essence of Provence" | Nov: "Europe's First Family: The Basques"

2005 Jan: "Caffeine" | Mar: "attack of the alien invaders" | May: "one fish, two fish, red fish, blue fish: why are coral reefs so colorful?" | Jul: "China's Great Armada" | Sept: "African Oil: Whose Bonanza?" | Nov: "The Secrets of Long Life"

2015 Jan: "The First Year" | Mar: "Fleeing Terror, Finding Refuge" | May: "It's Time for a Conversation" | Jul: "Stalking a Killer" | Sept: "Point of no Return" | Nov: "The Will to Change"

Research literature

Barthes, R. (1964/1977). *Image – music – text*. London: Fontana.

Bateman, J. A. (2014a). Genre in the age of multimodality: Some conceptual refinements for practical analysis. In P. Evangelisti Allori, J. A. Bateman, & V. K. Bhatia (Eds.), *Evolution in genre: Emergence, variation, multimodality* (pp. 237–269). Bern: Peter Lang.

Bateman, J. A. (2014b). *Text and image: A critical introduction to the visual/verbal divide*. New York: Routledge.

Bateman, J. A. (2014c). Multimodal coherence research and its applications. In H. Gruber & G. Redeker (Eds.), *Pragmatics of discourse coherence: Theories and applications* (pp. 145–177). Amsterdam: Benjamins.

Bateman, J. A. (2008). *Multimodality and genre: A foundation for the systematic analysis of multimodal documents*. New York: Palgrave Macmillan.

Bateman, J. A., Evangelisti Allori, P., & Bhatia, V. K. (2014). Evolution in genre: Emergence, variation, multimodality. In P. Evangelisti Allori, J. A. Bateman, & V. K. Bhatia (Eds.), *Evolution in genre: Emergence, variation, multimodality* (pp. 9–16). Bern: Peter Lang.

Bateman, J. A., Wildfeuer, J., & Hiippala T. (2017). *Multimodality: Foundations, research and analysis. A problem-oriented introduction*. Berlin: Mouton de Gruyter.

Bazerman, C. (1994). Systems of genres and the enactment of social intentions. In A. Freedman & P. Medway (Eds.), *Genre and the new rhetoric* (pp. 79–101). London: Taylor & Francis.

Bednarek, M., & Caple, H. (2017). *The discourse of news values: How news organizations create newsworthiness*. New York, NY: Oxford University Press.

Bednarek, M., & Caple, H. (2012). *News discourse*. London: Bloomsbury.

Bell, A. (1991). Audience accommodation in the mass media. In H. Giles, J. Coupland, & N. Coupland (Eds.), *Contexts of accommodation: Developments in applied sociolinguistics* (pp. 69–102). Cambridge: Cambridge University Press.

Bhatia, V. K. (2014). *Worlds of written discourse: A Genre-based view*. London: Bloomsbury.

Bhatia, V. K. (1993). *Analysing genre: Language use in professional settings. Applied linguistics and language study*. London: Longman.

Brighton, P., & Foy, D. (2007). *News values*. Amsterdam: Benjamins.

Brock, A. (2015). Comedy Panel Show, Dramedy und Improv-Comedy: Zur kulturellen Ausdifferenzierung komischer Fernsehgenres in Großbritannien. In S. Neuhaus, H. Diekmannshenke, & U. Schaffers (Eds.), *Das Komische in der Kultur* (pp. 193–208). Marburg: Tectum.

Bucchi, M., & Trench, B. (2014). Science communication research. In M. Bucchi & B. Trench (Eds.), *Routledge handbook of public communication of science and technology* (pp. 1–14). London: Routledge.

Bucher, H.-J. (1996). Textdesign – Zaubermittel der Verständlichkeit? Die Tageszeitung auf dem Weg zum interaktiven Medium. In E. W. B. Hess-Lüttich, W. Holly, & U. Püschel (Eds.), *Textstrukturen im Medienwandel* (pp. 31–59). Frankfurt am Main: Peter Lang.

Caple, H. (2018). News values and newsworthiness. In *Oxford Research Encyclopedia of Communication*. Oxford: Oxford University Press.

Caple, H. (2013). *Photojournalism: A social semiotic approach*. Basingstoke: Palgrave Macmillan.

Caple, H. (2008). Intermodal relations in image nuclear news stories. In L. Unsworth (Ed.), *Multimodal semiotics: Functional analysis in contexts of education* (pp. 125–138). London: Continuum.

Caple, H. (2006). Nuclearity in the news story: The genesis of image-nuclear news stories. In C. Anyanwu (Ed.), *Empowerment, creativity and innovation: Challenging media and communication in the 21st Century* (pp. 1–12). Adelaide: Australia and New Zealand Communication Association and the University of Adelaide.

Caple, H., & Bednarek, M. (2010). Double-take: Unpacking the play in the image-nuclear news story. *Visual Communication, 9*(2), 211–229.

Caple, H., & Knox, J. S. (2012). Online news galleries, photojournalism and the photo essay. *Visual Communication, 11*(2), 207–236.

Davis, M. (2005). *More than a name: An introduction to branding*. Lausanne: AVA.

Draper, R. (2013, October). The power of photography. *National Geographic*, pp. 28–37.

Economou, D. (2012). Standing out on critical issues: Evaluation in large verbal-visual displays in Australian broadsheets. In W. L. Bowcher (Ed.), *Multimodal texts from around the world: Cultural and linguistic insights* (pp. 246–269). Basingstoke: Palgrave Macmillan.

Economou, D. (2008). Pulling readers in: News photos in Greek and Australian broadsheets. In E. A. Thomson & P. R. R. White (Eds.), *Communicating conflict: Multilingual case studies of the news media* (pp. 253–280). London: Continuum.

Galtung, J., & Ruge, M. (1965). The structure of foreign news: The presentation of the Congo, Cuba and Cyprus crisis in four Norwegian newspapers. *Journal of Peace Research, 2*(1), 60–90.

Hawkins, S. L. (2010). *American iconographic: National Geographic, global culture, and the visual imagination. Cultural frames, framing culture.* Charlottesville: University of Virginia Press.

Hitchcock, S. T. (2013). *Visions of earth: National Geographic photographs of beauty, majesty, and wonder.* Washington: National Geographic.

Iedema, R., Feez, S., & White, P. R. R. (1994). *Media literacy (Write it right literacy in industry research project – Stage 2).* Sydney: Metropolitan East Disadvantaged Schools Program.

Jewitt, C. (2017). What next for multimodality? In C. Jewitt (Ed.), *The Routledge handbook of multimodal analysis* (pp. 450–455). London: Routledge.

Johns, C. (2013, October). Editor's note. *National Geographic*, n.pag.

Johnson, S., & Prijatel, P. (1999). *The magazine from cover to cover: Inside a dynamic industry.* Lincolnwood: NTC Publishing Group.

Knox, J. S. (2017). Online newspapers: Structure and layout. In C. Jewitt (Ed.), *The Routledge handbook of multimodal analysis* (pp. 440–449). London: Routledge.

Knox, J. S. (2007). Visual-verbal communication on online newspaper home pages. *Visual Communication*, 6(1), 19–53.

Lemke, J. L. (1999). Typology, topology, topography: Genre semantics. Retrieved from http://academic.brooklyn.cuny.edu/education/jlemke/papers/Genre-topology-revised.htm

Lenk, H. E. H. (2017). ISA oder RST? Ein Vergleich der Illokutionsstrukturanalyse und der Rhetorical Structure Theory an zwei Texten aus dem Helsinkier Kommentarkorpus. In H. W. Giessen & H. E. H. Lenk (Eds.), *Persuasionsstile in Europa III: Linguistische Methoden zu vergleichenden Analyse von Kommentartexten in Tageszeitungen europäischer Länder* (pp. 143–177). Hildesheim: Olms Verlag.

Liu, Z. (2005). Reading behavior in the digital environment: Changes in reading behavior over the past ten years. *School of Library and Information Science*, 61(6), 700–712.

Lomborg, S. (2014). *Social media, social genres: Making sense of the ordinary.* New York, NY: Routledge.

Luginbühl, M. (2014a). Genre profiles and genre change: The case of TV news. In J. K. Androutsopoulos (Ed.), *Mediatization and sociolinguistic change* (pp. 305–330). Berlin: de Gruyter.

Luginbühl, M. (2014b). *Medienkultur und Medienlinguistik: Komparative Textsortengeschichte(n) der amerikanischen "CBS Evening News" und der Schweizer "Tagesschau".* Bern: Peter Lang.

Mann, W. C., & Thompson, S. A. (1988). Rhetorical structure theory: Toward a functional theory of text organization. *Text*, 8(3), 243–281.

Miller, C. R. (1984). Genre as social action. *Quarterly Journal of Speech*, 70, 151–167.

Orlikowski, W. J., & Yates, J. (1994). Genre repertoire: The structuring of communicative practices in organizations. *Administrative Science Quarterly*, 39(4), 541–574.

Pflaeging, J. (2019). Beyond genre names: Diachronic perspectives on genre indexation in print magazines. In A. Brock, J. Pflaeging, & P. Schildhauer (Eds.), *Genre emergence: Developments in print, TV and digital media* (pp. 73–104). Frankfurt am Main: Peter Lang.

Pflaeging, J. (2017). Tracing the narrativity of *National Geographic* feature articles in the light of evolving media landscapes. *Discourse, Context & Media, 20*, 248–261.

Poynter. (Producer). (2015, May 14). *Photo caption advice from National Geographic* [Video]. Retrieved from https://www.youtube.com/watch?v=3K-V4nTlAn0

Püschel, U. (1992). Von der Pyramide zum Cluster: Textsorten und Textsortenmischung in Fernsehnachrichten. In E. W. B. Hess-Lüttich (Ed.), *Medienkultur – Kulturkonflikt: Massenmedien in der interkulturellen und internationalen Kommunikation* (pp. 233–258). Wiesbaden: VS Verlag für Sozialwissenschaften.

Ryan, W. E., & Conover, T. E. (2004). *Graphic communications today*. Clifton Park, NY: Thomson/Delmar Learning.

Schildhauer, P. (2016). *The personal weblog: A linguistic history*. Frankfurt am Main: Peter Lang.

Stöckl, H. (2015). From text linguistics to multimodality: Reflections on definitions, transcription, and analysis. In J. Wildfeuer (Ed.), *Building bridges for multimodal research: International perspectives on theories and practices of multimodal analysis* (pp. 51–75). Frankfurt am Main: Peter Lang.

Stöckl, H. (2010). Textsortenentwicklung und Textverstehen als Metamorphosen: Am Beispiel der Werbung. In H. Stöckl (Ed.), *Mediale Transkodierungen: Metamorphosen zwischen Sprache, Bild und Ton* (pp. 145–172). Heidelberg: Winter.

Stöckl, H., & Pflaeging, J. (2018). Populärwissenschaftliche Magazine der Geisteswissenschaften als Gegenstand der medienvergleichenden und multimodalen Textlinguistik. In M. Luginbühl & J. Schröter (Eds.), *Geisteswissenschaften und Öffentlichkeit – Linguistisch betrachtet* (pp. 107–138). Bern: Peter Lang.

Swales, J. M. (1990). *Genre analysis: English in academic and research settings*. Cambridge: CUP.

White, P. R. R., & Thomson, E. A. (2008). The news story as rhetoric: Linguistic approaches to the analysis of journalistic discourse. In E. A. Thomson & White, P. R. R. (Eds.), *Communicating conflict: Multilingual case studies of the news media* (pp. 1–23). London: Continuum.

Zenith. (2018a). Daily time spent reading magazines per capita in the United States from 2010 to 2018 (in minutes). In Statista – The Statistics Portal. Retrieved May 27, 2019, from https://www.statista.com/statistics/186944/us-magazine-reading-habits-since-2002/

Zenith. (2018b). Daily time spent reading newspapers per capita in the United States from 2010 to 2018 (in minutes). In Statista – The Statistics Portal. Retrieved May 27, 2019, from https://www.statista.com/statistics/186934/us-newspaper-reading-habits-since-2002/

Zenith. (2018c). Average daily time spent per capita with the internet in the United States from 2010 to 2018, by device (in minutes). In Statista – The Statistics Portal. Retrieved May 27, 2019, from https://www.statista.com/statistics/645604/united-states-daily-time-per-capita-internet-device/

6 Previewing News Stories

How Contextual Cohesion Contributes to the Creation of News Stories

Sameera Durrani

1 Introduction

Kress and van Leeuwen (2006, p. 43) describe how the form of a narrative is put together through two kinds of cohesion: internal and contextual cohesion. Internal cohesion refers to the way elements cohere internally within an image, for example, all the visual elements that make up a single photograph, such as color, camera angle, and camera shot. Contextual cohesion looks at how signs cohere externally with their context, for instance, where a photograph is placed on the page, and how it interacts with the text. The domain of *visual communication* and *social semiotics* has focused in detail on crafting frameworks that analyze both: internal cohesion in photography (see, for instance, Bednarek & Caple, 2012; Caple, 2013) and individualized elements of page design (see e.g., Economou, 2008, 2010; Pflaeging, 2017). The proposed framework aims to analyze both as a single unit – moreover, one with predictive potential, where lead images impact on how subsequent verbal text is to be read. This chapter, therefore, introduces a system of analysis, termed *Compositional Narrative Devices* (hereafter *CND*). This framework illustrates how the interaction of the *representational* content of images with specific elements of page design – picture size, picture placement, compositional balance (Caple, 2013) – creates mini-narratives. These narrative snapshots, when anchored within the verbal context unit (Economou, 2010), create a preview for the reader, in terms of what to expect from the story. In this way, representational and compositional choices exist in a symbiotic relationship to generate quick, predictive comprehension of the news feature.

2 Researching Contextual Cohesion: An Overview

Research within the domain of visual communication tends to study the representational and compositional metafunctions separately, the former studied primarily by those interested in *photojournalism* research, while the latter is of interest to semioticians (see Wignell, et al. this volume for an explanation of metafunctions). Internal cohesion and or the representational metafunction is the focus of papers that examine photojournalism and conflict (see, e.g., Durrani & Mughees, 2010; Fahmy, 2004; Griffin, 2004; Griffin & Lee, 1995; King & Lester, 2005; Klaus & Kassel, 2005; Parry, 2011). Studies focusing on the *compositional metafunction*, specifically contextual cohesion, tend to examine layout in terms of separate units, focusing on design principles, and not image content. For instance, social semiotic research has investigated the meaning potential of the layout and design features of software interfaces (see, for example, Djonov & van Leeuwen, 2013; Engebretsen, 2012; O'Halloran, Tan, Smith, & Podlasov, 2010). Research has also looked at the use of compositional strategies in the assemblage and sequencing of educational materials, such as websites (Djonov, 2008) and history textbooks (Bezemer & Kress, 2009; Derewianka & Coffin, 2008). A more integrated approach is taken by Economou (2006, 2008, 2010). She examines the interplay between images and the accompanying salient texts (such as headlines and captions), and analyzes the manner in which evaluative meanings are inscribed onto images via this interaction. This framework has been adapted into the design of the CND framework.

The relationship between layout and images is an area of interest for multimodal researchers who examine the increasing interplay of images and text in digital media. Knox (2007) looks at the semiotic evolution of a new grammar of visual design in English-language online newspapers. He notes that this grammar interacts with existing verbal practices in English-language newspaper reporting, and appears to exist across national and cultural boundaries. In another study investigating the *Sydney Morning Herald* news website's use of thumbnail images as an example, Knox (2009) demonstrates how the traditional divide between the verbal and visual is becoming blurred. This hybrid online environment has led to the creation of new potential genres, as noted by Caple and Knox (2012), in their study of online news galleries. This chapter draws inspiration from that work – it examines the visual-verbal compositional formats extant within the print media, and looks at how some of these have been extended into, or are the forerunners of, what exists now in digital media.

3 Research Design: A View of *Time Asia* through a Semiotic Lens

The data for this chapter have been derived from a longitudinal study documenting semiotic conventions in photojournalism. To this end, it samples from a prestigious publication that gives priority to the visual in its layout preferences, and that has remained in print for an extended period of time: *Time* magazine, specifically its Asia edition. *Time Asia* has been in print since 1946. It is a leading English-language weekly, targeting elite audiences in the Asia-Pacific region (Rohn, 2010). As the study focuses on two countries from this region – Pakistan and Iran – this edition is a suitable choice for this project. A total of 840 images were sampled from a period extending across three decades (1981–2010). Both Iran and Pakistan have experienced significant socio-political upheavals within these three decades, and, therefore, this time period was selected because of representational implications for the data set, not directly relevant to the analysis presented within this chapter (see Durrani, 2018, for further analyses of the representational implications).

3.1 Analysing Contextual Cohesion: Situating the CND System within Visual Research

This chapter is drawn from a larger research project that takes an interdisciplinary approach to examining the evolution of national images in *Time* magazine. It examines questions of *form* (compositional choices – how a picture is put together), as well as *content* (what exists within the picture – representational elements). Debates regarding the *form* of photographs are addressed with the help of ideas drawn from the realm of film studies and social semiotics, while findings about representation are addressed with the help of perspectives from cultural studies (see Durrani, 2018). As this chapter confines itself primarily to compositional issues, it takes a social semiotic view (Caple, 2013; Kress & van Leeuwen, 2006). It examines internal cohesion in images, as well as external cohesion, as it affects page layout. These concepts are introduced in the following text, in turn.

According to Kress and van Leeuwen (2006, p. 43), the meaning conveyed by an image relies on two types of cohesion. Internal cohesion refers to the way different elements combine within an image. In contrast, external, or contextual cohesion, accounts for how signs combine externally with the surrounding elements on the page. As noted earlier, studies on photojournalism overwhelmingly focus on the photographs themselves; the methodologies adopted pay much less attention to the manner in which contextual cohesion subtly enhances and modifies the meanings of both the image and the text within which it is encapsulated.

Drawing on and extending the work of theorists who have created original analytical systems for examining internal cohesion (Caple, 2013; Kress & van Leeuwen, 2006), this chapter proposes a new framework that can be applied to foreshadow how certain semiotic combinations result in certain kinds of narratives, that allow a reader to capture the essence of a story in a single glance, as is demonstrated via in-depth qualitative analysis of relevant examples. This framework, as indicated earlier, is denoted by the term Compositional Narrative Devices (CND), used here to refer to strategies whereby elements of page composition come together to provide a synopsis or preview of the content of a news article. To draw on film terminology, these mini-narratives serve as previews/trailers. With their help, the reader can grasp the essence of the news article with a cursory glance, and then decide whether to read the rest of the article. CNDs represent a means of categorizing contextual (external) cohesion.

3.2 *Methodology*

The study that forms the basis for this chapter is based on a purposive sample of 840 photographs captured during a 30-year period of news coverage of Pakistan and Iran by *Time Asia*. These images include the cover of the magazine, as well as photographs from consistently recurrent sections of *Time Asia* notable for their use of image-dominant layouts. These include soft/hard news-based feature articles (news features, lifestyle features, issue-based features, profile features, and explanatory/supplementary features), photo features, photo essays, interviews, *Time Asia* Person of the Year, and *Time Asia*'s annual selection of the year's most memorable photographs.

For the purpose of analysis, all photographs, alongside a scan of the page on which they appeared, were entered into and analyzed with an electronic relational database management system, Microsoft Access. A relational database allows for data and relationships among aspects of data to be stored in the form of tables (Caple, 2013). The database makes it possible to recall any aspect of data from large sample sets and to analyze them efficiently and instantaneously, qualitatively as well as quantitatively.

The Microsoft Access database consisted of 840 entries, or *forms*. Each entry contains two images: the photograph, and a scan of the full page on which the photograph appears. The pre-designed quantitative analysis, based on deductive reasoning, is focused primarily on internal cohesion of the photograph, as is traditional for photojournalism-based studies. Qualitative analysis of the scanned pages uploaded into the database yielded evidence of unexpected patterns of contextual cohesion. This led to the construction of the system, derived inductively, as is traditional for semiotic systems of analysis (see e.g., Kress & van Leeuwen, 2006), discussed in the following pages.

4 Compositional Narrative Devices: Constituent Elements

The CND system investigates how the interrelation of four elements into a contextually cohesive system generates specific, standard *narrative types*. These elements are *represented participants*, *relative picture placement*, *picture size*, and *verbal context unit*:

Represented participants. This term, taken from Kress and van Leeuwen (2006), refers to the people portrayed within the photographs.

The analysis of these participants is carried out with the help of terminology from Kress and van Leeuwen (2006), as well as category systems established specifically for this research. In specific terms, it draws on the idea of a particular typology of represented participants – participant status (elite vs. ordinary). These elements draw on aspects of internal cohesion, and as is demonstrated in the analysis, their significance can be modified by the manner in which they are integrated with cues that define external cohesion.

Galtung and Ruge (1965) argue that the actions of famous people are seen by news selectors as having more consequence; readers are also expected to identify with them. Over the years, this concept has been modified and applied by researchers in different ways (Harcup & O'Neill, 2001). It may be seen as corresponding to the news value of Prominence (Bednarek & Caple, 2012). This research uses the term *elite actor* to identify such individuals. These are represented participants identified by name within the verbal context unit. They are generally well known within the public sphere, and their photographs recur regularly within the sample. They may belong to elite professions (politics, entertainment, sports, human rights activism, etc.). The database enables the identification of such actors (e.g., Ayatollah Khomeini). The separation of elite and ordinary actors enables differentiated analysis of the way in which they are placed within visual narratives. In the context of this chapter, as demonstrated in the analysis, certain ways of configuring external cohesion align more strongly with elite actors, while others are more likely to be employed for ordinary actors.

Relative picture placement. This refers to the placement of the image(s) on a page. This is analyzed with the help of the balance network, an analytical framework designed to analyze the manner in which composition enhances the newsworthiness of an image (Caple, 2013). It was originally designed to assess internal cohesion only. This chapter argues and, with the help of qualitative analysis, demonstrates, how the application of this system can be extended to analyze external cohesion. Broadly speaking, the balance network consists of two broad categories (Bednarek & Caple, 2012; Caple, 2013).

a   *Isolating:* This refers to images that single someone or something out and make that element the focus of attention, for example, a portrait of Obama. Isolating images focus a viewer's attention on one element in the frame. The Isolating configuration has three subtypes: Isolating Centered Single, Centered Triptych, and Axial. These subtypes can focus attention on one element either singly (Isolating Centered Singled, where only one element dominates the frame) or in relation to other elements; in Centered Triptych, the central element is framed on both sides by two accompanying elements. In the Axial configurations, the dominant element is brought forward by angling it in a way that it ends up in a corner of the picture, and is the most visible component (Caple, 2013).

b *Iterating:* This refers to images where regular, repeated patterns between several elements occur, and are depicted in the image frame in relation to each other, for example, a group of soldiers saluting a flag. The notion of iterating comes from the repetition or regular/symmetrical patterning of elements within the image frame (e.g., a group of marching soldiers) (Caple, 2013). The Iterating configuration is sub-divided into two more categories. The first is Dividing (when there are two elements in the frame). This includes Dividing Matching, where two elements are captured while engaging in similar activities (e.g., a picture of two soldiers saluting the flag); Dividing Mirroring (e.g., a photo of a girl's reflection in the mirror), and Dividing Facing (e.g., two politicians facing each other and shaking hands). The second category is Serializing (when there are more than two elements in the frame). This includes Iterating Serializing Matching (when a configuration of elements matches, e.g., a photo of a police identification line-up of criminals); Serializing Mirroring (when a configuration of multiple elements is reflected in a surface); Serializing Facing (when two groups of elements face off, say, protestors vs. police); and Serializing Scattered (where randomly configured elements convey a chaotic impression, say, an unruly crowd of protestors or a random group of students milling outside a classroom).

Picture size. While placement refers to where the picture is placed on the page, size refers to how much space is taken up by it. Therefore, picture size is an indicator of salience; it provides a way of measuring which themes and actors are given more salience. Qualitative analysis of the impact of picture size is integrated where needed.

Verbal context unit. The cohesive unit of meaning potential generated by the combination of these cues complements the narrative established by the Verbal Context Unit (VCU). The VCU is the salient text which appears beside the photograph. It is standard practice amongst researchers working on photojournalism to make use of a unit of text that assists in circumscribing the meaning of the photo. Headlines and captions are standard inclusions in a VCU (see, for instance, Fahmy & Kim, 2008; Parry, 2010, 2011). The VCU in this study includes the headline, caption, and the *stand-first*, a term appropriated from Economou (2010). The stand-first is defined here as the short paragraph that accompanies the headline, distinguished from the remaining text with a font size and weight smaller than that of the headline, but bigger than that of the remaining text.

The CND system establishes links between the representational and compositional metafunctions in a way that provides a degree of predictability for the narrative type that is promoted by the VCU. Representation analysis focuses on what Kress and van Leeuwen (2006) term as relations between represented participants, that is, the conceptual representations encoded into the image. A single image may comprise many such conceptual representations. The central argument, as conveyed through analysis of relevant examples, is that certain CNDs are used to integrate certain kinds of actors into specific narratives in predictable patterns.

5 Page Design in *Time Asia*: Introducing Compositional Narrative Devices

Each compositional collocation represents a specific kind of narrative device; as snapshots/synopses, they offer predictive value in terms of what the reader can expect from the article. The following sections discuss these subtypes, alongside examples, and an explanation of the kinds of relations they foreshadow. The analysis draws on Kress and van Leeuwen's (2006) social semiotic framework as well as Caple's (2013) balance network. It uses mathematical symbols and descriptive labels to better capture and foreshadow the essence of the narrative strategy each configuration represents. Six devices are discussed: contradiction, asymmetric sets, contrast, gallery, subsets, and banner.

5.1 Contradiction: →← Face-Off

The *Contradiction* CND is an adversarial one (see Figure 6.1). It typically represents two antagonists from opposite sides of a given spectrum, at loggerheads, which is why a mathematically inspired symbol for contradiction, →←, is used to represent this collocation. In predictive terms, it foreshadows outright hostility/competition between two parties, usually elite actors, who represent two sides of a political spectrum.

The Face-off configuration, which recurs at various points within the data, is characterized by several consistent composition choices. Two pictures are placed along the horizontal axis opposite each other, almost literally facing-off (see example given earlier). This example is a mock-up of a two-page spread from February 9, 1981, that juxtaposes a photo of the Iranian Supreme leader Ayatollah Khomeini against a picture of an American official negotiating with the American government, during the Iranian hostage crisis. The headline reads *Wheeling and Dealing*. This example is typical of most cases, where the participants face each other. These configurations rely on a bi-directional transactional narrative process between two interactors, where each participant is both the Actor and the Goal (Kress & van Leeuwen, 2006, p. 67). The gaze of the two represented participants does not quite connect, as they are represented within two separate images. Aesthetically, in terms of the balance

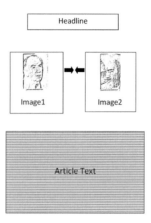

Figure 6.1 CND type 1: Face-off.

network, as applied to contextual cohesion (Caple, 2013), Face-off may be seen as an Iterating Dividing Facing configuration.

The antagonistic resonance of this CND can be further emphasized with another variation, based on the direction of the gaze of the represented participants. In some instance from the sample, the two participants face away from each other, a compositional choice that perhaps serves to further highlight the unbridgeable divide between the two antagonists portrayed. For example, a two-page spread from September 24, 1990, displays two represented participants facing away from each other. The context is the First Gulf War, and what is seen as Iran's opposition to this war. The headline reads *Call to Arms*. The two represented participants are President George Bush Senior and Ayatollah Khamenei. Equal-sized photographs, both medium shots, composed as Isolating-Centered-Single images, are placed at opposite ends of a double-page spread. Both show the represented participants actively gesturing. President Bush points a finger at the camera in a stance and manner reminiscent of the iconic Uncle Sam recruitment posters. Ayatollah Khamenei raises his hand skywards, in a gesture which evokes other photos in *Time Asia* that show Ayatollah Khomeini. Such gesturing and postures add to the adversarial visual narrative, as do the somber expressions of both represented participants.

Given the antagonism between the American and Iranian governments, it is somewhat predictable that this configuration recurs at different points in time in the coverage of U.S.-Iran relations, with elite actors from both sides personifying the hostile relations. George Bush Junior and President Ahmadinejad are also paired up in the 2000s in a Face-off configuration on a two-page spread in a news feature published on May 22, 2009. The headline reads *Why Not Talk?* Two photos, both in the Isolating-Centered-Single format, appear to face each other from opposite ends of the double-page spread. A cut-out photo of Ahmadinejad, an extreme close-up, is placed at the left end; the image takes up the whole page. The caption reads *CORRESPONDENT: Ahmadinejad's letter criticizes U.S. policies but hints at a possible openness to dialogue*. The caption of the photograph, which shows Bush, reads, *DECIDER: Bush has ruled out face-to-face talks until Tehran abandons its nuclear program*. However, unlike previous examples of the Face-off →← configuration in the data sample, this one features an imbalance in photo size. Ahmadinejad's photo dwarfs Bush's image in terms of size. Possibly, this is a visual allusion of the extent to which each side is eager to negotiate. As the stand-first explains, *A missive from Iran stirs a call for direct negotiations over Iran's nukes. Here is why the U.S. is not tempted*.

It is worth noting that while these examples are from print journalism, the face-off configuration can be found in digital news media as well. On September 22, 2017, Buzzfeed published an article titled *Here's everything you need to know about New Zealand's elections*. Right at the top of the web page is a picture of the two opposing politicians, incumbent Prime Minister Bill English and challenger Jacinda Ardern, literally facing off against each other, in a format that perfectly fits the first example discussed in this section.

5.2 Asymmetric Pairs (A>B). And the Contestants Are…

Asymmetric Pair is another adversative configuration; however, unlike the first category, it may be interpreted as hierarchical. This configuration, to use Kress and van Leeuwen's (2006, p. 79) terminology, employs a classificational process that relates participants to each other in terms of an overt taxonomy. This is accomplished with the help of relative picture size, as well as relative picture placement. Kress and van Leeuwen (2006, p. 79) examine how the size and placement of elements create asymmetric, taxonomical relations with reference to internal cohesion. This CND extends their ideas to external cohesion. The represented participants tend to be elite actors, who may be antagonists, but are depicted in an asymmetrical power relation. The anticipatory value of this CND, then, lies in illustrating a hierarchical adversative relationship between two elite actors who are central to the news story.

According to Kress and van Leeuwen (2006), classificational processes relate participants to each other in terms of a kind of relation, a taxonomy: at least one set of participants will play the role of subordinates with respect to at least one other participant, the superordinate. Taxonomies may be covert or overt. An overt taxonomy is arranged in

132 *Sameera Durrani*

terms of levels. It shows a higher degree of (explicit) ordering. It may represent and name the superordinate within some type of tree structure. Given that overt taxonomies are usually *chained*, they involve *intermediate* participants, termed as *interordinate*, who will be superordinate with respect to some of the other participants, and subordinate with respect to others. The participants may be realized verbally, visually, or both verbally and visually, but the process is always visual (Kress & van Leeuwen, 2006, pp. 79–80).

A mock-up of an example of this CND is shown in Figure 6.2. The news story documents an election contest between two Pakistani politicians, Benazir Bhutto (Figure 6.2, image 3) and Nawaz Sharif (Figure 6.2, image 2). The headline reads: *No holds barred* (*Time Asia*, August 28, 1989). This is a typical example of an Asymmetric Pair CND.

Similar to the Face-off configuration, the Asymmetric Pair configuration makes use of two individual images of two antagonists, both depicted in the Isolating-Centered-Single configuration. (The balance network is applied here with reference to external cohesion.) This allows for a clear identification of the participants in the depicted contest. These images are sometimes (though not always) placed on opposite pages. In terms of page composition, however, these images are placed in an Isolating-Axial configuration, placed at a diagonal angle. This allows for a taxonomical structure, as the image that is placed higher qualifies as the superordinate, while the image that is placed lower, qualifies as the subordinate. The process of ordering the represented participants is

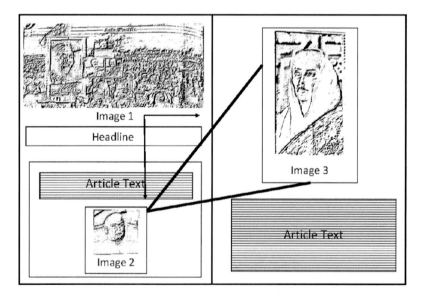

Figure 6.2 CND type 2: Asymmetric pairs.

realized visually, but as demonstrated in the examples discussed in this section, the verbal context unit also supports the structure of the taxonomy. With the help of placement and salience cues, one represented participant is discursively constructed as having more power than the other; the verbal context unit contains information which reinforces the asymmetrical power relations between two 'contestants'.

The mathematical symbol used to symbolize this is A > B, which denotes a hierarchical relation. One represented participant (A) is always placed in a more salient position in relation to another one (B). The double-page configuration may contain other pictures as well; these represented participants may be seen as interordinates, who provide axillary information about the narrative strand (e.g., image 1 in Figure 6.2). The two large lines denote the relation between the superordinate and subordinate represented participants, while the small arrows represent the relations between them and the interordinates. The interordinates are represented participants whose inclusion adds to the visual narrative, but they are not the key actors, as the captions confirm.

Key examples of this CND emerge from a particular narrative thread in the data for Pakistan, which concerned the political chaos and the consecutive and closely spaced elections of the 1990s. The contestants are two political rivals, Benazir Bhutto and Nawaz Sharif, who alternated as Pakistan's prime ministers within that decade. The hierarchical taxonomical structure reflected in the visual composition of the page is supported by the text. The verbal context unit of the two examples, published in *Time Asia* on August 28, 1998 (see Figure 6.2), and October 22, 1999 (in *Time Asia*), identifies Bhutto as the incumbent prime minister; she is in power, while Nawaz Sharif is the adversary who challenges her. The visual cues reinforce that impression, by placing larger images of her on the upper half of one page, while placing smaller images of her rival Sharif on the lower half of the opposite page.

Two other examples (published in *Time Asia* on November 5, 1990, and February 17, 1997) are from news features about Nawaz Sharif's victories over Bhutto in elections. Here, he receives the larger pictures, placed above Bhutto's. His photographs are given visual ascendance over Bhutto's, as a reflection of their mutual power dynamic at those points in time. In terms of aesthetic balance, this configuration may be identified as Isolating Axial. In all of these examples, the larger, upper picture seems to dominate the narrative, as well as the viewer's field of vision.

Within the sample, Benazir Bhutto's narrative contains the most recurrent examples of this configuration. The placement of her images on a page is reflective of the rise and fall of her fortunes. During the 1980s, the rival against whom her images are juxtaposed is General

Zia-ul-Haq, her chief political rival at the time, who had executed her father, former Prime Minister Zulfikar Ali Bhutto (Tran, 2007). One example appears on August 1, 1988, where her smaller-sized image is placed above, below Zia's, at a diagonal, in an article titled "Crisis of Confidence". Her photo appears above Zia's in a feature story that documents Zia's death and heralds her as the next potential leader (*Time Asia*, August 29, 1988), although this is not an A < B configuration. Her photos continue to stay on top until August 20, 1990, when she is depicted in a smaller photo placed at diagonal at the bottom of page, below that of a politician who helped dismiss her government. Her picture appears at the bottom of the page, in an article aptly titled "Bhutto's sudden fall". From there onward, there is visual evidence of a game of alternating musical chairs, of sorts. The visual narrative documents elections won and lost, and amidst political crises, the placement of her image goes up and down the page, usually changing places with images of her chief political rivals; in the 1990s, Nawaz Sharif, and in the 2000s, General Musharraf and Sharif. The 2000s are a mixed bag, in compositional terms; three compositional configurations from this decade may be coded as A > B. Bhutto is at the bottom in two cases (e.g., an article titled "The New Odd Couple", published in *Time Asia* on September 3, 2007, places her picture below that of General Musharraf) and relatively centered in the final one – below Nawaz Sharif, but above General Musharraf (*Time Asia*, September 4, 2007). As the article discusses how the exiled Nawaz Sharif's return to Pakistan threatens Musharraf, her picture serves as an interordinate, rather than superordinate or subordinate.

In sum, Benazir's profile offers an interesting diachronic case study in how picture placement can play a critical role in mediating and representing power relations, and is exemplary of how power dynamics between elite actors are configured using this CND.

5.3 Contrast: A ≠ B. When Two Worlds Clash

This compositional configuration is also an antagonistic one. However, it differs from the first two in a few ways. The antagonism is reflected via symbolic processes depicted in the images themselves, reinforced further by the verbal context unit and other elements of page composition (e.g., placement, size, contrast). The key element here is the presence of two images characterized by differing symbolic processes, the connotations of which clash with each other. Symbolic processes, according to Kress and van Leeuwen (2006, p. 105), are "about what a participant means, or is". This CND foreshadows a clash of ideologies, conveyed through ordinary actors personifying symbolic processes. This differs from the previous antagonistic configurations, which rely on elite actors.

Previewing News Stories 135

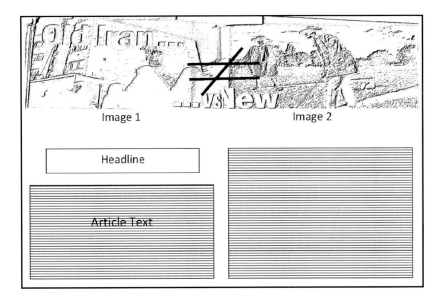

Figure 6.3 CND type 3: Contrast.

In terms of Balance, this compositional configuration may take the form of Iterating-Dividing-Facing (if both pictures are accorded the same salience, as with the Face-off configuration) or Isolating-Axial (if one picture is given salience over the other, as with the Asymmetrical Pairs). This CND tells a story of two worlds placed at opposite ends of a spectrum, a theme of contrast; hence, the mathematical term $A \neq B$ (see Figure 6.3 for an example of this type).

Some of the most pertinent examples of this device available within the data set concern and illustrate issues of gender, religion, and culture. The story in Figure 6.3 concerns the transformative processes at play within Iranian society in the late 1990s. The image on the left side, a low-angle shot, shows a group of women veiled in black, with a mural of Ayatollah Khomeini in the background. This image may be seen as a symbolic attributive one.[1] The human participants (the veiled women) are at rest. The symbolic attributive object, made salient with the help of its size and placement within the image and the low-camera angle, is the mural of Ayatollah Khomeini, which looms over the women. Khomeini's portrait is presented here, it seems, as a symbol of the Iranian Revolution of 1979 and all the political and cultural changes it brought with it.

The veiled women themselves may be seen as carriers with attributes that reinforce the visual motifs and connotations associated with the Islamic Revolution: they are a faceless group, dressed conservatively, their faces not clearly visible. These visual attributes are throwbacks to how Iranian women are depicted in the data during the 1980s (see Durrani, 2018). The mood of the image hints at the oppressive atmosphere associated in Western news narratives with the narrative of the Iranian Revolution. It is created with a combination of representational narrative tools (Kress & van Leeuwen, 2006) such as circumstance (the setting – the looming mural on the smooth, implacable high walls, which seem to fence in the veiled, faceless women) and conceptual tools, specifically, analytical processes (the veiled women, carriers with specific attributes) and the symbolic attributive object (the mural of Ayatollah Khomeini).

The image placed directly opposite, which matches it in size and placement, seems to invert all of these tools. It is a low-angle shot which shows two women wearing modest but modern attire, playing golf. The representational devices used here are starkly different. The circumstance, specifically the setting, is a golf course; the blue sky, the green grass, and the light colors worn by the women create a sense of space and openness. The golf club, which may be categorized as a circumstance of accompaniment, indicates a Western sport not conventionally associated with Iranian women. The image is dominated by a non-transactional action process. A non-transactional process, it may be noted, is one that has no *goal*, is not 'done to' or 'aimed at' anyone or anything; it simply showcases a single actor. It is analogous to the intransitive verb in language, that is, the verb that does not take an object (Kress & van Leeuwen, 2006, p. 63), and here it amounts to a woman playing golf, as well as a reaction process, as one female player (Reactor) looks at another (Phenomenon).[2] These women, then, are engaged in the process of doing something, as opposed to their counterparts, who are passive recipients of both a diegetic gaze (from Ayatollah Khomeini, in the mural) and a non-diegetic one (the reader's). In conceptual terms, the analytical processes are very different. The foregrounded female golf player is very much individualized, with her face clearly visible, her figure salient against the background: her attire and accessories are more Westernized (she is wearing jeans, a short tunic, a hat, and is carrying a golf club). Together, the conceptual and representational tools create a mood that suggests a narrative of openness, modernization, and, through the use of the interpersonal function, empowerment. While the first image uses a low angle to accord power to the mural, the second one makes use of a low angle to represent and empower the female golfer.

The contrast is further emphasized with the help of the headline: *Old Iran … vs. New*. The headline text is integrated into the pictures in a way that echoes what van Leeuwen (2010) calls the *new writing aesthetic*. The font type and size are the same, echoing the sameness of picture size; however, the placement and color are in direct contrast. *Old Iran* is printed on the top half of the first photograph, in a stark, intimidating black, emblazoned across the mural of Ayatollah Khomeini. *New* is printed in white, at the bottom of the second picture, in keeping with the lighter colors of the second picture itself. In a sense, the headline text color choices seem to visually echo associations with the symbolism of light vs. dark, white vs. black, and, in this way, may convey connotations of good versus bad.

Another example occurs in a feature article from the data for Pakistan, in the aftermath of 9/11 (*Time Asia*, October 1, 2001). The story illustrates the deepening divisions in Pakistani society along religious lines; it uses two different A ≠ B configurations to convey this theme. As with the Iranian example, the A ≠ B configuration is used here to explore intertwining themes of politics, religion, and gender. It employs representational and conceptual tools similar to the ones stated earlier.

The first example is a two-page spread with the headline "One Family Divided". The feature article talks about a progressive poetess, Attiya, and how her family is split along religious lines – a phenomenon increasingly true of Pakistani society at large. The larger image on the top features a transactional uni-directional process: a group of men gaze at a pile of burning television sets. The image foregrounds a symbolic attributive object – a burning pyre of television sets. Television sets are seen here as a symbol of Westernization; the fire a symbolic act of its destruction. The exclusively male crowd in the background serves as a circumstance of accompaniment, a prop, an extension of the locative circumstance, that is, the setting. True to the conventions which govern the A ≠ B compositional device, the image below reverses some of these elements. The first is the gender of the represented participant – the 'progressive' face is a woman. Where the previous image backgrounded the human-represented participant, this one foregrounds her. The colors of the flame, the central defining feature of the symbolic attribute object which dominates the first image, seems to be echoed here in the locative circumstances, in the form of a painting in fiery colors. The interactive elements are also in contrast to each other. The crowd of men is photographed in a long shot, at social/public distance, while the poetess is depicted with a medium close-up, at close personal distance. Furthermore, she is accorded a low-angle shot, which places her in a position of power relative to the viewer, whereas the image above is taken at an equal-angle shot. In terms of the balance network, the composition here is Isolating-Axial; the picture of religious activists burning televisions is given salience over the image of progressive poetess Attiya Dawood, by virtue of its placement on the page.

The next two pages of the article continue with the use of the A ≠ B compositional narrative device, though here, the contrast seems to have moved on to a younger generation of represented participants. These two images exemplify how quantification may not always be able to grasp the significance of data, and how some of the significance of images may be lost if analysis is confined to the contents of an individual image itself.

While the represented participants are, in representational terms, engaged in simple activities – one photograph shows a group of young girls in a shopping complex, whereas the other depicts a group of students – the contrast is the significant element which mediates the meaning of these images. Both are analytical images (Kress & van Leeuwen, 2006), where the carriers in each possess inverted possessive attributes with reference to the other. The first photo on the left side shows a group of young women in colorful Western clothes in a mall, while the other shows a group of female students similarly clad in austere white shawls. There is also a contrast in terms of interactional cues. The faces of the girls in the image on the left side, the one with girls in Western clothes, are clearly visible, and one of them looks directly toward the camera, in an equal-angle shot. In contrast, the image on the right shows students in a high-angle shot, with their faces and gaze obscured by the hijab, reminiscent of the conventions that govern the photographs of Iranian women in the 1980s. In terms of composition, the configuration employed here is Iterating-Dividing-Facing.

Gender seems to be a recurrent element within the clash thesis. Another example comes from the coverage of Iran's reformist President Khatami (*Time Asia*, January 19, 1998). It is a variant of the A ≠ B compositional device. In an Isolating-Centered-Triptych configuration, Khatami's picture punctuates two images which show very different sides of Iran. The left side shows a young woman putting on make-up in the mirror. In terms of possessive attributes, she wears a scarf with bright colors. She is in the middle of a specific activity, not merely passively posing for the camera. There are strong vectors connecting her gaze with her reflection. Vectors are also visible in her hand, which she extends toward her face to apply lipstick. The image on the right represents the right-wing ideologies of old Iran, even though the carrier is a young boy. It is dominated by a symbolic attributive object, a burning American flag, which may be seen as a representation of old, traditional political animosities. The image on the left is a woman; the circumstance of accompaniment is a lipstick, which may be seen as a symbol of Westernization and progress. As with the other examples, this instance contains the key hallmarks of this CND: ordinary actors personifying opposing ends of a theological or political debate are placed next to each other, illustrating the depth of the gulf.

5.4 (A+B+C): Gallery. Summing Up a Story in Pictures

This compositional narrative device is, perhaps, the print equivalent of its ubiquitous online version (see Figures 6.4 and 6.5 for examples). It can be further sub-divided into two categories: photobook and filmstrip.

Figure 6.4 shows the mock-up of a gallery where a compilation of snapshots is assembled to provide a synopsis of a given event. This

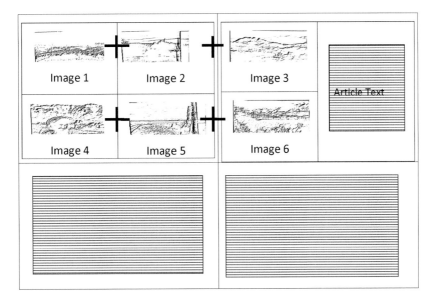

Figure 6.4 CND type 4: Gallery (Photobook format).

example contains six photographs of Pakistan's northern areas, giving the reader a snapshot of the lives of its residents (*Time Asia*, April 2, 2007). The images may be accompanied by separate captions or a single composite one.

The photobook format (see Figure 6.4) can be seen as an unstructured analytical process. Kress and van Leeuwen (2006, p. 94) define this is an analytical process where "they show us the Possessive Attributes of the Carrier, but not the Carrier itself, they show us the parts, but not the way the parts fit together to make up a whole"; here we see the parts of a region, though the parts do not fit together to make up the exhaustive picture of a whole. The unified caption introduces this gallery with these words: "A portfolio of scenes from the Afghanistan-Pakistan border provides a glimpse of the territory where the Taliban roam". The most ubiquitous use of it within digital media would be Instagram, where users can go to great lengths to coordinate the overall photobook 'look' of their profile overview.

Galleries may also be used to tell a story in a chronological fashion; this is described here as the filmstrip format. One example comes from *Time Asia*, May 6, 2003 (a mock-up is provided in Figure 6.5), which may be seen loosely as a temporal analytical process (Kress & van Leeuwen, 2006, p. 94), although the photos are not arranged in a strictly linear temporal sequence. The essential characteristic of temporal analytical processes is that they are realized by timelines: the participants

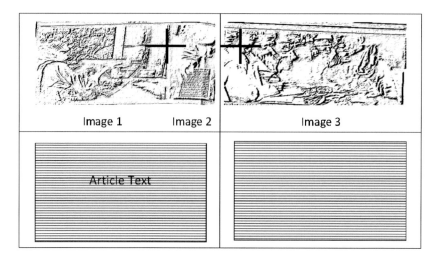

Figure 6.5 CND type 4: Gallery (Filmstrip format. Temporal sequences).

are arranged on an actual or imaginary line, usually horizontal, sometimes vertical. Timelines need not be straight, and they may involve all kinds of geometrical symbolism (Kress & van Leeuwen, 2006, p. 94). Here, the arrangement is horizontal only; hence, the connections between the images are denoted with plain + symbols.

While no typographical line demarcates the timeline in a gallery format, the sequence of arrangement does imply a temporal sequence (Caple & Knox, 2012). The events do tell a story, though the order in which the pictures are placed is not strictly linear. The temporal analytical format of the gallery (filmstrip format) singles out key actors or events that help illustrate the story under discussion. In both cases, the verbal context unit weaves all three images into a single narrative thread. One example from the corpus data (*Time Asia*, August 3, 1998) shows a former Iranian hostage taker, a former hostage, and an old photograph of the hostage from the days of the crisis. The stand first reads "A dramatic meeting between a former American hostage and one of his captors could be a powerful symbol of reconciliation".

Another example (Figure 6.5) shows a militant, an image from religious seminaries which are seen as places that produce militants, and religious activists who support militants. The caption reads, "Rogues No More?", while the stand-first adds, "Pervez Musharraf is attempting to tame Pakistan's secret service". At stake is the war on terrorism. Here, the text of the VCU is a more salient part of the page design. It incorporates color in a very notable manner. As van Leeuwen (2011, p. 11) notes, one instance of the ideational function of color comes from the modern corporation using specific colors to denote their unique identities; the same may be said of using colors to denote a national 'brand'. The red font used for the word *Iran*, and the green font used for the word *Rogues* may allude to colors from the Iranian and Pakistani flags, respectively. The colors are echoed in other parts of the VCU and add to the holistic design aesthetic. From a balance network perspective, both types of galleries fall into the Iterating-Serializing-Matching category in terms of the way they are placed on the page. Both ordinary and elite actors can comprise the subject matter, the designation flowing from who/what is emphasized in the news story.

5.5 Subsets/Insets: B ⊆ A. Story Plots and Subplots

This is a compositional device used often in newspapers as an inset picture. In terms of news narratives, this compositional device places a larger photo of the key actors/activities central to the story (the photographic equivalent of the main plot) next to a smaller one which depicts minor characters/actors, or the subplot (see Figure 6.6). Following the equation, the smaller photo B is a subset of the narrative process depicted

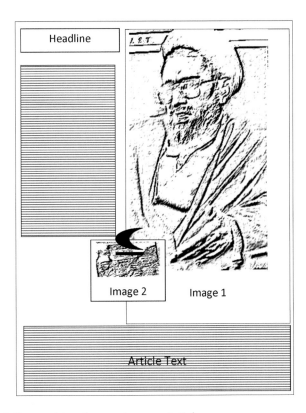

Figure 6.6 Compositional narrative type 1: Subsets.

in the large photo A. This is similar to how television narratives construct episodes around a main storyline A and a minor storyline B. With reference to the balance network, this configuration is Isolating-Axial. The larger photo and the actor(s) represented in it are more salient in terms of size and placement, while the smaller ones are less so. In terms of representational meanings, this may be seen as a conceptual, classificational device, a covert taxonomy that works to hierarchically organize certain represented participants over others with the help of image size and placement. The represented participants in the larger photograph placed in the upper half of the page may be seen as superordinates, while the rest are subordinates.

Unlike Asymmetric Pairs, there is no use of interordinates, and the relationship between the superordinate and subordinate is more about salience than hierarchical power relations between two different actors. For example, a story from August 20, 2001, titled "The Evil that Men Do", shows two Pakistani women victimized by feudal landlords in the superordinate photo, with smaller images of them with their families from the past superimposed at the bottom edge of the photo as subordinate photographs.

5.6 Banner ↔

This is a compositional device in which the width of the picture creates an effect of salience; the double-headed arrow symbol is used here to visually indicate the manner in which it extends from one side of the page to the other (as shown in Figure 6.7). The original photo shows the corpse of an Iranian soldier; the headline reads, "Carnage in the Marshes" (*Time Asia*, April 1, 1985).

This format consists of a photograph that foregrounds a scene or a represented participant with the help of what may be described in cinematic terms as a wide shot, to create a banner or film poster effect. The way it stretches across the top of the page is reminiscent of the gallery-filmstrip format; the key differences here are image size (somewhat less than half page) and the number of images (single, as opposed to multiple). A single image tells a clear story; the verbal context unit is used in a more supporting role here. This format showcases both elite and ordinary actors. It translates well to digital formats. The Pakistani newspaper *Dawn* uses this format to illustrate lifestyle and entertainment features. An example would be a feature on Pakistan's first Oscar winner, Sharmeen Obaid Chinoy (Zubair, 2016).

6 Conclusion

This chapter has introduced a new analytical framework for analyzing contextual cohesion in a modular, encapsulated format. The system, termed Compositional Narrative Devices, interrelates the representational

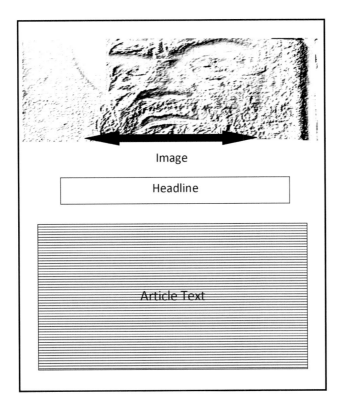

Figure 6.7 Compositional narrative type 6: Banner.

and compositional metafunctions, has predictive value, as well as potential transferability to the digital medium. It may be useful for researchers working within digital media to interrogate the existence of these and other potential CNDs within that realm. While the system is derived inductively from qualitative diachronic analysis, it is hoped that this new lens will provide researchers with a new, holistic way of examining and unpacking the potential inherent within contextual cohesion and the influence it exerts on the meaning-making potential of a news story.

Notes

1 Symbolic attributes are objects with one or more of the following characteristics: (1) they are made salient in the representation in one way or another; for instance, by being placed in the foreground or through exaggerated size, (2) they may be pointed at by means of a gesture, (3) they look out of place in the whole, in some way, (4) they are conventionally associated with symbolic values (Kress & van Leeuwen, 2006, p. 105).
2 It is worth remembering here that when the vector is formed by an eyeline, by the direction of the glance of one or more of the represented participants,

the process is reactional and is said to involve a Reactor and a Phenomena. The Reactor is the participant who does the looking; the Phenomenon may be formed either by another participant, the participant at whom or which the Reactor is looking, or by a whole visual proposition, for example, a transactional structure (Kress & van Leeuwen, 2006, p. 67).

References

Bednarek, M., & Caple, H. (2012). *News discourse*. London: Continuum.

Bezemer, J., & Kress, G. (2009). Writing in multimodal texts: A social semiotic account of designs for learning. *Visual Communication, 8*(3), 247–262.

Caple, H. (2013). *Photojournalism: A social semiotic approach*. Basingstoke: Palgrave Macmillan.

Caple, H., & Knox, J. (2012). Online news galleries, photojournalism and the photo essay. *Visual Communication, 11*(2), 207–236.

Derewianka, B., & Coffin, C. (2008). The visuals in history textbooks: Some pedagogic issues. In L. Unsworth (Ed.), *Multimodal semiotics: Functional analysis in contexts of education* (pp. 187–200). London: Continuum.

Djonov, E. (2008). Children's website structure and navigation. In L. Unsworth (Ed.), *Multimodal semiotics: Functional analysis in contexts of education* (pp. 216–236), London: Continuum.

Djonov, E., & van Leeuwen, T. (2013). Between the grid and composition: Layout in PowerPoint's design and use. *Semiotica, 197*, 1–34.

Durrani, S. (2018). Absence in visual narratives: The story of Iran and Pakistan across time. In M. Schröter & C. Taylor (Eds.), *Exploring silence and absence in discourse: Empirical approaches* (pp. 65–93). Basingstoke: Palgrave Macmillan.

Durrani, S., & Mughees, S. (2010). The pictorial image of Pakistan in *Newsweek* and *Time*: Pre and post 9/11. *Journal of the Research Society of Pakistan, 47*(1), 1–31.

Economou, D. (2010). Having it both ways? Images and text face off in the broadsheet feature story. In V. Rupar (Ed.), *Journalism and meaning making: Reading the newspaper* (pp. 175–193). Cresskill, NJ: Hampton Press.

Economou, D. (2008). Pulling readers in: News photos in Greek and Australian broadsheets. In E. Thomson & P. R. R. White (Eds.), *Communicating conflict: Multilingual case studies of the news media* (pp. 253–280). London: Continuum.

Economou, D. (2006). Big picture: The role of the lead image in print feature stories. In I. Lassen, J. Strunck & T. Vestergaard (Eds.), *Mediating ideology in text and image: Ten critical studies* (pp. 211–233). Amsterdam: John Benjamins.

Engebretsen, M. (2012). Balancing cohesion and tension in multimodal rhetoric. An interdisciplinary approach to the study of semiotic complexity. *Learning, Media and.Technology, 37*(2), 145–162.

Fahmy, S. (2004). Picturing Afghan women: A content analysis of APWire Photographs during the Taliban regime and after the fall of the Taliban regime. *The International Journal for Communication Studies, 66*(2), 91–112.

Fahmy, S., & Kim, D. (2008). Picturing the Iraq War: Constructing the image of war in British and U.S. press. *International Communication Gazette, 70*(6), 443–462.

Galtung, J., & Ruge, M. (1965). The structure of foreign news. *Journal of Peace Research*, 1(1), 64–91.

Griffin, M. (2004). Picturing America's 'War on Terrorism' in Afghanistan and Iraq: Photographic motifs as news frames. *Journalism: Theory, Practice and Criticism*, 5(4), 381–402.

Griffin, M., & Lee, J. (1995). Picturing the Gulf War: Constructing an image of war in *Time*, *Newsweek* and *U.S. News and World Report*. *Journalism Quarterly*, 72(4), 813–825.

Harcup, T., & O'Neill, D. (2001). What is news? Galtung and Ruge revisted. *Journalism Studies*, 2(2), 261–268.

King, C., & Lester, P. (2005). Photographic coverage during the Persian Gulf and Iraqi wars in three U.S. newspapers. *Journalism and Mass Communication Quarterly*, 82(3), 623–637.

Klaus, E., & Kassel, S. (2005). The veil as a means of legitimization: An analysis of the interconnectedness of gender, media and war. *Journalism: Theory, Practice and Criticism*, 6(3), 335–355.

Knox, J. (2009). Visual minimalism in hard news: Thumbnail faces on the SMH online home page. *Social Semiotics*, 19(2), 165–189.

Knox, J. (2007). Visual and verbal communication on online newspaper home pages. *International Communication Gazette*, 6(1), 19–53.

Kress, G., & van Leeuwen, T. (2006). *Reading images: The grammar of visual design*. London: Routledge.

O'Halloran, K. L., Tan, S., Smith, B. A., & Podlasov, A. (2010). Challenges in designing digital interfaces for the study of multimodal phenomena. *Information Design Journal*, 18(1), 2–21.

Parry, K. (2011). Images of liberation? Visual framing, humanitarianism and British press photography during the 2003 Iraq invasion. *Media, Culture and Society*, 33(8), 1185–1201.

Parry, K. (2010). A visual framing analysis of British press photography during the 2006 Israel-Lebanon conflict. *Media, War and Conflict*, 3(1), 67–85.

Pflaeging, J. (2017). Tracing the narrativity of National Geographic feature articles in the light of evolving media landscapes. *Discourse, Context and Media*, 20, 248–261.

Rohn, U. (2010). *Cultural barriers to the success of foreign media content: Western media in China, India, and Japan*. Frankfurt: Peter Lang.

Tran, M. (2007). A moderate success? *The Guardian*, Retrieved February 17, 2016, from http://www.theguardian.com/uk/2007/oct/18/pakistan.benazirbhutto

van Leeuwen, T. (2011). *The language of color*. Routledge, London.

Workman, A. (2017, September 22). Here's everything you need to know about New Zealand's election. *Buzzfeed*. Retrieved from https://www.buzzfeed.com/aliceworkman/its-literally-a-choice-bro?utm_term=.hp23ZORPW#.muD2EnpY3

Zubair, H. (2016, March 2). We need to change the conversation about Sharmeen Obaid Chinoy: Here's how. *Dawn*. Retrieved from https://images.dawn.com/news/1174916

Commentary
Image-Centricity and Change in Journalistic Cultures

Martin Luginbühl

Both contributions of this section relate to the concept of *image-centricity* by analyzing mass media texts of the last 30 years. While the contribution of Jana Pflaeging focuses on dynamic changes in genre ecologies, the analysis of Sameera Durrani identifies visual-textual configurations of news articles with narrative implications.

Jana Pflaeging's article shows in a very convincing manner how image-centric stories became predominant over time in a leading popular science magazine. These changes may be specific for this kind of medium to the extent that they can be observed in the case of this magazine. However, the general trend toward image-centricity is also noted in studies looking at other news media like newspaper front-pages (e.g., Caple, 2013, or Stöckl, 2015, who also point to the importance of aesthetic image appeal), new newspaper genres (e.g., Caple, 2013, discussed in the article), or online newspapers genres (Knox, 2007, who observes an increasing frequency of images in newsbites). In addition, important magazines have often proven to be places where changes in text design originate. So even if the clarity of changes observed by Pflaeging may be due to the popular magazine in question, it seems very clear to me that the general tendency observed – toward more, bigger, and especially more meaningful images within the overall coverage and a changing form and purpose of the accompanying verbal text – is a general tendency. And as we are dealing with a general tendency here, I would like to point out some methodological aspects of Pflaeging's study that seem important to me.

While it is common for pragmatic reasons to limit research to the emergence of *one* new or the change of *one* single genre (or in the case of the front-pages or homepages on a subset of usually quite specific genres), Pflaeging's study takes an integral look at entire genre profiles of the magazine in question (using very skillful DVs as heuristic tool), which is complemented by an in-depth qualitative genre analysis. The analysis of single genres or genre subsets is, of course, essential to describe and understand genre changes, as the stylistic design of genres, that is, the form of genres is meaningful. As a case in point, Pflaeging elaborates on this using the example of news values, which not only relate to the news content that is covered, but which are *construed* (Bednarek & Caple, 2017) in many cases, for example, by picture design aspects or by verbal emphases in the captions. This is how – and this seems crucial to me – the editorial staff fosters its identity and establishes, passes on, and – as can be seen in the diachronic perspective – changes its journalistic culture. Cultural norms and values can only be negotiated if they are communicated, and this means they have to be materialized in some way (see Linke, 2009), be it on the verbal, the typographical, the pictorial, or the multimodal level, that is, dependent on a specific multimodal combination. It is this mandatory materialization of cultural norms and values that makes the analysis of the generic micro level crucial for a holistic understanding of genre emergence and change.

But – as de Saussure pointed out – the meaning does not lie in the form itself – it comes 'from the side', that is, the value of a sign depends on the entire sign system, its paradigmatic and syntagmatic relations. This is why a look beyond the micro level of single genres is important for understanding (and not only describing) genre emergence and change.

Pflaeging's analysis combines micro-level analysis with the meso level in what I have called *genre profiles* (Luginbühl, 2016), which are part of the genre ecology of a community of practice. In my view, this level is indispensable if we want to relate changes in genre design to the macro level of journalistic identities and cultures. It is Pflaeging's combined look at genre style and genre profiles that paint a very clear picture of the growing empowerment of images, as it not only shows that *Visions of Earth* is an ancestor of *Visions*, but also and most of all that it can be directly linked to changes over time in the predominant *Feature Article*. *Visions* is some kind of a spin-off genre. At the same time, the analysis shows that changes in genre repertoire can also be related to style changes within the dominant genre feature article, namely, the growing share of double pages with one image and caption only. So what can be seen is a strong trend within the genre of feature article that culminates in the early 2000s in the emergence of a new genre, in which the empowerment of the image becomes condensed.

Sameera Durrani's contribution deals with image-centricity of another kind. Her analysis does not look at diachronic changes (although the corpus consists of newspaper articles from *Time Asia* of 1981–2010), but at the way pictures and their integration in the text design of newspaper articles frame the news stories.

Focusing on contextual cohesion within the paradigm of social semiotics, she shows how image content, especially the represented participants, picture size, and picture placement in the page layout, together with salient text passages like headlines or captions, create story previews. *Contrast*, for example, is expressed by the combination of contrasting image content, the placement of the pictures on the newspaper page next to each other, and salient verbal text within and below the pictures. It is especially intriguing how Durrani extends the Balance Network concept from internal picture cohesion to external cohesion between picture, page layout, and verbal text. On a methodological level, thus, it would have been important to learn more about the way these strategies have been identified, how distinct or fuzzy they are, and if they are all equally important during the period investigated.

I strongly agree that the identified patterns of image content types and page design create previews for the reader, but I am not sure if the term *narrative* is best suited for the phenomena described. Durrani argues that the compositional devices identified create "mini-narratives" and that compositional narrative devices (CNDs) integrate actors into narratives. The term *narrative* is also used in works on news narratives (see Bird & Dardenne, 2009; Fiske, 2011; Johnson-Cartee, 2005). But the term *narrative* refers in these works not to a certain static state of affairs, but – like in the classic definitions of narrative within literary studies (e.g., Genette, 2010) – to a (at least transitory) change of state: Fiske (2011, p. 295) – referring to Todorov – writes of a "basic narrative structure in which a state of equilibrium is disrupted, the forces of disruption are worked through until a resolution is reached", or Johnson-Cartee (2005, p. 159) understands narrative as a "story with characters, scene descriptions, conflict(s), actions with motives, and, ultimately, resolution(s)". Looking at Durrani's devices, it seems to me that most of them depict static constellations, but not dynamic events that include a change of state. They express "hostility/competition between two parties", "a hierarchical adversarial relationship between two elite actors", or "a clash of ideologies". While the CNDs probably are part of news narratives realized by the entire newspaper articles, the CNDs themselves seem rather to produce a *framing* of the events reported than a preview of the events themselves. This term seems to capture better what Durrani has in mind: "the essence of the news article".

Both chapters could be further elaborated to understand the establishment, tradition, and change of journalistic culture (sensu Hanitzsch, 2007) in more detail. This research perspective is already mentioned or at least implied by both authors, for example, by referring to professional identities.

Pflaeging relates the trend toward image-centricity mainly to a popularization strategy. In her analysis, she relates this strategy to the construction of news values such as Unexpectedness, Proximity, Personalization, Aesthetic Appeal, or Superlativeness (see Bednarek & Caple, 2017), which again can be related to changing communicative generic purposes and thus changing professional identities. And, I would add, they should also be related to different audiences that are targeted or constructed by this strategy. Further analysis could look at the (picture and verbal text) content realized, how they create these news values, and at shifts that can be observed – it is a very interesting finding that people have become the most prominent main image participants; this could be related to ideological questions, for example, to what extent the magazine tells less about nature itself and more about modern people's relations to (and dreams or imaginations of) nature. This may allow for further and more detailed ideological interpretations of genre and genre profile changes; for example, the emergence of Aesthetic Appeal in leading readers into the story in a very specific way; the changing picture-to-running text ratio which comes with a shift in information packaging; and the diminishing importance of Proximity and the absence (as it seems at least in all examples given) of certain news values (e.g., Negativity) and topics (e.g., environmental pollution).

Questions regarding journalistic culture are also highly relevant for Durrani's analysis. An analysis based on the strategies described could ask to what extent they lead journalists to realize framings that fit and therefore reinforce existing ideologies in the context of certain discourses. And although Durrani's analysis takes into account texts from 30 years, a diachronic aspect on the strategies could shed light on changes and stabilities in journalistic cultures asking questions such as the following: which strategies emerged or disappeared since the 1980s; what about their frequency?

In addition, further analysis could ask how these changes interact with changes in the media market, technological developments, changes in editorial staff, and other aspects that have proven to be relevant for journalistic cultures. As trends related to these manifold aspects can interact in complex ways, it also would be desirable if further research could look at smaller time intervals, and especially ask for short-term trends that have not been successful and thus have been dropped again after short time. While – in the case of Pflaeging's analysis – the overall trend toward more popularized content presentation is obvious, we also have to take into account the possibility that these trends are not usually absolutely continuous. They may give this impression if we look at data with a 10-year interval. A more fine-grained corpus may show twists and turns in genre change, and thus in journalistic culture change.

References

Bird, E. S., & Dardenne, R. W. (2009). Rethinking news as myth and storytelling. In K. Wahl-Jorgensen, & T. Hanitzsch (Eds.), *Handbook of journalism studies* (pp. 205–217). New York, NY: Routledge.

Bednarek, M., & Caple, H. (2017). *The discourse of news values: How news organizations create newsworthiness.* New York, NY: Oxford University Press.

Caple, H. (2013). *Photojournalism: A social semiotic approach.* London: Palgrave Macmillan.

Fiske, J. (2011). *Television culture* (2nd ed.). Milton Park: Routledge.

Genette, G. (2010). *Die Erzählung* (3rd ed.). Paderborn: Fink.

Hanitzsch, T. (2007). Deconstructing journalism culture: Towards a universal theory. *Communication Theory, 17*(4), 367–385.

Johnson-Cartee, K. S. (2005). *News narratives and news framing: Constructing political reality.* Lanham: Rowman & Littlefield.

Knox, J. S. (2007). Visual-verbal communication on online newspaper home pages. *Visual Communication, 6*(1), 19–53.

Linke, A. (2009). Stil und Kultur. In U. Fix, A. Gardt, & J. Knape (Eds.), *Rhetorik und Stilistik* (pp. 1131–1144). Berlin: de Gruyter.

Luginbühl, M. (2016). Genre profiles as intermediate analytical level for cultural genre analysis. In N. Artemeva, & A. Freedman (Eds.), *Genre studies around the globe: Beyond the three traditions* (pp. 251–274). Lexington: Trafford.

Stöckl, H. (2015). Bewegung auf der Titelseite: Ausdifferenzierung und Hybridisierung durch Sprache-Bild-Texte. In S. Hauser, & M. Luginbühl (Eds.), *Hybridisierung und Ausdifferenzierung: Kontrastive Perspektiven der Medienanalyse* (pp. 235–259). Bern: Lang.

Part 3

The Relative Status of Image and Language

7 Image-Centric Practices on Instagram
Subtle Shifts in 'Footing'

Helen Caple

1 Introduction

Many of the discursive practices of the contemporary media sphere are undeniably image-centric. News reporting, for instance, increasingly relies on images to tell stories: newspapers have for a long time published stories where an aesthetically-motivated image combines with minimal verbal text as *image-nuclear news stories* (Caple, 2008a, 2008b, 2013); the digitization of news products has allowed for the easy production of online news galleries (Caple & Knox, 2012, 2015) alongside other multimedia news genres (Engebretsen, 2012); and the templated formats of social media applications such as Facebook and Twitter have fully integrated visual storytelling as they take on the role of news retailers (Bednarek & Caple, 2017). Through the transition from news websites to news applications for Internet-enabled smart devices, page design has increasingly become more visual (Knox this volume; cf. Knox, 2007, 2010, 2014), with image-headline-lead macros now commonly used as the entry point into a news story (Caple, 2017). Thus, images have become central both in design and semantic terms.

As the contributions to this volume attest, such forms of image-centricity are not the exclusive domain of the news media. Advertisements and magazines have become increasingly image-centric, and the templated interfaces of social media platforms give prominence to images. *Instagram*, for example, is inherently image-centric, having been created for the purpose of viewing and sharing photographs. Users are encouraged to capture, edit, and post images online in close to real-time; and as co-founder and CEO, Kevin Systrom, states, by engaging with the visual content on Instagram "you're literally getting a view of what's happening in the world right now" (cited in Blake, 2014). Since its inception in October 2010, Instagram has come to dominate the social media arena (Blake, 2014), and is second only to its parent company Facebook in the number of active users (one billion monthly users as of September 2018, Statista, 2018). As a shared space, Instagram allows users to share images and videos (using Internet-enabled smart devices) on a particular topic or event. Users range from official government sources, news outlets, businesses, and other organizations to members of the public and their pets. The verbal text associated with these image-posts spans from the absolute minimal, as in no words or one or two words and/or metadata (hashtags, @mentions), through short descriptions of the visual content, to lengthy treatise on matters of import to the Instagrammer making the post.

With its primary function being to share photographs, the addition of verbal text could be viewed as somewhat of an afterthought on Instagram. Indeed, on any device, the default setting for viewing another Instagrammer's posts is grid format, three images wide, with no appended verbal text visible. To access any associated verbal text, the viewer has to click on an image (or change the page settings), and is taken to that particular post where verbal text and metadata appear alongside the image. The inclusion of metadata in a post, such as the *hashtag*, makes sense in terms of making this a *social* media, as hashtags increase the searchability and visibility of the post, connecting Instagrammers to each other and encouraging the formation of networks and communities of users (Bruns & Burgess, 2015; Highfield & Leaver, 2014; Hochman & Manovich, 2013; Zappavigna, 2012). Where verbal text is added to the caption space, it opens up the opportunity for dialogue between Instagrammers, as they comment on what is visually depicted and/or verbally stated, thus providing another way to commune with each other (see Siever & Siever, this volume).

In my research on Instagram, I have found that the caption space is highly likely to include verbal text alongside metadata, ranging from the minimal (interjections and nominal groups) to the maximal (sentences and paragraphs). Instagrammers use this space to fix the meaning of the image, naming participants, what they are doing and where they are, but they also do much more besides. This chapter explores the relations between the visual and verbal components of the Instagram post. It also examines how these elements relate to other data that make up the Instagram post, such as username, bio note, and avatar. To do this, I draw on previous work examining captioning practices in news storytelling (Caple, 2013; Caple & Knox, 2015, 2017). I also draw on Goffman's (1981) notion of *footing* to explore how subtle shifts in *production format* and projection have a profound effect on the production and reception of an Instagram post and on the ways in which Instagrammers do or do not align with their audiences.

2 The Relative Status of Images and Words

While there is no denying the fact that there is an "essential incommensurability" between images and words (Lemke, 1998, p. 110; Unsworth & Cléirigh, 2011, p. 156), images and words do enter into relations with one another. One could describe this relationship most elementally as showing and naming, by drawing on their most fundamental affordances: "image *shows* what takes too long to *read*, and writing *names* what would be difficult to *show*" (Kress, 2010, p. 1, italics in original). Studies examining the *relations between words and images* are numerous (see Martinec & Salway, 2005, pp. 339–341, or Zhao, 2010, pp. 197–200 for reviews of early work on intersemiosis). However, since this chapter draws quite specifically on previous work on image nuclearity, and extends it into analyses of *social media*, I briefly review this approach here. This study draws on the traditions of systemic functional linguistic/SFL-inspired social semiotics, and here I focus on research involving single static texts.[1]

2.1 Image Nuclearity

In previous research, I have argued for the centrality of news photography in the functional structure of a particular type of news story – the image-nuclear news story (INNS) – where a headline and salient photograph function as the nucleus of the story, while the attendant verbiage in the caption text acts as a satellite to this image-headline nucleus (Caple, 2006, 2008a, 2013). This additional verbiage does not extend beyond the caption. Such stories overwhelmingly make use of a very large (covering up to 50 percent of the printed page), aesthetically motivated photograph that draws the reader into the page. In virtually all of these stories, the photo and headline enter into a form of visual-verbal play, drawing on allusions to popular culture, literature, or historical record that are re-contextualized both visually and verbally (Caple, 2013). I use the term *image-nuclear* here because the image is an obligatory or structural element of the nucleus of this news story genre.

The image-headline nucleus, and the visual-verbal play between the two, form the launch pad into the story that is contained within the caption space. The logico-semantic relations between the image-headline nucleus and the caption text are functionally organized as experiential orientation and contextual extension. Experiential orientation functions to set the scene and introduce the image participants, their activities, and circumstances. It also usually disambiguates the visual-verbal play established in the nucleus. Thus, the verbal and visual components of the INNS together clarify and sharpen audience understanding of the event at that particular moment of image capture. In Martinec and Salway's (2005) logico-semantic terms, this is an example of elaboration between language and image. Liu and O'Halloran (2009, p. 379) similarly refer to this as "intersemiotic comparative relations" where image and language may be viewed as semiotic reformulations of each other and lead to "experiential and textual convergence".

Since the verbal text in the INNS never extends beyond the caption, the caption may have the additional task of connecting the moment captured in the photo to the wider news event – its newsworthiness – and is thus extratextual to what is represented in the photo. Clauses that elaborate on the wider news context in the INNS are labeled *contextual extension* and position the events in the photo in relation to an activity sequence that may reconstruct proceedings either side of the captured moment in the photo or that may reflect on the event. Thus, we associate contextual extension with a shift in time/tense choice (Caple, 2013, pp. 134–135). In Martinec and Salway's (2005, p. 350) logico-semantic terms, this would be an example of extension or enhancement between language and image. Again, Liu and O'Halloran (2009, pp. 379–381) refer to these semantic relations as "intersemiotic additive relations", where related but different messages are linguistically and visually presented, and "intersemiotic consequential relations" where semiotic messages enable or determine each other.

Posts to Instagram may display similar logico-semantic relations between image and verbiage. This is particularly true when an Instagrammer photographs a third party that is not known to her, and the caption text is written from an impersonal third-person perspective. However, it is far more common for the Instagrammer to know the person(s) being photographed, or even to photograph herself. In such instances, point of view is more likely to be both visually and verbally construed from the first-person perspective. In such posts, image and verbiage enter into what Martinec (2013) terms *complementary status relations*, and the syntagm is constructed across the image-text boundary. Section 4 explores these logico-semantic relations and introduces four functions of the Instagram post based on the analysis of these relations.

In addition, shifts in source and perspective (both visually and verbally construed) offer a great deal of flexibility to the creators of Instagram posts; such flexibility allows an Instagrammer's dexterity and innovation with this platform to come to the fore. To explore these novel practices, I use Goffman's (1981) notion of *footing*, explained here and taken up in the analysis in Section 5.

2.2 Footing: Production Format and Projection

In this study, I am also concerned with the source of a post, that is, the being attributed with the responsibility for the creation of a post, the position being established in the post, and their relationship with the subject matter of the post. Goffman (1981) provides a useful way of getting at the source of an utterance through his notion of *footing*. He takes a trinocular view of the production format of an utterance, proposing the performance of three separate roles in the creation of an utterance: those of animator, author, and principal (Goffman, 1981, p. 144). The "animator" is the "talking machine", the one who utters the words, or as Goffman (1981, p. 144) puts it, "an individual active in the role of utterance production". The "author" is the one who has "selected the sentiments that are being expressed and the words in which they are encoded" (Goffman, 1981, p. 144), while the "principal" is "someone whose position is established by the words that are spoken, someone whose beliefs have been told, someone who is committed to what the words say" (Goffman, 1981, p. 144). Often, these three roles are conflated into one *speaker*. However, being able to separate these three roles in the production of an utterance is very helpful for this study. In the following paragraphs, I introduce how I adapt the roles in Goffman's production format for the analysis of the Instagram post.

While Goffman (1981) originally devised production format for spoken discourse, it can be adapted to describe the production format of the Instagram post. When he refers to the animator as a *talking* machine, Goffman is suggesting that this is a physical function, rather than a social role. In the Instagram post, we might consider the animator, or *reading machine*, to be the digital device, with the Instagram interface installed through which posts are created by the Instagrammer and viewed and read by audiences. In essence, Instagram is the *vehicle* through which Instagrammers communicate with their audiences. In this sense, Instagram is the *publisher-animator*. In relation to the role of author, one might assume that an Instagrammer captures and uploads the photograph, and writes the words accompanying it, to their own Instagram account on their own digital device. Thus, Instagrammer is *author*. Likewise, if social media is said to be an expression of the self, then in the most congruent of realizations, the Instagrammer would also be *principal*, and committed to the position established through the post.[2] Such posts, I would argue, operate on a personal level, involving the self and close associates, and maintaining a first-person perspective.

Alternatively, the Instagrammer may choose to take a more impersonal or objective stance in a post, working with the ideas and images of others and shifting to third-person perspective. In such instances, I would argue that the Instagrammer acts more like an *editor*, and while the Instagrammer is author, she will not necessarily be principal. Further, the Instagrammer may invite collaboration on a post, resulting in a multiplication of perspectives within the post, opening up the opportunity for dialogue within the post as well as with other Instagrammers. Here, the Instagrammer may be acting as *endorser* or even *ventriloquist*. As will become clear in the analysis to follow, the role of ventriloquist is particularly pertinent to the dataset being examined in this chapter, as the sources co-present in an Instagram post do not necessarily need to be human. In sum, an Instagrammer might post *as* herself, or *about* someone else, or *in* someone else's words, or even *for* someone else, and to do so, I would suggest, involves subtle shifts in footing.

The role of projection (direct and indirect quotation) is also important in relation to production format, as it provides a means of conveying words that are not our own. This is what Goffman (1981, p. 150) calls the "embedding function of much talk". Whether this embedded talk is attributed to the self or another person/being in an Instagram post is important in this study, because it allows the Instagrammer to either align herself closely with or distance herself from the propositions or evaluations being conveyed. To give a brief example, an Instagrammer may photograph an object or landscape that is currently in her view, and may include herself or part of herself in the image frame, for example, photographing her own hand holding a coffee cup. Any verbal text added to such a post would most likely be written from the first-person perspective, for example, *I really needed this*, where *this* refers to the coffee in the photograph. In such instances, the verbal component is dependent on the visual content for disambiguation. Both visual and verbal elements emanate from the same person, and there is a conflation of author and principal. However, should the Instagrammer choose to quote another person's words or ideas (writing instead: *I'd rather take coffee than complements just now*), an embedded principal in the form of an external source (here, Louisa May Alcott) would be introduced through this intertextual reference. Thus, the role of principal is shared because: (1) quoting another person's words from first-person perspective and without a caveat suggests that the Instagrammer endorses the position encoded in these words, and (2) while Alcott is the original author of these words, the Instagrammer has re-contextualized them in the Instagram post and in relation to her own photograph and position as a coffee drinker.

By exploring this negotiation of roles through subtle shifts in footing, especially around the conflation or separation of these roles and projection, there is much to be learned about how Instagrammers encode certain messages in their posts and through these enact social relations with their audiences and other social media users. Before discussing the analysis, however, the next section introduces the dataset explored for this study.

3 Instagram as Object of Study

Social media applications such as Twitter have long been noted as spaces for the public to "voice a political opinion or present an emotional response" (Zappavigna, 2012, p. 173), and thus to enact social relations with other users and their audiences. Instagram is similar in this regard. However, given its inherent image-centricity, it does so through both visual and verbal resources.

In this study, the focus is directed at posts made by members of the public regarding a significant political process: the *Australian federal election* of July 2016. Specifically, it examines posts that used the hashtag *#dogsatpollingstations* and that were posted on the day of the election, 2 July, 2016 (further explanation of the choice of topic and hashtag is given in the next section). The study investigates the Instagram post from the perspective of text as meaning, and examines the semantic systems that are operationalized in identifying particular configurations of

Image-Centric Practices on Instagram   159

meaning. The aim is to uncover how images and words relate to each other in Instagram posts, thus revealing their functional structure, as well as how they enable shifts in footing. These visual-verbal interactions allow Instagrammers to present political opinions in a novel form that masks the extent to which they are committed to the opinions being presented. Figure 7.1 shows an Instagram post from the #*dogsatpollingstations* dataset with the parts of the post labeled.

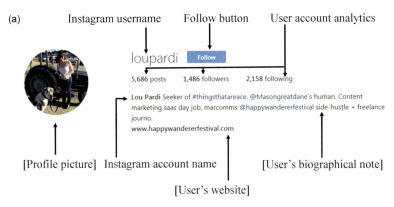

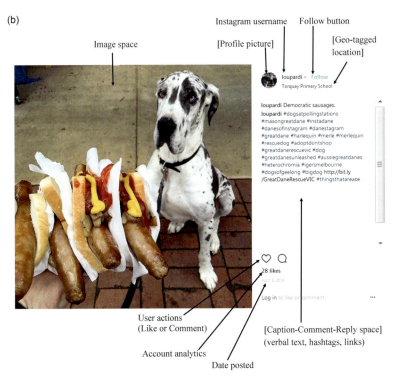

Figure 7.1 The anatomy of an Instagram post as viewed on a computer screen (Instagrammer and Post) (Post reproduced with permission).[3]

Like other social media platforms, Instagram makes use of a templated format, which is prescriptive in pre-deciding the appearance and distribution of key components. Kvåle (2016, p. 262) suggests that such control may lead to and legitimize certain bureaucratic processes. However, while the layout is restricted, Instagram places almost no restriction on the meanings generated in these spaces. As shown in Figure 7.1, the Instagram template consists of a space for something that is *image-like* (configurations include still image [+text], moving image [+text], text-as-image), a space for something that is *caption-like* (ranging from a single word, interjection, emoticon, or metadata, to sentences and paragraphs), which is combined with a space for something that is *comment-reply-like*. Information about the Instagrammer in the form of a handle (username), an avatar, bio note, and contact details (e.g., website) is visible at the top of a person's feed. Analytics, commonly used in social media, like the number of followers/following, posts made, likes for a post, appear either with the biographical information or on a post. The date the post was made also appears with the actual post (when viewing a single post). With slight variation across devices, two layout formats are available: a grid view, showing three images across, with all frames squared and no verbiage, or a post view, which is a scrolling list where each post (in an Instagrammer's feed) is shown with its attendant verbiage.

In its first iteration in 2010, Instagram restricted the image to a square frame. However, more freedom is now offered in terms of the shape and orientation of the image. Multiple images in a gallery-style format may also be presented in one post. As a platform created for the purpose of sharing photographs, there is no doubting the dominance or *firstness* of images in the construction of an Instagram post. However, the visual space can also be occupied with an image of written text, thus demonstrating the fact that language always attempts to reassert its dominance in any medium (see van Leeuwen, this volume, on new writing). In the dataset examined here, for example, the Australian Greens Party offered a number of text-as-image templates that users could post: one states *This Saturday I'm voting Greens* in white letters against a green background.

The data examined in this chapter are a small companion dataset to a larger case study investigating news reporting and social media use around the Australian federal election of 2016.[4] This companion dataset consists of 92 Instagram posts that made use of the hashtag #dogsat-pollingstations, posted on Instagram on July 2, 2016, the day of the federal election. There are three key reasons for focusing on this particular dataset. The first is that it was a trending hashtag on the day of the election. The second is that when compared with the other datasets collected (posts using #*ausvotes* and #*democracysausage*), posts using #*dogsatpollingstations* were much more likely to include a reference to a political party than posts in either of the other datasets. The third reason is because 22 accounts in this dataset are owned by dogs (ascertained by looking at the user avatar, username, and account-owner biography), and, as anthropomorphized beings, they make a total of 26 posts. The fact that animals are presented as the owners of an Instagram account makes these posts particularly relevant to an analysis of shifts in footing.

Also important to note here is the fact that the #*dogsatpollingstations* hashtag proved to be a very good *visual topic marker*: 96 percent of all images have dogs as subject matter, and 90 percent of all images are set either inside or outside a polling station. Only four images are potential outliers in this dataset, since they do not depict either dogs or polling stations. Further general findings on the make-up of the #*dogsatpollingstations* dataset (hereafter the DAPS dataset) are given in Caple (2018), along with qualitative linguistic and semiotic analyses, which demonstrate how political preferences are linguistically and visually expressed in each post. The focus in this chapter shifts to an examination of the functional structure of the Instagram post as a "modal ensemble" (Kress, 2010, p. 28), uncovering the ways in which visual and verbal semiotic resources interact with each other in posts.

4 Analysis: The Functions of Instagram Posts

In the analysis that follows, I begin from the assumption that the being that owns the Instagram account is the being that takes the photograph and writes the caption and posts both to Instagram. Therefore, I call on readers to engage in the suspension of disbelief that dogs can be Instagrammers in their own right, photographing, writing, and posting their own images and thoughts to Instagram. The necessary human intervention in the creation of these posts, while understood to be present, is effectively elided (i.e., the human ventriloquist remains hidden). However, the extent to which this intervention eventually becomes explicit in a post and interferes with meaning making is discussed in the next section in relation to shifts in footing. This section introduces four functions of the Instagram post by examining the logico-semantic relations between the visual and verbal components of the post.

> IMPERSONAL PERSPECTIVE: REPORTING on the experiences of others, *telling* audiences what is happening at that image moment

A number of Instagram posts in the DAPS dataset share similarities with the image-captioning practices of news reporting and take an objective or impersonal stance toward the topic of the post. The Instagrammer photographs a third party (a dog) who may or may not be known to her, and there is a clear separation of the Instagrammer and the photographed. The verbal text in the caption shares the characteristics of news-image-captioning practices in that it is experientially oriented toward the image content, disambiguating the participants (dogs) and the happenings that they are involved in (the federal election) to different degrees of explicitness. At the same time, the images specify the verbal content by showing audiences the location, number, and breed of dogs photographed. Thus, language and image may be viewed as semiotic reformulations of each other (elaboration), and the meanings realized verbally and visually tend not to extend beyond the moment captured in the image.

At their least specific, captions in reporting posts consist of noun phrases where the image participants are either referred to in the most generic terms, labeled as dogs, or in terms of the activity they are taking part in, for example, snoozing or relaxing. However, pre-modification of the noun does specify which dogs these are: "election" dogs (e.g., *Election day doggos*; *Election dogs. Waiting.*). This specification of the noun *dog* places the dogs within the context of the election event that was happening that day. In addition, nominalization of the activities they are engaged in also allows for the condensing of multiple meanings into the nominal group: so not just relaxation, but *post-voting relaxation*. Thus, while such captions may appear generic in labeling the image participants, they are very specifically associated with a particular event – the federal election – through pre-modification of this labeling.

Alternatively, the image participants are named in the verbal text using a proper name, for example, *Bouncer*. These captions mostly consist of full sentences. The processes largely retell the activity sequence that is visually depicted, for example, *Pip meets George* [image: very small dog (Pip) stands facing very large dog (George)]; some elaborate further to indicate the preferences/allegiances associated with these activities, as in: *This is Annie **casting her #democracysausage vote** at Yeronga State School today!* Thus, we learn not just that they are voting, but also who or what they are voting for. Voting preferences are also visually depicted through the inclusion of posters, placards, and other voting paraphernalia associated with a particular party (see Caple, 2018, for further discussion of such affiliative practices).

Word-image play features here and across the whole dataset. In relation to captions consisting only of noun phrases, the word play is based on the blending of words, for example, dog and democracy are used to form the portmanteau *Dogmocracy*. The photograph in this post depicts the combination of a dog with election paraphernalia; thus, the play spans both image and verbiage as they reconstrue each other as visual/verbal play.

Across this section of the data, evaluation is attributed to a third party, not the Instagrammer, which is again similar to the attribution practices of news reporting, where a journalist would attribute evaluation/stance to a quoted source. Thus, while there are a small number of captions that are attitudinally loaded, this attitude is attributed to the photographed third party. In reporting posts, I would contend that the Instagrammer is acting as author/editor, with the photographed third party as principal. The caption texts in these posts may report the emotional state of the image participants (dogs in all cases), for example, *bored, disappointed*, in relation to aspects of the election (here, the length of the campaign, and the lack of a sausage sizzle, respectively)[5], as well as report negative assessments (judgment) about the political process, for example *Ted is not down with this absentee voting malarkey*. Here, the coupling of the interpersonal (attitude – underlined) with the ideational (aspects of the election process – in bold font) allows for the formation of bonds (Martin, 2007; Stenglin, 2004) around which Instagrammers may rally, that is, other Instagrammers may share these evaluations of the political process and thus align with the Instagrammer editing this post (discussed further later, and in the next section).

PERSONAL PERSPECTIVE: COMMENTING on own or shared experiences, *looking together* with audiences at the moment captured in the image

---

If reporting posts are about the experiences of others (not the Instagrammer), then commenting posts sit at the opposite end of the spectrum in focusing on the self (the Instagrammer). In commenting posts, we see a shift in point of view to that of the Instagrammer (first-person perspective in the verbiage), and the Instagrammer is also likely to be photographed. Image and verbiage are still focused on the moment photographed, elaborating on the photographed phenomenon, and verbiage and image enter into dependency relations, where fragments (prepositional phrases and non-finite clauses, i.e., rheme only) in the verbal text rely on the visually represented subject (Theme) for disambiguation. These are what Martinec (2013, pp. 151–152) refers to as *complementary status relations*, and the syntagm is constructed across the image-text boundary.

Figure 7.2 presents two examples of commenting posts where canine Instagrammers share pictures of themselves, and in the verbiage comment on what was going on at the moment photographed. This gives a sense of looking together with the audience. Since the Instagrammer/commentator is photographed, the verbiage elides the subject, giving intermodal dependency relations between Instagrammer, image, and verbiage. The shared commentary, verbally reconstrued, might look something like:

Here I am … *with Aunty Angela!!* [Example 1 in Figure 7.2]
In this picture I am … *Braving the Canberra cold for the coveted #democracysausage* [Example 2 in Figure 7.2]

Figure 7.2 Examples of commenting posts (Posts reproduced with permission: Post in Example 2, courtesy of Aimee Castrission/axelandteddy).

Image-Centric Practices on Instagram 165

Such posts are also likely to be evaluative (of the self). For example, in Example 2 in Figure 7.2, this canine Instagrammer positively evaluates himself as being "brave" in the face of Canberra's very cold winter weather (positive judgment : social esteem : tenacity in Martin & White's, 2005 terms). In commenting posts, the Instagrammer is author and principal.

While not present in the DAPS dataset, I would posit that there is another type of commenting post, where the Instagrammer shares her thoughts and feelings on an external phenomenon, which may be represented visually in place of the Instagrammer. In such posts, the Instagrammer is personally invested in the topic of the post and is sharing her own thoughts/feelings on the topic, which means that they are also highly evaluative. Example 3 in Figure 7.2 comes from the #*ausvotes* corpus. Again, we might reconstrue this post verbally as: This is … *Not quite the celebration of sausage sizzles and cake sales I'm used to …* #*ausvotes*, where "this" is the sterile, imposing visual depiction of an Australian embassy in a far-off land.

PROJECTED PERSPECTIVE: CONVERSING with audiences

In written text, locutions and ideas (speech and thought) can be introduced and attributed to a source through the use of projection (Halliday & Matthiessen, 2014, p. 509). Verbal and mental processes (e.g., *say, think*) are used to link the speech/thought to the speaker/thinker (Example 1 in Figure 7.3). In comic books, direct speech and thought are connected to speakers and thinkers through the use of dialogue balloons and thought balloons (Martinec & Salway, 2005, p. 352; Kress & van Leeuwen, 2006, p. 68). Thus, in comics, verbal and mental processes are visually mediated through speech and thought bubbles (Example 2 in Figure 7.3). In Instagram posts, I would contend that both the visual *and* linguistic markers (speech/thought balloons and verbal/mental processes) are elided yet still inscribe the projection of direct speech and thought (Example 3 in Figure 7.3). In comic books, locutions are more likely to be directed at other characters in the narrative. However, the locutions in Instagram posts are typically directed toward audiences.

In Instagram posts using projection from the DAPS dataset, the source of the utterance is depicted in the image and the quoted utterance may be realized in a number of verbal forms, for example, as a statement: *I'm just here for the sausage sizzle*; question: *Where's my Democracy Sausage?*; or command: *Make sure that you vote Labor in both houses*. These are principally voiced from the first- and second-person perspective. In conversing posts, we see a shift in focus between verbiage and image, where logico-semantic relations of expansion hold and the verbal text adds new related information (extension). Those that are realized through statements tell audiences more about the state of mind of the

166 *Helen Caple*

Example 1:

"I'm just here for the sausage sizzle," <u>said</u> Freda.

Figure 7.3 Projection in written text (1), cartoons (2), and the Instagram post (3) (Post reproduced with permission).

image participants: specifically in this dataset, their thoughts and feelings about the federal election. In conversing posts, the Instagrammer is typically author and principal.

Conversing posts are dialogic, and in order to disambiguate the participants, the recipient of the message needs to engage with the Instagram post as a whole, including image, verbal text, and metadata such as account holder. The assumption here is that there is a conflation of the producer of the post, the image participant, and the owner of the

Image-Centric Practices on Instagram 167

account, that is, the Instagrammer is also the photographed. The complicating factor of this being a dog in this dataset will be discussed further in relation to Goffman's (1981) notion of *footing* in the next section.

> **AFFECTIVE PERSPECTIVE: REACTING** to an external phenomenon, *showing* audiences how you feel about something

A captioning practice that has become prevalent on a number of social media platforms (e.g., Twitter, Facebook, and Instagram) involves the use of conjunctions to link the verbal (cause) and visual (consequence) components of the post. This is often realized in other social media platforms through the abbreviation 'tfw', meaning 'the feeling when'. In the DAPS dataset, this is realized verbally through a *When ...* clause connecting the verbal and visual element. Here, *when* is acting not as a temporal marker but rather as a causal conjunction. The verbal text realizes the cause, while the image realizes the consequence, most frequently in the form of an emotional reaction. The example in Figure 7.4 demonstrates this phenomenon.

The post shown in Figure 7.4 makes use of this verbal cause-visual consequence structure. In this post, a dog stands over a voting paper at a pine table. He is wearing a bandana emblazoned with the Australian flag, which suggests that he is fervently patriotic. This adds to the sense that

Figure 7.4 A reacting post (Post reproduced with permission: Courtesy of douglas_von_puglas).

he takes his democratic duty to vote in the federal election very seriously, and thus compounds the extreme frustration the dog expresses as he glares directly at the audience through the camera lens. The cause of his extreme emotion is revealed in the verbal text: his lack of self-control in the face of the sausage sizzle, and therefore the inconvenience of having to participate in the postal vote. One might reconstruct this intersemiotic relationship verbally as: This is what you look like … *When you're made to vote at home because you have no self-control at #democracysausage sizzle.* This is another instance of complementary status, where words and image co-construct a syntagm (Martinec, 2013, p. 151).

Reacting posts also establish an intersemiotic consequential relation. We cannot fully understand the source (or trigger) of the emotional reaction in the image without attending to the verbal text where the cause is revealed. Likewise, we cannot fully appreciate how this happening has affected the protagonist without attending to the visual text where the emotional response is revealed. It must be noted here, however, that this image also makes sense in its own right, as the source of the dog's frustration could also be the sheer size and complexity of the ballot paper on the table that he has to fill in.

An important feature of reacting posts is hence the combination of a visually realized emotional response with a verbally realized ideational account of cause. This visual-verbal combination is an example of coupling across both metafunction (ideational/interpersonal) and mode (image/verbiage) (Caple, 2008b; Martin, 2000; Painter, Martin, & Unsworth, 2014, p. 143; Zhao, 2011, p. 144). Zappavigna (2012, p. 16) discusses the coupling of ideational and interpersonal meaning in the service of *bonding* on the social media platform Twitter (verbally construed through hashtags). A similar conclusion can be drawn from this Instagram data in that the coupling of visual interpersonal meaning with verbal ideational meaning creates the ideal conditions for shared humor and empathy with the image participant and creates a space for Instagrammers to bond and form social relations around this shared experience.

To summarize this section, four functions of the Instagram post have been introduced: reporting, commenting, conversing, and reacting. Shifts in perspective and subject matter of both the verbal and visual elements in the post allow the Instagrammer and audience to connect with each other in ways that are less or more inclusive. The fact that the Instagrammer (in this dataset) may be non-human allows for novel practices on Instagram, and I turn now to a discussion of such practices through the lens of footing.

5 Playing with the Participants: Subtle Shifts in Footing

One of the most interesting and innovative aspects of the discursive construction of social media posts is the way in which footing can be manipulated. In the case of Instagram, this is further complicated through the combination of both verbal and visual elements in a post, where the source of an utterance could be the Instagrammer, the photographed, or a third party external to both. Such shifts in footing may result in a humorous effect, may signal how we (dis)associate ourselves with certain beliefs and values, or, when footing is misaligned, may also lead to confusion. As noted earlier, in using the term *footing* I am borrowing from Goffman (1981, p. 151) who states that "when we shift from saying something ourselves to reporting what someone else said, we are changing our footing".

In Section 4, I presented the most congruent (i.e., typical) realizations of Instagram posts, as they occurred in the DAPS dataset. In this section, I discuss departures from the norm, in order to demonstrate how such deviations may lead to confusion or may reveal the ingenuity of the Instagrammer. Departures from the norm also allow Instagrammers to introduce attitudinal meaning (realized both visually and verbally) into their posts while maintaining distance between themselves and the attitudes being expressed, the need for which will be discussed in the final section. Figure 7.5 presents the posts to be discussed.

In relation to footing, the roles of author and principal are assigned to the Instagrammer in Example 1 in Figure 7.5. As noted earlier, this claim is contingent on the willingness of audiences to suspend disbelief that a dog, as an anthropomorphized non-human, is able to behave in the same way as a human. Thus, the role of the human ventriloquist remains hidden, allowing audiences to suspend disbelief and view the post as authored by the *principal* – the dog. This means that in this post, we engage with a canine Instagrammer.

The congruency of Example 1 in Figure 7.5 is made even clearer when we compare that post to the almost identical post in Example 2 in Figure 7.5. Here the canine Instagrammer, Axel, is also captured eating a democracy sausage. However, the intervention of the human dog owner is made transparent through the shift in perspective in the verbal component of the caption. Rather than being directly *voiced* by Axel, as a conversing post, point of view in the utterance shifts to the more impersonal third person and Axel is talked *about*, thus presenting more like a reporting post. Axel talking about himself in the third person seems strange or even pretentious. The resulting clash between Axel as Instagrammer and therefore producer of the post, and the human ventriloquist making their intervention transparent through the verbal text may lead to confusion about where this message emanates from and who is committed to the position being put through the message.

Continuing with the democracy sausage theme, Example 3 in Figure 7.5 is a good example of how the necessary human intervention in the creation of a dog's post can be played with. Like Example 1, Example 3 is also a congruent realization of footing: the canine Instagrammer, Misha, is author and principal. This is an example of a conversing post, and Misha directly addresses the audience. At the same time, the direct address 'you' realized

Figure 7.5 Examples of shifts in footing in Instagram posts (Posts reproduced with permission: Post in Example 2, courtesy of Aimee Castrission/axelandteddy).

Image-Centric Practices on Instagram 171

Figure 7.5 (Continued).

verbally in combination with the direct eye-contact realized visually also acknowledge the human ventriloquist on the other side of the camera. Such a configuration of verbal and visual elements plays with the fact that there is a necessary layer of human intervention in the production of a pet's Instagram post. In this post, there is a sophisticated pattern of shifting between footing, and audiences need to hold both the 'naturalized' footing (dog as author/principal) and the shift to acknowledging the human ventriloquist in view at the same time. By simultaneously holding these two perspectives in view, audiences can appreciate the playful manipulation of footing, and observe that the dog is addressing both the audience *and* its human overlord.

Another way in which footing may be manipulated is shown in Example 4 in Figure 7.5. This is another congruent post, where the canine Instagrammer is both photographed and source of the command in the projected verbal text. However, the additional participant in the image, Adelaide Labor candidate Kate Ellis, albeit via a poster, adds an additional voice to this call to vote. Thus, there are two potential *principals* in this post, who may be committed to the point being made. In this post, the dog is effectively sharing the stage with his preferred candidate.

A similar phenomenon of sharing the stage can be seen in Example 5 in Figure 7.5. In this post, the human Instagrammer has taken a photograph of a third party – a dog. The caption is an instance of projection that could emanate from both the image participant, the dog, and the account holder, the human. Such clever blurring of footing elides who the *principal* is. Such blurring of voices could be a useful strategy for making indirect comments on controversial issues, because it adds a layer of distance, or at least ambiguity, between *principals*. The implications of this added layer of complexity through the blurring of voices are discussed in the final section of the chapter.

6 Summary: Letting our Pets Speak for us

In conclusion, re-examining this dataset using Goffman's *footing* has revealed how the subtle shifting between *speaker roles* masks who is responsible for a set of ideas. This is particularly important for this dataset since this blurring of perspectives is common in this dataset. It occurs in 26 percent of the posts. Furthermore, 50 percent of all posts also reveal voting preferences (Caple, 2018). Compared with two other datasets also collected in relation to the federal election (6,299 posts to #*ausvotes*; 927 posts to #*democracysausauge*), the DAPS dataset is much more likely to include references to a political party. This leads to the question of whether allowing pets to speak for their humans creates a space for the Instagrammer to be bolder. Thus, can more openness be achieved through such indirectness?

Bell (1991, p. 70) contends that in mass communication fractures in the communication process have significant consequences for language production. I would argue that the addition of our pets as *author/principal* can be viewed as a fracture in the communication process in other mass-mediated practices, those of social media. On Instagram, the subtle shifts in the conflation and separation of speaker roles between pets and their human ventriloquists put different demands on the work that image, language, and the spaces in between need to do to make meaning. Openly stating political preferences on social media may trigger a range of responses from audiences, not all of them pleasant. The ability to play with footing, blurring the role of *principal* within a post, or merely assigning *principal* to a pet, allows the human ventriloquist to remain in the background. Thus, by channeling political preferences through a third party, in this case a pet, the Instagrammer adds distance between themselves and their ideas, creating humor and a sense of solidarity with audiences, rather than hatred and vitriol: a useful strategy for keeping the trolls in their caves. Long may the Dogs-of-Instagram reign.

Acknowledgments

I am immensely grateful to Hartmut Stöckl for first imagining and then enacting a volume of this nature, to Jana Pflaeging for her careful stewardship of the book project, and to John S. Knox for his ongoing and exacting critique of my work. This research was supported by an Australian Research Council DECRA: Project ID DE106100120.

Notes

1 A number of studies have dealt with intersemiosis in hypertext (Zhao, 2010), between sequences of still images (Caple & Knox, 2012, 2015; Engebretsen, 2012; Lim, 2007) and in moving images in documentary/news/filmic discourse (Meinhof, 1994; Montgomery, 2007; Tseng, 2008; Tseng & Bateman, 2011, 2012; van Leeuwen, 1991, 2005). See Caple (2013) for further discussion of this research.
2 Bell (1991, pp. 36–44) adapts Goffman's production format to describe producer roles in news language, adding further division of roles to account for the different levels of responsibility for the linguistic form as well as news content. For example, he assigns the role of principal to the institution (news organization) because news executives/newspaper proprietors set the editorial policies which affect news language: "A proprietor's definition of what will be treated as news and how it is to be reported has linguistic repercussions" (Bell, 1991, p. 40). I do not assign the role of principal to Instagram, as it does not exert control over what Instagrammers choose to photograph, write, and publish, beyond fulfilling its legal obligations around obscene content.
3 Square brackets [ ] indicate that this feature is optional, e.g. the Instagrammer may choose not to upload a profile picture or a bio note.
4 The sausage sizzle is a cultural icon of Australian elections. Voting usually takes place at local primary schools, which on the day of the election usually set up a barbeque to sell sausages in bread, also known as 'democracy sausages', as part of their fund-raising efforts.
5 The study is part of a larger project investigating the ways in which citizens and organizations outside of journalism are re-shaping and re-defining photojournalistic practice through their engagement with the digital economy (ARC DECRA Project ID: DE160100120), and addresses the project aim of examining the extent to which the Australian news media is in line with the expression of public sentiment through social media platforms on events of cultural, political, and historical significance.

References

Bednarek, M., & Caple, H. (2017). *The discourse of news values: How news organisations create newsworthiness*. New York, NY: Oxford University Press.

Bell, A. (1991). *The language of news media.* Oxford: Blackwell.
Blake, J. (2014, December 10). Instagram now bigger than Twitter. *BBC Newsbeat.* Retrieved from http://www.bbc.co.uk/newsbeat/article/30410973/instagram-now-bigger-than-twitter
Bruns, A., & Burgess, J. (2015). Twitter hashtags from ad hoc to calculated publics. In N. Rambukkana (Ed.), *Hashtag publics: The power and politics of discursive networks* (pp. 13–28). New York, NY: Peter Lang.
Caple, H. (2018). "Lucy says today she is a Labordoodle": How the dogs-of-Instagram reveal voter preferences. *Social Semiotics, 28,* 1–21.
Caple, H. (2017). Results, resolve, reaction: Words, images and the functional structure of online match reports. In D. Caldwell, J. Walsh, E. W. Vine, & J. Jureidini (Eds.), *The discourse of sport: Analyses from social linguistics* (pp. 209–227). London: Routledge.
Caple, H. (2013). *Photojournalism: A social semiotic approach.* Basingstoke: Palgrave Macmillan.
Caple, H. (2008a). Intermodal relations in image nuclear news stories. In L. Unsworth (Ed.), *Multimodal semiotics: Functional analysis in contexts of education* (pp. 125–138). London: Continuum.
Caple, H. (2008b). Reconciling the co-articulation of meaning between words and pictures: Exploring instantiation and commitment in image-nuclear news stories. In A. Mahboob & N. Knight (Eds.), *Questioning linguistics* (pp. 77–94). Newcastle: Cambridge Scholars Press.
Caple, H. (2006, December). Nuclearity in the news story: The genesis of image nuclear news stories. In C. Anyanwu (Ed.), *Empowerment, creativity and innovation: Challenging media and communication in the 21st century. Refereed proceedings of the Australia and New Zealand Communication Association international conference.* Adelaide: Australia and New Zealand Communication Association and the University of Adelaide.
Caple, H., & Knox, J. S. (2017). How to author a picture gallery. *Journalism: Theory, Practice and Criticism.* Advance online publication.
Caple, H., & Knox, J. S. (2015). A framework for the multimodal analysis of online news galleries. *Social Semiotics, 25*(3), 292–321.
Caple, H., & Knox, J. S. (2012). Online news galleries, photojournalism and the photo essay. *Visual Communication, 11*(2), 1–30.
Engebretsen, M. (2012). Balancing cohesion and tension in multimodal rhetoric: An interdisciplinary approach to the study of semiotic complexity. *Learning, Media and Technology, 37*(2), 145–162.
Goffman, E. (1981). *Forms of talk.* Philadelphia: University of Pennsylvania Press.
Halliday, M. A. K., & Matthiessen, C. M. I. M. (2014). *Halliday's introduction to functional grammar* (4th ed.). London: Routledge.
Highfield, T., & Leaver, T. (2014). A methodology for mapping Instagram hashtags. *First Monday, 20*(1), 1–11.
Hochman, N., & Manovich, L. (2013). Zooming into an Instagram city: Reading the local through social media. *First Monday, 18*(7). Retrieved from https://firstmonday.org/ojs/index.php/fm/article/view/4711/3698
Knox, J. S. (2014). Online newspapers: Structure and layout. In C. Jewitt (Ed.), *The Routledge handbook of multimodal analysis* (2nd ed.) (pp. 440–449). London: Routledge.

Knox, J. S. (2010). Online newspapers: Evolving genres, evolving theory. In C. Coffin, T. Lillis & K. O'Halloran (Eds.), *Applied linguistics methods: A reader* (pp. 33–51). London: Routledge.

Knox, J. S. (2007). Visual-verbal communication on online newspaper home pages. *Visual Communication, 6*(1), 19–53.

Kress, G. (2010). *Multimodality: A social semiotic approach to contemporary communication.* London: Routledge.

Kress, G., & van Leeuwen, T. J. (2006). *Reading images: The grammar of visual design* (2nd ed.). London: Routledge.

Kvåle, G. (2016). Software as ideology: A multimodal critical discourse analysis of Microsoft Word and SmartArt. *Journal of Language and Politics, 15*(3), 259–273.

Lemke, J. (1998). Multiplying meaning: Visual and verbal semiotics in scientific text. In J. R. Martin & R. Veel (Eds.), *Reading science: Critical and functional perspectives on discourses of science* (pp. 87–113). London: Routledge.

Lim, V. F. (2007). The visual semantics stratum: Making meaning in sequential images. In T. Royce & W. Bowcher (Eds.), *New directions in the analysis of multimodal discourse* (pp. 195–213). Mahwah, NJ: Erlbaum.

Liu, Y., & O'Halloran, K. L. (2009). Intersemiotic texture: Analyzing cohesive devices between language and images. *Social Semiotics, 19*(4), 367–388.

Martin, J. R. (2007, September). *Intermodal reconciliation: Mates in arms.* Plenary address at the ASFLA Conference, University of New England, Armidale.

Martin, J. R. (2000). Beyond exchange: APPRAISAL systems in English. In S. Hunston & G. Thompson (Eds.), *Evaluation in text: Authorial stance and the construction of discourse* (pp. 142–175). Oxford: Oxford University Press.

Martin, J. R., & White, P. R. R. (2005). *The language of evaluation: Appraisal in English.* Basingstoke: Palgrave Macmillan.

Martinec, R. (2013). Nascent and mature uses of a semiotic system: The case of image–text relations. *Visual Communication, 12*(2), 147–172.

Martinec, R., & Salway, A. (2005). A system for image-text relations in new (and old) media. *Visual Communication, 4*(3), 337–371.

Meinhof, U. H. (1994). Double talk in news broadcasts: A cross-cultural comparison of pictures and texts in television news. In D. Graddol & O. Boyd-Barrett (Eds.), *Media texts: Authors and readers* (pp. 212–223). Clevedon: Open University Press.

Montgomery, M. (2007). *The discourse of broadcast news: A linguistic approach.* London: Routledge.

Painter, C., Martin, J. R., & Unsworth, L. (2014). *Reading visual narratives: Image analysis of children's picture books.* Sheffield: Equinox.

Statista. (2018). Number of monthly active Instagram users from January 2013 to June 2018 (in millions). Retrieved from https://www.statista.com/statistics/253577/number-of-monthly-active-instagram-users/.

Stenglin, M. K. (2004). *Packaging curiosities: Towards a grammar of three-dimensional space* (Unpublished doctoral dissertation). University of Sydney, Sydney.

Tseng, C. (2008). Cohesive harmony in filmic text. In L. Unsworth (Ed.), *Multimodal semiotics: Functional analysis in contexts of education* (pp. 87–104). London: Continuum.

Tseng, C., & Bateman, J. A. (2012). Multimodal narrative construction in Christopher Nolan's *Memento*: A description of analytic method. *Visual Communication, 11*(1), 91–119.

Tseng, C., & Bateman, J. A. (2011). Chain and choice in filmic narrative: An analysis of multimodal narrative construction in *The Fountain*. In C. R. Hoffmann (Ed.), *Narrative revisited: Telling a story in the age of new media* (pp. 213–244). Amsterdam: John Benjamins.

Unsworth, L., & Cléirigh, C. (2011). Multimodality and reading: The construction of meaning through image-text interaction. In C. Jewitt (Ed.), *The Routledge handbook of multimodal analysis* (pp. 151–163). London: Routledge.

van Leeuwen, T. J. (2005). *Introducing social semiotics*. London: Routledge.

van Leeuwen, T. J. (1991). Conjunctive structure in documentary film and television. *Continuum, 5*(1), 76–114.

Zappavigna, M. (2012). *Discourse of Twitter and social media*. London: Continuum.

Zhao, S. (2011). *Learning through multimedia interaction: The construal of primary social science knowledge on web-based e-texts* (Unpublished doctoral dissertation). University of Sydney, Sydney.

Zhao, S. (2010). Intersemiotic relations as logogenetic patterns: Towards the restoration of the time dimension in hypertext description. In M. Bednarek & J. R. Martin (Eds.), *New discourse on language: Functional perspectives on multimodality, identity, and affiliation* (pp. 195–218). London: Continuum.

8 Emoji-Text Relations on Instagram
Empirical Corpus Studies on Multimodal Uses of the Iconographetic Mode

Christina Margit Siever and Torsten Siever

Translated by Hartmut Stöckl

1 Introduction

Communication in digital media, especially on *social media*, is today primarily of the multimodal kind. On image-centric communication platforms such as *Instagram*, *Snapchat*, or *Flickr*, images have come to play an ever more significant role and have led to a diversification of the types of *intermodal relations*. Jovanovic and van Leeuwen (2018, p. 687) aptly describe the situation by saying that "social media platforms are increasingly providing us with new visual resources for realizing both initiating moves and responses, so making it possible to replace words and sentences with emoticons, stickers, and so on". Despite the popularity of such "visual social media", multimodal communication in these digital media is still strongly under-researched in comparison with purely text-/language-based forms of communication (cf. Highfield & Leaver, 2016, p. 47). We, therefore, wholeheartedly agree with van Leeuwen's (2006, p. 154) claim that "in the age of 'new writing' it has become imperative to analyze and evaluate documents multimodally, rather than on the basis of the linguistic text alone, however important language is, and will always remain". There is as yet little research on the social media platform Instagram, especially from a linguistic point of view (cf. Kuhlhüser, 2017; Page, Barton, Unger, & Zappavigna, 2014).

Addressing multimodal communicative processes on Instagram generally, the present chapter specifically studies one typical kind of intermodal relation, namely, *emoji-text relations* (in analogy to *text-image relations*, cf. Bateman, 2014). Of course, other types of inter- and intramodal relations also occur on Instagram (see Caple, this volume), but we will address these only in passing. The chapter proceeds as follows. First, we will provide some general information on the medial characteristics of Instagram and its image-centric nature (Section 2). Building a foundation for the *empirical corpus work*, Section 3 outlines what we label as *iconographetic communication* and provides a theoretical discussion of the *semiotic qualities of emoji*. While Sections 4 and 5 briefly introduce the corpus and some interesting quantifications, Sections 6 and 7 will present primarily qualitative analyses of emoji-use on Instagram with a strong emphasis on emoji-text relations, outlining in this fashion major aspects of iconographetic communication. The chapter closes with a brief summary and outlook (Section 8).

2 Instagram as an Image-Centric Communication Platform

Instagram counts as an image-centric multimodal digital platform for communication, whose app allows use on mobile devices[1] and has been available for Apple devices since October 2010, for Android devices since April 2012, and for Windows devices since November 2013. Users with a valid account will continuously be shown a timeline consisting of various posts, which contain either a static image or a short video.[2] Initially restricted to a square format and requiring filter processing, images can now be created freely on any mobile device. Desktop and laptop computers, however, allow only for the reading of posts, not creating them. Being one of the fastest growing social-sharing communities with currently (June 2018) more than one billion users[3] (cf. Figure 8.1), Instagram came sixth place in an April 2018 ranking, after Facebook, YouTube, WhatsApp, Facebook Messenger, and WeChat.[4]

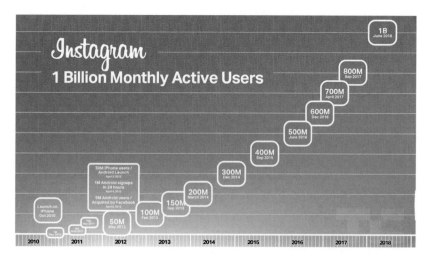

Figure 8.1 Numbers of monthly active Instagram users worldwide between 2010 and June 2018 (in millions of users).[5]

From 70 million uploaded images in 2016, the figure increased to 95 million images at the start of 2017, and is a trend that is likely to continue.[6] The gender distribution of Instagram users appears very balanced: in April 2018, in all, 50.7 percent of users were female and 49.3 percent were male.[7] Regarding user age, out of the Instagrammers in Germany at that time, for instance, 56.5 percent were between 13 and 24 years old, another 17.3 percent between 25 and 29, amounting to a total 75 percent of users being under 30 years old.[8] It seems, therefore, a likely assumption that the multimodal communication in our corpus (cf. below) has predominantly been produced by young people.

2.1 Communicative Characteristics of Instagram

What a typical Instagram profile looks like is shown by Caple (this volume), and it is clear that either a static or a dynamic image constitutes the focal point of any post, which may then be accompanied by an *image caption* and *comments*. These, in turn, may contain *hashtags* and *@-mentions*, both of which are hallmarks of Instagram communiqués. What is more, however, captions and comments frequently contain emoji, which may themselves function as hashtags. Manikonda, Hu, and Kambhampati (2014, p. 4) state that over 50 percent of all Instagram posts do not contain any comments. Compared with Flickr posts, whose images include comments in 74.5 percent of the cases (Siever, 2015, p. 346), one may conclude that the level of verbal interaction on Instagram is low. Even if images include comments, the communiqués are relatively short: the average comment in our current corpus contains only 44.7 characters (with a standard deviation of 57.1). Manikonda et al. (2014, p. 4) even registered an average comment length of only 32 characters. Again, in comparison with Flickr, comments there tend to be slightly longer: in a study involving two different sub-corpora, 95.4 and 55.4 characters were established, respectively (Siever, 2015, p. 347). One of the reasons for the comparatively low level of verbal engagement on Instagram could lie with its restriction to mobile devices, whose screens and keyboards are more cumbersome and time-consuming to type at. On the other hand, Instagram also shows relatively weak community building in comparison with other platforms. Whereas the social networking site Facebook[9] requires social and communicative relations to be reciprocal, *social sharing* sites usually merely require the following of other users, thus splitting the community into followers and following. Mutual following is, of course, also an option, but while on Flickr 68 percent of the users follow one another, it is only 14.9 percent on Instagram (cf. Manikonda et al., 2014, p. 3). Consequently, it seems that on Instagram the user motive of sharing outweighs the one of networking. For this very reason, Manikonda et al. (2014, p. 5) refer to Instagram as an "asymmetric social awareness platform".

2.2 Image-Centricity on Instagram

Instagram may be regarded as facilitating a prototypically image-centric form of communication. This is because an image constitutes the central part of any post, be this static JPGs or dynamic MP4-videos. The present corpus (cf. below), however, attests only 3.2 percent videos, which allows for the cautious observation that static images seem to dominate image use in Instagram posts. These static images are predominantly photographs; however, some texts, graphic elements, and emoji also occur in *pictorial function* (cf. Figure 8.2).

Posting content thus necessarily entails using images in the sense of uploading a JPG- or MP4-file and consecutively commenting on it verbally. Jovanovic and van Leeuwen (2018, p. 678) suggest that for the communicative platforms Instagram, Snapchat, and Flickr, "their design therefore facilitates the use of visual modes (photographs, illustrations, drawings, information graphics and all other pictorial forms) as initiating moves". Image-centricity on Instagram may and should be studied in a syntactic and semantic perspective. Nöth (2001, p. 2) specifies the syntactic relation between text and image as the temporal or spatial relation between the two semiotic modes. In terms of space, clearly on Instagram, images dominate. This is evident from how a user's timeline or profile displays the posts, namely, with the image visible, but only parts or none of the captions in immediate sight. If *captions* are displayed, they occupy only a little space below the image, so that any scrolling action primarily makes the images perceivable. Longer captions are automatically interrupted after one or two lines. It is the technological affordances of the medial platform that give prominence to the images and produce an image-centric layout. This kind of pictorial dominance affects the navigation through the posts that is determined and led by the images.

Whether or not the semantic relation of text and image in a given Instagram communiqué is image-centric, after all, depends on which semiotic mode plays the central semantic role, that is, whether or not it is the image that conveys the major part of the message. Besides such

Figure 8.2 Various types of communiqués on Instagram: (a) photograph, (b) photo + text + emoji, (c) photo + text, (d) graphics + text, (e) text only.

text-image relations as discrepancy, contradiction, or redundancy, which seems to bear little relevance to image-centricity, Nöth (2001, p. 3) distinguishes between dominance and complementarity. These two types of text-image relations are united by the fact that in this case the information is deployed in both semiotic modes and needs to be integrated. While complementarity requires a balance between the modes, in dominance one mode takes center stage, that is, either "dominance of the picture" or "dominance of the text" (Nöth, 2001, p. 3). Barthes (1977, p. 38) in this regard talks about "text supporting image ('anchorage')" versus "image supporting text ('illustration')" (Martinec & Salway, 2005, p. 343). In order for an analysis of Instagram-posts to use those categories for distinguishing between text- or image-centricity, they would first need to be operationalized (cf. Caple, 2013, Chapters 5 and 6).

The present chapter, however, puts the emphasis on a type of image-centricity produced by an intensive use of emoji. While initial social-web comments were predominantly verbal, an increase in pictorial signage can be observed in written communication since emoji were coded in Unicode. Emoji may not only be seen as image-centric due to their pictorial nature, this is also due to their text-structuring (in relation to verbal syntax and layout) and coherence-conducive functions, which will be described toward the end of this chapter. Similarly, van Leeuwen (2006, p. 139) states that a major part of today's communication does not rely on linguistic means for cohesion, but uses layout, color, and typography instead. As emoji are a typical feature of Instagram-communication occurring in captions, comments, as well as hashtags, and can even be superimposed on images (see Figure 8.2), Instagram communiqués are thus doubly image-centric: they put an image center stage and accompany it by writing that contains pictorial characters. Not surprisingly, and consequently, there is an increased potential for diverse inter- and intramodal relations on Instagram.

2.3 Instagram Stories: The Epitome of Image-Centricity

The enormous growth of Instagram can partly be attributed to its new *story function*, which had already been familiar from Snapchat and has been available in WhatsApp (under the name 'status') since February 2017. Stories entail a number of static or dynamic images presented and shared in a slideshow, only to be automatically deleted after 24 hours. This time limit proved to be a useful instrument of increasing Instagram's impact, as many users apparently did not want to miss any story and therefore ended up spending more time on the platform. Figure 8.3 shows a multimodal story about ice cream, which comes as the fourth in a series of ten images (identifiable from the top bar).

Figure 8.3 Sample image from an Instagram story.

Images posted in stories can be post-produced through the application of filters and the insertion of emoji, stickers, typed and hand-written text, drawings, hashtags, and music. For the very reason that many diverse semiotic resources may be combined, such stories seem ideal objects of multimodal research; they enable a whole host of intra- and intermodal relations. Stories also appear special with regard to their image-centric qualities: in contrast to the conventional Instagram-post, images in stories must be complemented by signage from other semiotic modes right in or superimposed on the image, not next to it.

Let us look more closely now at the image in Figure 8.3. It consists of a photograph which contains intradiegetic[10] text, that is, the name of the baker's shop selling the ice cream (*Bachmann*), but also extradiegetic text, that is, text added to the photograph in post-production (*they had the same idea: ice cream*) and the reference to the temperature 26°C, which Instagram automatically provides on the basis of GPS-data. Along with location and time, such indications form the meta-data contextualizing the image. The English utterance in the top-center position functions as a title of the image with *they* deictically referring to the queue of people shown in the image. *Ice cream*, however, is not part of the image – this verbal information thus is crucial for a full understanding of the image. In addition, the Instagrammer has inserted two extradiegetic images of ice cream. Further down, the question *Shall I cue up?* in Swiss German is integrated into the image along with possible answers *Yes* (+ Ice cream emoji) and *no, certainly not* (even though one cannot directly answer, however, one can reply to the story's image with a message). It is necessary for the recipient to read the ice cream emoji or the expression *ice cream* in the title in order for them to understand the pragmatic impact of the communiqué: should I queue up for an ice cream despite the long queue? The brief explanation of this example shows that analyzing such stories is likely to be very revealing for the study of multimodal meaning making.

3 The Semiotics of Emoji and Iconographetic Communication

Emoji-mediated communication is above all characterized by a blurring of the usual distinctions between writing and the image, as emoji characters can take over functions usually performed by writing (cf. Schmitz, 2003, p. 246). The emulation of written language functions by emoji has become so easily possible because, since October 2010, emoji can be rendered in *Unicode* (version 6.0), a standard for all written characters in all languages and sign systems of the world. This means that emoji can occur side by side with language characters and mix with them in lines and blocks of writing. This common practice naturally raises questions about the semiotic qualities of the emoji signing mode. Albert (in press) discusses the place of emoji in between words and images; he concludes that they cannot be equated with either, which is why he argues emoji are "a phenomenon sui generis somewhere between images and logograms". As Dürscheid and Siever (2017, p. 268) have advocated, one should refer to emoji not as logograms, but as ideograms. This is because in contrast to logograms, which represent a phonetic form, ideograms stand for a term or concept. It is interesting in this respect that emoji, depending on the way they are graphically signed in different fonts, may either be drawings or pictograms. Figure 8.4 demonstrates that emoji may be situated on a continuum between iconic and symbolic signs. It is only in their concrete contexts of usage that we can tell whether they are being used in iconic or symbolic function. So, even if emoji can be seen to function as substitutes of language signs, they must not formally be treated as such, but they clearly classify as schematic-abstracting pictorial signs.

This is why communiqués that mix emoji with images and written text must be characterized as doubly multimodal as relations emerge between

184 *Christina Margit Siever and Torsten Siever*

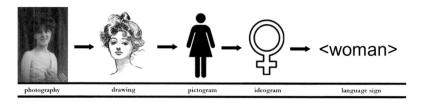

Figure 8.4 Continuum ranging from iconic to symbolic signs.

text and image and between text and emoji. Such a view is based on Jewitt's (2009, p. 301) definition of multimodality as "an object or text in which more than one semiotic mode combine as resources for meaning making" and singles out the Instagram post as a (doubly) multimodal text. If in such posts and stories the propositions distribute across both modes, we are dealing with cases of *semantic complementarity*. As emoji function on the same level as written language signs, we are dealing with a special case of multimodal communication, which we would like to refer to as *iconographetic communication* (cf. Siever, 2015, p. 281). In this term, *icono-* stands for all kinds of pictorial signs, irrespective of whether they are iconic or symbolic; *-graphetic* stands for written signs. Section 6 will address the analysis of such forms of iconographetic communication.

4 The Instagram Corpus

The corpus utilized in the present chapter was compiled in the research project *What's up, Switzerland*,[11] specifically in its sub-project B *Language Design in WhatsApp: Icono/Graphy*, which studies the use of emoji in WhatsApp communication.[12] In order to also compile a German-speaking Instagram-corpus, Instagram posts containing the hashtag #*heute* (German for today) and at least one comment in German were selected. A neutral hashtag was deliberately chosen in order to obtain a maximum thematic diversity of posts in the corpus. Based on the initial choices, further posts were selected by tracing the profiles of people who commented and picking their first image, and so forth.[13] In this fashion, only one post was picked from each user in order to integrate as many different users in the corpus. Overall, the corpus contains 6,142 posts by unique users, representing altogether 30,442 users who are either first post writers or commentators. Out of these 6,142 posts, 96.7 percent contained a caption devised by the writer of the post. The captions have an average of 340.2 characters, however, factoring in a standard deviation of 322. Generally, Instagram does not restrict the number of characters in the captions and comments, only the number of hashtags possible is limited to 30; however, comments may add new ones. This and the standard deviation allow for the conclusion that captions range from very short to relatively extensive, the latter, among others, conditioned by text in a number of different languages. Multimodality is already achieved by image-caption relations, but the corpus, in addition, contains a total of 94,152 comments, which yield an average number of 15.3 comments per dataset.[14] We may compare our data with a study by Manikonda et al. (2014, p. 4) which represents a corpus of 1 million unique users. By comparison with their study where an image was supplemented with an average of 2.55 comments, our 15.3 comments per dataset seems a high figure. However, we need to consider that due to our method of sampling, no datasets without comments were contained, whereas Manikonda et al. (2014, p. 4) feature 41.3 percent of posts without a single comment.

5 General Emoji Stats for Instagram

Even though *hashtags* are considered to be perhaps the most typical feature of Instagram communication, the number of posts containing emoji, namely, 95.9 percent, even exceeds the number of posts containing at least one hashtag, namely, 85.7 percent. According to a worldwide survey of Instagram, only 47 percent of all Instagram posts in Germany initially (2015) contained emoji.[15] The survey also pinpoints clear country-specific differences in emoji usage: ranging from a mere 10 percent in Tanzania, up to 63 percent in Finland. As our figures demonstrate, the rapid increase in emoji-use on Instagram, as discernible from Figure 8.5, continued in Germany. Figure 8.5 also shows how strongly emoji-use correlates with technological infrastructure. Whereas initially hardly any emoji occurred, their use rapidly increased when Apple devices made an emoji keyboard available. When Instagram was launched on Android devices, emoji-use figures declined because even though the number of posts rose, emoji-use remained on the same level, as an emoji keyboard only became available on Android devices one and a half years later.

To the best of our knowledge, Instagram features the highest rate of emoji-use: whereas in WhatsApp only every 43rd token represents an emoji, on Instagram every 34th character is an emoji.[17] In all, 77.7 percent of all Instagrammers in our corpus use at least one emoji; figures of emoji-use in the corresponding WhatsApp corpus are considerably higher: for German, there are 84.8 percent, and for Swiss German, 95 percent of users using emoji at all (cf. Ueberwasser & Stark, 2017, p. 115). It needs to be said, however, that the corpora are not fully comparable; generally, when compiling the Instagram corpus, only one post per user was collected, whereas the WhatsApp corpus includes several messages from single users.

Looking at individual parts of WhatsApp messages, emoji-use varies and is at a lower level: on average, 20.3 percent of the German messages,

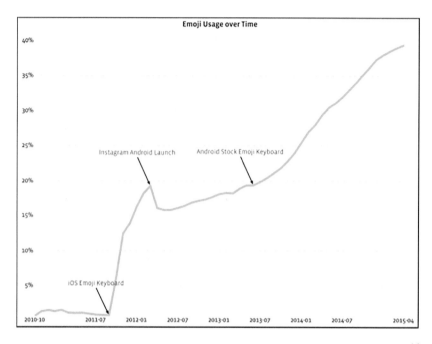

Figure 8.5 Emoji-use on Instagram worldwide (October 2010 to April 2015).[16]

25 percent of the Swiss German ones, and only 14.4 percent of the French WhatsApp messages contain emoji (cf. Ueberwasser & Stark, 2017, p. 115). On Instagram, by comparison, 69.6 percent of captions and 79.1 percent of the comments contain emoji. In all posts that contain a caption, an average of 2.6 emoji occur, whereas within the posts containing emoji at all, an average of 3.6 emoji occur. Comments overall contain 1.6 emoji, on average, whereas it is an average of 2 emoji in those post alone that contain emoji.

Figure 8.6 surveys the ten most used emoji in our corpus and affords a first glimpse of their functionality. An interesting emoji-hashtag correlation immediately emerges: the first four emoji all contain hearts symbolizing love, which corresponds with the second hashtag rank for #love.[18] Not insignificantly, perhaps, the like-button on Instagram is not a thumbs-up pictogram but a heart, which may have an influence on emoji-use. The ten most frequently used emoji feature five smileys as well as the person-raising-hand-emoji (including both woman and man raising hand). Finally included here are also two gestures, namely, the thumbs-up emoji and the ok-hand emoji. The first signals consent or confirmation, while the second may be understood, in this cultural context, as meaning okay. In the German-speaking world, it is also used as expressing praise in the sense of very well or excellently done.

Emoji-Text Relations on Instagram   187

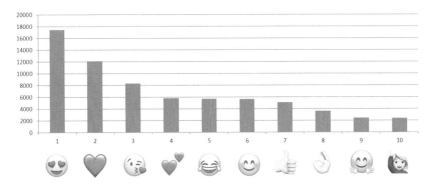

Figure 8.6 Ten most frequently used emoji in the corpus.

Figure 8.7 Ten most frequently used emoji in hashtags.[19]

The company *Curalate* has conducted a survey of emoji used in hashtags (Figure 8.7). The ten most frequently used emoji there are very similar to the results in our study Ranks 1 and 2 are reversed, rank 3 is identical. The emoji smiling face with smiling eyes, two hearts, face with tears of joy, and thumbs-up are represented in both top-ten lists.

In conclusion, we can state that the most favorite emoji are primarily facial expressions that express positive emotions such as love and happiness. Object-based emoji, however, are much more rarely used. It is only among the 20 most frequent emoji that such object emoji like cherry blossom (rank 11) or sun (rank 17) occur, which may, for instance, refer to the posted image. We will focus mainly on such object-based emoji in the following sections when we explore the functions of emoji on Instagram.

6 Exploring Emoji Functions – Emoji as Part of a Proposition

In this section we address the functions emoji may have in iconographetic communication on Instagram. Schlobinski and Watanabe (2003, p. 30) – to our knowledge among the first linguists to describe emoji function in an explorative study of Japanese text messaging – distinguish between what they called a modal function and a referential function. To add modality to a message means to modify the verb phrase. Similar to modal particles, emoji can reinforce or weaken the illocutionary force of an utterance or lend an utterance a subjective perspective. Example 5 illustrates this: the rolling on the floor laughing emoji at the end of the caption indicates that emoji-use in the previous sentence was felt to be funny. If an emoji functions to add modal meaning to a message, linguistic utterances are merely modified. Danesi (2017, p. 10), too, speaks of *visual tone* being added to an utterance. In all these cases, the resulting multimodal communication is text-centric. This is very different when emoji are used in referential function. Schlobinski and Watanabe (2003, p. 30) define these uses as cases where emoji that refer to extra-linguistic objects come to occupy the position and function of a noun. As demonstrated elsewhere (cf. Siever, 2015, p. 303), emoji may also substitute for such word classes as verbs, adjectives, and even prepositions, but they may also substitute for only parts of words, so emoji can become constituents of compounds (both in head and modifying positions) or form the nominal base in a suffix derivation. What is more, even whole syntactic units such as prepositional phrases can be replaced by an emoji. Finally, a whole set of emoji may work together to evoke a semantic frame and thus come to stand for an entire word and its concept. In what follows, diverse examples will be analyzed to illustrate the various uses of emoji found in the present corpus.[20]

6.1 Emoji as Nouns

Replacing nouns in utterances (cf. Examples (1)–(7)) can count as the classic case of emoji-use in referential function. The first four examples demonstrate how the lexemes *sun, pizza, airplane*, and *cherries* have been substituted by the respective emoji. However, as can be seen in the case of the pizza-emoji, another function is involved here, which will be discussed later – the emoji simultaneously helps structure the text and takes over the function of sentence-final punctuation.

1 *Oh, you really did make something delicious for a drink there* 🍷 🍒
   ☀️😊 *Sleep well and hopefully the* ☀️ *comes back again* 😊 ☀️
2 *Super yummy! I love* 🍕 *Have a great day!* ❤️
3 *All will go well on the* ✈️ 😊 *and such lovely legs* 🍒
4 *K- for* 🍒

5 With 🎩, charm and 🍈! ✌
6 The symphony was absolutely 🔨
7 Good 🍀🍀
8 By now the weather is at its best and we can leave the umbrella behind 🌂 ☀ we went shopping 🛍 and will enjoy a delicious ☕ and 🍰 ☕

Interestingly, in Examples (5)–(7) the emoji express figurative meanings: (5) alludes to the film series *The Avengers* [German title: *Mit Schirm, Charme und Melone*], and the melon emoji does not refer to the type of fruit here but to the bowler hat [German *Melone* = bowler hat; melon]. Such classic cases of polysemy become unequivocal through the use of the emoji or, alternatively, provided there is a suitable context, they may be used to bring out a visual/pictorial pun. Similarly, *hammer* in (6) does not refer to the tool but metaphorically stands for something great and fantastic. Likewise, the clover in (7) is not meant literally but clearly stands symbolically for luck (cf. Danesi, 2017, p. 59). By contrast, in (8), all emoji literally represent the object in question, but it is interesting that the two linguistically unconnected emoji *coffee/cake* evoke the co-ordinated noun phrase 'coffee and cake' [*Kaffee und Kuchen*].

9 My 💅 remain bright.
10 thanks we worked hard like 🐴🐴 and tomorrow is going to be a full day, too.
11 Sooo sweet your little 🐶🐶🐶!!! Good night 😘

Examples (9)–(11) demonstrate further cases of noun substitution, specifically those where nouns take the plural and thus tend to be replaced by multiple emoji repetition. The nail emoji in (9) already depicts more than one finger, thus making repetition superfluous, but in (10) and (11) horse and dog emoji are doubled or tripled. In (10), this is necessitated by the plural of the phrase, while in (11), even though the statement is about one dog only, the user apparently felt they could emphasize the illocutionary effect of the utterance by the repetition. It will be interesting to see whether a convention of emoji-use for handling plurals will evolve and stabilize in future.

12 How happy I was when the ♥-man came and took over the fun part.
13 This is the coolest birthday cake ever. Thanks to my ♥woman
14 This went straight to the ♥ and the lyrics I should take to ♥. Thanks😘

Examples (12)–(14) raise the question of whether emoji stand for the uninflected or the inflected form, that is, whether they represent the root or the grammatical word. In (14), the user must have assumed that the emoji represents the root, which is why they decided to add the inflectional ending (-en) for the phrase 'to take something to heart' [German: *zu Herzen nehmen*]. Example (29), later, shows an opposite case, where a phrase that requires noun inflection did not add it to the emoji. Both (12) and (13) additionally show that appending inflectional suffixes to emoji may either use hyphenation (12) or not (13).

15 Have a good ✶ day all of you.
16 Have a nice Saturday night and a really good ✶-day 🌞🌞🌞🌞

Examples (15) and (16) also exhibit different uses of hyphenation in the case of the compound noun *Sunday*, where the root (sun) was substituted by the emoji. What is interesting here is the varying handling of capitalization – against expectations, both users opt for capitalized *Tag* [day] rather than small letters. While the hyphen in (16) – in addition to the context of *Saturday night* – narrows down the interpretation to Sunday, in (15) the same emoji-language combination could be read as representing 'sunny day'. It is equivocal readings of emoji and their language-links like these that pose challenges to identifying and quantifying emoji functions. In the present example, the missing space and the fact that the message was posted on a Sunday make an adjective interpretation less likely.

17 Busy ✶a-let 📱[21]

The corpus even contains one example (17), where a diminutive suffix was appended to an emoji that represents the root using a hyphen. Variation in hyphenation, generally, is frequently found with compounds (18–23), and it would be revealing to see whether this is subject to historical change. In German, hyphenation in more complex compounds prefers the hyphen for those cases that are not yet (fully) lexicalized. A plausible hypothesis then would be to assume that hyphenated root-emoji linking is likely to decrease, a trend that might be facilitated by an increase in iconographetic communication and its growing naturalness in daily use.

18 *This looks like a party for two* 🎉🎊🎁🎈 *♥lichen Glück✶wunsch on your wedding anniversary my Schnubbel✶ be embraced* 🤗 *and* ♥*ed* 🌞🌞🌞♥🌸[22]
19 *Have a great weekend with your loved ones and make yourselves really comfortable in this* ✶*weather* ☺ *will we perhaps fire up the stove for the first time?* 😊*.*
20 *I'll book such a flight to Costa Rica*✶*for us with the Visa*▬ *right away*
21 *Good morning dear [Christian name]! Be successful dear [Christian name] in your first day and in between a* ☕*-break will always be a good idea.* ✶♥☺
22 *Protein-milk*🥛 *with* 🍌 *-puree*
23 *Good m*♥*rning, my sweetheart! Magnificent* 🌅 *Set! Have a good start to the new week!* 🌞

Examples (18–23) demonstrate that different elements of compounds may be substituted by emoji. In *Schnubbel*🐷, the head noun refers a person called Bine (short for Sabine) and thus helps constitute a word or visual play. ☀weather (19) and ☕-break (21) represent the type where the emoji substitutes for the modifier, whereas in Visa💳 (20) the opposite case of an emoji replacing the head noun can be seen at work. Complex compounds, such as 'Haftpflicht-Versicherungsgesellschaft' [personal liability insurance company], are often spelled with at least one hyphen for better legibility. Examples (22) and (23) show similar complex compounds: 🥕-🍆-puree (hyphenated) and ✨set (without hyphen) (the dizzy emoji and the glitter emoji are interchangeably used here.). In (18), we encounter an emoji linking modifier and head noun (Glück🍀wunsch [literally: luck + wish]), creating semantic redundancy as the clover leaf symbolically represents good luck.

6.2 *Emoji as Verbs and Adjectives*

The last example (18) also contains another interesting case of emoji being inflected – heart + en-infinitive verb suffix [German *herzen*]. Other uses (24–26), however, suggest that verbs are being fully realized by emoji as in (24), where the heart metonymically and symbolically stands for love. Since it was very effectively used in the 1970s in a campaign for New York (I ♥ NY), the heart emoji has come to mean 'love' in numerous contexts (cf. Schmitz, 2011, p. 80).

24 *I ♥ you favorite […]* ♥👯
25 *½ a bunch of parsley (as you like up to) 1 bunch of coriander (I ♥ coriander 🌿).*
26 *am very late already ☺ have to dash, to still drink ☕ and* 🚿 *…*

In (26), the last emoji represents the verb 'to shower', whereas the remaining emoji are either substitutions of nouns ('coffee') or, as the smiley, add modal meaning to the utterance, function as a punctuation mark, and signal syntactic structure.

27 *Thanks to German Rail my last night was once again really* 💩*, this morning made it all worse, when I woke up ill.*
28 *My 1.* 🚗 *was a Mini mayfair 1989. Will get my 3. today and in between I drove something else. But this go-kart feeling: simply* 🆒😋

Adjectives are realized by emoji comparatively less frequently. In (27), the pile-of-poo emoji represents the adjective 'shitty'; in (28), the cool button is used instead of the adjective 'cool'. What is more frequent, however, is to express morphological parts of adjective meaning through emoji.

29 ♥*a lovely good morning and a good start to the new week*♥ *I would like to* ♥*-ily thank you for all the many, kind comments und direct messages, you are all so nice and kind, I wouldn't want to miss you anymore!!* ♥*After the holidays I will have more time again than only sharing out* ♥*!!*
30 *good morning* ☺☺☺☺ *a fine* ☀*y Sunday in the North*♥
31 ☺☀ *a good morning* ☺ *wish you a beautiful* ☀☀*y Sunday* ☺☀☺☀☀☺
32 ☺ *yes today Berlin too is nice and* ☀☀☀*y simply beautiful* ♥☺♥

Whereas (29) shows another case of hyphenated adjective suffix appending, that is, ♥-ily, (30)–(32) realize the adjective 'sunny' by putting the emoji in the base-of-derivation function, with the type and number of the emoji varying.

33 *The apple-related quality* 😂 *can be seen clearly, the difference is too big not to be noticed* 👆 *and yet Frieda was* 🐽*-sweet* 😂😂😂

In (33), the prefix-like intensifier 'sau' (meaning [very/damn]) in the adjective 'sausüß' [very sweet] is expressed through the pig nose emoji. Beyond the morphological structure of the emoji-text relation, this example raises the interesting question of how users utilize versions of emoji (e.g., pig, pig-face, pig-nose). Also, it is relevant to note that the face-with-tears-of-joy emoji does not, as in many other cases, relate to a whole utterance but to a syntactic phrase only, namely, *apple-related quality*. This expression also appears in the caption of the post as *apple-related image quality*, and it seems likely that the person writing intends to mock this linguistic coinage (apple-related most likely relates to the brand *Apple*).

6.3 Emoji for Semantic Frames

In order to represent rather abstract concepts, users often employ a combination of many emoji capable of evoking an entire semantic frame. Ziem (2014, p. 2) defines frames as "conceptual knowledge units that linguistic expressions evoke", and he goes on to explain that

> language users call up these frames from their memories to grasp the meaning of a linguistic expression. Accordingly, knowing what an expression means and how it is to be used means having a certain cognitive structure at one's disposal that is conventionally associated with an expression. (Ziem, 2014, p. 2)

34 *Dear [Christian name], we're especially going to ElPampa (to the Allgäu) so that our kids and us can experience* 🏔☀🐄🐴🐷🐔🐑🌲🌳

The lemma 'nature' in the Duden (2012) contains the following definition: "totality of all plants, animals, waters and stones as part of the earth's surface or a particular region". In (34), the emoji used depict almost all of these aspects (stones, animals, plants, weather), thus cumulatively representing 'nature'.

35 🗿🐌🌱
36 *Have a wonderful* 👰🤵💍💒
37 *All the best* ♥️👰💍🤵😘*, from me, too*

Examples (35–37) relate to the 'wedding' frame; in (35), for instance, the three emoji constitute the caption and symbolize bride (bride with veil), bridegroom (top hat), and wedlock (ring), respectively. It is interesting that the hashtag #nowordsneeded specifically alludes to the emoji-only caption, while, nevertheless, other hashtags (i.e., #weddingday, #hochzeitstag) have been added to contextualize the caption and the image itself, which, in turn, contains text (wedding day) and many hearts. In (36), the emoji specify the nature of the day that the caption refers to as having arrived (the big day has come). In this post, whose emoji-comment interestingly has not been integrated into the syntactic structure of the elliptic utterance, image, hashtag, and caption help to cue the reader into the wedding frame. In (37), a post about the first wedding anniversary of a couple is similar in its adoption of the frame-semantic principle. However, there is variation in the use of emoji: man in tuxedo instead of top hat, and heart emoji signifying a marriage based on love. The utterance-final emoji face blowing a kiss may well be interpreted as having a modal function. The sequence of emoji from heart to bridegroom may also be read as standing for a prepositional phrase (*All the best from me, too, to your wedding anniversary*).

6.4 Emoji Standing in for Prepositional Phrases

Examples (38) and (39) also demonstrate cases where emoji may plausibly be interpreted as representing a prepositional phrase.

38 *Today, I will go to Berlin on the spur of the moment* ✈️
39 *Good morning, dear [Christian name]* 💕 *@30758************ and dear [Christian name]* 💕 *@19586************* 😘💕 *... my mum* 👵*went back home again* 🏠🚗💨

In (38), the airplane emoji may safely be read as 'on the plane'. In (39), things are slightly more complex: the combination of house, car, and dashing-away emoji can, on the one hand, be interpreted as an illustration of 'going home', which would produce a semantic relation of redundancy. On the other hand, there is an element of semantic complementarity involved as the car emoji specifies the type of 'going', which means it may likely be read as 'in the car'.

6.5 Emoji as a Substitute for Complex Propositions

Example (40) shows a posting along with a fragment of the corresponding caption; (41) and (42) are comments relating to this post. The caption (40) starts with an image title in caps framed by two crystal ball emoji, which is then extended after the dots. The caption makes it clear that the image had already been taken a weak ago, which is why it cannot relate to the weather but rather alludes to the practice of clairvoyance with the help of crystal balls.

40 Usr1288: 🔮 *A LOOK THROUGH THE BALL* 🔮 *[…] does not promise anything good* 🔮☂ *weather-wise today …*
41 Usr4381: ☁☀ *Morrrning* ☁☀ *have a good Tuesday* ☀ *and all the same* ☔ *we'll have the* ☀ *in our hearts*
42 Usr15672: @Usr1288 *Morning!* ☀ *Hope your weather is nicer …* ☁☁☁☁☁☂

Interestingly, the reply (41) to the statement made in Example (40) may be paraphrased as: 'It doesn't matter how bad (and rainy) the weather is going to be, we have the sun in our hearts'. The second reply (42) finally expresses the entire proposition with the help of emoji; the writer chose a number of cloud-emoji (including the sun-behind-cloud) plus the closed umbrella emoji. The latter utterance-final emoji refers back to the opened umbrella used before construing the proposition that, thanks to the weather situation described, umbrellas need not be opened. The iconographetic statement made would thus be: 'I hope it will not rain'. The word 'rain', even though a central theme in this posting, is not used once.

6.6 Limits of Emoji Interpretation

A number of our examples have already indicated that interpreting emoji is not always easy and unequivocal; linguistic criteria alone are not sufficient in the analysis. In any analysis, it is paramount not to generally equate emoji with words or word classes, but instead to enquire into exactly how propositional content and pragmatic functions are expressed through the multimodal interrelation between text and emoji.

43 Usr3348: *I wish you a wonderful Thursday and a lot of sun* ☀ *perhaps today will be better* ♥☺♥☺♥
44 Usr4376: *Good morning* ☀ *I wish you a nice* ☀ *Thursday* ☺☀♥

Examples (43) and (44) are comments by two different users on the same posting who do not refer to one another. They show that emoji-use to illustrate statements is a typical pattern and raises non-trivial questions of their interpretation. The first comment (43) uses a sun emoji, which is used to structure the utterance as this is also the case with the coffee cup emoji in Example (44). In the second comment (44), the sun emoji in front of 'Thursday' might be plausibly interpreted as the adjective 'sunny', but it may be an equally adequate interpretation to view it as a means to structure the utterance or, alternatively also, to specify 'nice Thursday'. As emoji interpretation faces a number of problems, further research would do well to integrate interviews with users in order to ascertain which functions emoji are intended to perform and how they are actually understood.

7 Emoji-Functions: 'Grapho-Stylistics', Semantics, Pragmatics, and Utterance Structuring

Emoji may not only be used as parts of propositions but can also perform independently. Apart from the modal function already mentioned, they can function as allographs, cohesive devices, deictic elements, structuring devices, as hashtags, and as a way of specifying a statement. The following sections will explain these functions with the help of selected examples.

7.1 Emoji as Allographs

Over and above substituting emoji for lexical and syntactic units, they may be used as allographs for individual letters. As Examples (45–48) show, the emoji are in some way more or less graphically similar to the letter they substitute (e.g., sooooo great a photo, cf. (46); wooow, (45)). What is more, semantic relations can be established between the allograph and the lexical environment, as in Example (47), where 'happy t☺t' stands for 'happy tongue out Tuesday', with the tongue emoji filling in for the grapheme 'o' in *out* and at the same time relating to 'tongue'.

45 W   w
46 S☺☺☺☺☺ T☺LLES (great) 🌿🌸🍃🌱🌱PHOTO 🌿💚 LIZZIE 🍃💚 Good weekend 🌸🌺🌺🍃
47 Happy t☺t
48 ☀ g☺☺d m☀rning, dear ones ☺☺☺ ... it's 'bip on' today 📅 so we can fortify ourselves 🍞☕🥐 before we take a walk ☺☺☺! Not for nothing do we say 🍎☺: "an apple 🍎 a day keeps the doctor 👨‍⚕️💊 away!!!" ... 💚 ROSALIE 💚 and I ... will be spending the rest of the day ☀ making preparations 🎂🎉 for papa-bear's 🐻🎂 birthday 🎁! [...]

In Example (48), the phrase 'good morning' makes use of the coffee cup emoji for the obvious reason that many people's mornings are characterized by this drink. The apple emoji in 'morning', however, points to the rest of the text: the posted image shows a child who has just eaten an apple (the apple itself is not shown, only the bib). The caption talks about fortifying oneself, alluding to the proverb 'an apple a day keeps the doctor away', with context thus providing an appropriate reading of the image. Apart from the allographic use of the emoji, the example is also revealing as many of its parts are illustrated with suitable emoji. This kind of consistent illustration or decoration of the verbal text may be seen as a subgroup of the modal function because the partial semantic redundancy reinforces the illocution of the message.

7.2 Emoji as Semantic Specifiers

Emoji may not only reinforce a message, they may also specify it. Whereas the car emoji in (49) seems a mere decoration of the noun 'Vollgas' [full blast], the racing car further down in the reply to the utterance is used for specifying the intended meaning, resulting in some kind of a pictorial joke.

49 Usr1488: *All these things have their place in life, each one at a time. Where there's no peace, there's no full blast 🚗 Usr1487: @Usr1488 quite right! Here we go, I'll lend you my 🏎️ 😊*
50 *After the first onset of winter 🌨️ the animals 🐂🐄🐏 were driven from their alpine pastures here at the Haimingerberg. [...]*

In Example (50), communicators talk about animals being driven from their pastures and accompany this by emoji of ox, cow, and ram. This could either be seen as a mere decorative function, but may also be viewed as specifying which types of animals were driven down into the valley, in this case cows and sheep, and not goats, perhaps.

51 *Good morning [Christian name], how sweet the two 🐺🐺 nice Friday 😊😊🐺🐺*

Example (51) is a comment on a picture showing two cats, and while both emoji clearly refer to the photo, the wolf-face emoji was chosen twice even though 10 cat emoji would have been available. It remains in the dark whether by mistake the wrong emoji was picked or whether the user intentionally and ironically opted for the wolf to refer to the cats.[23] Finally, it should be clear that not every concept or object (in the widest sense) can be depicted using emoji. Even though the Unicode Consortium annually adopts new emoji, they can never do full justice to the world's complexity.

7.3 Emoji Functioning as Cohesive Devices

As Examples (52) and (53) demonstrate, emoji can also be used in order to build cohesion between two parts of text.

52 *That's where I'd like to live!* 🏠
53 *haha, that's right* ⏰⏰⏰ *@Usr13553*

The comment in (52) relates to a posting that showed the watercolor of a house, and the house emoji, together with the local adverb 'that's where/there', points to that very house. The local adverb alone can function as a deictic element, but the house emoji is a backward reference to the pictorial house in the emoji. Example (53) is the reply of the person posting the image to User 1, who had written: *I'm curious to see the new solution & good luck ... the clock is ticking.* The reply features the @-mention that states what the writer refers to, but it also displays three alarm clock emoji, which symbolically represent time passing and thus refer to the utterance of the other user. Here, emoji-use serves to take up the verbal statement of a previous comment. Generally, repetition – be this through text or emoji – is necessary on Instagram as another means (alongside @-mentions) to make clear which post or image users are referring to.

7.4 Emoji as Deictic Elements

Emoji can also take over the function of deictic elements, which may be seen at work in captions pointing to photos (cf. Examples (54–56)). Example (54) non-verbally points to a garden path a child walks on in one of the photos.[24] In Examples (55) and (56), it is a combination of emoji and adverb (so) that does the pointing to the image.

54 ✻*New paths*✻ *You can find new ways even in the garden* 🖼 *[...]*
55 ❤❤❤ *today I'm running around like this* 💦 ❤❤❤ *[...]*
56 *Exactly THIS* 🔝 *is what my diner looked like last night. [...]*
57 *really good image* 👆😊

Examples (56) and (57) are both comments on the same posting. The second top arrow emoji simultaneously fulfills two functions: it represents the indeclinable adjective 'top' and it also deictically points to the image in the elliptical sentence, which was mentioned in the previous sentence. In (57), a syntactic ellipsis is filled with the index-pointing-up emoji, which refers to the image.

7.5 Emoji as Structuring Devices

So far, emoji-use was discussed as either emoji substituting for text (in referential function) or adding modal meanings to it (modal function).

Two further functions shall now be discussed that especially serve structuring and orientation (structuring function) on sentence and/or text level.

58 Good morrrrning ♥● You look great ☺ Ease into the Friday ♥
59 Good morning honey ●♥ what a breathtaking image ●♥♥ wish you a great day ☺♥♥
60 Hi,hi ☺ had just commented on your last image ☺ but gladly again on this beautiful one: ♥♥♥☀Good morning little angel ♥☺♥! I wish you a marvelous Thursday with lots of sunshine ♥♥☀♥☀ Sending you a huge box ● ♥ full to the brim with kisses ●●●●

In Examples (58–60), the emoji function as structuring devices on the sentence level, that is, they take over functions of punctuation. Interestingly, the editors of the Duden were recently asked whether emoji ought to be placed in front or following the punctuation mark if it was to refer to the entire sentence. The recommendation given for complete sentences is to place emoji only after the punctuation mark, a practice analogous to footnote numbers.[25] However, as the examples demonstrate, this practice is not always being followed – instead, emoji are often used as a substitute for punctuation marks. This would seem to make good sense as emoji, just like punctuation marks, fulfill a structuring function. As emoji are a hallmark of informal digital communications, where correct punctuation is of rather secondary importance, it appears to make little sense to use both punctuation marks and emoji. The recommendation by the Duden, however, signals just how important emoji are in current communication.

61 Gesunder Apfelkuchen - Low Carb und super Werte. Was will man mehr?! ☺
    ● Rezept vor einiger Zeit bei @33616** gesehen und leicht abgeändert ☺
    Schönes Wochenende euch! ☺
    .
    🌟 70g Instant Oats / gemahlene Haferflocken
    🌟 1 Ei
    🌟 50g Magerquark
    🌟 15g Proteinpulver (zB Vanille)
    🌟 70ml Milch
    🌟 Süßstoff, Flavdrops o.Ä
    🌟 1 Apfel
    .

[Healthy apple cake - Low carb and great values. What else could you ask for?! [ ] [ ]

Emoji-Text Relations on Instagram 199

Got the recipe from @33616** a while ago and have changed it slightly [ ] Have a nice weekend everyone! [ ]
70 g instant oats | ground oats
1 egg
50 g low-fat curd
15 g protein powder (e.g. vanilla)
70 ml milk
sweetener, flavoring, etc.
1 apple]

Emoji may not only be used for structuring on sentence level but also help to structure entire texts. When postings are written in more than one language (cf. 61), the two language versions can be separated by a series of emoji. Also, as, unlike on Flickr, title and caption of an image are not formally segregated, emoji may conveniently be used to structure text within the text accompanying the image in order to increase readability.

62 Usr3105: #throwbackwednesday #glowcon #düsseldorf
Am Wochenende wurde ich (zum wiederholten Mal) darauf angesprochen, ob mich die Drogerien dafür bezahlen, dass ich ihre Produkte poste.. ☺☺ Die Antwort ist NEIN.
Fakt ist - ich interessiere mich (überwiegend) für das Thema #beauty und die meisten meiner Follower offenbar ebenso ☺ Ich poste Produkte, weil sue entweder für mich interessant sind oder ich davon ausgehe, dass sie für jd von euch interessant sein könnten.
Es ist immer wieder so n komisches Gefühl, wenn ich gefragt werde, warum ich Produkte poste und kein Geld dafür verlange. Es ist blöd, als wäre ich bescheuert und man hätte mich mit Dreck übergossen ☺☺
#lebenundlebenlassen ☺☺☺
☐☐☐☐☐☐☐☐☐☐
Блин, накипело немного.. На выходных меня в очередной спросили, мой ли это аккаунт или я пишу рекламу для магазинов. От таких вопросов я всегда прихожу в ступор. Понятно, что для кого-то инста просто что то типо альбома. Для кого то же это способ самовыражения и возможность общаться с единомышленниками. Да, я выставляю фото продуктов, но только потому, что мне это кажется интересным или мне кажется, что то из этого может быть интересным для моих подписчиков. Как будто грязью обливают.. Каждый раз, чесслово.. Надоело ☺

[Usr3105: #throwbackwednesday #glowcon #düsseldorf
At the weekend I was (yet again) asked if I get paid by drug stores for posting about their products [ ] [ ] The answer is NO.
For some people, insta is like an online photo album, for some it's an opportunity to express themselves and/or to exchange views. It's a fact that I'm (mostly) interested in #beauty, apparently just like most of my followers [ ] I post about products because either they are interesting to me or I believe they are interesting to some of you. It's always a strange feeling when I get asked why I post about products and do not charge anyone for doing so. It is stupid, as if I were dumb and I always get mud slung at me [ ] [ ]
liveandletlive [ ] [ ] [ ]
[ ][ ][ ][ ][ ][ ][ ][ ][ ]
[Russian version of previous part of the message]]

Sometimes emoji also function as bullet points in enumerations, especially in recipes when ingredients are listed (cf. 62). This not only increases graphic clarity, it also makes the messages more colorful in the sense of producing an eye-catching effect.

7.6 Emoji as Hashtags

A last function to be discussed briefly here is the use of emoji as hashtags.

63 *Pumpkin pasta casserole*⬤⬤ *#Vegan* ⌇*#Germanyde #pumpkin*⬤*#mienoodles#peas(GoodBio) #vegetable stock*⬤*#onion#garlic*⬤*#smoked tofu*⬤*#herbs*⬤*#soy oats cuisine*⬤*#cheese(#[brand name])* ⬤

One posting in the corpus, for instance, makes use of the hashtags ##⬤⬤ ⬤⬤⬤ and #⬤⬤, which exclusively consist of emoji, but combinations with letter-writing also occur (cf. 63). In the case of single emoji hashtags, as in #⬤, we may find a sensible emoji-based alternative here for multilingual tagging.

The *emoji functions* discussed in this chapter cannot be seen as an exhaustive description of the functionality of emoji. What we have described is based on our observations of the given corpus, and it is likely emoji are being put to different uses in other contexts by other users. Finally, we must pay attention to the fact that usually a single emoji may well fulfill a whole range of functions simultaneously (cf. Albert, in press).

8 Outlook

The present chapter has demonstrated that Instagram is an image-centric form of communication in two ways: first, as on many other social-sharing sites or photo-communities, images form the focal point of meaning making, and, second, communication about the image is also heavily image-centric itself. This is because – as we were able to empirically demonstrate here – Instagram is the communicative platform with the most intense emoji-use. Using German-language data, the study showed that combinations of emoji and text may substitute for nouns, verbs, and adjectives. The substitution may also merely affect morphological units smaller than words. The chapter has also shown that emoji on Instagram often perform in a structuring function. In addition, we pointed out that emoji enter into complex semantic relations with text and become part of the overall proposition of a message. The most frequently employed function of emoji, however, is to add and modify modal meanings of verb phrases, a function well known from the conventional ASCII-emoticons. In conclusion, iconographetic communication as discussed in this chapter can be called image-centric in the semantic sense, if the text message alone would be unintelligible without emoji.

As there are country- and language-specific differences in the use of emoji, future research would do well to carry out appropriate contrastive analyses of emoji-use in iconographetic communication, both from a quantitative and qualitative perspective. Also, studies comparing emoji-use on different platforms would be recommendable. Diachronic studies, on the other hand, could help ascertain whether or not emoji-use intensifies/changes or whether conventions have emerged and stabilized. The focus of the present study was on Instagram postings, but linguistic and multimodal research could certainly address other objects such as emoji-use in the genre of bios (cf. Example (64)).

64 Photos 📷 of an amateur 📸. The 🌍 with my 👀

It is especially the currently fashionable Instagram stories that would be a worthwhile site for multimodal research, as relations between text, image, and sound seem particularly complex in this genre.

Notes

1 The name Instagram is a blend from 'instant' and 'telegram', which points to the fast posting of images via a smart phone (cf. Kuhlhüser, 2017, p. 86).
2 Since June 2018, also longer films may be published on Instagram through IGTV (Instagram Television): press.com/blog/2018/06/20/welcome-to-igtv.
3 Source: https://instagram-press.com/blog/2018/06/20/welcome-to-igtv.
4 Source: https://www.statista.com/statistics/272014/global-social-networks-ranked-by-number-of-users.
5 Source: https://de.statista.com/statistik/daten/studie/300347/umfrage/monatlich-aktive-nutzer-mau-von-instagram-weltweit.
6 Source: https://www.omnicoreagency.com/instagram-statistics.
7 Source: https://www.statista.com/statistics/802776/distribution-of-users-on-instagram-worldwide-gender.
8 Source: https://www.crowdmedia.de/blog/instagram-nutzerzahlen-deutschland.
9 Friendships on Facebook are always mutual. However, since September 2011, one can also follow the postings of another user.
10 For the terms intradiegetic and extradiegetic text, see Burger and Luginbühl (2014, p. 180).
11 This is a Sinergia-project of the Swiss National Fund led by Elisabeth Stark (CRSII1_160714). Thanks go to the *Universitäre Forschungsschwerpunkt Sprache und Raum* (University Research Priority Program Language and Space) for providing the funding to compile a comparative corpus.
12 A parallel corpus was compiled to be able to compare the use of emoji in different digital communication platforms.
13 The method chosen has a disadvantage: As first images have only recently been posted, they will have generated only few comments, which are then taken up into the corpus. For example, an image posted in September 2017 initially only had 71 comments, while in May 2018, there were already 135. This means that our corpus ultimately represents only part of the comments that images may generate.

14 For technical reasons, only the first 40 comments of a posting could be fed into the corpus, which is why the statistics are only based on 63.134 comments.
15 Source: https://instagram-engineering.com/emojineering-part-1-machine-learning-for-emoji-trendsmachine-learning-for-emoji-trends-7f5f9cb979ad. It is not clear whether 'text' here refers to caption or comments, or perhaps even both.
16 https://instagram-engineering.com/emojineering-part-1-machine-learning-for-emoji-trendsmachine-learning-for-emoji-trends-7f5f9cb979ad.
17 The figures for WhatsApp were established in the current research project mentioned earlier.
18 In the present corpus, there are 400 occurrences of the hashtag #love; in 136 cases, these very same postings contain another one of the top-four emoji.
19 Source:https://www.curalate.com/blog/the-top-100-most-popular-instagram-emojis/.
20 All examples of posts and comments in this chapter are originally German and have been translated.
21 The German original 'fleißiges Bienchen' is closest to the English phrase 'busy little bee'.
22 A sensible translation reflecting emoji-use adequately is only possible in part. 'Herzlich' in 'herzlichen Glückwunsch' literally means 'heartily', while Glückwunsch contains the two morphemes 'luck' and 'wish'.
23 Depending on the operating system in use and its fonts, the style of the emoji differs.
24 Of course, there is always a semantic relation between a caption and an image, as it is the caption's function to point to the image.
25 Cf. https://www.srf.ch/kultur/netzwelt/neue-duden-empfehlung-der-duden-weiss-wo-das-emoji-hingehoert.

References

Albert, G. (in press). *Beyond the binary? Emoji as a challenge to the image-word distinction*, 65–79.
Barthes, R. (1977). *Image music text*. London: Fontana.
Bateman, J. A. (2014). *Text and image: A critical introduction to the visual/verbal divide*. London: Routledge.
Burger, H., & Luginbühl, M. (2014). *Mediensprache: Eine Einführung in Sprache und Kommunikationsformen der Massenmedien* (4th ed.). Berlin: de Gruyter.
Caple, H. (2013). *Photojournalism: A social semiotic approach*. Basingstoke: Palgrave Macmillan.
Danesi, M. (2017). *The semiotics of emoji: The rise of visual language in the age of the internet*. London: Bloomsbury.
Duden. (2012). *Das große Wörterbuch der deutschen Sprache* (4th ed.). Mannheim: Dudenverlag.
Dürscheid, C., & Siever, C. M. (2017). Jenseits des Alphabets: Kommunikation mit Emojis. *Zeitschrift für germanistische Linguistik, 45*(2), 256–285.
Highfield, T., & Leaver, T. (2016). Instagrammatics and digital methods: Studying visual social media, from selfies and GIFs to memes and emoji. *Communication Research and Practice, 2*(1), 47–62.

Jewitt, C. (Ed.). (2009). *The Routledge handbook of multimodal analysis.* London: Routledge.
Jovanovic, D., & van Leeuwen, T. (2018). Multimodal dialogue on social media. *Social Semiotics, 28*(5), 683–699.
Kuhlhüser, S. (2017). #fernweh #wanderlust #explore: Reise-»Erzählungen« auf Instagram. *Rhetorik, 36*(1), 84–108.
Manikonda, L., Hu, Y., & Kambhampati, S. (2014). Analyzing user activities, demographics, social network structure and user-generated content on Instagram [PDF file]. Retrieved from https://arxiv.org/pdf/1410.8099.pdf
Martinec, R., & Salway, A. (2005). A system for image-text relations in new (and old) media. *Visual Communication, 4*(3), 337–371.
Nöth, W. (2001). Word and image: Intermedial aspects. *MedienPädagogik, 1,* 1–8.
Page, R., Barton, D., Unger, J. W., & Zappavigna, M. (2014). *Researching language and social media: A student guide.* London: Routledge.
Schlobinski, P., & Watanabe, M. (2003). SMS-Kommunikation – Deutsch/Japanisch kontrastiv: Eine explorative Studie. *Networx, 31.* Retrieved from http://www.mediensprache.net/networx/networx-31.pdf
Schmitz, U. (2011). Blickfang und Mitteilung: Zur Arbeitsteilung von Design und Grammatik in der Werbekommunikation. *Zeitschrift für Angewandte Linguistik, 54,* 79–109.
Schmitz, U. (2003). Text-Bild-Metamorphosen in Medien um 2000. In U. Schmitz & H. Wenzel (Eds.), *Wissen und neue Medien: Bilder und Zeichen von 800 bis 2000* (pp. 241–263). Berlin: Schmidt.
Siever, C. M. (2015). *Multimodale Kommunikation im Social Web: Forschungsansätze und Analysen zu Text-Bild-Relationen.* Frankfurt am Main: Peter Lang.
Ueberwasser, S., & Stark, E. (2017). What's up, Switzerland? A corpus-based research project in a multilingual country. *Linguistik Online, 84*(5), 105–126.
Van Leeuwen, T. (2006). Towards a semiotics of typography. *Information Design, 14*(2), 139–155.
Ziem, A. (2014). *Frames of understanding in text and discourse: Theoretical foundations and descriptive applications.* Amsterdam: John Benjamins.

9 "And then he Said … No one has more Respect for Women than I do"

Intermodal Relations and Intersubjectivity in Image Macros

Michele Zappavigna

1 Introduction

Social media platforms are becoming increasingly visual (Adami & Jewitt, 2016), with images being an important means of both sharing experience and enacting social commentary. Many of the texts published on these platforms feature only a small amount of verbiage, presented either as an appendage to the visual image, or embedded within it as an overlay referred to as a *caption*.[1] This chapter explores a visual practice that has become prevalent in contemporary digital discourse: sharing *image macros*, a type of meme featuring an image with superimposed text. Image macros are an example of an image-centric practice since they require the presence of a visual image for the meaning making, often a form of humorous critique, to be realized. These types of texts achieve meme status through social media users producing their own versions, altered across particular parameters (distinguishing memes from virally shared images). Iterations of a particular image macro will typically involve changing the text that occurs in combination with the image. This text will often conform to a particular *phrasal template* (e.g., "And then he said" + reported speech). However, as is the case with the *And then he said…* image macro considered in this chapter (Figure 9.1), the image itself may also be modified within particular parameters (e.g., different images of people laughing).

Producing an image macro is "an act geared toward fashioning semiotic belonging", allowing users to rally around some shared value or stance (Zappavigna, 2012, p. 103). Using a specialized corpus of *And then he said…* image macros, this chapter investigates how intersubjectivity (Zhao & Zappavigna, 2017) is co-construed through visual and verbal meanings. Developing a system network for analyzing the quoted social media voice (Zappavigna, 2017, 2018), the chapter explores how these meanings combine to produce different kinds of perspectives/points of view. The aim is to expand *social semiotic modeling of intermodal intersubjectivity*, as well as to explore how political ideas are negotiated in highly intertextual ambient arenas.

Meme is a folk term for the "novel online phenomenon" whereby digital texts are mimicked, modified, and shared (Dynel, 2016, p. 662). These texts proliferate across online social networks and are particularly common on social media platforms such as Twitter, Instagram, and Facebook. They may be thought of as *microgenres* since they repeat visual/verbal patterning in predictable ways,[2] but are much more condensed than texts that have typically been termed *full genres* within linguistics (e.g., recounts and narratives (Martin & Rose, 2008)). Beyond digital discourse, memes include phenomena recurrently shared in social life, for instance, a range of faddish or 'catchy' multimodal phenomena such as "popular tunes, catchphrases, clothing fashions, architectural styles, ways of doing things, icons, jingles etcetera" (Knobel & Lankshear, 2007, p. 199).

Internet memes tend to be humorous, witty, or satirical texts, and typically make use of some form of intertextual reference (e.g., a popular phrase in a film) to make a comment on another domain of experience (e.g., politics). Thus, understanding Internet memes requires a theory of how intersubjectivity (relations between different perspectives) is intermodally construed. *Intersubjectivity* (as it pertains to visual texts) refers to "the possibility for difference of perspectives to be created and this difference to be shared between the image creator and the viewer" (Zhao & Zappavigna, 2017, p. 1). A major dimension of the discursive function of memes is managing (and projecting) these perspectives. This function is enacted in highly intertextual, highly visual ambient environments such as social media, where performing a stance about a social issue is often what is at stake. These environments are *ambient* in the sense that they foster not only dialogic communication in explicit interactions but also forms of communion around shared practices such as hashtagging and the production of memes where users are not necessarily involved in direct exchanges (Zappavigna, 2012, 2018).

This chapter will explore the semiotic resources involved in construing both visual and verbal perspective in image macros. This will involve considering how the image, the verbal text superimposed on the image, as well as the post in which the macro is embedded work together to make intersubjective meanings. Memes appear particularly amenable to expressing different kinds of point of view due to their ability to traverse contexts, allowing meanings made in one context to be applied in another context. The particular image macro that will be explored in this chapter is derived from a set of *And then he said…* memes (ATHS macros, hereon). These feature a caption in which the upper portion above the image introduces a voice quoting another voice (often a political voice) whose quoted verbiage is presented in the lower portion below the image. The upper and lower captions are superimposed on an image of visual participants laughing (Figure 9.1). As Figures 9.1 and 9.5 suggest, this is most commonly realized as an underspecified 'he' in the upper caption.

Figure 9.1 Google image search for "and then he said" (search conducted on March 22, 2018).

As the Google search in Figure 9.1 indicates, the image of former US secretary of State, Hillary Clinton, and US President, Barak Obama, laughing uproariously is one of the most common instances of this type of meme. This type of text proliferated in 2016–2017, around the time of the US presidential election and during the early term of the Trump administration (see also Figure 9.3). Image macros featuring this image typically use it to negatively critique this administration, and are an example of the kind of humor that tends to proliferate during election campaigns (Shifman, Coleman, & Ward, 2007). As Figure 9.1 shows, the same macro structure also features historical images of conservative politicians (e.g., former US President Ronald Reagan). These tend to critique right-wing positions more broadly. The amenability of memes for this kind of political expression perhaps arises out the fact that "the combination of static image and malleable text offers a simple means of visual-discursive political expression not requiring specialist technical knowledge or ability" (Ross & Rivers, 2017, p. 287), and able to be applied across digital platforms.

2 Previous Research into Memes

Investigating the function of memes in digital communication has been undertaken across the areas of media studies and communication, as well as, more recently, linguistics and multimodal discourse analysis. The focus has been on interpreting their social function and role in media ecologies, and also on exploring memes as a form of visual rhetoric (Davis, Glantz, & Novak, 2016; Huntington, 2013, 2016; Jenkins, 2014). When applied in Internet studies, the concept of a meme has been used to broadly describe "units of popular culture that are circulated, imitated, and transformed by individual Internet users, creating a shared cultural experience in the process" (Shifman, 2013, p. 367). Online memes are usually humorous texts, typically requiring knowledge of a particular context to appreciate the witty intertextual references made. They often transform something from its original context and apply it to a new context through forms of repackaging such as mimicry, or by remixing via digital multimedia manipulation (Hill, Monroy-Hernández, & Olson, 2010; Mitchell & Clarke, 2003; Shifman, 2014). For instance, a source text may be modified by substituting items within a visual or verbal template.

Most studies trace the concept of a meme back to Dawkins's (2006) original coining of the term *meme* to capture the idea that cultural units could proliferate via imitation in a manner analogous to genes. However, we might question the extent to which semiosis can be reduced to imitation, which is but one of the vast repertoires of choices available to humans as they make meaning. Indeed, some scholars have suggested that the meme is an impoverished concept of "the old semiotic idea of sign, in somewhat new clothing, and reintroduced with some bombast" (Kilpinen, 2008, p. 220) and that it reduced the role of human agency in communication and culture (Shifman, 2012). Scholars adopting a semiotic perspective have argued that rather than following the somewhat crude metaphor of virality drawn from memetics, memes are "better understood by the semiotic model proposed by Peirce" and thought of "as systems of signs with the tendency to take up a flexible, intelligent translational habit" (Cannizzaro, 2016, p. 582).

Memes have proliferated across a range of social media platforms such as Facebook (du Preez & Lombard, 2014), Instagram, and Twitter, and across a range of domains of commentary, for instance, politics and religion (Aguilar, Campbell, Stanley, & Taylor, 2017). Some studies claim that memes represent a new form of literacy (Knobel & Lankshear, 2007; Procházka, 2014). There has been a recent concentration of work considering memes in relation to the 2016 US presidential election. For example, the concept of *spreadable spectacle* has been used to explore the "heightened distrust, polarization, and partisanship" observed during this election where the *alt-right* (alternative right) movement enlisted memes such as Pepe the Frog to fuel this negative discourse (Mihailidis & Viotty, 2017, p. 452). Many of the memes that circulated were used for the *delegitimization* of a political target (Ross & Rivers, 2017). The two candidates were central targets, for instance, memes targeted at Trump sought to delegitimize him "on the basis of his assumed persona, his alleged personal affairs, and his questionable policies" (Ross & Rivers, 2017, p. 299). Memes aimed at villainizing Clinton have had a long history in American politics, and Trump and his surrogates created many new iterations riffing on his theme of *Crooked Hillary* (Kellner, 2017).

Knobel and Lankshear (2007, p. 207) suggest that in order to discursively analyze online memes, various dimensions need to be considered, such as the referential or ideational system involved in their meaning, the contextual or interpersonal systems involved in the social relations they enact, and the ideology or worldviews that they convey, in terms of the values and beliefs that they construe. From an interpersonal perspective, memes are generally "deployed for social bonding rather than for sharing information" (Zappavigna, 2012, p. 101). Knobel and Lankshear (2007, p. 218) propose taxonomizing memes in terms of their purpose, distinguishing between *social commentary purposes*, *absurdist humor purposes*, *Otaku or manga fan purposes*, and *hoax purposes*. The ATHS image macro that will be considered in this chapter appears closest to Knobel and Lankshear's (2007, p. 219) social commentary type, where "participating [...] marks somebody as being a person of a particular kind who has particular desirable characteristics and worldviews within groups or social spaces committed to critiques of power and inequity".

3 Image Macros

Image macros are a form of image-verbiage combination shared prevalently via social media. The term is believed to have derived from the Something Awful forum where a macro was a form of shortcut[3] that could be used to activate a default image. The caption text superimposed above and below the image in a macro is often rendered in Impact, Arial, or Comic Sans font, with bold white lettering and black outlining (e.g., Figure 9.1). In addition, it also often will include "Internet orthographic alterations" (Rintel, 2013, p. 257). Image macros may be produced by adding the same caption to a range of images, or by appending different iterations of a caption to the same or similar images (Davison, 2012, p. 125). While these texts can be hand-generated, they are often produced via a captioning tool (e.g., Meme Generator https://memegenerator.net) where the user manually enters the text and the tool defines the position of the words in relation to the image (above and below the image). Image macros seem to endure longer than other kinds of meme media (such as video), perhaps due to the ease with which iterations can be created via these captioning tools (Wiggins & Bowers, 2015).

Because of their humorous nature and the fact that the humor often hinges on the caption-image relation, image macros have been seen as a kind of visual-verbal joke (Dynel, 2016, p. 670). In addition, they often feature benign imagery such as cute animals, even when they are used to make a biting or insightful commentary on a social issue. One of the first, and most enduring forms of image macro, is the Lolcat (Miltner, 2014). These feature an image of a cat with an amusing caption and are sometimes referred to as *cat macros*. Variations of Lolcat memes have endured for a long time due to their wide appeal and ability to be used to comment on topics across many different contexts (Zappavigna, 2012). They are also part of a running joke that the Internet is meant for consuming cat pictures. Another popular animal macro is *Advice Animals* such as *Confession Bear* which features "a sad looking Malayan sun bear 'confessing' to something silly, shameful, taboo, or embarrassing" (Vickery, 2014, p. 1). All of these types of macros can be used simply for humorous frivolity or to enact more potent social commentary.

The ATHS macro in Figure 9.3 is an example of an image macro featuring a "phrasal template" in its caption (Zappavigna, 2012, p. 101). Examples of captions appended to the image of former US Secretary of State Hillary Clinton and former President Barack Obama laughing include:

> And then he said no president in history has been treated as unfairly as me
> And then he said no one has more respect for women than I do
> And then he said who knew health care could be so complicated!

Each of the aforementioned is a quotation of comments made by Donald Trump in his campaign and early presidency. These captions conform to the general phrasal template with the following structure (where [ ] represent customizable slots in the template, and the word in italics indicates the linguistic feature that can occupy the slot, where this is restricted):

> Upper caption: And then [*pronoun*] said
> Lower caption: [...]

Image macros often embed phrasal template memes in the caption in this way. A *phrasal template meme* typically consists of a frame that stays relatively constant, into which users can insert their own (usually humorous) iterations. Rintel (2013, p. 256) refers to this potential as *templatability* of memes, "a product of the human capability to separate ideas into two levels – content and structure – and then contextually manipulate that relationship". The lower caption of the ATHS macro is often some form of hyperbolic statement or a statement that casts the projecting voice (referenced via the pronoun) in a negative light by implying negative judgment, as we will see later. When posted to a social media service, a meme will also often be accompanied by a hashtag. Sometimes the hashtag itself will encapsulate the meme, referred to as a *hashtag meme* (Zappavigna, 2018).

4 Dataset

The data analyzed in this chapter are the ATHS image macro described above. A grounded theory approach (Strauss & Corbin, 1994) was applied, which involved using 'and then he/she/I/they said' as a search term to query Google, Twitter, and Instagram for examples of images incorporating this caption. This involved iteratively sampling instances of this image macro for the image-caption-post-tag relations summarized in Figure 9.4. Sampling ceased when saturation of description was reached, that is, at the point at which collecting additional data did not appear to modify the description of these relations (i.e., the description of the relations was exhausted). I then began to qualitatively consider how these relations could be integrated with the framework for considering intersubjectivity and the *quoted voice* in *social media* developed in Zappavigna (2017). This framework is described in the next section.

5 Voice, Perspective, and Intersubjectivity

The notion of *voice* is important to understanding memes shared in social media environments. The notion of a discursive voice derives from Bakhtin's (1986, p. 89) idea that "all our utterances [...] [are] filled with others' words, varying degrees of otherness and varying degrees of 'our-own-ness'".[4] Social media texts always have heteroglossic meaning as their starting point, as producing a genuinely monoglossic text is largely impossible in the ambient environment. A post always enters into a relation with the other posts (and hence other voices and perspectives) that are co-present in the social stream, and is always in this sense closer to 'talk' than 'text'. In addition, the voice of the user is always present in the text via the user profile, as I will explain later. As soon as some form of social tag is used, other potential voices are invoked (Zappavigna, 2018). This understanding of the heteroglossic nature of meme discourses is in accord with Dancygier and Vanelanotte's (2017, p. 591) exploration of image macros as "view-point driven multimodal constructions". These authors suggest that image macros are intersubjective in the sense that they depend on the viewer recognizing "certain sets of beliefs and certain frames, and also assume that viewers are likely to share the discourse viewpoint ultimately expressed by the whole construction" (Dancygier & Vandelanotte, 2017, p. 591).

Central to the ATHS macro is the ability to use both language and image to present multiple perspectives/points of view in the one text, and to find humor in various kinds of tension. While Bakhtin (1986, p. 120) noted, "infinite gradations in the degree of foreignness (or assimilation) of words, their various distances from the speaker", most theories of *point of view* and stance adopt some version of a primary/secondary voice distinction. For instance, Sinclair's (1988) distinction between stances that are *averred* by the author or *attributed* to a source is similar to Martin and White's (2005) notion of *authorial and non-authorial evaluation*, and to Hunston's (2000) categorization of sources into *self* and *other*. In addition, White (2012, p. 66) has noted that secondary voices are often dialogistically multiple, with the primary voice indicating

> a dialogistic stance on the part of the secondary voice". For example, "reporting verbs may have a double functionality of indicating both the 'stance' of the primary authorial voice vis-a-vis the attributed material and the 'stance' of the secondary, quoted source towards this material. (White, 2012, p. 63)

The next section develops a method of exploring these ideas of voice in relation to *quotation practices* in social media that are at the heart of visual-verbal meaning making in the ATHS image macro.

5.1 Projection and the Quoted Voice

The grammar of reported speech, or *projection*, is central to the ATHS macro. How quotation is managed in social media texts is very interesting due to the expanded meaning potential for quoting other people's material within your own post. For instance, platforms will often incorporate technical affordances that allow the user to republish other people's material within their post, for example, 'retweeting' on Twitter, 're-pinning' on

Pinterest, or 're- blogging' on various blog platforms. In addition, social media texts will often quote other texts without using any punctuation resources such as quotation marks, instead relying on the ambient audience's ability to resolve important cultural moments from either their observations of what has been happening in the social stream, or from knowledge of the relevant contextual meaning, particularly in relation to political or crisis events that are prominent at the time (Zappavigna, 2017).

Quotation practices on social media are part of a broader practice of negotiating intersubjectivity, that is, how different perspectives are managed in texts. The ATHS macro relies on intersubjective manipulation of multiple perspectives, and the ability of both image and text to "open up" or "close down" (Martin & White, 2005, p. 103, 110) the dialogic space available to different textual viewpoints. One way in which the perspective of other voices is managed in discourse is through direct and indirect quotation. While it might be tempting to view understanding quotation as relatively simple, to be interpreted only by resolving who is the source of propositions or proposals in a text, attribution in fact involves a complex discourse semantic patterning that foregrounds how well or how inadequately our models of discourse cope with the intersubjective nature of communication.

As semiotic resources, quotation and attribution can function to positively assess a source and a stance as valuable, or to distance the authorial voice from both the source and the stance. In the ATHS macro, the central stance appears in the lower caption in the macro structure and is linguistically projected as an indirect quote by the upper portion of the caption. The source is underspecified as he/she/they, without resolving what would usually be an endophoric reference. If the image macro conforms to the default structure, the projection is usually construed as an indirect quote, for example:

> Upper caption: And then he said
> Lower caption: who knew health care could be so complicated!

In terms of how the text is managing relations between voices, this indirect quote may be classified as assimilated extra-vocalization (Figure 9.1). Extra-vocalization is a concept derived from White's (1998) work on 'journalistic' voices in which he developed the systems of extra-vocalization and intra-vocalization as a means for exploring the heteroglossic play of voices in news reporting.[5] According to White's framework, extra-vocalization is where external voices are visibly included in a text, for example, through explicit quotation. On the other hand, intra-vocalization integrates other voices "as part of the author's own utterances, rather than as an explicitly external voice or discourse" (White, 1998, p. 127). White (1998, p. 124) identifies two further choices for extra-vocalization: *insertion*, where the external voice is inserted into "the text without modification or recontextualisation" (e.g., directly reported speech), and *assimilation*, where the external voice is "merged to some degree with that of the text" (e.g., indirect speech).

In Zappavigna (2017), I further developed the system of assimilation to distinguish between contextually abduced and co-textually abduced vocalization in order to account for the particular meaning potential afforded by Twitter as a communicative channel. Contextually abduced extra-vocalization implicates a source that is unnamed in the co-text through contextual knowledge (e.g., knowledge that a particular phrasing is an Internet meme). For instance, in the example shown on the network, Trump's utterance that "Nobody knew that health care could be so complicated" (from the image macro in Figure 9.3) is provided with no attribution. Instead, the audience must abduce the attribution from their knowledge of the political context.

On the other hand, co-textually abduced extra-vocalization is the case where the source may be inferred by being named somewhere in the co-text. The example shown in the network names Trump via a hashtag, though does not involve Trump in grammaticalized projection. In this case, the audience may infer a relation between Trump and the intra-vocalized material. The use of *abduction* as a concept here, relating to how sources are implicated rather than inscribed, is drawn from the suggestion of Bateman and Wildfeuer (2014, p. 183) that an "inherent property of the discourse semantic stratum in any semiotic mode is that it operates abductively: i.e., as a process of defeasible hypothesis formation" (Figure 9.2).

The other optional system considers whether the source is instantiated through metadata such as @mentions, retweets, or hashtags. It is the beginning of attempting to systematize how multimodal features, for example, interactive metadata and layout, interact with meanings made in the written verbiage or 'body' of posts. Meta-vocalization, a form of quotation that optionally coordinates with extra- and intra-vocalization, is realized through the use of mode-related features such as social metadata, for instance, hashtags, and channel-specific features such as retweets and naming accounts via @username. Meta-vocalization could be used to imply the origin of a direct quote by implicating a source, or it could assist in contextually or co-textually abducing the source of an intra-vocalized indirect quote.

5.2 Multimodal Projection

The projection involved in social media posts is not just linguistic, and not just limited to the 'body' of the post. It may incorporate other people's material re-published within a post and involve images (both created by the original poster or sourced from another user or resource) (Zappavigna, 2017). Returning to the example of the ATHS macro,

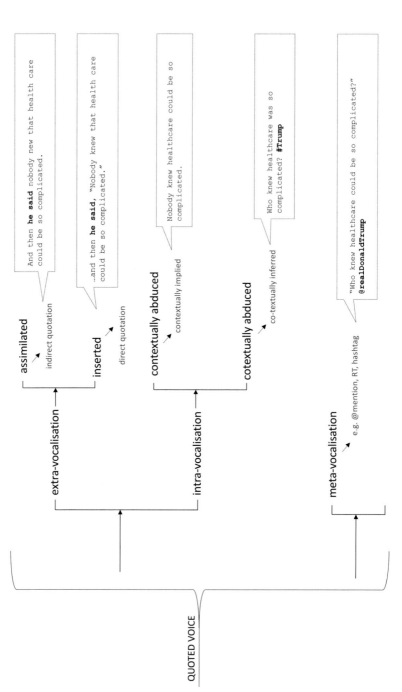

Figure 9.2 A system network for exploring the quoted voice in social media discourse (based on Zappavigna, 2017, 2018).

Intermodal Relations and Intersubjectivity 215

the meme itself, when posted to a social media service such as Twitter, can be involved in both multimodal projection and embedding in the sense that it be realized as part of the body of the post (and hence the projected discourse of the user identified in the user profile), as well as being part of another user's material that is re-posted inside the body of that post (Figure 9.3). Within social media services, the user profile has special semiotic status in terms of multimodal attribution and text production, occupying an 'anchoring' role, indicating that the discourse within the stream of unfolding posts is authored by a single user. In one sense, all of the posts that are published within the account are 'projected' by the user profile. Other people's posts as well as images (such as the ATHS image macro) can also be embedded in the post, creating various kinds of intersubjective relations, as we will see in Section 6. The extent to which this material is ambiguous in terms of attribution depends on the affordances of the particular social media platform. For instance, on Twitter, it is obvious when another person's tweet has been embedded, but less clear when an image is embedded. In addition, the extent to which the 'classic' image macro structure is realized depends on the type of post into which the macro is incorporated, and there may be instances where the caption is realized in the body of the post and not superimposed on the image, or, as in Figure 9.3, part or all of the caption is co-realized in the body of the post.

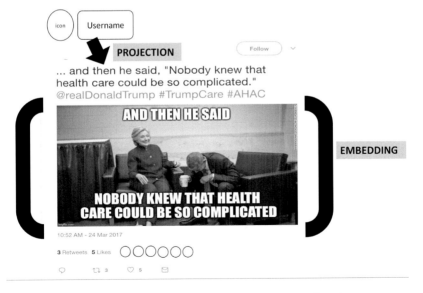

Figure 9.3 Multimodal projection and embedding in a social media post.

5.3 The Role of Images in Projection

Having laid out a way of exploring the complex terrain of linguistic and multimodal quotation in social media, it is now possible to explore in more detail the particular role that images can play in social media quotation practices. In terms of the ATHS macro, the caption is the projected speech of one of the represented laughing participants, although we typically cannot tell which. This relation is invoked rather than inscribed as there are no visual equivalents to linguistic "surface features" (Fairclough, 1992) (such as quotation marks) realized in the form of speech bubbles or other visual resources. There are two layers of projection in play, as the represented participants are depicted as reacting to the linguistic projection construed in the caption itself (discussed in the previous section).

6 Image-Caption-Post-Tag Relations in the ATHS Image Macro

Figure 9.4 shows the image-caption-post-tag relations in operation in the ATHS image macro, that is, the possible relations between the image and its caption, the verbiage in the body of the social media post, and any appended social tags (e.g., hashtags). The potential relations are numbered in the first diagram, and examples are provided to the right. The numbers in the diagram correspond to the analyzed relations:

1 *Embedding (echoing)* – the multiple voices managed within the image macro are 'embedded' in the social media post (see Figure 9.3 on embedding versus projection). There is an 'echoing' relation in the example of the stance in the meme, with the process of 'laughing' that is inscribed visually in the meme, being co-inscribed in the verbiage of the tweet.
2 *Reference resolution* – The underspecified endophoric reference 'he' in the image is made explicit in the verbiage of the tweet through 'you' combined with the mention of @realdonaldtrump used to direct the communication at Trump's Twitter account. If the reference is unresolved in the body of the post, this will be a text-intertext relation and rely on the reader's knowledge of the intertextual meanings in the context in order to make the text cohesive (see Section 7).
3 *Linguistic projection* – The verbal process (*said*) in the upper caption projects the verbiage in the lower caption.
4 *Visual projection* – The verbiage in the upper and lower captions is visually projected as the speech of the represented participants. This is invoked via the image macro structure, and we can only 'read' this relation if we understand the genre.
5 *Tagging* – The hashtag creates a heteroglossic relation with other potential tags in the social media stream. It simultaneously affords a relation both with the post (and embedded meme) and with other tags in the stream.

Figure 9.4 Image-caption-tag-post relations in a social media post containing an image macro and two examples.

The projecting clause (*and then he said*) in the right-hand example in Figure 9.4 is positioned within the body of the post, rather than inside the image macro, in contrast to the middle example. This realization in the body of the tweet appears to have become the more frequent realization for the caption of an image macro on social media platforms, and an example where the affordances of the platform influence the structure of the text. It has implications in terms of resolving the attribution: is the quoted material the verbiage of the user to which the participants in the image are reacting, or is it the verbiage of one of these participants? I will return to this type of cohesion/coherence problem at the end of the chapter. Whether the structural integrity of other kinds of image macros breaks down in a similar way will require a larger study of multiple types of memes.

If we approach the image-caption relations from an ideational perspective, considering how both language and image are being used to represent experience, a number of dimensions of meaning appear significant:

- Who are the laughing visual participants?
- Who is the 'he/she/they' realized as a projecting voice in the top caption?
- What is the semantic domain (field) referenced in the projected material?
- What is the relationship between the above dimensions?
- In what sense are these ideational relations cohesive and/or coherent?

In order to interpret the projected material as conforming to the particular meme type, the reader needs to infer that one of the laughing represented participants is the projecting voice in the caption. The visually projecting voice in the image may either be 'specified' (e.g., a readily identifiable public figure such as a US president or film character) or 'generalized' (e.g., unidentified people or subject positions such as professionals) (Figure 9.5). There is potentially a one-to-one mapping between the linguistic projecting voice and the visual projecting voice that the reader/viewer is left to infer in terms of a 'minimal mapping' (Zhao, 2010, 2011). For example, Hillary Clinton in the image macro shown in Figure 9.3 can be inferred as the projecting voice in the upper caption. However, as we will see in Section 7, the discursive relations involved can actually be quite complex to unravel and are not always cohesive (even if coherent).

Where the represented participants are not identifiable as a known public figure, they are likely to be interpreted as representing a subject position, across the types shown in Figure 9.5, allowing the text to play with meanings about what are views commonly held by this type of persona. For example, the first example in row 4 invokes a generalized subject position of a doctor or a nurse, playing on the reader's ideas about what these professionals must think when they administer a painful procedure. This kind of relation is also often used to parody social norms and common mindsets that may be attributable to broad groups

Intermodal Relations and Intersubjectivity 219

Figure 9.5 Examples of different types of visually projecting voices.

of people. It is also similar to the tendency noted by Dancygier and Vandelanotte (2017, p. 584) for certain types of image macro memes to employ "fictive" quotes "in order to typify characteristic behaviour". For example, in the *size doesn't matter* example in row 3 featuring laughing women, the indirect quote is fictive in the sense that it cannot be directly attributed to an identifiable persona. However, as in this example, it can be difficult to know what is being parodied: is it the laughing participants who hold these views or the fact that the view itself is worthy of ridicule? We will return to this idea in Section 7. By way of contrast, when one of the laughing visual participants is an identifiable politician, the quoted material appears more likely to be read as expressing the view of a single persona rather than of an entire subject position or group, although the quotation can be presented as emblematic of an entire political stance.

7 Coherent but not Cohesive?

While exploring the image-text relations in Internet memes shared via social media can illuminate interesting dimensions in meaning making, the problem of accounting for the constantly shifting intertextual environment in which these texts are produced is very real. The notion of *context collapse* has been employed in media studies to understand the author-reader/viewer relation, where it refers to the impossibility of a user being able to exhaustively assess, and attune to, the various parameters of a given context. This difficulty arises because the social media audience is largely unknown or irretrievable for the social media user as it may be both vast and anonymous (Wesch, 2009; Marwick & boyd, 2011).

Social media texts in fact seem to problematize some of the basic assumptions that we make in linguistic analysis and how we can apply linguistic categories that have been developed for studying older forms of textual production (Zhao, 2015). According to Halliday and Hasan (1976, p. 23), a text may be thought of as discursively coherent in two ways: "it is coherent with respect to the context of situation, and therefore consistent in register; and it is coherent with respect to itself, and therefore cohesive". However, there are ways that a social media text can be coherent but not necessarily cohesive, due to the flexibility that is afforded by social media platforms in terms of construing (and playing with) intersubjectivity.

For instance, consider the image macro in Figure 9.3 (depicting Barack Obama and Hillary Clinton laughing). This text is an example of a social media post that is coherent but not cohesive.[6] Resolving just whose perspective is being represented in this text is challenging due to the inherent ambiguity of the visual/verbal relations. The following is the verbiage construed in the body of the post:

> …and then he said "Nobody knew that healthcare could be so complicated." @realDonaldTrump #TrumpCare #AHAC

The embedded image macro also contains the following caption:

> **Upper caption:** AND THEN HE SAID
> **Lower caption:** NOBODY KNEW THAT HEALTHCARE COULD BE SO COMPLICATED

Consider the following "reference chain" (Martin, 1992, p. 140), incorporating both linguistic and visual participants:

> he – @realDonaldTrump – Barack Obama (visual participant) – Hillary Clinton (visual participant)

This chain is not cohesive since the 'he' is not referring to Barack Obama or Hillary Clinton. Instead, the reference (and hence the mockery) is directed at Trump who is not visually represented. One would expect a 'you' reference, since the text is addressed to Trump (via the mention @realdonaldtrump). As readers, we can recognize, however, that the represented participants are laughing at Trump, even though the text is not actually cohesive in strict linguistic terms. This capacity will have arisen through either exposure to a set of similar instances of this meme or to discourse mocking Trump. It may also arise with exposure to the image macro structure more generally as readers are socialized into being able to recognize the likely image-text relations.

Such a lack of cohesion is more obvious in the image second from the left in the top row of the table in Figure 9.5. This text has the following caption:

Upper caption: AND THEN HE SAID
Lower caption: HEALTH CARE IS A RIGHT!

The visual participant who is depicted as speaking (via an open mouth that looks to be mid-sentence, and a pointing gesture) is Trump himself, even though the caption is mocking Trump's position on health care. If we try to determine who the 'he' in this text refers to, we can either assume it is the visually represented Trump (and the image is showing us his act of saying), or it is a persona who is not represented (but we know from the political context that this is not a reasonable conclusion). In either case, the humor is 'broken' by our attempts to resolve the reference and make the text cohesive.

In social media texts such as those discussed in this chapter, some sort of ritualized dimension appears to be in play. The essential function appears to be performing a *stance* in which cohesiveness is not necessarily important, perhaps due to the larger textual coherence offered by the 'anchoring' affordance of the social media profile. This anchoring function means that all posts in a user's stream are, in effect, the projected verbiage of their user profile. Thus, all memes that are embedded within these posts relate back to the identity being constructed via the profile (as well as to each other). Add to this the multiple perspectives that are introduced via social tagging and the fact that other users' texts can be embedded within a post without attribution, and it can be very difficult to interpret in a stable way what is going on within the "cacophony of voices" that are realized in the social media environments in which memes proliferate (Zappavigna, 2018, p. 100). In this sense, what happens inside one social media post as a 'text' cannot be divorced from what is going on before, after, and in tandem with that post in the stream, and it seems to make little sense to think of a post in non-dialogic isolation. If we follow Zhao's (2010, 2011) minimum-mapping hypothesis to its logical conclusion, interpreting what is going on at the level of an individual post will involve determining what pushes a semantic bridge too far, such that it breaks the cohesion of the text's reference chain. However, if cohesion in not an important function, and posts can be coherent without being cohesive, the utility of interpreting image-text relations at this level remains to be seen.

8 Conclusion

This chapter has explored the meanings made in image macros when they are shared on social media platforms. The focus was on understanding the meanings made in the ATHS image macro as a starting point for considering what is a very complex semiotic practice. The image macros studied in this paper are an example of memes aimed at *delegitimization* that negatively evaluates a target (Ross & Rivers, 2017). Unsurprisingly, the ATHS macro has regularly been applied to Donald Trump since the 2016 presidential election, and can be seen as part of a set of memes originating at this time that sought to delegitimize Donald Trump "on the basis of his assumed persona, his alleged personal affairs, and his questionable policies" (Ross & Rivers, 2017, p. 299).

Producing and sharing memes of this kind on social media platforms draws on a range of visual and textual resources that are inflected by the affordances of these platforms as *semiotic technologies* (Zhao et al., 2014).[7] Accounting for this complexity has meant that this chapter has drawn on a range of theoretical concepts. In order to understand how image and text function in image macros, we explored the notions of voice and intersubjectivity to examine the way in which these texts use various multimodal quotation strategies to manage the multiple perspectives that they construe. This meant that we needed to consider issues of multimodal projection and embedding, both internally within the image macro, and in terms of the relations construed between the image macro and the social media post itself, as well as with social tags. I introduced a system network for exploring the quoted social media voice designed to assist in explicating these relations.

A number of image-caption-post-tag relations have been identified in this chapter that are central to the ATHS macro, and likely are involved in other image macros that incorporate linguistic and visual quotation. These were embedding (of the image within the social media post), reference resolution (of the 'he' in the caption), linguistic projection (within the caption), *visual projection* (between the image and the caption), and tagging (where the hashtag relates to the post and also to other tags). In exploring these relations, in particular reference resolution, it became apparent that the interplay of voices in social media texts is so flexible that it is possible for texts to be coherent but not strictly cohesive. This is because social media platforms prioritize intersubjectivity, giving users multiple ways to project and embed other voices in their texts and to associate their text with other texts in the unfolding social stream.

Notes

1 Note this use of *caption* is the term which proliferates on the Internet for the verbal text superimposed on the image in an image macro and is different to the Instagram captions explored in Caple, this volume.
2 They may be argued to have stabilized as a recognizable text type (or set of text types) since researchers have begun to consider how to automate their production (Oliveira, Costa, & Pinto, 2016).
3 A *macroinstruction* in computing is a type of shorthand used to enter large (often repeated) text.
4 This is related to Voloshinov's (1986, p. 103) suggestion that all utterances are necessarily construed with an *evaluative accent*, that is, they invoke value judgments implicated in particular ideological systems. The idea that

speakers and writers "encode their point of view" in any utterance they produce is also seen in corpus-based approaches to stance (Stubbs, 1986, p. 1).
5 These ideas regarding (what?) are a more elaborated and nuanced modeling of what Fairclough (1992, p. 104) deals with at the level of structural or typographic features in his notion of *manifest intertextuality* whereby other texts can be "'manifestly' marked or cued by features on the surface of the text, such as quotation marks" or be seamlessly incorporated into the wording of the text.
6 I am indebted to Sumin Zhao for pointing this out to me in our ongoing digital theorizing via text message.
7 A forthcoming special issue of the journal *Social Semiotics* considers social media in relation to the concept of semiotic technology.

References

Adami, E., & Jewitt, C. (2016). Special issue: Social media and the visual. *Visual Communication, 15*(3), 263–270.

Aguilar, G. K., Campbell, H. A., Stanley, M., & Taylor, E. (2017). Communicating mixed messages about religion through Internet memes. *Information, Communication & Society, 20*(10), 1498–1520.

Bakhtin, M. (1986). *Speech genres and other late essays*. (V. McGee, Trans.). Austin: University of Texas Press.

Bateman, J. A., & Wildfeuer, J. (2014). A multimodal discourse theory of visual narrative. *Journal of Pragmatics, 74*, 180–208. Retrieved from http://www.sciencedirect.com/science/article/pii/S0378216614001830

Cannizzaro, S. (2016). Internet memes as Internet signs: A semiotic view of digital culture. *Sign Systems Studies, 44*(4), 562–586.

Dancygier, B., & Vandelanotte, L. (2017). Internet memes as multimodal constructions. *Cognitive Linguistics, 28*(3), 565–598.

Davis, C. B., Glantz, M., & Novak, D. R. (2016). "You can't run your SUV on cute. Let's go!": Internet memes as delegitimizing discourse. *Environmental Communication, 10*(1), 62–83.

Davison, P. (2012). The language of Internet memes. In M. Mandiberg (Ed.), *The social media reader* (pp. 120–134). New York: New York University Press.

Dawkins, R. (2006). *The selfish gene* (30th anniversary ed.). Oxford: Oxford University Press.

du Preez, A., & Lombard, E. (2014). The role of memes in the construction of Facebook personae. *Communicatio, 40*(3), 253–270.

Dynel, M. (2016). "I has seen image macros!" Advice animals memes as visual-verbal jokes. *International Journal of Communication, 10*, 660–688.

Fairclough, N. (1992). *Discourse and social change*. Cambridge, UK: Polity Press.

Halliday, M. A. K., & Hasan, R. (1976). *Cohesion in English*. London: Longman.

Hill, B. M., Monroy-Hernández, A., & Olson, K. (2010, May). Responses to remixing on a social media sharing website. *Proceedings of the fourth international AAAI conference on weblogs and social media* (pp. 74–81). Washington, DC: The AAAI Press.

Hunston, S. (2000). Evaluation and the planes of discourse: Status and value in persuasive texts. In S. Hunston & G. Thompson (Eds.), *Evaluation in text: Authorial stance and the construction of discourse* (pp. 176–207). Oxford: Oxford Unversity Press.

Huntington, H. E. (2016). Pepper spray cop and the American Dream: Using synecdoche and metaphor to unlock Internet memes' visual political rhetoric. *Communication Studies, 67*(1), 77–93. doi: 10.1080/10510974.2015.1087414

Huntington, H. E. (2013). Subversive memes: Internet memes as a form of visual rhetoric. *AoIR Selected Papers of Internet Research, 3*. Retrieved from https://journals.uic.edu/ojs/index.php/spir/article/view/8886/7085

Jenkins, E. S. (2014). The modes of visual rhetoric: Circulating memes as expressions. *Quarterly Journal of Speech, 100*(4), 442–466.

Kellner, D. (2017). Brexit plus, whitelash, and the ascendency of Donald J. Trump. *Cultural Politics, 13*(2), 135–149.

Kilpinen, E. (2008). Memes versus signs: On the use of meaning concepts about nature and culture. *Semiotica, 2008*(171), pp. 215–237.

Knobel, M., & Lankshear, C. (2007). Online memes, affinities, and cultural production. In M. Knobel & C. Lankshear (Eds.), *A new literacies sampler* (pp. 199–227). New York: Peter Lang.

Martin, J. R. (1992). *English text: System and structure*. Philadelphia, PA: John Benjamins Publishing.

Martin, J. R., & Rose, D. (2008). *Genre relations: Mapping culture*. London: Equinox.

Martin, J. R., & White, P. R. R. (2005). *The language of evaluation: Appraisal in English*. New York, NY: Palgrave Macmillan.

Marwick, A. E., & boyd, d. (2011). I tweet honestly, I tweet passionately: Twitter users, context collapse, and the imagined audience. *New Media & Society, 13*(1), 114–133.

Mihailidis, P., & Viotty, S. (2017). Spreadable spectacle in digital culture: Civic expression, fake news, and the role of media literacies in "post-fact" society. *American Behavioral Scientist, 61*(4), 441–454.

Miltner, K. M. (2014). "There's no place for lulz on LOLCats": The role of genre, gender, and group identity in the interpretation and enjoyment of an Internet meme. *First Monday, 19*(8).

Mitchell, G., & Clarke, A. (2003). Videogame art: Remixing, reworking and other interventions. *Proceedings of the 2003 DiGRA International Conference: Level Up* (pp. 338–349). Utrecht: Utrecht University.

Oliveira, H. G., Costa, D., & Pinto, A. (2016, June). One does not simply produce funny memes! – Explorations on the automatic generation of Internet humor. In F. Pachet, A. Cardoso, V. Corruble, & F. Ghedini (Eds.), *Proceedings of 7th International Conference on Computational Creativity* (pp. 238–245). Paris: Sony CSL

Procházka, O. (2014). Internet memes – A new literacy? *Ostrava Journal of English Philology, 6*(1), 53–74.

Rintel, S. (2013). Crisis memes: The importance of templatability to Internet culture and freedom of expression. *Australasian Journal of Popular Culture, 2*(2), 253–271.

Ross, A. S., & Rivers, D. J. (2017). Internet memes as polyvocal political participation. In D. Schill & J. A. Hendricks (Eds.), *The presidency and social media: Discourse, disruption, and digital democracy in the 2016 Presidential Election* (pp. 285–308). London: Routledge.

Shifman, L. (2014). The cultural logic of photo-based meme genres. *Journal of Visual Culture, 13*(3), 340–358.

Shifman, L. (2013). Memes in a digital world: Reconciling with a conceptual troublemaker. *Journal of Computer-Mediated Communication, 18*(3), 362–377.

Shifman, L. (2012). An anatomy of a YouTube meme. *New Media & Society, 14*(2), 187–203.

Shifman, L., Coleman, S., & Ward, S. (2007). Only joking? Online humour in the 2005 UK general election. *Information, Communication & Society, 10*(4), 465–487.

Sinclair, J. M. (1988). Mirror for a text. *Journal of English and Foreign Languages, 1*, 15–44.

Strauss, A., & Corbin, J. (1994). Grounded theory methodology: An overview. In N. Denzin, N. & Y. Lincoln (Eds.), *Handbook of Qualitative Research* (pp. 273–285), London: Sage.

Stubbs, M. (1986). 'A matter of prolonged field work': Notes towards a modal grammar of English. *Applied Linguistics, 7*(1), 1–25. Retrieved from http://applij.oxfordjournals.org/content/7/1/1.short

Vickery, J. R. (2014). The curious case of Confession Bear: The reappropriation of online macro-image memes. *Information, Communication & Society, 17*(3), 301–325.

Voloshinov, V. N. (1986). *Marxism and the philosophy of language* (L. Matejka & I. R. Titunik, Trans.). Cambridge, MA: Harvard University Press.

Wesch, M. (2009). Youtube and you: Experiences of self-awareness in the context collapse of the recording webcam. *Explorations in Media Ecology, 8*(2), 19–34.

White, P. R. R. (2012). Exploring the axiological workings of 'reporter voice' news stories—attribution and attitudinal positioning. *Discourse, Context & Media, 1*(2–3), 57–67.

White, P. R. R. (1998). *Telling media tales: The news story as rhetoric*. (Unpublished doctoral dissertation). University of Sydney, Sydney.

Wiggins, B. E., & Bowers, G. B. (2015). Memes as genre: A structurational analysis of the memescape. *New Media & Society, 17*(11), 1886–1906.

Zappavigna, M. (2018). *Searchable talk: Hashtags and social media metadiscourse*. London: Bloomsbury.

Zappavigna, M. (2017). "Had enough of experts": Intersubjectivity and quotation in social media. In E. Friginal (Ed.), *Studies in Corpus-Based Sociolinguistics* (pp. 321–343). London: Routledge.

Zappavigna, M. (2012). *Discourse of Twitter and Social Media: How we use language to create affiliation on the Web*. London: Continuum.

Zhao, S. (2015). Book review: Christian R. Hoffmann, Cohesive profiling: Meaning and interaction in personal weblogs. *Discourse & Communication, 9*(3), 373–375.

Zhao, S. (2011). *Learning through multimedia interaction: The construal of primary social science knowledge in Web-based digital learning materials*. (Unpublished doctoral dissertation). University of Sydney, Sydney.

Zhao, S. (2010). Intersemiotic relations as logogenetic patterns: The time factor in hypertext description. In M. Bednarek & J. R. Martin (Eds.), *New discourse on language: Functional perspectives on multimodality, identity, and affiliation* (pp. 195–218). London: Continuum.

Zhao, S., Djonov, E., & van Leeuwen, T. (2014). Semiotic technology and practice: A multimodal social semiotic approach to PowerPoint. *Text & Talk, 34*(3), 349–375.

Zhao, S., & Zappavigna, M. (2017). Beyond the self: Intersubjectivity and the social semiotic interpretation of the selfie. *New Media & Society, 20*(5), 1735–1754.

Commentary
Reflections on the Relative Status of Image and Language

Carey Jewitt

The three chapters in the section offer an exciting and thoughtful reflection on the changing developments in image-centric practices and how they shape the relative status of image and language. As Caple notes, scholars working with the visual will agree with the essential incommensurability of image and language and the significance of the need to understand the ways in which images and words "enter into relations with one another". The chapters explore how these relations unfold across the use of a range of social media in new and different ways, which, as Zappavigna argues, are "increasingly embedding images and other visual media into their texts". Emojis – perhaps the ultimate form of image-centric practice, are, Siever and Siever argue, "not only image-centric due to their pictorial nature, but also due to their text-structuring (in relation to verbal syntax and layout) and coherence-conducive functions".

The investigation that this section provides is focused on a range of contemporary multimodal social media practices, with an emphasis on the relative status of image and language, and this draws attention to the changing and slippery boundaries between the place of images in news reporting, advertisements, magazines, social media, Internet memes, and the potentials of looking across media to understand this complex landscape. Caple's exploration of Instagram via captioning practices in news storytelling is valuable in the ways in which she unpacks how meaning is understood through the interrelation of texts moving beyond standard ideas of illustration, anchorage, and so forth. She explores the complexity of "intersemiotic comparative relations", where image and language may be viewed as semiotic reformulations of each other and lead to "experiential and textual convergence".

Across the chapters, the authors' reflections on image-centric communication platforms such as Instagram, Flickr, Snapchat, or WhatsApp resonate for me with the very early days of researching the impact of digital technologies on our communication landscape. In particular, Zappavigna's analysis of image-text relations in Internet memes shared via social media raises the "problem of accounting for the constantly shifting intertextual environment in which these texts are produced" and the evocative notion of "context collapse" connected with examples in my early work of visual and written modes (Jewitt, 1997). I found collapsing and blurring boundaries between visual and written modal resources, modes, genres, and their boundaries in the digital translation of written novels into a digital multimodal text (Jewitt, 2002), multimodal literacies (Jewitt & Kress, 2003), games and identities (Jewitt, 2005), and explored the ways in which these changing resources shaped literacy and learning (Jewitt, 2008). The chapters in this section collectively make a case for the communicative significance of the image and its relationships with language, and the need to diversify the types of intermodal relations that we both produce and consume. These continuities and our collective understandings serve to develop new directions regarding how modes interact and interplay across the multimodal landscape in ways that are significant for digital communication.

The visual landscape mapped by this book is a wild and exciting one, a place of renewal and change spreading across the media landscape of magazines, advertising, news, and social media platforms. The chapters point to different ways in which the visual is named and the importance of naming and renaming as a social semiotic process, a key point that Kress (2015) makes through his work within social semiotics. How we name the visual matters as it frames the lens through which we view the media landscape – and marks what is included in and what is left out of that framing. It is interesting for me to reflect on how the *image* is now productively stretched in this changing landscape to cover a range of visuals – within which the editors include "photographs, illustrations, visualizations, and new writing/typography" (Stöckl, Caple, & Pflaeging, this volume). My use of the term *image* was in the past shaped, perhaps (too) constrained, by a fine-art training: leaving me stumbling in my early work within social semiotics between *image*, *visual*, and *visual image*, or feeling the need to name the medium of production – *photographic image*. It is significant to see *image* set free and on the rampage across the three chapters in this future-facing section. The renaming, the invention of new visual forms, mapped in the chapters is part of a recognition of the gravitational shift of image- and word-relations. Siever and Siever argue that new ways of describing image-word relationships extend beyond "discrepancy, contradiction, redundancy", "dominance", "illustration", or "anchorage". The chapters offer a range of useful new terms such as *image-nuclear* (Caple) in which "the image is an obligatory or structural element of the nucleus of this news story genre", and *image macro* (Zappavigna), "an image-centric practice since they require the presence of a visual image for the meaning making, often humorous critique to be realized".

The chapters show how the new image-language relationships that social media make available for making meaning serve to shape the visual, linguistic, and ultimately multimodal practices of users. These practices are central to how we communicate to develop, establish, and maintain our social relations through digital media, not only through the "transmission of content: rather they become the idiom of expressive intent" (Madianou, 2016, p. 126). She goes on to argue that we need to understand the affordances of media with attention to both their materiality and the sociality in which the relationships are enacted in relation to roles, normative expectations within relationships, culture, structures of power, and emotions. I see the chapters as being pertinent to this broader social context, providing theoretical and empirical insights on specific media and practices. Caple sets out the ways in which Instagram fosters the practices of capture, editing, and posting images and the use of language in particular ways. She points to four functions of the Instagram post that have been introduced into the repertoire of users: reporting, commenting, conversing, and reacting. Caple also shows how such shifts allow the "Instagrammer and audience to connect with each other in ways that are less or more inclusive". Zappavigna explores the highly intertextual and visual ambient environments of social media, arguing that "performing a stance about a social issue is often what is at stake", and investigates how this is achieved via shared practices such as "hashtagging and the production of memes where users are not necessarily involved in direct exchanges". Zappavigna also hones in on *direct* and *indirect* quotation practices on social media, and details how these "are part of a broader practice of negotiating intersubjectivity, that is, how different perspectives are managed in texts ... [and] the dialogic space available to different textual viewpoints". Sievers and Sievers explore the ways in which users create "visual tone" through their use of emojis, as well as the ways in which they are used as "extra-linguistic objects", enabling emojis to substitute for verbs, adjectives, and prepositions, or parts of words in which they become "constituents of compounds", or even come to stand for an entire word and its concept.

The chapters engage with the way in which the semiotic resources of different digital platforms are taken up by users, to get at the resulting construction of the user as producer and/or viewer. Key to that are the practices that the platform enables them to engage in and the relationships outside of the platform. For example, Caple points to the fact that it is far more common for an Instagrammer to know the person(s) being photographed, or even to photograph herself. The chapters point to how "[s]ocial media platforms engineer particular kinds of sociality even as their users develop norms around their use" (Baym, 2015, p. 51, in ref. to van Dijck, 2013). This raises the challenge of understanding how the design of semiotic resources – the place of image and language, and the relationships between them – differs across digital platforms and how it works to constrain and afford the practices of their users. Together, the chapters in this section explore this challenge, and together they remind us why this is paramount for understanding communication, for:

each device is not just added to the others, nor is its use substituted for a rival use. It is the entire relational economy that is 'reworked' every time by the redistribution of the technological scene on which interpersonal sociability is played out. (Licoppe, 2004, p. 142)

These chapters help us in our efforts to understand this communicational reworking.

References

Baym, N. K. (2015). *Personal connections in the digital age* (2nd ed.). Cambridge: Polity Press.
Jewitt, C. (2008). *Technology, literacy, learning: Multimodal approach.* London: Routledge.
Jewitt, C. (2005). Multimodality, 'reading', and 'writing' for the 21st century. *Discourse: Studies in the Cultural Politics of Education, 26*(3), 315–331.
Jewitt, C. (2002). The move from page to screen: The multimodal reshaping of school English. *Journal of Visual Communication, 1*(2), 171–196.
Jewitt, C. (1997). Images of men: Male sexuality in sexual health leaflets and posters for young people. *Sociological Research Online, 2*(2), 1–13.
Jewitt, C., & Kress, G. (Eds.). (2003). *Multimodal literacy.* New York, NY: Peter Lang.
Kress, G. (2015). Semiotic work: Applied linguistics and a social semiotic account of multimodality. *AILA Review, 28*, 49–71.
Licoppe, C. (2004). 'Connected' presence: The emergence of a new repertoire for managing social relationships in a changing communication technoscape. *Society and Space, 22*, 135–156.
Madianou, M. (2016). Ambient co-presence: Transnational family practices in polymedia environments. *Global Networks, 16*(2), 183–201.
van Dijck, J. (2013). 'You have one identity': Performing the self on Facebook and LinkedIn. *Media, Culture & Society, 35*(2), 199–215.

Part 4

Image-Centric Practices as Global Design Strategies

10 Multimodal Mobile News
Design and Images in Tablet-Platform Apps

John S. Knox

1 Introduction

Tablets provide a canvas with unique characteristics, by which news institutions and their readers can, respectively, distribute and access news. *Tablets* are screen-based and afford one or more scrolling screens, akin in some ways to the more traditional computer screen. They are also hand-held, affording a portrait orientation with sufficient 'real estate' on-screen to allow for design choices that are similar to print newspapers. Further, they allow news designers more layout choices than the smaller screens found on mobile phones, whose restricted size places inevitable limitations on news design.

Particularly since Apple released the iPad in 2010, *news apps* on tablets have become one important outlet for news institutions to reach audiences. Mitchell, Christian, and Rosenstiel (2011) found that in late 2011, a total of 11 percent of American adults owned a tablet, and of these, 53 percent accessed news daily on that device. Most tablet news consumers accessed news through browsers, but 21 percent used news apps exclusively, and another 31 percent used both news apps and browsers. From this small base, later studies indicate growing numbers of consumers of *mobile news* on tablets. In a study based on data from Sweden, Westlund (2014) found that mobile news (news delivered on tablets, smart phones, and in-between *phablets*) was accessed daily or weekly by approximately a third of the population of that country in 2012, and that news apps were the most common way of accessing mobile news from legacy news organizations. Newman, Fletcher, Kalogeropoulos, Levy, and Nielsen (2017, p. 9) reported that, in 2017, in a number of countries, more of the population with access to the Internet were accessing news from a mobile device than a computer, "giving a new lease of life to news apps". The percentage of people who accessed mobile news through tablets was lower than those doing so with smartphones (e.g., respectively and approximately: 25 percent vs. 80 percent in Australia; 30 percent vs. 55 percent in Germany; 26 percent vs. 67 percent in Hong Kong; 24 percent vs. 70 percent in Mexico; 25 percent vs. 50 percent in the UK; 20 percent vs. 55 percent in the USA), but these figures demonstrate that tablet-based news apps are used by large numbers of people internationally.

In short, the screen size and technological affordances of tablets provide unique design possibilities for tablet-based news apps. In addition, there are significant numbers of people consuming news internationally using tablet-based news apps. Together, these facts raise questions as to how the institutional authors of online news exploit the affordances of the tablet in their dedicated news apps.

In order to address such questions, this paper examines the *multimodal construal* of news in 12 English-language news apps from Australia, the UK, and the USA. These include legacy news institutions (e.g., *The New York Times*, *The Guardian*) and Internet-first news institutions (e.g., *BuzzFeed*, *The Huffington Post*). Taking a social-semiotic perspective on *news design* (e.g., Caple, 2013; Knox, 2014), this paper demonstrates how the design of news on these apps converges in a number of ways, and considers the extent to which mobile news on tablet-based apps can be considered image-centric (cf. Caple, 2013).

2 Mobile News, Multimodality, and Image-Centricity

Mobile news has been studied from a range of perspectives, including processes of news production (Westlund, 2013), and transformations in the social practices of news consumption, the nature of news, and the ways in which news events are construed and communicated (Sheller, 2015). A number of studies have looked at consumer and consumption patterns for mobile news, and whether factors such as existing news consumption, and social factors such as age and education might predict such usage (e.g., Chan, 2015; Chan-Olmsted, Rim, & Zerba, 2013; Thorson, Shoenberger, Karaliova, Kim, & Fidler, 2015; van Damme, Courtois, Verbrugge, & de Marez, 2015; Westlund & Färdigh, 2015). Looking at the relation between mobile news and society from a different perspective, Martin (2013) explored the social impact of mobile news as a force for democratization and social change. In terms of news design, Yu and Kong (2016) conducted an experimental study of user experience of design, and Dowling and Vogan (2015) looked at the relation between the tablet as a device and innovation in long-form journalism.

Despite this range of approaches and questions, to date, there appear to be no published studies in the literature dedicated to examining mobile news from a social-semiotic perspective. There have, however, been social-semiotic studies of print and *online news* that have direct bearing on the focus of the current study. The first is the seminal work of Caple on image-nuclear news stories (INNS), a specific genre of news story where language is secondary to a dominant, central image (e.g., Caple, 2013). Caple's study was of print newspapers, but building on this work, Caple and Knox (e.g., 2015, 2017) conducted a study of online news galleries, which consist of a series of images, each of which is likewise accompanied by language secondary to the image. Both the genre of INNS and the genres found in online news galleries (Caple & Knox, 2017) can be considered image-centric (to employ the terminology of the focus of the current volume), since image is essential to the genre: without it, the social goal of the genre cannot be achieved. Exactly how the term *image-centric* might be defined is discussed further at the end of this chapter.

The work of Caple, and of Caple and Knox, and its relevance to image-centricity, raises the question of the notion of genre used in their work and in this paper. This notion of *genre* follows the work of Martin and colleagues, where a genre is defined as:

> a staged, goal-oriented, purposeful activity in which speakers engage as members of our culture. Examples of genres are staged activities such as making a dental appointment, buying vegetables, telling a story, writing an essay, applying for a job, writing a letter to the editor, inviting someone for dinner, and so on. Virtually everything you do involves your participating in one or another genre. (Martin, 2001, p. 155)

From this perspective, genres are patterns of meaning that we identify as common across individual activities: activities which are often identified and analyzed as texts. The stages, or structure, of an individual text allows us to identify a generic pattern (or combination of generic patterns in complex texts) to which a text belongs. Linguistically, texts vary in terms of their choice of lexis, their grammar, their discursive patterns, and the extent to which they follow the staging of one or more genres. Genres will include obligatory (must be present) and optional (may or may not be present) structural elements for the successful achievement of the social goal. So genre is not deterministic; it is cultural patterning that we can use to help understand, analyze, and explain activities. This notion of genre and the presence of obligatory and optional stages in genre structures is relevant to the question of image-centricity, addressed near the end of this chapter.

Returning to social-semiotic studies of print and online news, another line of study central to the approach taken here is research on online newspaper *home pages* and the short headline-plus-lead-plus-link *newsbites*, and shorter headline-plus-link *newsbits*, that dominate them (e.g., Knox, 2007, 2014). Knox (2009c) studied the use of thumbnail images in newsbites, and found that the thumbnail images in the dataset of that study were dominated by close-cropped images of faces. He further found that the primary function of *thumbnail faces* in The Sydney Morning Herald online was "to personalize the story (with which the reader will engage for a matter of seconds), and to position the reader interpersonally in a way that is not possible with verbal text alone" (Knox, 2009c, p. 180; cf. Knox, 2009b). In terms of *systemic functional theory*, images were textually prominent (as visual hyper-theme) and involved in experiential relations of intersemiotic repetition with elements of the headline and lead (cf. Knox, 2010; Royce, 1998). That is, the 'same' content (to the extent that that is possible) was repeated in language and image. Separately, Knox (2009a, 2014) also found that some variations on newsbites had a large image that was spatially dominant over text. In all these cases, newsbites relied on language to achieve their social purpose, while images were an obligatory structural element in only some sub-types of newsbites and newsbits. The question of whether some sub-types of newsbites are image-centric was not explored in these studies, but this body of work is pertinent to the current study, since newsbites, newsbits, and similar genres are found on the home pages of the mobile news apps in this study.

The current paper builds on the work cited earlier, and examines (1) the design of tablet-based news app home pages and (2) the extent to which mobile news and the genres by which it is communicated are image-centric, in keeping with the call from Westlund (2015; p. 152) to "further theorize and conceptualize the area of mobile news (Peters, 2012; Westlund, 2008), critically reflecting upon what is known and also what is currently happening".

3 The Study

This paper draws on a dataset of screen captures from tablet-based news apps, collected over two 'constructed weeks' of Monday to Friday (a Monday from one week, a Tuesday from another, and so on, see Bell, 1991) from October to December 2015. Data used in this study were collected from the following 12 mobile news apps:

- *BuzzFeed* (USA)
- *The Australian* (Australia)
- *The Courier Mail* (Australia)
- *The Daily Mail* (UK)
- *The Daily Telegraph* (Australia)
- *The Daily Telegraph* (UK)
- *The Guardian* (UK)
- *The Huffington Post* (USA – since re-named HuffPost)
- *The New York Times* (USA)
- *The Sydney Morning Herald* (Australia)
- *The Times* (UK)
- *USA Today* (USA).

Due to the relative lack of research on mobile news from a social-semiotic perspective, this paper took a relatively conservative approach to the selection of media institutions to examine, drawing on data from major, well-known, and well-resourced English-language news organizations from the trans-Atlantic markets typical of much research into the mass media (i.e., the UK and the USA), and from a third, relatively minor market to provide a counterpoint to this perspective (i.e., Australia) (Knox, 2009a, p. 22; cf. Caple & Knox, 2012, p. 212). In addition, two relative newcomers to the news reporting space, *BuzzFeed* and *The Huffington Post*, were included in order to provide a counterpoint to the legacy news organizations.

The news on each app was analyzed in terms of the visual design of each app and the use of images. The aim was to identify patterns in the multimodal design of news on these apps, the roles of images, and the extent to which tablet-based mobile news can be considered to be image-centric. Initially, pages were scanned for visual similarities and differences. Early classification identified a number of apps that drew heavily on the visual design of print news, and a number that did not. Further investigation showed differences in design in terms of the design of news stories each app included, and also a tendency toward the use of columns, or the use of tiles in the visual design of the app home pages. This is detailed further in the following section.

4 News Design

As discussed, this study focuses on the design of home pages and the use of images in tablet-based news apps. The apps analyzed in this study provide a reader experience that is structurally similar to news websites. Each app has one or more home pages that provide entry points to 'full' versions of each story. These entry points are in the form of 'shorter' versions of the original story, either adapted or shortened for the home page.

There may be one home page for the entire app, or different home pages dedicated to different content of the app (e.g., international news, sport), and whether they are viewed as a single page or different pages depends on how the notion of *page* is understood and defined in online media. This is a complex question beyond the scope of this paper (see Zhao, 2011). Some apps take advantage of horizontal swiping as a means of navigation between home pages, and some rely on vertical scrolling and/or menus. These aspects of app design are beyond the scope of the current study and are not explored in any depth in this paper.

Regardless of the design of home pages in individual apps, the structural principal in the design of these apps is one where home pages with short versions of stories link to story pages with longer (or modally different) versions of those stories at a 'lower level' in the semiotic structure of the app. This is the same structural principal on which online newspapers are designed (see Knox, 2009a, 2014). This is not a claim about the technical architecture of websites and apps, but of the semiotic architecture of these texts.

Analysis of the home pages of the news apps led to the identification of three primary areas of choice in their design. Such areas of choice are theorized in systemic theory in system networks, which present choices as oppositions (see Figure 10.1). In the apps under analysis here, some of these oppositions can also be considered as end points or mid-points on a cline, with actual instances (e.g., the page composition of a particular app) falling more toward one choice or the other, rather than strictly 'within' a particular category (see Martin & Matthiessen, 1991, for discussion of typological and topological meanings). This is represented in the system network in Figure 10.1 by the diagonally-angled vertical lines.

The three areas of choice identified in this paper are: kind of reportage on the page, the composition of the page, and the visual metaphor of the page. Each of these is discussed in turn in the remainder of this section. Images are discussed in the following section.

Beginning with *reportage*, the apps differed in terms of whether they were dominated by newsbites, by newsbits, or by split stories. As discussed earlier, *newsbites* are short, multimodal 'bites' of news that emerged with the social and technological developments of online news sites. Newsbites emerged from a socio-historical and discursive environment where the interpersonal 'peak' of print news stories had moved to the front, and ultimately was able to *stand alone* (Knox, 2007; cf. Iedema, Feez, & White, 1994; White, 1997, 2003). This enabled online newspapers to take advantage of the role of website home pages within the structure of websites (see Djonov, 2007, 2008) and use newsbites as entry points to more detailed coverage 'deeper' in the website.

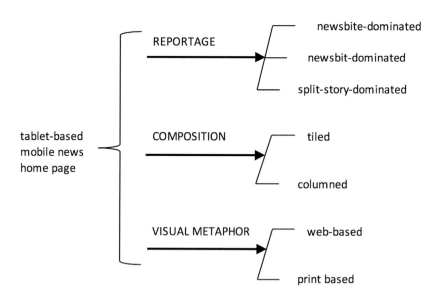

Figure 10.1 A system of news design on tablet-based news app home pages.

Because they must fit the design constraints of the home page (e.g., word limits), the wording of a newsbite commonly differs from the headline and/or lead of the linked story. Over time, collections of newsbites themselves have come to serve as news coverage on news websites, because they (1) include headline and lead, and therefore the key aspects of a given news story (according to the values of the news institution), (2) are often authored specifically for home pages, and (3) function as an endpoint for those news consumers who read only the newsbite without following the link (Knox, 2014, p. 448).

Linguistically, newsbites consist of headline and lead. "The lead pares the story back to its essential point, and the headline abstracts the lead itself" (Bell, 1991, p. 150). The news coverage provided by newsbites on home pages is illustrated by the following collection of newsbites from a home page of *The Sydney Morning Herald* app (December 29, 2015).

> *'I'll stab you, dog!'* [image of the event – woman holding a chisel]
> A woman who objected to a man sitting next to her pulled out a chisel and threatened to stab him.
> **Fatal weather rounds out an extreme 2015** [image of a bushfire]
> Record heat in southern Australia, tornadoes in Texas and 'biblical' flooding in UK.
> **Birmingham's public education a rarity** [mug shot of Simon Birmingham]
> In Malcom Turnbull's cabinet, Education Minister Simon Birmingham is unique.
> **Five cars damaged in Bellevue Hill fire** [image of burnt-out cars]
> Fire has destroyed cars in Bellevue Hill after fuel from one of the vehicles ignited.
> **Deputy Lord Mayor of Sydney dies** [mug shot of Robyn Kemmis]
> Sydney's deputy Lord Mayor Robyn Kemmis has died while on holidays in QLD.

Despite the pervasive use of newsbites on online newspaper home pages, and despite the apps using a website-like home-page-to-story-page structure as discussed earlier, only two of the apps studied used newsbites as the dominant news genre on the home page: *The Sydney Morning Herald* and *The New York Times*. Possible explanations for this are discussed further in the chapter.

The second approach to reportage is found in those apps whose home pages are dominated by *newsbits*, or headline-only stories. Headlines are "an abstract of the abstract" (Bell, 1991, p. 150) designed to capture attention. Collections of newsbits provide an even less-detailed coverage of the news than a collection of newsbites, and can therefore tend toward an index of stories rather than an overview. Consider the following selection of newsbits from *The Huffington Post* of October 19, 2015, which collectively give an orientation to the news with even less detail than the aforementioned collection of newsbites.

> **TIME TO FACE THE MUSIC** [image of US Congress building]
> *Stabbings In Jerusalem And West bank Leave Nearly 50 Dead* [image of protester throwing tear gas canister]
> *Gun Debate Goes Presidential* [head and shoulders shot of U.S. President Barack Obama]
> *Top Dem Slams Benghazi For False Claims Against Hillary* [head and shoulders shot of Democratic Congressman speaking behind a lectern]
> *2 Shot During 'Old West' Gunfight Reenactment in Tombstone* [image of 'old-style' Western gunfight]

This approach to reportage is taken by the apps of the two Internet-first news institutions studied, *BuzzFeed* and *The Huffington Post*, and also by *The Guardian*. It is not uncommon in these publications – especially *BuzzFeed* and *The Huffington Post* – for headlines to be noticeably longer than typical print headlines, presumably (in part at least) to compensate for the lack of a lead. Consider the following examples from *BuzzFeed* of October 19, 2015.

> *This May Be The Hardest "Harry Potter" Character Quiz You'll Ever Take* [still from Harry Potter film]
> *A Bride And Groom Went To A Kansas City Royals Playoff Game During Their Wedding* [head and shoulders shot of couple at baseball game]
> *The Ruins Of A Historic Church Are Rising Out Of A Reservoir* [aesthetic shot of church ruins]
> *After A Wedding Was Cancelled, A Bride's Family Turned Her Reception Into A Feast For The Homeless* [mid-shot of family]
> *This Baby Koala Wants A Hug And Doesn't Give A Fuck What You Think* [shot of koala on a toy koala in a home]

As can be seen from this list, *BuzzFeed* tends to ignore grammatical conventions typical of headlines (Halliday, 1985, Appendix 2). As the examples here demonstrate, nominal groups include deixis, verbal groups are made finite, and full Moods are included. This is also the case in some sections of *The Huffington Post*. This 'unusual' grammar – in terms of what is typical of news headlines – helps distinguish these apps discursively from the apps published by traditional media outlets, and may represent a deliberate strategy on the part of the publishers to differentiate themselves from legacy media and to appeal to a different audience. However, further research would be required to document the institutional processes involved, and to establish the motivation for these choices.

The third approach to reportage on the home pages studied is the dominant use of stories that 'jump' from the home page to the story page. In some print newspapers, some front-page stories 'break', often mid-sentence, with a link to an inside page (e.g., "continued p. 4"), and then continue on an inside page of the paper. In some news apps, this kind of split story can also be found, and the text begins anew on the story page with identical text to that on the home page. This approach to reportage is used by *The Australian*, *The Courier Mail*, *The Daily Mail*, *The Daily Telegraph* (Australia), *The Daily Telegraph* (UK), *The Times*, and *USA Today*.

In these news apps, both headline and lead break, sometimes mid-word, in some apps. Further, in all three apps that use newsbits (see examples above), the headlines sometimes break, so those apps (*BuzzFeed*, *The Guardian*, and *The Huffington Post*), while newsbit-dominated, also have some split stories (see the discussion of system networks and clines above). Examples follow from *The Daily Mail* of November 20, 2015.

> *BREAKING NEWS: Jihadists shouting 'Allahu Akbar' launch gun and gr...*
> *BREAKING NEWS: Police discover a THIRD body at the scene of the Paris...*
> *Paris prosecutors said the corpse wa...*
> *ISIS on the run: Sun sets on another day of heavy losses for terror group as R...*
> *Russian jets flew more than 100 com...*
> *EXCLUSIVE: Extraordinary selfie of Europe's first female suicide bo...*
> *EXCLUSIVE: A series of revealing new pi...*

This approach to reportage on the home page requires readers to jump to story pages to continue reading the story. The stories on home pages, then, are incomplete fragments of a story, in contrast to newsbites, which stand alone as bite-size news stories in their own right.

The use of split stories is a distinct point of contrast between news websites and apps, since the use of split stories is very unusual on news website home pages. Of the ten news institutions using split stories on their apps, only one (*The Times*) uses split stories on the home page of its website.

This difference between online newspaper home pages and news app home pages suggests that such tablet-based mobile news apps are:

- designed to appeal to print or print-oriented readers, because they draw on a print-news tradition of split stories that has not carried over to news websites (in further support of this, excluding the newsbit apps, six of the seven apps that use split stories also use a print metaphor – see later), or

- visually designed in such a way that including images is more important than avoiding a break in headlines and leads (see discussion of *The Daily Mail* later).

In summary then, the three approaches to reportage on the home pages of the apps are of using newsbites, newsbits, or split-stories as shown in Figure 10.1.

The second primary area of choice is of the *composition* of the page, and whether the news content is organized in tiles or in columns. A tiled design means that the individual news stories are framed by borders or backgrounding in a way that each story is a distinct visual unit – a 'tile' of its own. The following apps use a tiled approach to composition: *BuzzFeed*, *The Guardian*, *The Huffington Post*, *The Sydney Morning Herald*.

A columned approach to composition is a page design founded on an underlying grid of columns as is the historical basis for print newspapers. Such pages sometimes resemble a tiled design on some pages, but most of their pages resemble a design based on columns, and the framing conventions they use (white space, and/or incomplete thin borders) are similar to print, without complete framing of individual stories.

The following apps use a columned approach to composition: *The Australian*, *The Courier Mail*, *The Daily Mail* (which, uniquely in this dataset, uses tiles within its columns), *The Daily Telegraph* (Australia), *The Daily Telegraph* (UK), *The New York Times*, *The Times*, *USA Today*.

The third primary area of choice identified is the dominant *visual metaphor* of the page. The apps studied tend to draw on one of two metaphors, or some combination of the two (again, see discussion of system and cline earlier in the chapter). The first is the visual metaphor of the World Wide Web and online news: Apps using a web-based visual metaphor in this study are *BuzzFeed*, *The Daily Mail*, *The Guardian*, and *The Huffington Post*. These apps tend to use some of the following visual features: colored font, shaded or colored backgrounds on different areas of the page, and a minimal or non-traditional masthead. The masthead contributes to apps such as *BuzzFeed* and *The Huffington Post*, appearing more web-based, since they were first created as websites. However, this particular association may be limited to readers who are familiar with the history of news providers, especially the legacy news institutions.

The second visual metaphor is print news. Apps employing a print-based visual metaphor tend to use some of the following visual features: dominant, traditional, institutional masthead, white background, mostly black typeface, and/or typography typical of print news. Some of these apps use an initial front-page-like dominant image-headline combination as is common in print tabloids, with subsequent home pages resembling the inside pages of a print newspaper (e.g., *The*

Courier Mail, The Daily Telegraph (Australia)). *The Sydney Morning Herald*'s tiled design draws on the same front page visual conventions, but repeats this also on later home pages. Others use a broadsheet-like, black-print-on-white-background design obviously intended to resemble the appearance of a print newspaper (*The Australian, The Daily Telegraph* (UK), *The Times*). All these apps with the exception of *The Sydney Morning Herald* and *The Times* (which use their masthead on the first home page) include their distinctive, traditional masthead on every home page.

These three areas of choice – reportage, composition, and visual metaphor – are represented visually as a system network in Figure 10.1. Reading left to right, the entry condition (tablet-based mobile news home page) enters a curly bracket, meaning that a choice needs to be made from all three systems of REPORTAGE, COMPOSITION, and VISUAL METAPHOR. Each of these systems has angled square brackets, meaning one and only once choice is made from each, and these choices represent graded oppositions rather that definitive, categorical choices.

It is surprising, perhaps, that there is such a high degree of consistency in the semiotic structure of these apps and the visual conventions of their home page design. The fundamental structural principle of online news – home page leading to (home pages leading to) story pages (Knox, 2014, pp. 442–444) – has been transferred from web design to app design, suggesting that this is an approach to news delivery that suits the production processes of institutions, and/or one that meets the demands of news consumers. Alternatively, it may also indicate that news institutions are not well disposed to innovation, whether because of the nature of institutional practices, or the relative lack of resources in the current news environment.

The aforementioned system network generates 12 possible feature combinations, and the patterns of instantiation of the 12 apps analyzed are shown in Table 10.1.

Table 10.1 shows the patterns of instantiation in the dataset, demonstrating a clustering of apps (six of 12) that use a split-story-dominated, columned, print-based home page design, which can be viewed as 'overlaying' visual conventions of print news onto an online news text structure. As discussed earlier in relation to the use of split stories, it appears that these apps target readers who are inclined toward print news. It should also be noted that four of these six apps (the three Australian titles plus *The Times*) are owned by Rupert Murdoch's News Corporation, and there may be institutional practices common across these titles that are responsible for the similarities in visual design in these apps.

The second, smaller cluster of apps uses a newsbit-dominated, tiled, web-based design. It is interesting that this group includes the apps of the two Internet-first news institutions, *BuzzFeed* and *The Huffington Post*, as well as the app of a legacy institution, *The Guardian*. Figure 10.2

Table 10.1 Instantiation of tablet-based mobile news home pages in the dataset

• newsbite-dominated • tiled • web-based	–
• newsbit-dominated • tiled • web-based	*BuzzFeed* (note: headlines can split) *The Guardian* (note: headlines can split) *The Huffington Post* (note: headlines can split)
• split-story-dominated • tiled • web-based	–
• newsbite-dominated • columned • web-based	–
• newsbit-dominated • columned • web-based	–
• split-story-dominated • columned • web-based	*The Daily Mail* (note: tiled within columns)
• newsbite-dominated • tiled • print-based	*The Sydney Morning Herald*
• newsbit-dominated • tiled • print-based	–
• split-story-dominated • tiled • print-based	–
• newsbite-dominated • columned • print-based	*The New York Times*
• newsbit-dominated • columned • print-based	–
• split-story-dominated • columned • print-based	*The Australian* *The Courier Mail* *The Daily Telegraph* (Australia) *The Daily Telegraph* (UK) *The Times* *USA Today*

shows a tablet viewing the home pages of *The Daily Mail*, *The Daily Telegraph*, *The New York Times*, and *The Guardian*, respectively.

Overall, even the relatively limited contrasts in choice that have emerged in the meaning potential of tablet-based mobile news app design are taken up in a relatively limited distribution.

Multimodal Mobile News 245

Figure 10.2 Composite of shots of a tablet viewing the home pages of *The Daily Mail* (top-left), *The Daily Telegraph* (UK) (top-right), *The New York Times* (bottom-left), and *The Guardian* (bottom-right).

5 Images

Images are not included in the earlier discussion because they are not a design feature of the page, but of the story. Images occur in stories, not as page-design elements, though the visual design of stories and the inclusion (or not) of images obviously have implications for how a page looks.

246   *John S. Knox*

In four of the apps in this study, every news story must have an image due to the visual design of news stories: *BuzzFeed*, *The Daily Mail*, *The Huffington Post*, *The Sydney Morning Herald*. *USA Today* has an image in almost every story, and *The Guardian* is designed in a way that every screen on the home page has a large image. In every other app, every page in the dataset has at least one image, though it would be theoretically possible for some of them to have pages without images, given their design.

Four apps include images with captions: *The Australian* and *The New York Times* on several home pages, and *The Daily Telegraph* (UK) and *The Times* include a single large image-caption complex on their initial front-page-like home page.

While most images in the dataset are not accompanied by a caption, the images in the dataset do perform a range of functions typical of news images as identified by Bednarek and Caple (2012, pp. 114–118) who identify functions of news images including image as illustration (putting a face to a name), image as evidence (providing a visual record of an event), image as sensation (highlighting sensational themes such as violence and sex), image as evaluation (taking an evaluative stance), and image as aesthetic (composed for aesthetic appeal and value), or any combination of these. Table 10.2 provides examples of image functions and their accompanying headlines from the dataset.

This brief illustration of the array of image functions shows that the use of images in the news apps in the dataset is more diverse than the

Table 10.2 Examples of images from tablet-based mobile news apps performing different functions of news images

Image function	Example
Image as illustration	TV stars loved up [image: close up of couple looking into camera] (*The Courier Mail* 18/10/15)
Image as evidence	Irish dreams blown away by Argentina [image: Argentinian rugby player about to score with Irish player on the ground] (*The Times* 19/10/2015)
Image as sensation	'I hope he enjoys this': Marnie Simpson flaunts her stunning figure in … [image: composite of Marnie Simpson twice in lingerie] (*The Daily Mail* 19/10/2015)
Image as evaluation	Rwanda Aid Shows Reach and Limits of Clinton Foundation – caption: *Former President Bill Clinton and President Paul Kagame of Rawanda greeting medical students in 2012 in Kigali, Rawanda* [image: Clinton making eye contact and shaking hands with Rawandan medical students] (*The New York Times* 18/10/2015)
Image as aesthetic	The Ruins Of A Historic Church Are Rising Out Of A Reservoir [image: aesthetic shot of church ruins] (*BuzzFeed* 19/10/2015)

limited use of the online newspaper thumbnail images in *The Sydney Morning Herald* online as described by Knox (2009c) and discussed earlier.

In order to explain some of the issues at stake in designing how images are used as visual elements in home-page news stories in the apps (as opposed to how they function in news stories), the remainder of this section will focus on the design of image placement in *The Guardian* and *The Daily Mail*. *The Guardian* shares similarities with *The New York Times* and *The Sydney Morning Herald* in this regard (though there are also important differences), while *The Daily Mail* is unique among the apps and is chosen for that reason. The other apps also make different design choices, but many of the relevant design issues are raised in the discussion that follows.

The Guardian home page scrolls vertically. It is organized into visual sections under headings (e.g., *headlines, opinion, across the country, around the world*), and each of these sections fits closely to a single screen on a tablet. Each section has approximately 6–8 newsbits, with one large newsbit dominating the space visually (taking approximately a third of the space). This large newsbit always has an image. The smaller newsbits sometimes include images, and sometimes do not. Each section, then, has at least one large image, and typically another 1–3 small images in other newsbits.

In terms of news story design in *The Guardian* app then, images are obligatory in the large newsbit and optional in the small newsbits, and each section of the homepage is designed in such a way that at least one large image is included. In this way, news story design and page design interact in such a way as to ensure that each screen features one large image, and possibly more smaller ones.

The Daily Mail app uses a different design from *The Guardian* app. The home page of *The Daily Mail* is columned (*The Guardian* app is tiled). Each column represents a different section, and the reader can scroll the page horizontally to reveal more columns. Each column has a colored bar with *The Daily Mail*'s "M" logo extracted from the traditional print masthead, and the heading of the section (e.g., *Home, Showbiz, Femail, Sport, World News*). Each column can scroll vertically, independent of the other columns, providing for a unique navigation experience.

The first split story in each column has a large headline above a large image that spans the entire column. All subsequent stories in the columns are divided left-right (language left, image right). Thus, every story on the page has an image. This means that images are an essential element in the story design used on this home page, and the entire page is designed in a way that images are pervasive. Once again, news story design and page design combine to ensure that every screen viewed features images, but in a very different way from *The Guardian* app.

Thus, when considering images in the design of the home pages of these apps, the design of news stories, and of sections (vertical or horizontal), and/or whole pages need to be considered. Some apps design their stories in such a way that an image must be included; some apps design some stories in this way and take account of this in the design of pages/sections of pages.

In conclusion to this section, we can see that images perform a range of functions in these apps, and varying but important roles in news stories and on pages. All apps employ a combination of page and story design which results in images appearing on every page in the dataset, which raises the following question: are these tablet-based mobile news apps image-centric?

6 Image-Centricity

The impetus for the focus on *image-centricity* in this volume comes from the work of Caple discussed earlier, and her research on INNS, also called stand-alones by practitioners. These are news stories featuring a large, typically aesthetically striking image, accompanied by a headline and a caption that often goes beyond the function of a typical news image caption. The crucial issue in that work for the current discussion is that Caple built on the foundational work of Iedema et al. (1994), and their identification of the Nucleus-Satellite structure of news genres. In hard news stories (for example), paragraphs functioning as Satellites in the story all link back to, and expand on the headline-plus-lead Nucleus of the story, which allows for the re-arrangement of paragraphs and a non-linear form of story-telling.

In Caple's INNS, the image makes up part of the Nucleus of the story,[1] and this provides a structural rationale for the term *image-nuclear*. There are examples of image-nuclear stand-alones in the dataset of this study (on the first home page of *The Times*, which uses a print-based metaphor), so at least some of the stories in the dataset are image-nuclear, but, broadly speaking, there remains a question as to whether the home pages and news stories in the dataset of this story are image-centric, and, more fundamentally, what is meant by the term *image-centric*.

On the basis of the discussion in this paper, one possibility[2] would be to use the term image-centric to refer to texts where image is an essential element of the text, either in terms of:

A   the design of the text, as in news stories that are designed to always include an image (e.g., *The Daily Mail* in this dataset; cf. newsbites and newsbits analyzed in Knox, 2008, 2014, which may be designed to include or exclude an image), or

B   the structural elements of the genre, meaning that images are an obligatory, not optional, element of the genre (in the genre of newsbite, an image is an optional structural element; in the genre of stand-alone, an image is an obligatory element).

This would mean that image-centric is a superordinate term to image-nuclear. Image-nuclear news stories would also be image-centric by criterion B, since the image is an obligatory element in the genre (and they are image-nuclear because the genre itself has a Nucleus-Satellite structure – not all genres do).

The Guardian app has newsbits. Newsbits as a genre are not image-centric by criterion B, since an image is not an obligatory element in the structure of a newsbit. However, due to the page design and story design employed in the app, some of those newsbits must have an image (due to design choices, rather than the structure of the genre), so those texts are image-centric (by criterion A). At the same time, the home page of this app is image-centric by criterion A, since newsbits which must include an image are part of the page design.

Similarly, news stories in *The Daily Mail* are image-centric by criterion A, since each of them is designed in a way that an image must be included, and the home page of the app is likewise image-centric since it must include images due to the interaction between story design and page design.

This approach to the notion of image-centricity can be applied consistently, and at different levels of texts and of genres, and is not based on the size or frequency of images. This approach could be applied consistently to analyzing stories in print and online newspapers, and to analyzing print and online newspapers as macro-genres. It also allows for the sub-classification of image-centric texts and genres into those which are also image-nuclear (like stand-alones), and those which are image-centric but not image-nuclear (like the split stories in *The Daily Mail* app).

7 Conclusion

Mobile news, including mobile news on tablet-based apps, is widely read, and one important means by which Internet-first and legacy news institutions construe and deliver their product to news consumers; yet, it remains a relatively un-investigated area from the perspective of social semiotics. The tablet-based mobile news apps in the dataset of this study use a semiotic structure built around home pages providing overviews and entry points for readers, with links to story pages with longer and/or modally different versions of those stories, consistent with the semiotic structure of online newspapers. There is a high degree of convergence in the design choices made in these apps in terms of their home page design. Images are pervasive, and the images in the apps perform a range of typical functions of news images. At the same time, the design of individual stories, the inclusion of images, and the interaction between story design and page design differ between apps.

On the basis of this study, a proposal for the notion of image-centricity is made. This builds on the work of Caple (e.g., 2009) and ties notions of image-centricity explicitly either to design or to genre. As macro-genres, the tablet-based mobile news apps in this study are image-centric, but just as the apps deliver complex texts, the question of image-centricity at different levels is a complex one, requiring further investigation and theorizing in mobile news and in other areas.

Notes

1 Together with the Heading and the Prosodic Tail (an evaluative comment at the beginning of the caption).
2 See Stöckl (this volume) for detailed discussion of an alternative definition.

References

Bednarek, M., & Caple, H. (2012). *News discourse*. London: Continuum.
Bell, A. (1991). *The language of news media*. Oxford: Blackwell.
Caple, H. (2013). *Photojournalism: A multisemiotic approach*. Basingstoke: Palgrave Macmillan.
Caple, H. (2009). *Playing with words and pictures: Intersemiosis in a new genre of news reportage* (Unpublished doctoral dissertation). University of Sydney, Sydney. Retrieved from http://hdl.handle.net/2123/7024
Caple, H., & Knox, J. S. (2017). Genre(less) and purpose(less): Online news galleries. *Discourse, Context and Media, 20*, 204–217.
Caple, H., & Knox, J. S. (2015). A framework for the multimodal analysis of online news galleries: What makes a 'good' picture gallery? *Social Semiotics, 25*(3), 292–321.
Caple, H., & Knox, J. S. (2012). Online news galleries, photojournalism and the photo essay. *Visual Communication, 11*(2), 1–30.
Chan, M. (2015). Examining the influences of news use patterns, motivations, and age cohort on mobile news use: The case of Hong Kong. *Mobile Media and Communication, 3*(2), 179–195.
Chan-Olmsted, S., Rim, H., & Zerba, A. (2013). Mobile news adoption among young adults: Examining the roles of perceptions, news consumption, and media usage. *Journalism and Mass Communication Quarterly, 90*(1), 126–147.
Djonov, E. (2008). Children's website structure and navigation. In L. Unsworth (Ed.), *Multimodal semiotics: Functional analysis in contexts of education* (pp. 216–236). London: Continuum.
Djonov, E. (2007). Website hierarchy and the interaction between content organization, webpage and navigation design: A systemic functional hypermedia discourse analysis perspective. *Information Design Journal, 15*(2), 144–162.
Dowling, D., & Vogan, T. (2015). Can we "Snowfall" this? Digital longform and the race for the tablet market. *Digital Journalism, 3*(2), 209–224.
Halliday, M. A. K. (1985). *An introduction to functional grammar*. London: Arnold.
Iedema, R., Feez, S., & White, P. R. R. (1994). *Stage two: Media literacy*. A report for the Write it Right Literacy in Industry Research Project. Sydney: N.S.W. Department of School Education, Disadvantaged Schools Program.

Knox, J. S. (2014). Online newspapers: Structure and layout. In C. Jewitt (Ed.), *The Routledge handbook of multimodal analysis* (2nd ed.) (pp. 440–449). London: Routledge.

Knox, J. S. (2010). Online newspapers: Evolving genres, evolving theory. In C. Coffin, T. Lillis & K. O'Halloran (Eds.), *Applied linguistics methods: A reader* (pp. 33–51). London: Routledge.

Knox, J. S. (2009a). *Multimodal discourse on online newspaper home pages: A social-semiotic perspective* (Unpublished doctoral dissertation). University of Sydney, Sydney. Retrieved from http://hdl.handle.net/2123/7696

Knox, J. S. (2009b). Punctuating the home page: Image as language in an online newspaper. *Discourse and Communication, 3*(2), 145–172.

Knox, J. S. (2009c). Visual minimalism in hard news: Thumbnail faces on the smh online home page. *Social Semiotics, 19*(2), 165–189.

Knox, J. S. (2008). Online newspapers and TESOL classrooms: A multimodal perspective. In L. Unsworth (Ed.), *Multimodal semiotics: Functional analysis in contexts of education* (pp. 139–158). London: Continuum.

Knox, J. S. (2007). Visual-verbal communication on online newspaper home pages. *Visual Communication, 6*(1), 19–53.

Martin, J. A. (2013). Mobile news use and participation in elections: A bridge for the democratic divide? *Mobile Media and Communication, 3*(2), 230–249.

Martin, J. R. (2001). Language, register and genre. In A. Burns & C. Coffin (Eds.), *Analysing English in a global context: A reader* (pp. 149–166). London: Routledge.

Martin, J. R., & Matthiessen, C. M. I. M. (1991). Systemic typology and topology. In F. Christie (Ed.), *Literacy in social processes: Papers from the inaugural Australian Systemic Functional Linguistics Conference, held at Deakin University, January 1990* (pp. 345–383). Darwin: Centre for Studies of Language in Education, Northern Territory University.

Mitchell, A., Christian, L., & Rosenstiel, T. (2011). *The tablet revolution and what it means for the future of news*. Washington, DC: Pew Research Centre.

Newman, N., Fletcher, R., Kalogeropoulos, A., Levy, D. A. L., & Nielsen, R. K. (2017). *Reuters Institute digital news report 2017*. Oxford: Reuters Institute, University of Oxford.

Royce, T. D. (1998). Synergy on the page: Exploring intersemiotic complementarity in page-based multimodal text. *JASFL Occasional Papers, 1*(1), 25–49.

Sheller, M. (2015). News now: Interface, ambience, flow, and the disruptive spatio-temporalities of mobile news media. *Journalism Studies, 16*(1), 12–26.

Thorson, E., Shoenberger, H., Karaliova, T., Kim, E. A., & Fidler, R. (2015). News use of mobile media: A contingency model. *Mobile Media and Communication, 3*(2), 160–178.

van Damme, K., Courtois, C., Verbrugge, K., & de Marez, L. (2015). What's APPening to news? A mixed-method audience-centred study on mobile news consumption. *Mobile Media and Communication, 3*(2), 196–213.

Westlund, O. (2015). News consumption in an age of mobile media: Patterns, people, place, and participation. *Mobile Media and Communication, 3*(2), 151–159.

Westlund, O. (2014). The production and consumption of mobile news. In G. Goggin & L. Hjorth (Eds.), *The mobile media companion* (pp. 135–145). New York: Routledge.

Westlund, O. (2013). Mobile news: A review and model of journalism in an age of mobile media. *Digital Journalism, 1*(1), 6–26.

Westlund, O., & Färdigh, M. A. (2015). Accessing the news in an age of mobile media: Tracing displacing and complementary effects of mobile news on newspapers and online news. *Mobile Media and Communication, 3*(1), 53–74.

White, P. R. R. (2003). News as history: Your daily gossip. In J. R. Martin & R. Wodak (Eds.), *Re/reading the past: Critical and functional perspectives on time and value* (pp. 61–89). Amsterdam: John Benjamins.

White, P. R. R. (1997). Death, disruption and the moral order: The narrative impulse in mass media hard news reporting. In F. Christie & J. R. Martin (Eds.), *Genres and institutions: Social processes in the workplace and school* (pp. 101–133). London: Continuum.

Yu, N., & Kong, J. (2016). User experience with web browsing on small screens: Experimental investigations of mobile-page interface design and homepage design for news websites. *Information Sciences, 330,* 427–443.

Zhao, S. (2011). *Learning through multimedia interaction: The construal of primary social science knowledge in web-based digital learning materials* (Unpublished doctoral dissertation). University of Sydney, Sydney. Retrieved from http://hdl.handle.net/2123/8376

11 Images as Ideology in Terrorist-Related Communications

Peter Wignell, Sabine Tan, Kay L. O'Halloran, Rebecca Lange, Kevin Chai, and Michael Wiebrands

1 Introduction

The concept of *image-centricity* refers to the dominance of meanings construed in images over meanings construed in language in multimodal texts. Referring to Norris (2014, p. 90), Stöckl, Caple, and Pflaeging (this volume) state that "image-centricity clearly implies that images become the superordinate mode in a multimodal text, that the directionality of mode elaboration is from image to text/language and that the modes have different 'modal intensity' or 'weight'". They track a shift in image-centricity in media platforms from the 19th century to the present and show that this shift has accelerated with relatively recent rapid advances in digital technology. In journalism, "a fundamental shift towards visual story-telling" (Caple & Knox, 2015, p. 292) is noted, to the point that it is proposed that "story structure has shifted and images now tend to dominate the verbal text" (Bednarek & Caple, 2012, p. 111). This approach to image-centricity is addressed later in this chapter in the discussion of image and text relations in ISIS propaganda materials.

This chapter examines image-centricity and images as ideology in violent extremist-related communications from several directions. First, it considers the use of images and combinations of text and image to synthesize ideology into images displaying iconic artifacts. The initial data source for this exploration is material produced by the Islamic violent extremist organization, which refers to itself as Islamic State (herein after referred to as ISIS). This provides a baseline for analyzing how this group, as perhaps the most prominent violent extremist organization worldwide, foregrounds images in presenting itself and its ideology to the world. Second, much material produced by ISIS is repurposed through mainstream and social media, often taking images from their original context and recontextualizing them in a variety of different media. Some implications, both theoretical and practical, of such repurposing are discussed. The chapter concludes by offering some suggestions for potentially tracking the distribution of known and as yet undiscovered images in online sources through the use of automated image analysis tools which identify key objects in images.

The work reported on in this chapter is part of a larger continuing project, which aims to develop an approach to big data analytics that integrates multimodal discourse analysis with automated text and image analysis. The data for this project comes from Islamic violent extremist discourse, where "similar to conventional social multimedia, the messages exchanged in the 'extremosphere' typically consist of text and visual content" (Rudinac, Gornishka, & Worring, 2017, p. 245). In order to more fully understand how online violent extremist discourses operate as forces for radicalization and how aspects of this discourse are recontextualized, the issue of the meanings arising from the integration of language and images needs to be addressed.

Production and distribution of propaganda online has been a key feature of ISIS's efforts to propagate its agenda through explicitly presenting and attempting to legitimize its worldview and values (see Wignell et al., 2016), with the dual aims of enticing and pressuring supporters and potential supporters to participate in their *jihad*, to commit acts of terror (see Wignell, Tan & O'Halloran, 2017), and to maximize fear and disruption among people ISIS perceive to be their enemies. This material is typically multimodal and includes video and audio material as well as material containing combinations of static images and text. Although much of this material is in Arabic, some 'flagship' items are produced in other languages, with English being the most frequently used language other than Arabic (Zelin, 2015, p. 89). The most prominent and accessible English language material is found in the magazines *Dabiq* and *Rumiyah*. These magazines are carefully and professionally produced, and, although no new editions have appeared since September 2017, all issues of both magazines are readily accessible online. From July 14, 2014 to July 31, 2016, ISIS released 15 issues of *Dabiq* magazine. In September 2016, *Dabiq* was replaced by *Rumiyah* magazine, which has had 13 issues, the last issue being released in September 2017. These magazines have been the outlets through which ISIS most clearly articulates its whole agenda.

The approach taken here is to use systemic functional multimodal discourse analysis (SF-MDA, see O'Halloran, 2008) as an analytical and interpretive framework. There is an existing and growing body of work within and related to the SF-MDA tradition which examines the use of images and text-image relations in Islamic violent extremist discourse and the re-use of images across media and social media platforms (see O'Halloran, Tan, Wignell, Bateman, Pham, Grossman, & Vande Moere, 2016; Tan, O'Halloran, Wignell, Chai, & Lange, 2018; Wignell, O'Halloran, Tan, Lange, & Chai, 2018; Wignell, Tan, & O'Halloran, 2016, 2017; Wignell, Tan, O'Halloran, & Lange, 2017). This work has identified key patterns in both the use and re-use of text and images in and from violent extremist discourse.

This work began with detailed analyses of text, images, and text-image relations in examples of violent extremist materials (Wignell et al., 2016, 2017), and proposed a framework for extending the research into big data analysis (O'Halloran et al., 2016). It then extended the scale and scope of analysis to larger samples from larger datasets (Tan et al., 2018; Wignell et al., 2018) and trialed the use of natural language understanding tools on samples of text produced by ISIS, text which uses recontextualized ISIS images and reports on ISIS activities (Wignell et al., 2018).

Extension of this work into large datasets, however, requires empirical analysis and testing of observations to map discourse patterns and trends in order to identify similarities and differences between these sources. However, the sheer volume of material represents a major obstacle for analysts. It is simply not possible to manually analyze such a volume of material. For example, the initial dataset for this study consisted of the 15 issues of *Dabiq* magazine, containing 1,095 images, and the 13 issues of *Rumiyah* magazine, containing 750 images. Recontextualization of images is also widespread. Of the 1,095 images in *Dabiq*, 773 had been indexed on other webpages 96,576 times as of July 5, 2017 (Tan et al., 2018). One way around this issue is to develop tools for the automated analysis of text, images, and how they combine to make meaning. Large-scale analyses of language and images tend to consider the potential meanings of these modalities separately, whereas in actual instances of use, the meanings arise from a complex integration of the contributions made by images and language. As SF-informed automated analyses are not yet available (Bateman, McDonald, Hiippala, Cuoto-Vale, & Costetchi, 2019), the next best option is to use readily available image and language processing tools, apply an SF-MDA approach to inform the input and interpret the results through an integrated theoretical framework, and offer informed suggestions for further, more specific, training of the existing tools.

2 Theory

In addressing the questions raised in the Introduction, this chapter adopts a research framework which employs the qualitative social semiotic approach of SF-MDA with a view to using this analysis to inform future automated object recognition and image captioning to examine how the analysis of images might potentially be used to identify images related to violent extremism.

Multimodal discourse analysis is the study of meanings arising from the integration of language, images, and other resources in texts, interactions, and events and has emerged as an interdisciplinary field of research that provides new and developing frameworks for analyzing how language and images combine to communicate meaning (see Jewitt,

2014; Jewitt, Bezemer, & O'Halloran, 2016; Kress & van Leeuwen, 2001; O'Halloran, 2004). The approach is based on social semiotics, which studies how sign systems are used to create meaning in context (see van Leeuwen, 2005). SF-MDA (O'Halloran, 2008; O'Halloran et al., 2018) is derived from and builds upon the application of Halliday's systemic functional theory (SFT), where language, images, and other semiotic resources are viewed as resources for making meaning (see Halliday, 1978, 1994a; Halliday & Matthiessen, 2014). Such semiotic resources are viewed as networks of options from which choices are made in multimodal texts. Specifying those options and showing how they are made in particular artifacts provides a contextually motivated method for characterizing the communicative effects when texts and images are combined. SFT was first applied to language but has since been adapted and extended for application to the study of other semiotic resources and to multimodal texts and artifacts to account for the ways in which linguistic and non-linguistic resources combine and interact in communicating meaning (e.g., Kress & van Leeuwen, 2006; O'Halloran, 2008; O'Toole, 2011; van Leeuwen, 2005).

The key principles behind this approach are that language and other semiotic systems are regarded as resources for making meaning and are structured according to the functions for which the resources have evolved to serve in social contexts (see Halliday, 1994b). These functions are realized through what Halliday refers to as metafunctions. According to Halliday, meaning is organized around three kinds of meaning, or metafunctions, and these three metafunctions are realized through simultaneous choices in language and/or other semiotic systems. The *ideational* metafunction consists of two aspects: *experiential* meaning, which construes our experience and knowledge of the world and *logical* meaning, which makes connections between and among events in that world. The *interpersonal* metafunction organizes meanings for enacting social relations and expressing attitudes. The *textual* metafunction organizes meanings into coherent messages (e.g., Halliday, 1978; Halliday & Matthiessen, 2014). From an SF-MDA perspective, the metafunctional principle plays a crucial role in determining the underlying organization of semiotic resources and for investigating the ways in which semiotic choices combine and interact in multimodal texts. This investigation is complemented by concepts from social semiotics, critical discourse analysis, photography, film theory, and visual design (e.g., Kress & van Leeuwen, 2006).

This does not imply that systems which have been developed for the study of language can be directly superimposed on to meanings constructed through other forms of semiosis but, rather, that the principle of metafunctions underlies the semiotic resources through which humans make meaning (see O'Toole, 2011, for an illustration of the application of the metafunctional principle to the analysis of art and architecture). The messages in any communicative situation are characterized along these dimensions. That is, every act of meaningful communication will be about something, involve some kind of relationship among the participants, and be organized as cohesive and coherent text.

3 Image-Centricity in the ISIS Propaganda Magazines

The explanation of image-centricity outlined in Stöckl et al. (this volume) discusses the concept largely in terms of logical meaning: that is, in terms of status or dependency relations (see Martinec & Salway, 2005), which can be viewed in relation to Halliday's (1994a) logico-semantic relations and taxis and in terms of Martin's (1992) and Martin and Rose's (2003) conjunctive relations. The highlighting of logical connections between text and image, however, does not exclude the roles of other metafunctions. Stöckl et al. imply interpersonal and textual connections by saying

> text subordination to us may mean both a semantic centrality of the image that allows it to lead the interpretation of a multimodal text, and a perceptual dominance or salience given to the image that makes it the textual 'entry point' for reading paths and meaning construal. (Stöckl et al., this volume)

Wignell et al. (2018) take a metafunctional discourse semantic approach to examining image and text relations in extremist discourse. They identify three predominant functions of images in articles in the ISIS online magazines *Dabiq* and *Rumiyah*. They distinguish between (a) images which have a so-called documentary function, (b) images which have a so-called primarily symbolic function, and (c) images which exhibit a combination of documentary and symbolic functions. This categorization is not binary. Images are not exclusively in one category or another. The function of the images in context is a question of the degree to which metafunction(s) is/are foregrounded. For example, images with a primarily documentary function "depict or refer to specific (or generic) people actions, places or things. These images are typically captioned and can be related by both position and content directly to specific parts of their accompanying text" (Wignell et al., 2018, p. 7). They typically foreground ideational meaning.

The image and text in Figure 11.1 are from an article with the headline *The Capture of the 4th Regiment Base in Wilayat Shamal Baghdad*. The article is an account of an ISIS military operation involving the use of *istihhadyyin* ('martyrs', typically suicide bombers). The text of the

The battle commenced with the mujāhidīn attacking the main gate in order to pave the way for the istishhādī brothers to enter the base. This was after distracting all of the lookout posts. The gate was opened and the istishhādī brother Abū Muṣʿab al-Almānī entered the base driving an explosives-laden armored military vehicle carrying 7 tons of highly explosive substances. His mission was to target and destroy the base's command center. He entered and detonated his explosive vehicle, completely destroying the command center building.

Dabiq, Issue 9, p. 29

The istishhādiyyīn of Wilāyat Shamāl Baghdād rain destruction on the 4th Regiment base

Dabiq, Issue 9, p. 30

Figure 11.1 Image with primarily documentary function and a sample of the text in which the image is embedded (*Dabiq*, Issue 9, pp. 29–30).

article describes the operation, and the images provide examples as visual support for the text.

On the other hand, images with a symbolic/documentary or symbolic function align more closely with image-centricity. This alignment is not only with regard to dependency status – these images also tend to be textually foregrounded and strongly interpersonally loaded. Figure 11.2 is an example of an image with a symbolic/documentary function.

The image in Figure 11.2 is the lead image in an article which is one of a series entitled *Among the Believers Are Men*. These articles extol the 'virtues' of 'martyrdom' (in ISIS's interpretation of the word) and narrate 'highlights' of the life of the 'martyr', focusing on the deeds that led him to 'martyrdom'. The text is interspersed with citations from Islamic scripture which 'validate' the 'martyr's' actions. The image is documentary in that it identifies a specific 'martyr' (Abu Mansur al-Muhajir) in death. The image is staged in that the body has been posed to highlight the face and to show the wound in the man's forehead and at the same time showing him to appear to be peacefully at rest. It is symbolic in that the 'martyr' is used to provide a visual symbol of the 'virtues' of 'martyrdom'. The 'martyr' is identified as being born in Lebanon but raised in Australia. His nom de guerre, *al-Muhajir*, means 'the migrant', giving him additional symbolic status as a foreign fighter. The image is more textually foregrounded than the image in Figure 11.1, functioning as a kind of visual macro-Theme (see Martin & Rose, 2003, pp. 184–186).

Figure 11.3 shows an example of an image with a primarily symbolic function. The image and the text superimposed on it are taken from an article which is one of a series of articles entitled *Hikmah* ('wisdom').

Ideology in Terrorist-Related Communications 259

Figure 11.2 Image with a symbolic/documentary function (*Rumiyah*, Issue 1, p. 14).

These articles outline ISIS's interpretation of aspects of Islam. The image takes up the whole of the second page of a two-page article. As such, it functions textually as a kind of visual macro-New (see Martin & Rose, 2003, pp. 184–186). What makes the image predominantly symbolic is that the objects foregrounded in the image, the AK47 rifle and the image of Islamic scripture in Arabic, are not specifically identified in the text. The connection is by inference from the text. For example, the text mentions prayer and praying, which are symbolized in the image of scripture. The text also refers to *jihad*, killing that is noble, and blood being spilled, which are symbolized by the image of the AK47 rifle.

These three images exhibit what could be conceived as a multi-faceted continuum of image-centricity, differentiated according to metafunctional orientation. That is, the image in Figure 11.1 is embedded in the text of the article and is directly connected to events described in the article. The image is not textually prominent, and, while it does contain

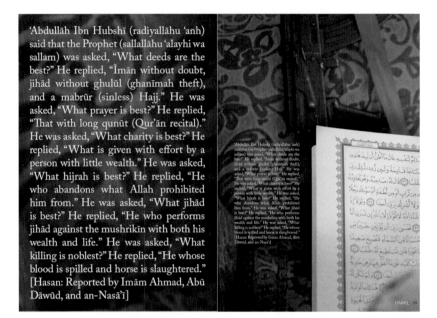

Figure 11.3 Image with a symbolic function and text superimposed over the image (*Dabiq*, Issue 9, p. 39) (Note: The text on the left of the image is the same text that is superimposed on the image. It has been copied and enlarged by the authors so that it is legible.).

interpersonal elements in the caption, its focus is predominantly ideational. The image in Figure 11.2 is also directly connected to the events in the article, but is textually prominent. It precedes the text of the article and, along with the article's title, occupies half of the first page of the article. As well as being textually prominent, it also has a strong interpersonal orientation through distilling the 'virtues' of a 'martyr' discussed in the text into the image of a 'real martyr'. The image in Figure 11.3 is even more textually prominent, occupying a whole page, while the text superimposed over the image occupies approximately one-eighth of the page and is placed so that it does not obscure either of the key objects in the image. In addition, as will be argued in the following discussion on iconization, the objects in the image have a strong interpersonal loading.

In the case of images with symbolic and symbolic/documentary functions, it is possible to view the relationship between text and image as somewhat analogous to the relationship between Token and Value in an identifying clause in systemic functional grammar (SFG) (see Halliday, 1994a, pp. 124–129). When applied to images with strong symbolic associations and accompanying text in the examples discussed in this chapter, the message of the text of the article is distilled into the image, which then serves to represent the key message of the text visually. Rather than the text elaborating the image, the relationship appears to work in both directions. While the image distils and condenses the message of the text, it is the image which is seen first by the viewer and is most salient textually and interpersonally, drawing the viewer/reader into the article. As such, the relationship in these cases is perhaps better regarded as one of complementarity, rather than superordination.

Image-centricity in the ISIS propaganda magazines can be accounted for through the principle of iconization (Martin, 2004; Martin & Stenglin, 2007; Martin & Zappavigna, 2013; Tann, 2013; Thomson, 2014). When considered in metafunctional terms, something becomes an icon when its ideational meaning is reduced and interpersonally charged meanings are concentrated, attached to it, and realized through various forms of semiosis such as words, people, objects, and practices, and in combinations of these. These are referred to as bonding icons, which then serve as emotional focal and rallying points for people (Martin, 2004; Martin & Stenglin, 2007). This is a different use of the term *icon* from its use in Peircian semiotics, where "the icon represents its object by virtue of resembling it" (Peirce, 1886/1993, p. 380). Interpreted through an SFT lens, Peirce's use of *icon* would be seen as relating primarily to ideational meaning, whereas the term as it is used here in relation to bonding icons has a largely interpersonal interpretation.

The principle of iconization has been applied to the function of images in material produced by ISIS and by another Islamic extremist group affiliated with ISIS (Wignell et al., 2016, 2017). This work demonstrates how ISIS (and others) use certain images to synthesize their worldview and espoused values into interpersonally charged bonding icons, which condense a whole set of meanings and associations into one thing. This work forms the foundations of the discussion of the function of images in ISIS's ideology stated later in the chapter.

Martin and Zappavigna (2013, p. 123) propose a set of options for types of bonding icons. These options and descriptions are summarized in Table 11.1.

Table 11.1 Bonding icon options (Adapted from Wignell et al., 2017, p. 434)

Type of bonding icon	Description
Icon Hero	People (or personifications) who are revered members of a community and exemplary role models.
Relic	Physical objects and images of physical objects such as flags and logos.
Creed Scripture	Written or spoken representations of scripture, including images of written scripture.
Enacted creed	Participation in rituals such as religious services, communal prayer, religious gestures.

The options outlined in Table 11.1 have been applied to images and components of images which function as bonding icons in ISIS propaganda material (see Wignell et al., 2016, 2017).

Selections from the set of bonding icon options shown in Table 11.1 can be seen in the images in Figures 11.2 and 11.3. In addition, the approach also provides a theoretical platform for analyzing how multimodal discourses are resemiotized over time in different contexts (Iedema, 2003), with a view to "tracing how semiotics are translated from one into the other as social processes unfold" (Iedema, 2003, p. 29). From this perspective, resemiotization inevitably leads to the construal of new meanings, which may function to either reinforce or negate earlier discourses through the recontextualization of meaning (Iedema, 2003).

Until recently, multimodal discourse analyses have largely been confined to close and detailed analysis of relatively small numbers of texts and artifacts. At the same time, many current approaches employing big data-based methodologies such as social network analysis, data mining, and other tools for analyzing large datasets continue to be grounded in content-and/or platform-focused analyses of, for example, online violent extremist messaging and interactions (e.g., Berger & Strathearn, 2013; Klausen, 2015). While such analyses can offer important insights about the content and spread of violent extremist messages, they remain so far insufficient for revealing communication strategies that rely increasingly on the deployment of a broad range of multimodal semiotic resources. Recent experimental approaches to the analysis of big cultural data (e.g., Manovich, 2017) have shown that combining traditional qualitative approaches with quantitative analysis, computational methods and visualization can prove useful for discovering, describing, and interpreting patterns in large datasets. The method adopted in this chapter represents a prelude to integrating an SF-MDA theoretical approach with automated image analysis. Such a mixed approach will offer an opportunity to bring together close multimodal analysis with data mining and automated analysis techniques to study patterns of recontextualization in the spread of violent extremist images in online media (O'Halloran et al., 2016) and to potentially provide means of identifying previously unidentified violent extremist material.

4 ISIS, Ideology, and Images in Context

This section discusses the role and function of images which serve as bonding icons in ISIS propaganda material, their role in synthesizing ISIS's ideology, and the role of image-centricity in presenting this ideology.

The foundations of ISIS's ideology are derived from the theology and practice of a small, extremist minority within Sunni Islam referred to as Jihadist Salafism. Jihadist Salafists are themselves a small sub-group of what is itself a minority Sunni Islamic faction referred to as Salafism, representing "only 3% of the world's Muslim population" (Rashid, 2015, p. 23). Jihadist Salafists adhere to a strict interpretation of Islamic scripture based on what they believe to be a reconstruction of the beliefs and practices of the generation of Muslims who were contemporaries of the Prophet Muhammad and the two subsequent generations (Stanley, 2005). They believe in a unified Islamic state with no separation between secular and religious life and a strict adherence to their own narrow and rigid interpretation of shari'a[1] (Egerton, 2011). The "austere, intolerant and muscular vision of Islam behind ISIS is jihadist Salafism" (Haykel, 2014, n. p.).

ISIS's ideological agenda is explicitly built in their propaganda materials. This is especially evident in the early issues of *Dabiq* magazine when ISIS was rapidly expanding and most actively recruiting foreign fighters and migrants. ISIS's ideology is encapsulated in an internally cohesive, self-reinforcing system (Wignell et al., 2016, 2017). ISIS builds a vision of an idealized world, founded on and ruled according to its interpretation of a re-imagining of the earliest Islamic practices (Wignell et al., 2016). This worldview is "actively and violently opposed to a polar opposite anti-world of 'near' and 'far' enemies: the world of *kufr* (non-belief): a world populated by apostate Muslims, idol worshippers, Crusaders and Jews" (Wignell et al., 2016, p. 18). The ISIS worldview is uncompromising, and its method of enforcing it can be summarized as 'join us on our terms or we will kill you' (Wignell et al., 2016, p. 10).

This worldview is composed of a set of values (see Wignell et al., 2016, 2017 for a discussion of ISIS values). ISIS explicitly presents the values behind their worldview in the first issue of *Dabiq* (p. 3). These values are presented with descriptions in Table 11.2. Note, it must be acknowledged that the values described in Table 11.2 have many interpretations in Islamic scholarship and practice. The descriptions here are based on ISIS's own narrow and rigid interpretation of Islamic values.

These values are synthesized into a set of largely visual bonding icons. The ISIS worldview, ISIS values, and bonding icons function together in a mutually reinforcing relationship where the set of values collectively form the worldview, which, in turn, endorses the values. Values are synthesized and exemplified in bonding icons, which, in turn, endorse the values. The bonding icons collectively serve to support the worldview and simultaneously exemplify it. These relationships are shown in Figure 11.4.

Each of the values put forward by ISIS in text is synthesized and exemplified by images containing bonding icons. Table 11.3 shows examples of ISIS bonding icons and the values they represent.

The images containing bonding icons tend to show concrete and symbolic visual examples of ISIS's worldview and values of ISIS that are built over quite substantial volumes of text. Much of the text of articles

Table 11.2 Summary of ISIS values (Adapted from Wignell et al., 2016, p. 11)

ISIS value	Description
Tawhid	Belief in the indivisible oneness of Allah. According to ISIS any worship other than this absolute monotheism must be punished and eliminated.
Hijrah	Originally, *Hijrah* referred to the migration of the Prophet Muhammad and his followers to Medina in 622CE. It has come to mean migration for the sake of Allah. ISIS consider *hijrah* to be obligatory.
Manhaj	Generally used to mean living according to Islamic principles and practices. ISIS interprets this to mean living according to a reconstruction/reimagining of the practices of the Prophet Muhammad and the earliest devotees of Islam.
Jam'ah	Refers to the Muslim community or *ummah*. According to ISIS, this means Muslims must live under the ISIS caliphate, be ruled by their caliph and their own narrow and rigid interpretation of shari'a.
Jihad	Jihad is also a term with many interpretations. According to ISIS, *jihad* implies a continuing military struggle against all 'non-believers'.

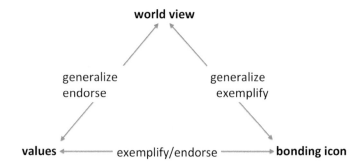

Figure 11.4 The relationship between the ISIS worldview, values, and bonding icons.

Table 11.3 ISIS bonding icons and values

Bonding icon type	Signified by	Value(s) represented
Heroes	References in text to Allah and the Prophet Muhammad (including inscriptions on the ISIS flag), ISIS leaders, mujahideen and 'martyrs'	jihad, manhaj, hijrah, tawheed
Relic	ISIS flag, AK47 assault rifle	tawheed, jihad
Scripture	Citations of scripture, images of text of scripture (in Arabic), inscriptions on ISIS flag	tawheed
Enacted creed	tawheed gesture,[2] communal prayer	tawheed, jam'ah (communal prayer)

contains citations from scripture, which provide a basis for the rationale for the ISIS vision of how the world should be. In order to make sense of much of the text, at least a working knowledge of Islamic scripture and some knowledge of Arabic are required. As an example, an extract from the text preceding the image in Figure 11.5 is included:

> To the extent that they were cursed by their own Prophets.
> {Cursed were those who disbelieved among the Children of Isrā'īl by the tongue of Dāwūd (David) and of 'Īsā (Jesus), the son of Maryam (Mary). That was because they disobeyed and [habitually] transgressed} [Al-Mā'idah: 78].
> In discussing the incident that led the Children of Isrā'īl to kill Yahyā (John the Baptist) ('alayhis-salam), we'll examine his name and the fact that it appears to foreshadow his martyrdom.
> Allah ta'ālā says, {(Allah said) "O Zakarīyā! Verily, We give you the glad tidings of a son whose name will be Yahyā. We have given that name to none before (him)} [Maryam: 7]. (*Dabiq*, Issue 5, p. 6)

The article, titled 'Yahya: Lessons from a shahid' (martyr), spans six pages and is about the martyrdom of Yahya (John the Baptist). The text of the article follows the pattern of the extract: relatively short narrative passages interspersed with citations from Islamic scripture. The text uses the story of John the Baptist, an ISIS hero, as an exemplar of a martyr. Figure 11.5 is an example of an image having what Wignell et al. (2018) describe as a symbolic function. That is, it depicts an unnamed example of an ISIS hero (a *mujahid* and therefore potential martyr), making an iconic gesture, accompanied by the ISIS flag. The image has no direct

Figure 11.5 Image containing relic, scripture (ISIS flag), hero (mujahid), and enacted creed (tawheed gesture) (*Dabiq*, Issue 5, p. 7).

connection to the wording of the text. Its connection to the text of the article is by inference and is symbolic.

While the text is likely to prove difficult for the lay reader, the image, on the other hand, catches the viewer's eye and provides a similar but condensed message. Unlike the text, the associations that the bonding icons distil are immediately accessible. The distillation of meaning is enhanced by the composite nature of the bonding icons, in this case containing four choices from the set of options (hero, relic, scripture, and enacted creed).

The flag itself is a relic, but the inscriptions on the flag are scripture, which refers to Islam's two foremost heroes, Allah and the Prophet Muhammad. The white banner at the top of the flag reads 'There is no god but Allah. Muhammad is the messenger of Allah'. The black writing and the white circle are meant to represent the seal of the Prophet Muhammad. The black writing translates as "Muhammad is the messenger of God" (Kovács, 2015, p. 55). The ISIS flag encapsulates all of the ISIS values. The value of *jihad* is represented by the *mujahid*, who, as well as holding the flag, is also showing his piousness by making the *tawheed* gesture (enacted creed) with his left hand. The bonding icons in this one image crystallize over six pages of text. Iconic images such as this are often placed in positions of textual prominence in their original context but can be readily detached from the articles they are connected to and re-circulated widely and easily as either free-standing artifacts in their own right or recontextualized in other media.

In general, the texts in which images with a primarily symbolic function were found were texts which outlined and built ISIS's interpretation of Islam. Images with a symbolic function typically contained ISIS icons such as ISIS flags and AK47 assault rifles and were typically found in positions of textual prominence in the texts in which they were embedded. Humans in these images were typically generic ISIS heroes, most often unidentified *mujahideen*. Images with a documentary function were often found in field reports of ISIS activities and were directly linked through proximity or captions to particular events in the accompanying text. Images having a symbolic/documentary function showed specific ISIS heroes, typically 'martyrs', and were textually prominent in articles which told of the 'martyr's' exemplary life and deeds. Images of foreign captives also often had a symbolic/documentary function in that they depicted real events but were used to show symbolically the humiliation of ISIS's enemies. The images with symbolic and symbolic/documentary functions tended to foreground the interpersonal and textual metafunctions, with textual choices locating interpersonal choices in positions of prominence in texts. Images with a documentary function tended to foreground the ideational metafunction (Wignell et al., 2018).

5 Images Recontextualized

Sets of meanings created multimodally through image and text relations in the image's original context can be replaced by other sets of meanings created by new image and text relations brought about through recontextualization. An image which had a particular relationship to its accompanying text in one context, once detached and recontextualized, can open up multiple possible new meanings. Reverse image searches were conducted using TinEye,[3] which identifies the websites where the image was found and the date when the sites were crawled. The recontextualization of the images is displayed graphically using the Multimodal Analysis Visualization application (O'Halloran et al., 2018). The red line on the graph shows when the image first appeared in *Dabiq* magazine (see Figures 11.6 (a and b)).

Tan et al. (2018) examined the redistribution of a sample of images and identified several broad patterns. Two of the characteristic patterns are shown in Figures 11.6 (a and b). Both of these images have been widely recontextualized: the image in Figure 11.6 (a) 541 times as on December 22, 2017; the image in Figure 11.6 (b) 1160 times as on January 15, 2018.

The pattern in Figure 11.6 (a) shows that the redistribution of the images is tied to a particular event or events that were considered newsworthy at the time. These events were typically either a terror attack against a Western country of the capture and murder of a "far enemy" (Tan et al., 2018). The image in Figure 11.6 (a) is of captive British journalist John Cantlie. The image appeared in Issue 4 of *Dabiq* and shows a spike and drop-off in redistribution, with the frequency of redistribution dropping consistently as time elapses. Figure 11.6 (b) has a very different pattern, which shows a consistent and relatively high level of redistribution enduring over time. Images of this type most often contain ISIS bonding icons (see O'Halloran et al., 2016; Wignell et al., 2016, 2017; Tan et al., 2018).

Wignell et al. (2018) also examined patterns of recontextualization of images by analyzing the functions of a sample of images in their context in articles in ISIS-produced materials and in their recontextualizations in a variety of online media and social media sites. In their recontextualizations, images with documentary and symbolic/documentary functions in their original contexts most typically functioned as documentary images in their new contexts as they were most often directly linked to some event or person in their new context. For example, the image in Figure 11.6 (a) has a documentary function in its recontextualisation. The article in which the image is embedded is about the captive British journalist John Cantlie.

Images, which initially functioned symbolically in ISIS materials, often also appeared to function symbolically in their new contexts, although differently from how they were used by ISIS. In their new contexts, they

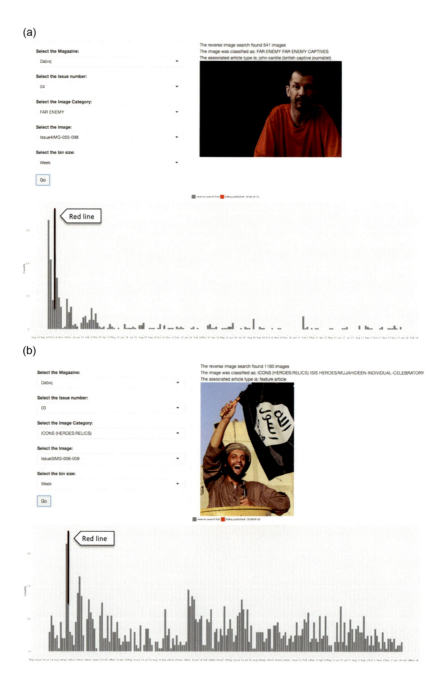

Figure 11.6 (a and b) Screenshots of two patterns of recontextualization of ISIS images.

appeared to function as stock images which had very little to do with the content of the article they were embedded in and were used simply to signify that the article was related to ISIS. They appear to function as floating signifiers (Lévi-Strauss, 1950). As such, the images are open to multiple different interpretations. That is, the articles using interpersonally charged ISIS icons to identify ISIS and which recirculate images of this type multiple times, open up the possibility of inadvertently distributing ISIS's message through their icons. This inadvertent publicity of ISIS through re-use of ISIS images in mainstream media has also been pointed out in O'Halloran et al. (2016).

6 Summary and Conclusions

This chapter has shown how ISIS's ideology, exemplified through its worldview and values, is condensed into bonding icons which are captured in images presented as part of ISIS's propaganda in materials produced by ISIS and that image-centricity plays a central role in these images being placed in positions of textual prominence. It has also shown that ISIS propaganda material is widely distributed and redistributed on the Internet through recontextualization of images in different textual contexts.

A key feature of publicly available ISIS materials is the use of bonding icons in images. Tracking of individual icons and combinations of icons is one possible way of identifying and tracking the distribution of ISIS and other violent extremist propaganda. However, while reverse image search tools can be used to find known images in circulation, other image-tracking techniques such as what is referred to as photo DNA (Farid, 2009; "New Technology Fights Child Porn", 2009) can be used to track images which have been substantially altered; in both cases, a source image is required to track from, just as with DNA testing, you need a sample of your DNA before you can find out who you are related to. While attempts are being made to identify and remove violent extremist materials from the Internet by Facebook, YouTube, Twitter, Microsoft, and other large companies,[4] there are many images and other propaganda materials which are still in circulation, and these are expected to increase, given the situation facing ISIS, as detailed in the following text.

A direction for future exploration in finding and tracking previously undetected images is through the use of image analysis tools such as DenseCap,[5] which can identify and caption key objects in images and, with additional training, hopefully more accurately caption them. In addition, the identification of more abstract features inferred from images would assist in identifying connections and associations between images and their accompanying text. The use of other automated image analysis tools such as Claraifai[6] and IBM Watson Visual Recognition,[7] in combination with DenseCap, could assist in this process, as these tools provide descriptive and inferential information about images which is not provided by DenseCap, which places bounding boxes around objects in an image and a caption for each bounding box.

Viewed in metafunctional terms, the identification and captioning of objects is based on ideational meaning: only things, attributes, locations, and some processes are identified. However, while features realizing textual and interpersonal meaning are not specifically identified, they can be inferred. For example, ISIS bonding icons can be identified by their ideational content as objects, but, since they function as bonding icons, these objects are also carrying a heavy interpersonal loading. Thus, identifying them as objects also identifies them interpersonally. Textual prominence can be inferred from the size and positioning of the bounding boxes. Figure 11.7 (a) shows DenseCap bounding boxes and captions for 20 objects identified in the image. Figure 11.7 (b) shows the same image, with the bounding boxes and captions reduced to two. The two most visually prominent features are bounded by the largest boxes. The other boxes appear to reduce in size in proportion to their decrease in textual prominence. Therefore, if DenseCap can be trained to successfully identify ISIS icons ideationally, some interpersonal and textual features are also included.

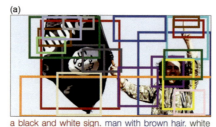

Figure 11.7 (a and b) Examples of DenseCap object recognition and captioning of an iconic ISIS image (*Dabiq*, Issue 5, p. 7).

Similarly, if DenseCap and other similar tools such as Clarifai and IBM Watson Visual Recognition could be trained to identify specifically the most readily identifiable members of the set of ISIS icons, then this retrieval option could prove effective in finding violent extremist images which contained one or more of these icons.

A combination of existing reverse image tracking and image analysis tools, which had been trained to recognize and correctly caption key ISIS icons and combinations of icons and which also incorporated natural language queries, would facilitate both the tracking of known images and the identification and tracking of previously unknown images. Both of these together would greatly enhance the identification and tracking of violent Islamic extremist propaganda online. Such tools would not be restricted to violent extremist material. Identification of and training in the recognition of key features of images associated with virtually any domain of human experience would enable these tools to be used to track the distribution of such images through the Internet.

Notes

1 *Shari'a* refers to Islamic law and jurisprudence. For a discussion of *shari'a*, see Quraishi-Landes (2015).
2 What we refer to as the *tawheed* gesture involves a raised index finger pointed to the sky, signifying the indivisible oneness of *Allah*.
3 TinEye (https://www.tineye.com/) identifies the websites and the date when these sites were crawled. TinEye creates a digital signature of the image and matches it with other indexed images in order to identify the sites in which the image appears.
4 https://www.theguardian.com/technology/2017/jun/26/google-facebook-counter-terrorism-online-extremism.
5 https://cs.stanford.edu/people/karpathy/densecap/ (See Johnson et al., 2016).
6 https://www.clarifai.com/demo.
7 https://www.ibm.com/watson/services/visual-recognition/demo/#demo.

References

Bateman, J. (2014). *Text and image: A critical introduction to the visual/verbal divide*. London: Routledge.
Bateman, J., McDonald, D., Hiippala, T., Couto-Vale, D., & Costetchi, E. (2019). Systemic functional linguistics and computation: New directions, new challenges. In G. Thompson, W. L. Bowcher, L. Fontaine, & D. Schönthal (Eds.), *The Cambridge handbook of systemic functional linguistics* (pp. 561–586). Cambridge, UK: Cambridge University Press.
Bednarek, M., & Caple, H. (2012). *News discourse*. London: Continuum.
Berger, J. M., & Strathearn, B. (2013). *Who matters online: Measuring influence, evaluating content and countering violent extremism in online social networks*. London: The International Centre for the Study of Radicalisation and Political Violence.
Caple, H., & Knox, J. S. (2015). A Framework for the multimodal analysis of online news galleries: What makes a 'good' picture gallery? *Social Semiotics*, 25(3), 292–321.

Egerton, F. (2011). *Jihad in the West: The rise of militant Salafism.* Cambridge, UK: Cambridge University Press.

Farid, H. (2009). A survey of image forgery detection. *IEEE Signal Processing Magazine, 26*(2), 16–25.

Halliday, M. A. K. (1994a). *An introduction to functional grammar* (2nd ed.). London: Arnold.

Halliday, M. A. K. (1994b). Systemic theory. In R. E. Asher (Ed.), *The encyclopedia of language and linguistics: Vol. 8.* Oxford: Pergamon Press.

Halliday, M. A. K. (1978). *Explorations in the functions of language.* London: Arnold.

Halliday, M. A. K., & Matthiessen, C. (2014). *Halliday's introduction to functional grammar.* London: Routledge.

Haykel, B. (2015, June 3). ISIS: A primer. *Princeton Alumni Weekly.* Retrieved from https://paw.princeton.edu/article/isis-primer

Iedema, R. (2003). Multimodality, resemiotization: Extending the analysis of discourse as multisemiotic practice. *Visual Communication, 2*(1), 29–57.

Jewitt, C. (Ed.). (2014). *The Routledge handbook of multimodal analysis* (2nd ed.). London: Routledge.

Jewitt, C., Bezemer, J., & O'Halloran, K. L. (2016). *Introducing multimodality.* London: Routledge.

Johnson, J., Karpathy, A., & Li, F. F. (2016, June). *DenseCap: Fully convolutional localization networks for dense captioning.* Paper presented at the 29th IEEE conference on computer vision and pattern recognition, Las Vegas, NV. doi: 10.1109/CVPR.2016.494

Klausen, J. (2015). Tweeting the Jihad: Social media networks of western foreign fighters in Syria and Iraq. *Studies in Conflict & Terrorism, 38*(1), 1–22.

Kovács, A. (2015). The "New Jihadists" and the visual turn from al-Qa'ida to ISIL / ISIS / Da'ish. *Biztpol Affairs, 2*(3), 47–69.

Kress, G., & van Leeuwen, T. (2006). *Reading images: The grammar of visual design* (2nd ed.). London: Routledge.

Kress, G., & van Leeuwen, T. (2001). *Multimodal discourse: The modes and media of contemporary communication.* London: Arnold.

Lévi-Strauss, C. (1950). Introduction a l'oeuvre de Marcel Mauss. *Mauss, sociologie et anthropologie* [Sociology and anthropology]. Paris: Presses Universitaires de France.

Manovich, L. (2017). Cultural data: Possibilities and limitations of digitized archives. In O. Grau (Ed.) with W. Coones & V. Rühse, *Museum and archive on the move: Changing cultural institutions in the digital era* (pp. 259–276). Berlin: De Gruyter.

Martin, J. R. (2004). Negotiating difference: Ideology and reconciliation. In M. Putz, J. van Aertselaer & T. J. van Dijk (Eds.), *Communicating ideologies: Multidisciplinary perspectives on language, discourse and social practice* (pp. 85–177). Frankfurt: Peter Lang.

Martin, J. R. (1992). *English text: System and structure.* Amsterdam: John Benjamins.

Martin, J. R., & Rose, D. (2003). *Working with discourse: Meaning beyond the clause.* London: Continuum.

Martin, J., & Stenglin, M. (2007). Materialising reconciliation: Negotiating difference in a transcolonial exhibition. In T. Royce & W. Bowcher (Eds.),

New directions in the analysis of multimodal discourse (pp. 215–238). Mahwah, NJ: Erlbaum.
Martin, J. R., & Zappavigna, M. (2013). Youth justice conferencing: Ceremonial redress. *International Journal of Law, Language & Discourse, 3*(2), 103–142.
Martinec, R., & Salway, A. (2005). A system for image-text relations in new (and old) media. *Visual Communication, 4*(3), 337–371.
New technology fights child porn by tracking its "PhotoDNA". (2009, December 15). *Microsoft.* Retrieved from https://news.microsoft.com/2009/12/15/new-technology-fights-child-porn-by-tracking-its-photodna/#sm.0001mpmupctevct7pjn11vtwrw6xj
Norris, S. (2014). Modal density and modal configurations. In C. Jewitt (Ed.), *The Routledge handbook of multimodal analysis* (2nd ed.) (pp. 86–99). London: Routledge.
O'Halloran, K. L. (2008). Systemic functional-multimodal discourse analysis (SF-MDA): Constructing ideational meaning using language and visual imagery. *Visual Communication, 7*(4), 443–475.
O'Halloran, K. L. (Ed.). (2004). *Multimodal discourse analysis*. London: Continuum.
O'Halloran, K. L., Tan, S., Wignell, P., Bateman, J., Pham, D.-S., Grossman, M., & Vande Moere, A. (2016). Interpreting text and image relations in violent extremist discourse: A mixed methods approach for big data analytics. *Terrorism and Political Violence, 31*(3), 454–474.
O'Halloran, K. L., Tan, S., Wignell, P., & Lange, R. (2018). Multimodal recontextualisations of images in violent extremist discourse. In S. Zhao, E. Djonov, A. Björkvall, & M. Boeriis (Eds.), *Advancing multimodal and critical discourse studies: Interdisciplinary Research inspired by Theo van Leeuwen's social semiotics* (pp. 181–202). New York: Routledge.
O'Toole, M. (2011). *The language of displayed art* (2nd ed.). London: Routledge.
Peirce, C. S. (1886/1993). An elementary account of the logic of relatives. In C. J. W. Kloesel (Ed.), *Writings of Charles S. Peirce: A chronological edition: Vol. 5. 1884–1886* (pp. 380–390). Bloomington: Indiana University Press.
Quraishi-Landes, A. (2015). The Sharia problem with Sharia legislation. *Ohio North University Law Review, 41*(3), 545–566.
Rashid, A. (2015). *ISIS: Race to Armageddon*. New Delhi: Vij Books.
Rudinac, S., Gornishka, I., & Worring, M. (2017, October). Multimodal classification of violent online political extremism content with graph convolutional networks. In *Thematic workshops '17. Proceedings of the thematic workshops of ACM multimedia 2017* (pp. 245–252). Mountain View, CA: Association for Computing Machinery.
Stanley, T. (2005). Understanding the origins of Wahhabism and Salafism. *Terrorism Monitor, 3*(14). Retrieved from http://www.jamestown.org/programs/tm/single/?tx_ttnews[tt_news]=528&#.Vlaqt7-6R4l
Tan, S., O'Halloran, K. L., Wignell, P., Chai, K., & Lange, R. (2018). A multimodal mixed methods approach for examining recontextualisation patterns of violent extremist images in online media. *Discourse, Context & Media, 21*, 18–35.
Tann, K. (2013). The language of identity discourse: Introducing a systemic functional framework for iconography. *Linguistics and the Human Sciences, 8*(3), 361–391.

Thomson, E. A. (2014). *Battling with words: A study of language, diversity and social inclusion in the Australian Department of Defence*. Canberra: Australian Government, Department of Defence.

van Leeuwen, T. (2005). *Introducing social semiotics*. London: Routledge.

Wignell, P., Chai, K., Tan, S., O'Halloran, K. L., & Lange, R. (2018). Natural language understanding and multimodal discourse analysis for interpreting extremist communications and the re-use of these materials online. *Terrorism and Political Violence*. Advance online publication.

Wignell, P., O'Halloran, K. L., Tan, S., Lange, R., & Chai, K. (2018). Image and text relations in ISIS materials and the new relations established through recontextualisation in online media. *Discourse & Communication, 12*(5), 535–559.

Wignell, P., Tan, S., & O'Halloran, K. L. (2017). Under the shade of AK47s: A multimodal approach to violent extremist recruitment strategies for foreign fighters. *Critical Studies on Terrorism, 10*(3), 429–452.

Wignell, P., Tan, S., & O'Halloran, K. L. (2016). Violent extremism and iconisation: Commanding good and forbidding evil? *Critical Discourse Studies, 14*(1), 1–22.

Wignell, P., Tan, S., O'Halloran, K. L., & Lange, R. (2017). A mixed methods empirical examination of changes in emphasis and style in the extremist magazines Dabiq and Rumiyah. *Perspectives on Terrorism, 11*(2), 2–20.

Zelin, A. Y. (2015). Picture or it didn't happen: A snapshot of the Islamic State's official media output. *Perspectives on Terrorism, 9*(4), 85–97.

12 Putting the Data Center Stage

Graphs, Charts, and Maps in the News Media

Martin Engebretsen

1 Introduction

Data visualization is a semiotic phenomenon of growing prevalence and impact in contemporary society – not least in the news media (e.g., Kennedy, Hill, Aiello, & Allen, 2016; Loosen, Reimer, & De Silva-Schmidt, 2017; Rinsdorf & Boers, 2016). Graphs, charts and maps – sometimes in animated or interactive forms – are used to contextualize news events, to add proof to verbal claims, and to activate the user in various ways (Engebretsen, Kennedy, & Weber, 2018). Sometimes, a data visualization works more or less as a stand-alone unit. In such cases, verbal elements have only supportive functions, in the forms of legends, explanations, or 'how-we-did-it' articles. This chapter investigates how these text formats, dominated by graphical expressions, represent discursive processes involving particular potentials of meanings and patterns of *intersemiotic interplay*. In the last sections, I discuss what kinds of media literacy they demand and how they influence the development of journalistic genres.

Greater access to datasets and better software for the visualization of numeric data are two of the driving forces behind the proliferation of data visualization (DV) in the news media. In almost all newsrooms of a certain size, priority is given to the building of cross-disciplinary teams tasked with producing data-driven news, in which DVs play a core role (Engebretsen et al., 2018). A news story on an epidemic outbreak will today be expected to be accompanied by a diagrammatic and cartographic representation of statistical, historical, and geographical information.

DV promises to make statistical material accessible and intelligible even for untrained users, and it can help users to see patterns and relations that otherwise would be difficult or impossible to detect (Bertin, 1967/2011; Few, 2004; Tufte, 2006). As such, DV is sometimes promoted as a guarantor of a fact-based discourse.[1] However, the *datafication* of society also raises questions concerning discursive focus and power (cf. Couldry & Yu, 2018). What cannot be measured and quantified will not be represented in a data-based discourse. Moreover, even though the data behind a DV are correctly measured, the visualization is still a product of many choices – concerning the data selected, the context in which it is placed, and the forms, axes, and scales applied in the actual visualization. Thus, although DVs may appear as objective reflections of the world, they perform discursive and often ideological work in the social contexts in which they are applied, comparable to that of words, photos, and video-clips. The digital footprint of a producer, of a human agent behind the DV, is thus an important factor in terms of trust and transparency.

In this chapter, I explore the discursive potentials of DVs in a news media context, based on these questions: *How can stand-alone data visualizations, as found on online news sites, be described as image-centric textual resources? What kinds of literacy do they demand and how do they affect journalistic genres?* The first question is prioritized. The study draws on investigations from several areas related to multimodal discourse analysis. Starting from a basic description of data visualization as a semiotic and discursive resource (Bertin, 1967/2011; Kress & van Leeuwen, 2006), I discuss some critical implications of the multimodal orchestration they represent. The interplay between the graphic expression and the verbal text elements is a particular focus. Moving from textual perspectives to interactional and cultural ones, the chapter will, in the closing sections, discuss the relation between DVs and media literacy, and their impact on news journalism. Two selected sample texts will illustrate and inform the theoretical discussions. Other empirical findings will also support the arguments, mainly collected from a recent text analysis of DVs on Norwegian news sites (Engebretsen, 2017) and from an interview study examining DV practices in Scandinavian newsrooms (Engebretsen et al., 2018).[2]

2 Core Concepts

The term *data visualization* refers to a visual representation of (most often numeric) data, created to amplify the cognitive processing and social application of the data represented (cf. Borgo et al., 2013; Cairo, 2013). DV is closely related to *information graphics*, but an infographic may not contain any numeric data at all, or may display data alongside other illustrations, like drawings or photographs. DVs come in a wide range of graphical forms and are often used in data-driven journalism as a tool for visual storytelling (Loosen et al., 2017; Weber, Engebretsen, & Kennedy, 2018).

When a DV appears with an individual title and in a layout framing it as an independent text, we may use the term *stand-alone data visualization*. This textual unit will often contain verbal elements, separated from or integrated within the area of the graphic model, forming what we may call a 'DV-cluster'. A stand-alone DV may be connected to how-we-did-it stories, or to a number of relevant news reports, as well as to fora for reader debate. However, it is not *dependent* on any of these related texts in order to work as a meaningful text unit.

3 Theoretical Framework

In the introduction to this volume, Stöckl, Caple, and Pflaeging define the concept of *image-centricity* within the framework of multimodal theory as a text-image relation where the image is superordinate in terms of semantic and functional weight. With reference to Barthes (1964/1977), they classify the text-image relation as one of *anchorage*, where the text, in cases of *strong* image-centricity, will anchor the entirety of the image, not only parts of it. Further, according to Stöckl et al. (this volume), in addition to a semantic centrality of the image, the image will function as an "[…] 'entry point' for reading paths and meaning construal" due to its perceptual dominance. Based on these definitions, they call for more detailed empirical investigations of the cohesive ties and semiotic interplay characterizing image-centric text types.

In order to respond to that call, this chapter builds on semiotic and social semiotic theory with a special focus on graphics. The French cartographer and semiologist Jacques Bertin is acknowledged as the founding father of a semiotics of graphics. In the book *Semiology of graphics* (original title is *Sémiologie graphique*, first published in 1967), he identifies three basic units that are visible as markings on the two-dimensional plane, namely, the *point*, the *line*, and the *area*. The visual appearance of these markings are determined by the variables *size, value, texture, color, orientation, position,* and *shape* (Bertin, 1967/2011). Bertin's system has been augmented and modified by a number of scholars and practitioners, taking, for example, three-dimensional and dynamic developments into account (see summaries in Halik, 2012). However, Bertin's basic units and variables are still authoritative in semiotic and linguistic approaches to DV.

More frequently cited in the context of multimodal studies is the book *Reading Images* by Günther Kress and Theo van Leeuwen (2006, first published in 1996). Drawing on the social semiotics of Michael Halliday (cf. Halliday, 1978), the two authors describe graphical language as a semiotic mode with particular capacities in the field of *compositional meaning*, creating coherence and structure in a given material, but also with specific qualities concerning the creation of *ideational* and *interpersonal* meaning potentials. Ideational meaning refers to how aspects of the (physical, social, or imagined) world are represented in a text or a cultural object, while interpersonal meaning refers to how the text constructs identities, social relations, and roles in the interplay between the participants in the process of communication. Kress and van Leeuwen (2006, p. 163) make an important distinction between iconic images – like photos – and images based on abstract visual forms – like graphs and charts – when it comes to their cultural value as *true* representations of reality, using the concept of *coding orientation*. While photos refer to reality according to a naturalistic coding orientation, in which detail, color, saturation, and resolution are regarded as criteria for truth-telling, graphs and charts are based on an abstract coding orientation, meaning that their ability to represent the real world "[...] is higher the more an image reduces the individual to the general, and the concrete to its essential qualities" (Kress & van Leeuwen, 2006, p. 165).

In a wider context, the increased use of DVs in journalism points to new forms of media literacy, and also to genre developments with interesting cultural implications. Jay Lemke (2006) underlines that our modern text culture, with highly complex, multimodal, and digital text forms, demands new forms of complex literacies, in which nuanced insights into the affordances of visual modes must be integrated. He calls for: "[...] a genuinely critical multimedia literacy to maintain our relative autonomy in making choices about what and who to believe, identify with, emulate, admire, scorn, or hate" (Lemke, 2006, p. 7). Within the field of journalism, the professional ethos is based on the ability of journalists to report on socially important events and conditions in a manner that is engaging, meaningful, and balanced (Mencher, 1997). As many commentators have noted, this ethos is challenged by certain conventionalized models of narrative storytelling (e.g., Engebretsen, 2000; Tuchman, 1978; Weber et al., 2018) and of the institutionalized news values regulating the journalistic production processes (cf. Bednarek & Caple, 2012, 2017). Factors that affect the development of the journalistic genres include changing technological and semiotic affordances, shifts in consumption patterns, as well as broader cultural developments (Engebretsen, 2006; Lüders, Prøitz, & Rasmussen, 2010). An interesting question is thus: will an increased use of DV strengthen fact-based news reporting, or will it rather lead to a situation where journalists become less visible as human agents in the public discourse, hiding behind a growing mantra of "show, don't tell"? I return to these questions in the last section of the chapter.

4 Related Work on Data Visualization

Being a cross-disciplinary field of study, research into DV includes a number of different trajectories. The most visible branch addresses the perspectives of practitioners, asking how numerical data can be visualized in an optimally clear and effective way (Few, 2004; Kirk, 2016; Mollerup, 2015; Tufte, 2001) and how to tell stories with data (Cairo, 2013, 2016; Nussbaumer Knaflic, 2015). In another, younger strand of literature, DV is discussed and investigated as a socially situated, discursive, and rhetorical resource in society. Building on semiotic theory by pioneers like Bertin (1967/2011) and Kress and van Leeuwen (2006), this strand of literature investigates how DV is applied in order to explain, convince, and tell stories in different domains of discourse, and how norms and conventions related to the language of graphics slowly emerge and spread. Furthermore, issues of participation and power are studied in this branch of DV literature (e.g., Engebretsen, 2013; Hullman & Diakopoulos, 2011; Kennedy et al., 2016; Lima, 2011; Weber et al., 2018).

The application of DV in journalism, as an aspect of the evolving practices of data journalism, has gained growing academic attention in recent years. Several commentators point out that data have become an important content element in news stories and, consequently, DV has become a formal element of growing impact and relevance (e.g., Ausserhofer, Gutounig, Oppermann, Matiasek, & Goldgruber, 2017; Engebretsen et al., 2018; Gynnild, 2013; Hannaford, 2015). Rinsdorf and Boers (2016) state that the increased application of DV in news discourse is indicative of a growing focus on background information and explanation in journalism. Research has also revealed that everyday data-driven news stories most often include static DVs in the forms of bar charts, line graphs, and maps (Stalph, 2017). In many newsrooms, toolboxes are developed in order to help ordinary journalists complement their own news stories with such visual material (Engebretsen et al., 2018). Specialist teams of developers and designers are thus able to concentrate on more advanced visualizations. Studies reveal that award-winning projects often offer interactive features, and sometimes include elements of animation (Loosen et al., 2017; Young & Fulda, 2017). Other early insights in the field of DV in journalism are offered by Appelgren and Nygren (2014), Appelgren (2018), Fink and Anderson (2015), Flew, Spurgeon, Daniel, & Swift (2012), Gynnild (2013), Karlsen and Stavelin (2014), Lewis and Westlund (2015), de Maeyer, Libert, Domingo, Heinderyckx, & Le Cam (2015), and Weber and Rall (2012). However, none of these studies offer a detailed investigation of DV as an image-centric, multimodal textual resource in the context of news discourse.

5 Notes on Methodology

This chapter aims to contribute to the investigation of image-centricity by analyzing and discussing two samples of stand-alone DV published on a major Norwegian news site. The analysis draws on multimodal theory, focusing on the interplay between graphic and verbal meaning resources within each of the three metafunctions – the ideational, the interpersonal, and the compositional (cf. Kress & van Leeuwen, 2006). Following the analysis, the findings are summarized with reference to the characteristics of image-centricity, as presented by Stöckl et al. in the introduction of this book, before they are discussed in relation to the concept of media literacy and to the development of news journalism.

280 *Martin Engebretsen*

One of the two DVs in the study functions as the main object of analysis, whilst the other one serves the purpose of comparison. Both sample DVs are found on the news site with the highest number of daily readers in Norway, VG.no, produced by the major news house Verdens Gang (VG). VG is among the leading actors in Scandinavia in terms of developing new forms of visual storytelling in journalism. The main sample text, Sample 1, is chosen because it represents an innovative type of DV, in the sense that it offers both interactive and dynamic features. At the same time, it represents the emerging journalistic practice of harvesting and processing publicly available data in a journalistic context (cf. Engebretsen et al., 2018). It also represents the kind of DV that relates directly to people's everyday lives, not only to distanced or abstracted patterns of change and development. The second sample text (Sample 2) is chosen because it complements Sample 1 in various ways. It represents another type of visualization; it uses verbal elements in a different way, and, finally, it relates to another domain of content, namely, international affairs.

The analysis, although following a systematic schema, is not meant to be exhaustive. It is designed to illuminate interesting aspects of the interplay between verbal (including numeric) and visual text elements in this specific domain of multimodal discourse.

6 The Data Samples

The Norwegian tabloid Verdens Gang (VG) will normally use a team consisting of a data journalist, a visual designer, and a programmer in productions that involve advanced forms of DV, like the two samples presented later in the text. In a personal interview, the editor-in-chief of VG, Gard Steiro, states that VG gives high priority to the development of DV as an integrated part of the newsroom practices.[3] The DV in Sample 1 (see Figure 12.1) offers a multimodal account of all of the 99,989 delays at Norwegian railway stations during 2016, answering questions concerning where the trains stopped, for how long, and for what reasons.

The DV is the dominant part of a multimodal text composed of several elements. It has a tripartite composition, where a zoomable map forms the backdrop, and a large menu element is located to the left of the map. The menu invites the user to search for data related to a specific train station and offers code information concerning the colors of the circles. A red circle means that the delay is caused by the train company, a blue circle means that infrastructural problems caused the delay, and a yellow circle indicates that other, external matters caused the delay. Directly under the map, the DV has a timeline in the form of a small locomotive moving on a 'railway'. On the part of the map showing the Norwegian mainland, there are circles of different sizes and in three different colors.

Figure 12.1 Sample 1: The DV, published on the news site VG.no, reveals the position, duration, and cause of all train delays at Norwegian railway stations during 2016. Downloaded from https://www.vg.no/spesial/2017/togstopp/. Reproduced with permission.

282   *Martin Engebretsen*

When clicking on a circle, the user will activate a pop-up box that provides detailed information about a train stop at a particular station on a particular date.

Thus, the graphic mode, in a form combining a topographic map with geometric shapes and colors, is the dominant mode of representation, while words and numbers represent co-active, but less prominent modes. Verbal – including numeric – text elements are subject to *pictorial integration*, in keeping with van Leeuwen's (2005, p. 13) terminology, indicating that they become part of the universe constructed by the pictorial elements. The user can choose whether she will use the auto-function and let the train run through the timeline of one year – with accompanying rapid changes in the pattern of circles on the map – or whether she will control the dynamics manually by placing the train on a selected date using the mouse or touchpad. A third choice is to filter the data by using the search options in the menu field.

Scrolling down the page, the user will find a section dominated by the written mode (see Figure 12.2). The section is divided into three columns, where the first explains what the graphic shows, the second explains criteria for the data processing, while the third identifies the sources on which the DV is based, in addition to crediting the individuals behind the application. Beneath the three verbal columns (not visible in the illustration), there is a discussion section, open for users to have their say about the presentation. The subordinate role of these verbal sections on the page is illustrated by the fact that they do not correspond directly to the main title of the page: "That is way the train stops". They only comment on details concerning the visualization presented above them, thus serving as 'meta-texts'.

The second sample DV is collected from the same news site as the first, VG.no. It is chosen because it illustrates the variety of visual models applied in the field of journalistic DV. The DV type applied in Sample 2 is the *mosaic plot*, distributing rectangles of different sizes and colors over a rectangular canvas according to numeric values in the represented datasets (as shown in Figure 12.3). The sample also illustrates strongly the issue of image-centricity, the verbal elements primarily having the role of connecting each country to its visual representation.

The DV is an integrated part of a 'special report' on the Middle East. The report consists exclusively of five DVs, each focusing on one aspect of the region in question, concerning political conflicts, religion, demography, and so forth. The purpose of the special report is to provide fact-based background information to the numerous news stories about political and cultural conflicts inside and between countries in this region. The DV presented in Figure 12.3 has *Demographic facts* as its title, and the ideational content of the visualization includes information regarding the population and prevalence of religions in 15 countries in the Middle East.

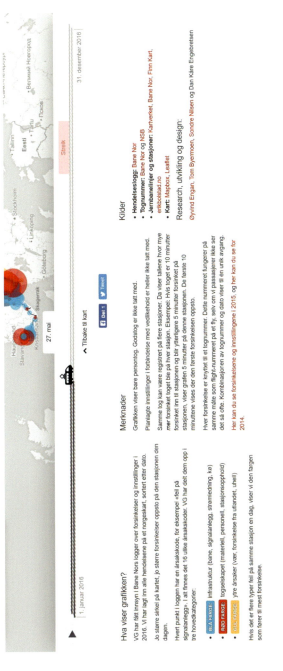

Figure 12.2 Directly below the visualization, verbal elements offer information concerning how the DV should be read and how it was made, as well as its data sources. Downloaded from www.vg.no/spesial/2017/togstopp/. Reproduced with permission.

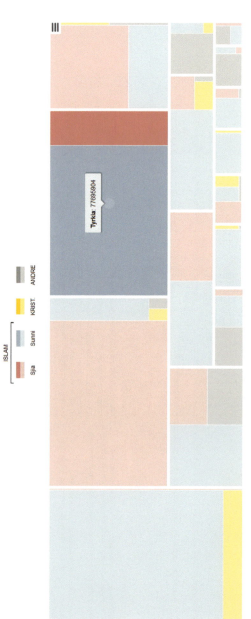

Figure 12.3 Sample 2: Mosaic plot showing the relative size of 15 Middle East countries according to population. The DV also indicates – by combinations of color – the relative prevalence of religions in each country. Downloaded from vg.no: www.vg.no/spesial/2016/midtosten/. Reproduced with permission.

7 Meaning Potentials and Intersemiotic Interplay

To investigate the construction of meaning potentials and the forms of intersemiotic interplay at work in stand-alone, journalistic DVs, the following section examines the different meaning dimensions in Sample 1, and compares the findings with relevant features from Sample 2. First, I look at the ways in which the DVs represent aspects of the world, and how the visual and the verbal modes interplay in this process of representation.

7.1 Ideational Meaning

In a DV, there are always visual codes at work (Engebretsen, 2017). Some of them will most often be intuitively interpreted by the user, due to strong conventions. In the case of Sample 1, we intuitively understand that the map and the position of a circle on the map refer to the position of a train delay somewhere in Norway. Most users will also be familiar with the conventions of the timeline, and thus intuitively understand the metaphoric connection between space and time in the representation of the train and the 'railway' beneath the map.

It is more demanding to interpret what is meant when some circles are blue while others are red or yellow. The connection between color and cause of delay is a non-intuitive code. That is, of course, why it is explained explicitly in the legend – positioned with high salience in the upper left area of the DV. The colors tell us *why* the train stops. But the legend does not say anything about another salient visual variable, namely, the size of the circles. For the user to gain a clear understanding of what size means, she has to read through the text elements beneath the graphic, where it is stated that size indicates the duration of the delay. This is hardly surprising, but other interpretations could also be possible, for example, number of passengers on the train in focus. Thus, size can be labeled a 'semi-intuitive' code.

Thus, in this sample text, ideational meaning is constructed mainly by visual codes, some intuitive, others non-intuitive. The non-intuitive codes are explained in the legend through verbal information. Together with the title, this code information thus functions as an anchorage of the visualization, as it explains the intended meaning of the image and guide the reader's attention. However, unlike the text-image relation we find in multimodal texts involving photographs, the verbal legend has the power to provide an otherwise meaningless visual variable with specific, situated meaning. Drawing on speech act theory (cf. Austin, 1962), we can say that the legend has a performative function, working as a subclass of anchorage. Moreover, verbal text elements (also including numbers) have ideational functions on a secondary level of interaction. If clicked by the user, each circle will display a text offering detailed

286 Martin Engebretsen

information about a particular train delay. Thus, following van Leeuwen (2005, p. 225), these text-elements function as a specification of the values indicated more vaguely by the size of the circles.

Other parts of the verbal text components, placed in the lower section of the DV cluster (see Figure 12.2), merely add contextual information, as described in the presentation of Sample 1. However, as we shall see later in the analysis, it does have an important role in the construction of interpersonal meaning.

Before returning to interpersonal meaning, we shall look at ideational meaning and intersemiotic interplay in Sample 2 (see Figure 12.3). In this DV, the size, color, and position of the rectangles carry ideational meaning, while form carries only compositional meaning. The countries are grouped by size. A country positioned to the right of or below another country has a smaller population than those positioned above or to the left. Position, thus, is a variable that informs the user about the relative size of population, not about relative geographical distance (as in Sample 1). The visualization is interactive and dynamic, providing information on several layers. To examine one country more closely, the user has to click on the relevant rectangle. The DV will then display only the chosen country, but in greater detail regarding the verbal and numeric information – similar to the pop-up text elements in Sample 1. Thus, the verbal text elements are used only for two purposes. Above the visualization, verbal text offers first a title for the DV ("Demographic Facts"), and then a legend, explaining the meaning of the rectangles and the colors. Again, we identify the cohesive type of anchorage, as the verbal text serves to explain the visual codes and guide the reader's attention. On the next level of interaction – the 'pop-up level' initiated by the user's clicking – the text elements work as a specification in relation to the values indicated more roughly by the visual forms.

An interesting difference between the two DVs is related to their affordances regarding ideational potentials, the kind of relations and proportions that are most easily expressed through the respective visual models. While the map-based DV has as its core capacity to inform about the relation between geographical position and certain data values, a mosaic plot is designed to *compare* data values connected to any kind of represented units – be it countries, groups, institutions, and so forth.

7.2 Interpersonal Meaning

DVs belong to a category of texts appearing as highly impersonal and fact-oriented (Kennedy et al., 2016). A bar graph or a scatter plot – seen as independent text units – offers little information about the human agent behind them. The power balance characterizing a DV-based discourse will often be textually constructed as very asymmetric, with the user relegated to a passive role of interpretation and acceptance

(Engebretsen, 2017). On the other hand, some users will approach DVs with a skeptical attitude, being aware of their rhetorical or even manipulative affordances (cf. Hullman & Diakopoulos, 2011; Wainer, 2016). Thus, the building of trust is crucial, in order for a DV to work according to newsroom intentions. Trust-building – interpersonal resources that are relevant to investigate in the context of journalistic, DV-based communication – includes all indications of the personality and qualifications of the persons behind the DV production.

In the case of the train-stop DV (Sample 1), we can point at both visual and verbal elements adding information about the producer. The little locomotive on the timeline is an iconic, visual element that stands out from the abstract geometrical forms, indicating a producer with a hint of playfulness and humor. Even more important to the producer-user relation is, however, the explicit verbal information about the producers, given in the text column to the right under the DV, which also offers links to their professional profile pages. This information has a relational and trust-building function. On the other hand, the style of writing in the entire text field below the visualization is of a very formal and distanced kind, with a minimum of first-person reference, evaluation, or modality markers (cf. Kong, 2014, p. 108).

Sample 2 differs clearly from Sample 1 in terms of the expression of producer information. Neither the graphic nor the verbal elements contain the digital footprint of a personal dialogue partner, except for three names offered at the top of the web-page (presented above the excerpts in Figure 12.3). These names, indicating the producers of the total DV-based report, are linked to email addresses, and thus facilitate direct contact between users and producers. This corresponds, however, to a standard convention in online news reporting, and does not stand out as a strong invitation to dialogue or negotiation.

Relevant to the investigation of user position are the ways in which the original data sources are accounted for. Journalistic DVs will sometimes include hyperlinks to the original datasets for the user to explore by herself. Such a practice indicates that the user is positioned as an active and qualified participant in the discourse, even though relatively few users will actually activate such links (Engebretsen et al., 2018). The same is true for the text elements accounting for the production process – from harvesting the data, filtering, and 'cleaning' them, to choosing a visual design for the DV. Such 'extra material' offers the user the position of a qualified evaluator, which is very different from the 'passive student' position.[4]

The DV in Sample 1 offers exact numbers from the original dataset (which appear when a circle is clicked) and also links to the data sources. Some information about the production process is also offered in the text field below the visualization, though not in any detail. Exact numbers and information about sources are offered also in Sample 2, however, without hyperlinks to the sources (source information is given above the title visible in the excerpt).

Another question that concerns the positioning of the user is related to interactive options. What kind of action is the user invited to perform in order to interact with the visualization or its makers, or with other users? In Sample 1, the user is offered a number of options related to exploration and communication. She can zoom in and out on the map, focusing, for example, on her own home station. She can manually manipulate the train, setting the date of investigation. She can also use the search bar to filter the data. And she can engage in a discussion forum, positioned right beneath the DV. Together, the semiotic and technological affordances highlighted here indicate an ideal user who is not only active and engaged, but also qualified for quality evaluation. The social tone of the producer is, however, ambiguous. The playfulness of the little train on the timeline does not harmonize very well with the strictly formal voice characterizing the verbal text elements. Thus, we can suggest there is an element of tension in the intersemiotic interplay in terms of tone and style.

In Sample 2, the user is offered less interactive options. Apart from scrolling down the page, or taking part in the discussion forum below the DVs, she can only click on the rectangles in order to focus on the properties of one single country. Compared to the target user of Sample 1, Sample 2 also constructs a user identity which implies an active and engaged participant. But the verbal text elements play a minor role in the construction of this identity, compared to the role of the graphic and technological elements.

7.3 Compositional Meaning

In multimodal analysis, compositional meaning is related to intersemiotic cohesion as well as to hierarchies of salience and to information value related to position (van Leeuwen, 2005). In the context of DV in the news media, the issue of *salience* is essential. The concept concerns two levels of presentation. First, how the DV, as a multimodal cluster, stands out from its textual environment, and second, how the different elements of the DV stand out from each other in order to be perceived and interpreted in the most meaningful sequence. DVs are not by convention supposed to be read from left to right, or from center to periphery. Different kinds of DV invite different reading paths, and to understand the 'logic' of a DV, a certain level of experience is required. The most important function of salience in many DVs is, however, to show a *pattern* of values, informing the user about minimum and maximum values, development over time, or other core characteristics of a dataset.

As seen in Figures 12.1 and 12.2, the train-stop DV is composed of three elements: the visualization, constituting the main element, the menu, integrated into the visualization to the upper left, and the verbal text element below the visualization. This organization of elements follows conventions of visual *information value* (van Leeuwen, 2005). The menu box is positioned to the upper left, thus signaled as general information of high value (cf. van Leeuwen, 2005, pp. 200–201). The larger text field offering information about the production process is placed at the bottom, and thus signaled as less important. Regarding the cohesive ties between the elements, the menu fits, according to van Leeuwen's concept of *information linking*, the category of Explanation, while the verbal element at the bottom can be labeled as Addition. Thus, on the macro level, the DV is following conventions for visual and multimodal cohesion in order to organize the intersemiotic interplay.

On the micro level, the picture is more complex. The visualization itself consists of a topographic map, abstract geometric forms (circles), and iconic elements (the little train and the railway), creating a mixed visual environment. It also offers specific dynamic qualities, as it can be read in both static and dynamic modes. In the automatic, dynamic mode, the shifting forms and colors 'dancing' on the map dominate the display to a degree that prevents the perception and interpretation of detailed ideational meaning. However, the larger patterns of the dataset, revealing the areas of the country that are most strongly affected by train stops, may be identified in the automatic mode. Likewise, the little train and the railway will stand out with high salience due to their iconicity and animation. The combination of abstract and iconic forms thus represents an aesthetic variation, and at the same time it carries a particular, symbolic form of meaning. While the iconic elements signal an affiliation with a certain environment (Norwegian topography) and a certain field of activity (traveling by train), the abstract circles signal the objectivity and precision of the dataset.

Sample 2 illustrates DV with a minimum of verbal text. Brief verbal elements are placed above the visualization, as well as inside it, the latter in the form of pop-up information. This composition guides the user to start with the general introduction (what the visualization is about) and the legend (explaining the visual codes), and thereafter retrieve (by clicking) and read the detailed information (names and numbers) as desired. Here, the categories of information linking (cf. van Leeuwen, 2005, p. 225) may be labeled Explanation and Specification, respectively.

8 Summing up: Forms of Image-Centricity in Data Visualizations

The examination of the two samples given above offers certain nuances in the exploration of how DVs function as image-centric forms in the news media. Taking the criteria offered by Stöckl et al. in the introductory chapter as a starting point, we can sum up the findings under three points. First, we can state that the sample DVs respond clearly to the main definition of image-centricity, as the graphic elements in the DVs are dominant both semantically and functionally, compared to the verbal elements. Yet, they also illustrate a specific characteristic of the text type. In order to constitute this dominant role in the interplay, the graphics in the samples need a legend, a verbally established explanation of the visual codes providing the abstract forms and colors with ideational meanings.

This brings us to the next point, focusing on the text-image relation of anchorage. In both sample DVs, the verbal text anchors the interpretation of the visualization, guiding the user on how to focus on the reading, and explaining what visual details are most important in the relevant context. But in addition to this anchoring function, the verbal legend has, as mentioned earlier, the performative, definitory function of constituting the semiotic relation between form and content. Unlike photography, and all other iconic signs, the abstract forms in a DV (e.g., circles and rectangles) do not carry any ideational meaning until they are connected to a legend, or a similar explanatory co-text. Without such explanations, they mainly carry compositional meaning, indicating internal proportions and relations between visual units.

Further, the level of image-centricity can be categorized as *strong* in both samples, as the main body of verbal elements anchors the entirety of the visualization, not only parts of it. However, on a secondary layer of information, both sample DVs offer exact numbers from the dataset as an interactive option. On this level, the pop-up text, functioning as a specification of the indications of values offered by the graphics, claims a temporary dominance in the text-image interplay.

Stöckl et al. (this volume) state that the image in an image-centric composition will serve as an entry point for reading paths and meaning construal. The two samples examined in this chapter suggest that this is not always the case with DVs. Because of the point made earlier, that the graphical elements of a DV will most often demand a verbal legend in order to serve their communicative purpose, such explanatory verbal elements will most often be placed in a position of high salience – high up, and/or to the left – sometimes integrated into the space of the actual visualization. This positioning responds to an anticipated reading behavior involving an initial establishment of visual codes. The bottom positioning of source information and how-we-did-it-stories (cf. Figure 12.2) indicate that this is information with a lower status. Yet, as the analysis indicates, these types of verbal background information can have an important function on an interpersonal level, establishing trust and positioning the user as an equal dialogue partner. Using a term from van Leeuwen (2005, p. 105), we can suggest that such elements of background information serve the function of "legitimizing", that is, attaching the social practice of DV production to the context in which it appears. The lack of such information in Sample 2 corresponds to findings in a broader study, indicating that this category of discursive elements is often neglected in journalistic DVs (Engebretsen, 2017).

Summing up these findings, we can suggest that stand-alone DVs found in the news media clearly constitute an image-centric text type, though with certain specific characteristics concerning the interplay between text and image distinguishing them from image-centric texts based on iconic images. Widening the perspective, we will, in the following section, look at the phenomenon of DV, including its image-centric characteristics, in relation to two sets of contextual frames. First, we will discuss DV in relation to literacy, and then in relation to the development of journalism.

9 Data Visualization and Media Literacy

DVs, presented as image-centric texts on online news sites, demand a complex form of media literacy from the viewer. Potter (2004, p. 58) understands *media literacy* as the ability to connect media content to one's own existing knowledge structures in a process that supports the achievement of one's own social goals. This requires an ability to process media content in a conscious and focused manner during exposure, and to build a repertoire of basic reading skills, including *analysis*, *abstraction*, and *evaluation*.

A field of literacy essential to users of DVs is the ability to quickly identify all codes necessary to interpret the meanings of the graphical expression. The 'vocabulary' of the graphical 'language' consists of a large number of DV types, each of them with the capacity to represent different kinds of ideational information: development over time, comparison between units, networks of connections, part-to-whole-relations, and so forth.[5] In order to quickly grasp the core information of a specific DV, the user will benefit greatly from having some insights into this vocabulary. It will help her to recognize the basic explanatory qualities of the DV-type in question, directly from the macrostructure of the visualization.

The user also needs to identify any visual features that do *not* carry intended meaning. In many visualizations, form, size, color, position, as well as surface texture, direction, and movement are coded parameters. However, in some cases, one or more of these parameters are randomly chosen, or chosen for aesthetic reasons, and thus remain uncoded. Due to a lack of strong conventions regarding the effects of possible choices related to graphical expression, these issues may result in challenges for the interpreter. Furthermore, a competent DV user must be aware that visual features stripped of ideational meaning may still carry both interpersonal and compositional meaning. To evaluate trustworthiness and to find ways to engage actively in the interaction with the DV, the user will need a certain level of 'social DV-literacy'. She should be able to identify and evaluate the footprint of the producer, and to adjust her own textual actions according to a conscious processing of the media content, asking the following question: How can this resource be relevant, useful, and engaging for me? For users to develop a media literacy that supports the kinds of advanced readings described earlier, involving analysis, abstraction, and evaluation, the interplay between verbal text and graphics plays a core role. This interplay is essential in the development of conventions regulating the discursive roles of all textual elements, and also the roles of the communication participants.

10 Data Visualization and the Evolution of Journalism

As stated earlier, many commentators have observed that DVs represent a text type of growing prevalence and impact in the news media – and thus in society. Following a discussion of the textual characteristics of the phenomenon, it is relevant to ask how they affect the genres of journalism. DV is closely related to several parallel trends in our contemporary culture, trends known as *datafication, visualization,* and *digitization.* In combination, these trends imply that many phenomena represented and discussed with words in the past are now represented by numbers, often in visualized forms, and they are integrated in digital discourses characterized by modulization and recontextualization (cf. Couldry & Hepp, 2017; Engebretsen, 2000). Based on the affiliation to these trends, and on the descriptions given in this chapter, we can point to several possible scenarios of genre change related to DV in the news media. It seems obvious that well-designed DVs have a strong potential to make complex matters easier to understand, regarding the identification of patterns, developments, correlations, and so forth. Moreover, DVs linked to trustworthy data sources add trustworthiness to the whole story. In that sense, the use of DV opens up the space for a more fact-based news discourse. This impact of DV on genre development was also emphasized by expert informants in a recent newsroom study (Engebretsen et al., 2018).

Further, it appears that creative applications of DV software and new techniques for visual storytelling – as promoted, for example, by the many awards in this field of practice – widen the range of journalistic formats, and also attract the attention of new user groups (cf. Engebretsen et al., 2018; Weber et al., 2018). Although the willingness of users to spend time and effort clicking on links and engaging in explorations of interactive data sets is a much contested issue (cf. Domingo, 2008; Young & Fulda, 2017), the fact that DV designers have invited users to engage freely with exploratory DVs is indicative of a desire to reach out to them.

The chances of experiencing the type of *personal relevance* that Potter (2004) calls for will often be enhanced by such applications of DV.

On the other hand, one possible outcome of a more widespread application of DV in the news is an even stronger focus on the aspects of life that can be measured and counted. This is a tendency that allows individual people, cases, and stories to lose value and status when numbers and "hard facts" are prioritized (cf. Larsen & Royrvik, 2017). The journalistic genres are recognized and legitimized by their supposed close relation to truth and reality. However, many aspects of our society can only be truthfully described and evaluated through interpretations of qualitative data and exchange of ideas and viewpoints. Journalists have historically been central providers of such 'narrative truths'. With the possibility to 'hide' behind quantified, objectivized, and indisputable data, one might fear that the subjective voice of the independent and socially engaged journalist will become weaker. DVs, with a minimum of verbal text elements – as we observed in Sample 2 – may push this development even further. However, further empirical studies, focusing on both production and reception, are needed in order to test the validity of these assumptions.

Acknowledgments

The research reported in this article was supported by The Norwegian Research Council (NFR) and The Norwegian Media Authorities (RAM). More results from the same project can be investigated on http://indvil.org/.

Notes

1. The popular provider of global health data, Gapminder.org, claims in their mission statement: "The mission of Gapminder Foundation is to fight devastating ignorance with a fact-based worldview that everyone can understand". Downloaded March 10, 2018 from: https://www.gapminder.org/ignorance/.
2. The chapter springs from the research project *Innovative Data Visualization and Visual-Numeric Literacy*, funded by the Norwegian Research Council 2016–2019. See indvil.org.
3. Personal interview with author, April 28, 2016.
4. In a recent analysis of 17 DVs published on four major Norwegian news sites, only two of them were accompanied by texts accounting for methodology (Engebretsen, 2017).
5. See e.g., https://datavizcatalogue.com/, explaining the affordances of 60 different types of DV.

References

Appelgren, E. (2018). An illusion of interactivity: The paternalistic side of data journalism. *Journalism Practice, 12*(3), 308–325.

Appelgren, E., & Nygren, G. (2014). Data journalism in Sweden. *Digital Journalism, 2*(3), 394–405.
Ausserhofer, J., Gutounig, R., Oppermann, M., Matiasek, S., & Goldgruber, E. (2017). The datafication of data journalism scholarship: Focal points, methods, and research propositions for the investigation of data-intensive newswork. *Journalism.* doi: 10.1177/1464884917700667
Austin, J. L. (1962). *How to do things with words.* London: Oxford University Press.
Barthes, R. (1964/1977). *Image – music – text* (S. Heath, Trans.). London: Fontana.
Bednarek, M., & Caple, H. (2017). *The discourse of news values: How news organizations create newsworthiness.* New York, NY: Oxford University Press.
Bednarek, M., & Caple, H. (2012). *News discourse.* London: Continuum.
Bertin, J. (1967/2011). *Semiology of graphics: Diagrams, networks, maps* (W. J. Berg, Trans.). Redlands, CA: ESRI Press.
Borgo, R., Kehrer, J., Chung, D., Maguire, E., Laramee, R., Hauser, H., & Chen, M. (2013, May). Glyph-based visualization: Foundations, design guidelines, techniques and applications. In M. Sbert & L. Szirmay-Kalos (Eds.), *Eurographics 2013. State of the art reports* (pp. 39–63). Girona: The Eurographics Association.
Cairo, A. (2016). *The truthful art: Data, charts, and maps for communication.* Berkeley, CA: New Riders.
Cairo, A. (2013). *The functional art: An introduction to information graphics and visualization.* Berkeley, CA: New Riders.
Couldry, N., & Hepp, A. (2017). *The mediated construction of reality.* Cambridge, UK: Polity Press.
Couldry, N., & Yu, J. (2018). Deconstructing datafication's brave new world. *New Media and Society, 20*(12), 4473–4491.
de Maeyer, J., Libert, M., Domingo, D., Heinderyckx, F., & Le Cam, F. (2015). Waiting for data journalism: A qualitative assessment of the anecdotal take-up of data journalism in French-speaking Belgium. *Digital Journalism, 3*(3), 432–446.
Domingo, D. (2008). Interactivity in the daily routines of online newsrooms: Dealing with an uncomfortable myth. *Journal of Computer-Mediated Communication, 13*(3), 680–705.
Engebretsen, M. (2017). Levende diagrammer og zoombare kart: Datavisualisering som nyskapende fortellerform i journalistikken [Living diagrams and zoomable maps: Data visualization as innovative form of storytelling in journalism]. *Norsk Medietidsskrift, 24*(2), 1–27.
Engebretsen, M. (2013). *Visuelle samtaler: Anvendelser av fotografi og grafikk i nye digitale kontekster [Visual conversations: Applications of photography and graphics in new digital contexts].* Bergen: Fagbokforlaget.
Engebretsen, M. (2006). Shallow and static or deep and dynamic? Studying the state of online journalism in Scandinavia. *Nordicom Review, 27*(1), 3–16.
Engebretsen, M. (2000). Hypernews and coherence. *Nordicom Review, 21*(2), 209–226.
Engebretsen, M., Kennedy, H., & Weber, W. (2018). Data visualization in Scandinavian Newsrooms: Emerging trends in journalistic visualization practices. *Nordicom Review, 39*(2), 3–18.

Few, S. (2004). *Show me the numbers: Designing tables and graphs to enlighten.* Oakland, CA: Analytics.

Fink, K., & Anderson, C. (2015). Data journalism in the United States: Beyond the "usual suspects". *Journalism Studies, 16*(4), 467–481.

Flew, T., Spurgeon, C., Daniel, A., & Swift, A. (2012). The promise of computational journalism. *Journalism Practice, 6*(2), 157–171.

Gynnild, A. (2013). Journalism innovation leads to innovation journalism: The impact of computational exploration on changing mindsets. *Journalism, 15*(6), 713–730.

Halik, L. (2012). The analysis of visual variables for use in the cartographic design of point symbols for mobile augmented reality applications. *Geodesy and Cartography, 61*(1), 19–30.

Halliday, M. A. K. (1978). *Language as social semiotic: The social interpretation of language and meaning.* London: Arnold.

Hannaford, L. (2015). Computational journalism in the UK newsroom: Hybrids or specialists? *Journalism Education, 4*(1), 6–21.

Hullman, J., & Diakopoulos, N. (2011). Visualization rhetoric: Framing effects in narrative visualization. *IEEE Transactions on Visualization and Computer Graphics, 17*(12), 2231–2240.

Karlsen, J., & Stavelin, E. (2014). Computational journalism in Norwegian newsrooms. *Journalism Practice, 8*(1), 34–49.

Kennedy, H., Hill, R., Aiello, G., & Allen, W. (2016). The work that visualization conventions do. *Information, Communication and Society, 19*(6), 715–735.

Kirk, A. (2016). *Data visualisation: A handbook for data driven design.* Los Angeles, CA: Sage.

Kong, K. (2014). *Professional discourse.* London: Cambridge University Press.

Kress, G., & van Leeuwen, T. (2006). *Reading images: The grammar of visual design* (2nd ed.). London: Routledge.

Larsen, T., & Royrvik, E. (Eds.). (2017). *Trangen til å telle: Objektivering, måling og standardisering som samfunnspraksis.* Oslo: Scandinavian Academic Press.

Lemke, J. (2006). Towards critical multimedia literacy: Technology, research, and politics. In M. McKenna, L. Labbo, R. Kieffer, & D. Reinking (Eds.), *International handbook of literacy and technology: Vol. 2* (pp. 3–14). Mahwah, NJ: Erlbaum.

Lewis, S., & Westlund, O. (2015). Big data and journalism: Epistemology, expertise, economics, and ethics. *Digital Journalism, 3*(3), 447–466.

Lima, M. (2011). *Visual complexity: Mapping patterns of information.* New York, NY: Princeton Architectural Press.

Loosen, W., Reimer, J., & De Silva-Schmidt, F. (2017). *Data-driven reporting – An on-going (r)evolution? A longitudinal analysis of projects nominated for the data journalism awards 2013-2016.* Hamburg: University of Hamburg, Hans-Bredow-Institut für Medienforschung.

Lüders, M., Prøitz, L., & Rasmussen, T. (2010). Emerging personal media genres. *New Media & Society, 12*(6), 947–963.

Mencher, M. (1997). *News reporting and writing.* Madison, WI: Brown & Benchmark.

Mollerup, P. (2015). *Data design: Visualising quantities, locations, connections.* London: Bloomsbury.

Nussbaumer Knaflic, C. (2015). *Storytelling with data: A data visualization guide for business professionals*. Hoboken, NJ: Wiley.

Potter, J. (2004). *Theory of media literacy: A cognitive approach*. Thousand Oaks, CA: Sage.

Rinsdorf, L., & Boers, R. (2016, July). The need to reflect: Data journalism as an aspect of disrupted practice in digital journalism and in journalism education. In J. Engel (Ed.), *Promoting understanding of statistics about society. Proceedings of the roundtable conference of the International Association of Statistics Education (IASE)*. Berlin: ISI/IASE.

Stalph, F. (2017). Classifying data journalism. *Journalism Practice, 12*(10), 1332–1351.

Tuchman, G. (1978). *Making news: A study in the construction of reality*. New York, NY: Free Press.

Tufte, E. R. (2006). *Beautiful evidence*. Cheshire, CT: Graphics Press.

Tufte, E. R. (2001). *The visual display of quantitative information*. Cheshire, CT: Graphics Press.

van Leeuwen, T. (2005). *Introducing social semiotics*. London: Routledge.

Wainer, H. (2016). *Truth or truthiness: Distinguishing fact from fiction by learning to think like a data scientist*. New York, NY: Cambridge University Press.

Weber, W., Engebretsen, M., & Kennedy, H. (2018). Data stories: Rethinking journalistic storytelling in the context of data journalism. *Studies in Communication Sciences, 18*(1), 191–206.

Weber, W., & Rall, H. (2012, July). Data visualization in online journalism and its implications for the production process. In E. Banissi (Ed.), *IV 2012. Proceedings of the 16th international conference on information visualization* (pp. 349–356). Washington, DC: IEEE Computer Society.

Young, M. L., & Fulda, J. (2017). What makes for great data journalism? A content analysis of data journalism awards finalists 2012–2015. *Journalism Practice, 12*(1), 115–135.

Commentary
Image-Centric Practices as Global Design Strategies

Teal Triggs

We are in the midst of a Fourth Industrial Revolution, an age characterized by ubiquitous devices, transmedia storytelling, and where data visualization strategies dominate. The three chapters (10, 11, and 12) included in Section 4 of this collection bring together case examples for developing and interrogating criteria and methods in defining image-centricity within the context of contemporary news media practice. What is shared by these three case examples is the foregrounding of design and its corollary strategies to generate new ways of approaching image-centricity and genre development. John S. Knox argues for a consideration of the design and technological affordances of tablet-based news apps and how these might be exploited in application and across geographic boundaries: he takes as his starting point the home pages of internationally recognized news apps from Australia, the USA, and the UK, and building upon the work of Caple (2013) links image-centricity to design and genre. Peter Wignell et al. focus on a visual interrogation of editorial design for Islamic State's online magazines *Dabiq* and *Rumiyah*: they explore the ways in which communication strategies use patterns and recontextualization to promote an ideological construction in forming a fundamental worldview. Martin Engebretsen focuses on how the newsroom and its journalists are increasingly relying on the visualization of data-driven evidence making accessible to users statistical, historical, or geographical information material in diagrammatic or cartographic representations: he provides examples drawn from Norwegian online news sites to evidence a new kind of multimodal interplay, a form of media literacy and a nuanced definition of image-centricity.

The juxtaposition of these three essays identifies a gap in academic studies which might benefit from taking into account a design-led perspective on the construction of image-centricity for global design strategies. The study of image-centricity has increased exponentially with social and online media platforms such as Instagram, Pinterest, Snapchat, Facebook, and Twitter. The image is ever-more prominent, especially in the way it is used to *lead* in the communication of news stories, information messaging, and promotion. Used effectively, images rapidly grab the attention of a tech-savvy readership. Whilst image-centricity may be analyzed through a social-semiotic approach, a more nuanced understanding of design knowledge and methods is equally needed. One thing does not negate the other: it is simply a question of getting the fullest picture via a variety of methods.

In its purist sense, design is concerned with the "planning, inventing, making and doing" (Cross, 1982, p. 221) in the realization of new products, and includes services, systems, networks, and experiences. Design informs how we communicate with people as an activity; that is, a "process of conceiving, programming, projecting" (Frascara, 2004, p. 2) and "constructs, represents and contests the social world" (Jewitt, van Leeuwen, Scollon, & Triggs, 2002, p. 7). Design according to Kazmierczak (2003, p. 47), is "an interface for meaning making, or simply the design of meaning" and holds "semiotic systems such as images, layout and typography" (Bednarek & Caple, 2014, p. 136). The inherent ways in which designers design for "encounters" (Atzmon & Boradkar, 2017, p. 2) may help to shed light on the creation of meanings in new kinds of socio-technological contexts. In exploring what Knox, Wignell et al., and Engebretsen have to offer, we might also consider asking: what does the designer bring to this discussion of image-centricity as a producer of meaning in the study of multimodal artifacts? To do this, I would suggest the potential role for design is best described as *mediated actions*, encompassing the designer as producer, designing for audiences, and designing as storytelling.

Designer as Producer

The rise of mobile news media apps, as Knox describes, suggests we have access to news from anywhere in the world, at speed, and at any time of the day or night. Such unprecedented access in news reporting results in new kinds of challenges for journalists and designers in determining effective ways to communicate this. Knox's chapter is excellent, and sufficiently detailed in his discussion on reportage, composition, and visual metaphor. However, taking the designer's process into consideration may offer an enhanced perspective. Thus, an interview with Alex Breuer, the creative director of *The Guardian*, elucidates the rationale behind the newspaper's ground-breaking rebranding in 2014 (Alderson, 2014). A design strategy was adopted to evolve a new design and brand language that was consistent across all platforms. Breuer states that he began with "a new responsive design built around the key proportion of the core image size" (Alderson, 2014, n. p.) used across platforms. Equally, a redesign was needed to adapt to "the readers' changing needs" and to an "evolving global news organisation" (Alderson, 2014, n. p.). Since 2014, the design of *The Guardian* home page has been iterative, with initial language systems built around color, customized icons, commissioned typeface (*Guardian Egyptian*), greater personalization, flexible formatting, and refresh animation. It is only by looking at this side of the story, as well, that we can fully understand the complexity and challenges of such new technology.

Designing for Audiences

Technology has afforded publishers' greater access to extending their reach to audiences across geographic borders, and with it all the associated complexities of language and visual representation. My second example considers the role of the audience and global design strategies. Whereas tablet-based news-media apps, as described by Knox, are drawing from previous design approaches found in print newspapers, Wignell et al. show how editorial design has impacted online digital magazines (in this case, the design of *Dabiq* – an ISIS-related, English-language online magazine produced between 2014 and 2017).

We learn from Wignell et al.'s findings that English-language publications such as *Dabiq* and subsequently *Rumiyah* are used as tools for radicalization of individuals from afar, employing literary conventions and Western symbolism, editorial design, and multimodal image-making strategies. The role of the editorial designer in this process of meaning making is made manifest in the construction of text-image relations as iconic artifacts. Images move easily across cultural borders, are recontextualized, and are picked up by the mainstream press to find new meaning as another form of propaganda.

Whilst Wignell et al. present useful insights into image-centricity and image tracking, the study offered by design researchers Scheuermann and Beifuss (2017) suggests a more detailed visual analysis of the typographic design and layout of *Dabiq*. It takes a designer's eye to discern the shifts in typographic and graphic placements in *Dabiq*, thus making it possible to suggest that its "editorial design is subjected to a multitude of changes" (Scheuermann & Beifuss, 2017, p. 63) in ISIS design policy. Scheuermann and Beifuss (2017, pp. 72–73) conclude in their study of the magazine that ISIS "up to six different designers might have been involved in a single issue", "including at least one designer, who might be trained as a graphic designer in the western hemisphere". Such an analysis may inform how designers engage with global design strategies and, in this case, for the development of "graphic design of future counter-terrorism activities" (Scheuermann & Beifuss, 2017, p. 9). A case might be made for design-led research which sits alongside more conventional image-centric approaches offered by Wignell et al. and others. The design of *Dabiq* and *Rumiyah* becomes an 'encounter' between publisher, designer, and reader, thereby establishing connections for the reader as an active participant in the process of meaning making. As Buchanan (1985, p. 6) has pointed out, design rhetoric is "an art of shaping society, changing the course of individuals and communities, and setting patterns for new action".

Designing as Storytelling

My third example suggests the role of the designer as a digital storyteller of information in the production of data visualizations. Graphical forms have the power to communicate, in an immediate manner, complex messages; although as Weber cautions, "not every infographic is a visual narrative or tells a story…" (Weber, 2017, p. 250). Engebretsen explores data visualization as "a semiotic phenomenon of growing prevalence in contemporary society". Within a context of media literacy, his primary example is from the Norwegian tabloid *Verdens Gang* (VG) – an online news site. Whilst Engebretsen gives brief mention of the perspectives offered by practitioners in the design of data visualization, citing the writings of Per Mollerup and Edward Tufte, he does not fully develop the practitioner's position in his essay. Yet, he acknowledges that "the visualization is still a product of many choices", and that decisions have to be made that inform not only the selection of data but "the context in which it is placed", and ultimately, the transformation of complex data into graphic forms. But perhaps here more could be made of the decision-making process and methods used by designers in their everyday work.

One example which sits outside of the field of news media may provide a clue in moving toward a design-led perspective on data visualization (small and big) and the everyday. In 2011, designers Barbara Hahn and Christine Zimmermann wrote about their collaborations with statisticians and how they employed design-based methods in the development of "knowledge visualisations" (Hahn & Zimmermann, 2011, p. 72) for the Bern University Hospital Inselspital. "Knowledge visualisations" in this case refers to "a form of knowledge transfer that uses all types of graphic media to guarantee an effective transfer of information" (Hahn & Zimmermann, 2011, p. 72). An in-depth set of visual experiments using reflective research provided the basis for visualizations focusing on daily hospital routines including hospital waiting times, decubitus risks, ward routines, and patient discharge. The design-led process not only precipitated effective visualizations, but also made "aspects visible that were lost or not visible in the statistical evaluations" (Hahn & Zimmermann, 2011, p. 80). The new insights which could be deduced from their visualizations contributed directly to the improvement of patient care (Hahn & Zimmermann, 2011, p. 83). In this way, *thinking like a designer* was crucial to the way in which the research questions were framed, and the data harvested and visualized. The manner in which designers utilize a "designerly form of activity that separates it from typical scientific and scholarly activities" (Cross, 1982, p. 223) might be a welcome addition to the studies of image-centricity as a global design strategy.

Design as addressed from a different discipline can be useful, but also creates distance. The more active inclusion of the designer (e.g., interviews, design ethnography, visual analysis, experimental practices) might provide a fuller picture of decision-making, intentions, and audience interaction and evaluation. For all the chapters' strengths – and there are many – the gap is in a lack of engagement with design as a lived experience. The fourth Industrial Revolution is here, and in the age of fake news, it is more important than ever to understand information flows. Designers are a crucial part of those flows and require to be contextualized in the same way as any other semiotic approach.

References

Alderson, R. (2014, June 3). Behind the scenes: *The Guardian's* creative director on their new app. *It's Nice That*. Retrieved from https://www.itsnicethat.com/articles/behind-the-scenes-guardian-app

Atzmon, L., & Boradkar, P. (Eds.). (2017). *Encountering things: Design and theories of things*. London: Bloomsbury.

Bednarek, M., & Caple, H. (2014). Why do news values matter? Towards a new methodological framework for analysing news discourse in Critical Discourse Analysis and beyond. *Discourse & Society, 25*(2), 135–158.

Buchanan, R. (1985). Declaration by design: Rhetoric, argument, and demonstration in design practice. *Design Issues, 2*(1), 4–22.

Caple, H. (2013). *Photojournalism: A multisemiotic approach*. Basingstoke: Palgrave Macmillan.

Cross, N. (1982). Designerly ways of knowing. *Design Studies, 3*(4), 221–227.

Frascara, J. (2004). *Communication design: Principles, methods, and practice*. New York: Allworth Press.

Hahn, B., & Zimmermann, C. (2011). Visualizing daily hospital routine. *Design Issues, 27*(3), 72–83.

Jewitt, C., van Leeuwen, T., Scollon, R., & Triggs, T. (2002). Editorial. *Visual Communication, 1*(1), 5–8.

Kazmierczak, E. T. (2003). Design as meaning making: From making things to the design of thinking. *Design Issues, 19*(2), 45–59.

Scheuermann, A., & Beifuss, A. (Eds.). (2017). The visual rhetoric of 'IS': An editorial design case study of the 'IS' Magazine Dabiq'. *HKB Research Paper No 16*. Bern: University of the Arts HKB.

Weber, W. (2017). Interactive information graphics: A framework for classifying a visual genre. In A. Black, P. Luna, O. Lund, & S. Walker (Eds.), *Information design: Research and practice* (pp. 243–256). London: Routledge.

Index

aesthetics 1, 28, 77, 79–80
advertising 3, 79
affordance 58, 93, 215, 228, 278; modal 45–47; technological 13, 180, 211, 222, 234, 288, 297
allograph 195–196
ambient environment 205, 211, 228; *see also* social sharing
analysis: automated image 254–255, 262, 269; diachronic 10, 102–104, 111, 143, 147–149; multimodal genre 26, 34–38, 87–88, 104–114; narrative 123, 125–129, 148; representational 123, 125, 128–129; synchronic 100, 104–107; systemic functional multimodal discourse (SF-MDA) 254–256
anchorage 6–7, 23, 226, 227, 277, 285, 286, 290; *see also* relay
angle (shot): equal 137, 138; high 138; low 137
app(lication): mobile/news 233–237, 249, 297, 298; WhatsApp 178–179, 185–186, 226
article: feature 3, 98–100, 110–114, 126, 134, 147; magazine 98, 104, 116–117, 125–126, 146, 257–262, 263; newspaper 24–25, 38–39, 44, 49–50, 87, 146, 148
atomization 12, 39, 117

big data analytics 254, 255, 262
bonding: icon(s) 261–266, 269–270; value 263–264

caption 20–23, 26–31, 35, 72, 105, 108–111, 115–116, 128, 139, 147, 154–155, 161–162, 179–181, 204, 205, 209, 216, 226, 246, 248, 255, 270; scope of 38, 105, 114, 184–185

carrier 67, 135–138, 139
chart 19, 73–81, 275–279; *see also* diagram
circumstances 53, 67, 101, 155
coherence/coherent 1, 30, 47, 66, 181, 218, 219–221, 226, 277
cohesion/cohesive: external/internal 123–127, 131, 148; multimodal 1, 7, 21, 24, 83, 181, 288–289; tie(s) 7, 20, 22, 24, 35, 38, 277, 289
color 35, 64, 66, 68–70, 73, 78, 80, 123, 137, 181, 277, 278, 285, 286, 291
composition/compositional: analysis 126–128, 288–289; dominance 7, 15, 277; structure 34–35, 88; *see also* layout
compositional narrative device 125, 126–129, 148; types of 129–142
configuration *see* layout
contextual extension 23, 35, 36, 38, 106, 115, 116, 155–156; *see also* experiential orientation
corpus/data 24–25, 87–88, 90, 104–105, 107–111, 124–125, 147, 149, 165, 184–188, 204, 236–237

data visualization *see* visualization
datafication 275, 292
design 78, 124, 233–234, 237–245, 249, 298–300
diagram 30; types of 73–81
digitization 153, 292
discourse: image-centric 21, 42, 58, 257, 279; Islamic violent extremist 254, 271; multimodal 21, 43, 58, 89–90, 254, 255, 262, 276, 280

editorial 21, 28, 30, 32
emoji 65, 79, 183; as adjective 191; as cohesive device 197; as deictic

Index

element 197; emoji-text relation 181; functions of 188; as noun 188; as prepositional phrase 193; as proposition 188, 194; as semantic frame 192; as semantic specifier 196; semiotic qualities of 183–184; as structuring device 195; as verb 191

enhancement *see* text-image relation

evaluation (stance) 162, 211, 246

experiential orientation 11, 22, 23, 36, 106, 115, 116, 155; *see also* contextual extension

explainer 30

extension *see* contextual extension

Facebook 79–80, 153, 167, 179, 208, 269, 297

feature article *see* article

footing 154, 156–158, 161, 168–172

font *see* typography

framing *see* typography

gallery 30–31, 129, 138–141

gaze 129, 130, 136, 137, 138

genre 20–21, 102–103; change/development 20–21, 54, 65, 90, 102–104, 117, 146–147, 201, 227, 292; emergence 21, 87, 104, 117, 146–147; family 20, 23–25, 34, 38, 87; frequency 31–34, 98; profile 31–34, 99, 102–104, 147; repertoire 14, 22, 25, 34, 39, 98, 103–104, 107, 147; space 14, 23–25, 36, 88; macro- 32, 249; micro- 205

goal 73, 74, 129, 136

grapho-stylistics 195–196

graph 275, 277–278, 279; *see also* diagram

graffiti 55–57, 89

grid *see* layout

hashtag 154, 158, 160–161, 179, 184, 185, 187, 200, 210, 228; *see also* social media

headline 5, 20, 22, 115, 128, 147, 153, 155, 235, 239–240, 248

homepage 26, 146, 235–237, 247, 297; design types 237–238, 244

iconographetic communication (mode) 183, 201

identity 68, 78–79, 104, 147, 221, 288

ideology 262–266

image: centrality/central 12, 20, 22, 23, 58, 64, 87, 115, 155, 277; conceptual 28, 36, 38; documentary 257–259, 266, 267; dominance/dominant 7, 20, 24, 103, 115, 180, 277; narrative 36, 73, 123; macro 204, 209–210, 222; nuclearity/nuclear 5, 22–23, 47, 87, 97, 101, 115–116, 155–156, 227, 248–249; nuclear news story 20, 22–23, 97, 100–101, 155, 234, 249; participant 53, 106, 110, 111, 113, 126–127, 129, 149, 154, 168, 216, 218; type 36–37

image-caption-post-tag relation 216–219, 222

image-caption cluster 3, 21

info(rmation)graphic 30, 276, 300

information linking 37, 289; explanation as 289; specification as 289

information value 288, 289

Instagram 139, 154, 156, 157, 158–161, 177–183, 200, 210, 228; post 154, 156–157, 161–172, 179, 180, 184, 216, 228; story 181–183

intermodal relation 52, 53, 177, 182, 204, 277

intersemiotic 7, 20–21, 24, 37–38, 53, 155–156, 168, 226, 235; (inter)play 21, 275, 285–289

intersubjectivity 205, 210, 212, 220, 222, 228

intertextuality/intertextual 30, 31, 32, 34, 38, 44–45, 47–48, 86, 89, 205, 219, 226, 228; direct/referential forms of 45; intermodal forms of 47; intra-modal forms of 47; typological forms of 44, 45

intertextual reference: image indexing 50; image metatextualization 50; image quotation 49; image resemiotization 56; image transcription 52; image transformation 54

ISIS (Islamic State of Iraq and Syria): propaganda 254, 257, 269, 299; ideology 262–263, 269

journalism 2, 21, 100–102, 115, 116–117, 234, 253, 278–280, 292–293; news 87, 276; photo 79, 116, 123–126; popular science 97

layout 34–35, 64, 66, 70–73, 88, 91–92, 103, 105, 111–114, 115–116, 124, 147, 160, 180–181, 213, 226, 233, 276; *see also* composition/compositional, structure, typography
legend 30, 118, 275, 285–286, 289–290
logico-semantic relation *see* relation

magazine 2–3, 227; online 254–255, 257, 297, 299; print 19, 28, 65, 69, 71–73, 97–98, 102–104, 116–117, 124–125, 146
map 19, 76–77, 275, 279; *see also* diagram
marketization 77–83
meaning: ideational (representational) 77, 168, 208, 218, 256, 261, 266, 270, 277, 279, 285–286, 289–290, 291; interpersonal (interactive) 77, 82, 168, 208, 238, 256, 257, 261, 266, 270, 277, 279, 286, 291; potential(s) 36, 46, 58, 73, 101, 124, 128, 143, 213, 244, 255, 275, 277, 285–289; textual (compositional) 124, 128, 143, 277, 279, 286, 288–289, 290
media 10, 14, 30, 227–228, 253, 292, 300; digital 5, 78, 124, 131, 139, 143, 157, 173, 207; literacy 208, 227, 275–276, 278, 291–292, 297; online 3, 21, 26, 30, 39, 108, 117, 124, 146, 153, 205, 208, 237, 254, 262, 297; social (platform) 3, 19, 153–154, 155, 157–158, 168, 172, 177, 204–205, 207–209, 212, 215–216, 219, 221, 222, 226–227, 253, 267, 297
meme 204–205, 207–208, 209, 222, 226
metaphor 45, 208, 285; multimodal 30; visual 238, 242, 243, 298
metafunction *see* meaning
mode/modal 5–7, 19, 23, 44, 46, 64, 67, 87, 90–92, 168, 180–181, 183–184, 213, 227, 253, 277, 282; elaboration 6–7, 253; intensity 6, 253; weight 6, 253, 277
mosaic plot 282, 284, 286
multimodality/multimodal 1, 5, 7, 19, 24, 39, 44, 86–88, 97, 184, 234; construal 7, 234, 257, 262, 277; construction of social reality 43–44, 211, 297; text 5–9, 20–21, 23, 44, 103, 184, 227, 278, 280

new writing *see* typography
news: app *see* app(lication); design 19, 124, 146–147, 233–234, 237–245, 279; hard 28, 34, 102, 115, 126, 248; media 5, 19, 44, 100, 124, 146, 153, 236, 275, 299; online 2, 21, 26, 30, 49, 50, 124, 153, 234–235, 249, 276, 291, 297; reportage 10, 238–243, 298; room 275–276, 279, 280, 292, 297; soft 28, 34, 102, 126
newsbite/newsbit 19, 26, 39, 146, 235–236, 238–239, 248
newspaper 21, 49, 141, 153, 249, 298; online 26, 49, 146, 234–235, 237–245; print 20, 26, 31, 38, 44, 87, 100, 117, 146, 243, 299
newsworthiness *see* news values
news value 5, 21, 22, 101–102, 110, 116, 148–149, 278; aesthetic appeal 101, 107, 110, 148, 149, 246; personalization 107, 110; proximity 101, 107, 148, 149; superlativeness 101, 107, 110, 115, 148; timeliness 101; unexpectedness 107, 110, 115, 148
nucleus 22, 23, 26, 34, 45, 47, 49, 50, 52, 55, 58, 97, 115, 118; *see also* satellite
nuclearization 12

participant *see* image, participant
pattern: genre/generic 38, 87, 88, 103, 104, 117, 205, 235; layout 3, 105, 111–114, 115; textual 24, 36, 88, 205, 275, 297
performative function 285, 290
photograph/photography 1, 2, 3, 8, 20, 32, 47, 97–98, 123, 126, 153, 156, 158, 227, 256, 290
picture/pictorial: characters 181; relative placement 126, 127, 131; size 123, 126, 128, 147, 298; superiority effect 46
point of view *see* angle
PowerPoint 64, 65, 68, 80, 82
preview 26–27, 28, 31, 33, 123, 126, 148
process (verb): analytical 66, 136, 139; bi-directional 129; classificational 131;

non-transactional 136; transactional 129, 137, 144; uni-directional 137
production format 154, 156–158, 173
projection 154, 156–158, 165, 211–213, 222; multimodal 213–215, 222; visual 216, 222
prosodic tail 22, 23, 28, 35, 97, 100–101, 115, 250

quotation practice 157, 211–215, 216, 228
quoted voice 165, 204–205, 210–215, 218, 222

recontextualization 262, 267, 269, 292, 297; patterns of 267–269, 297; *see also* intertextual reference, image resemiotization
relation: logico-semantic 7–8, 104, 115, 155–156, 161, 165, 257; status 1, 6–8, 11, 19, 22–23, 156, 163, 168, 181, 226–227, 257
relative status *see* relation, status
relay 6–7, 23; *see also* anchorage
representation *see* meaning
rhetorical structure 22, 114, 115, 118

salience 7, 12, 14, 26, 39, 68, 69, 70, 104, 116, 128, 257, 285, 288–289, 290
satellite 22, 34, 45, 47, 49, 55, 58, 101, 115, 116, 118, 155, 248, 249; *see also* nucleus
semantic complementarity 6, 181, 184, 261; *see also* text-image relation
semiotics/semiotic 5, 83, 183–184, 261, 262, 277; social 12, 13, 123, 125, 155, 227, 249, 256, 277; technology 223
sharing *see* social sharing
shift 1–5, 10, 19–22, 34, 80, 86, 98–100, 117, 118, 148–149, 253; *see also* genre, change
SmartArt 73, 80
social sharing 153, 160, 178, 179, 200, 204, 208, 222, *see also* social media
social media *see* media/social (platform)

speaker role 157, 172
split story 241–244, 247
stand-alone 97, 248, 249; data visualization 275, 276, 291
story intro 26–27, 28, 31–33
systemic functional linguistics/theory (SFL/SFT) 7, 20, 155, 235, 254, 256, 260
system network 127, 142, 204, 214, 222, 238, 241, 243, 256

tablet 233–234, 236, 241, 244, 246, 249, 299
taxonomy: covert 142; overt 131
template 2, 10, 49, 64, 72–73, 78, 153, 160, 204, 207, 210
text-image relation 1, 5–9, 11, 14, 22–23, 34, 36, 37–38, 47, 87–88, 105, 107–108, 154–155, 177, 213–215, 221, 226, 254, 277, 285, 290; complementary 3, 6–7, 156, 163, 168; *see also* anchorage, emoji-text relation, relay
textuality 65–68; inter/inter 9, 30, 31–32, 34, 38, 44–45, 47, 89, 158, 204, 205, 207, 223, 228; trans/trans 1, 9, 42–43, 44, 47, 58
texture 37–38, 83, 110, 277, 291
thematic structure 34–35, 88
theme/rheme 163, 235, 258
Twitter 153, 158, 168, 205, 208, 210, 211, 213, 215, 269, 297
typography 65, 69–70, 73, 86, 113, 227, 298

Unicode 181, 183, 196

vector 73–74, 91, 92, 138, 143
verbal context unit 123, 126, 128, 133
verbiage 160, 163, 204, 213, 216, 218; –centricity/–centric/–nuclearity/–nuclear 4–6, 20–23, 25, 33, 115, 155–156
visualization 1, 8, 19, 30, 33, 73, 275, 276, 278–279, 280, 289–292, 297, 300
vocalization 212–213

web page *see* home page